YUKON
PLACES AND NAMES

MW01706832

WWW.YUKONPLACESANDNAMES.COM

Produced by the Surveys and Mapping Branch, Ottawa, Canada, 1976.

Établie par la Direction des levés et de la cartographie, Ottawa, Canada, 197

YUKON
PLACES AND NAMES

Second Edition

R.C. Coutts

Moose Creek Publishing
PR Services Ltd.
Whitehorse, Yukon
Canada

Copyright © 1980 by R.C. Coutts

Design and typesetting by The Typeworks, Mayne Island, B.C.
Additional production and typesetting by PR Services Ltd., Whitehorse, Yukon

Index map reproduced with permission of the Surveys and Mapping Branch, Department of Energy, Mines & Resources, Ottawa.
Names listed in this book are normally found on maps of the National Topographic Series, scale 1:250,000.

Indexes and ordering instructions can be obtained free of charge from:

Canada Map Office
Surveys and Mapping Branch
Department of Energy, Mines & Resources
615 Booth Street
Ottawa, Ontario
K1A 0E9

or

Mac's Fireweed Books
203 Main Street
Whitehorse, Yukon
Y1A 2B2

Canadian Cataloguing in Publication Data

Coutts, Robert C., 1918-
Yukon: Places & Names

ISBN 0-88826-085-7 hardcover
ISBN 0-88826-085-2 paperback
1. Names, Geographical – Yukon Territory.
2. Yukon Territory – History, Local. I. Title.
FC4006.C68   917.19'1'0032   C80-091167-9
F1093.C68

Cover Design: K-L Services, Whitehorse, Yukon
ISBN 0-9688440-3-0

Second Edition 2003
Moose Creek Publishing
PR Services Ltd.
Printed in Canada
McAra Printing
Calgary, Alberta

FOREWORD

For any country, its names are a part of its history. From the beginning they have been a necessity; they are the means by which inhabitants and particularly explorers tell others where they have been and what they have seen. Indeed, without names, maps, records and books would be unintelligible.

When we see names in books or on maps we often take these for granted, thoughtless of asking ourselves whence they came or whether there is a meaningful story in their origin, but if we are curious where do we find out? Heretofore, there has been no handy reference for this information on names in the Yukon Territory which with its growth of population and expanding development, badly needs a published record of the history of its names. In YUKON PLACES and NAMES, Robert C. Coutts gives us a book which fills this need admirably.

For him, its compilation has been a labour of love, occupying years of research through old manuscripts, maps, books and all sorts of sources of information including mining records and private diaries. This work has taken him to many parts of Canada and to the United States in his hunt for original sources of names. From this he has produced a convenient alphabetical list of Yukon names, giving the features they apply to, their locations and historical background. In many instances this includes tales of the men who discovered the features, how they chose the names and who or what the names commemorate, in addition to accounts of those whose names the features bear. The author gives historical accounts not only of the well-known, established names in common usage but also of lonely creeks and hills, and long-abandoned localities in the hinterlands rarely now remembered, whose stories fade with passing years.

Besides supplying the history of these out-of-the-way places, this volume will make a most useful contribution to resurrecting these old names. When new strikes are made on old ground, where the early names were in obscure records and generally unknown, newcomers are prone to introduce new names. Here is a bulwark against such errors. Throughout its length the book by its very nature supplies a store of historical notes and fills an important place among the historical references for the Yukon Territory.

Five years of experience as representative for the Yukon Territory on the Canadian Board on Geographical Names gave me a very real appreciation of the need for such a work as this book and it gives me great satisfaction that this need has now been so well filled. The author points out that a number of names have been omitted for lack of information and almost daily we see new names established. It is my earnest hope that as time goes on, revised editions, in the same style but containing the missing names and giving the new ones, will follow, keeping the record up to date.

Hugh S. Bostock
Ottawa

INTRODUCTION

"Names are the pegs from which history is hung."
– Henry Schoolcraft.

The work contained in this book began around 1970 as a hobby. When first prospecting in the southeast Yukon and Cassiar country, I was naturally interested in the history of an area about which I had read and been told so much. Becoming curious about the origin or meaning of a Yukon place name, I found that there was often no answer, or conflicting ones. Alone of Canada's provinces and territories almost nothing has been written on this subject. On reading the early literature it often appeared that the modern name was not that given originally and that in many cases the name and its meaning had been altered or changed. I began to search for the true origins of these names. Gradually, the people and the stories behind the names began to live for me and many were more interesting than much of the fiction written about the territory. As the stories unfolded and extended, my interest became more serious but no less enjoyable. Many newly learned facts revealed other stories and puzzles to be traced and solved.

The stories set down here are almost entirely contained in the written accounts of those who took part in or were close to the events. Little is from hearsay, unless confirmed by other statements or accounts. In cases of conflict the earliest or most obvious story is given: in some cases, two or more equally reliable but differing accounts are recorded and the reader may choose between them.

The stories of most of the early explorers are well-known but those of the common people who opened and developed the country are often remembered only in the name of a feature where they pioneered. As builders of a country their names should not be forgotten. This is an attempt to record some of these stories. This Yukon is a hard and demanding country. For the most part it has always attracted the more self-reliant, individualistic and adventurous types of people. They were people worth knowing and people worth remembering.

The first known white man to set foot in the Yukon Territory was John Franklin, the famous English Arctic explorer. During his second expedition in 1826, he travelled the Arctic coast from the mouth of the MacKenzie River westward into what is now Alaska. Many of the Yukon's coastal features, including Herschel Island were named by him at that time. However, the first feature in the Yukon to be given a name by white men was Mount St. Elias in the southwest corner of the territory. Seen from the sea on St. Elias Day, 16 July 1741, it was named by Vitus Bering while he was exploring the coast of Alaska for the Russian government.

The next group of names was given in the period between 1839 and 1850. Robert Campbell of the Hudson's Bay Company entered the central Yukon by way of the Liard, Frances and Pelly Rivers. Campbell established the courses of the Frances, Pelly and Yukon Rivers and built trading posts on or near each of them. He named these rivers and many of their tributaries. Later in the same period John Bell and Alexander Hunter Murray of the same company, crossed the northern Yukon from the MacKenzie River and established Lapierre House and later, Fort Yukon.

From 1880 on, the early prospector-miners arrived and in their wanderings gave names to many of the streams where they found gold and to the mountains they used as landmarks. Up to this time the prospectors and explorers retained many of the old native names.

Lieutenant Frederick Schwatka, US Army, came over the Chilkoot Pass and rafted quickly down the Yukon River in June and July 1883, conducting the first rough survey of its course. Ignoring the names known to the natives, traders and miners he renamed most of the principal streams, lakes and outstanding features along the river after his Army superiors and prominent academicians of his day.

Dr. George Mercer Dawson, Director of the Geological and Natural History Survey of Canada (and one of Canada's outstanding explorer-geologists), in 1887 ascended the Liard and Frances Rivers from the Stikine and descended the Pelly to its junction with the Yukon, surveying the rivers and topography as he went. His maps and reports, which included all available information concerning the Territory and its inhabitants, were of such high quality that they are still classics of their kind today. He repudiated much of Schwatka's nomenclature, retaining many of the original names.

William Ogilvie, DLS, of the Department of the Interior, ran a precise survey in 1887-88 from Pyramid Harbor near Haines, Alaska, up Chilkoot Inlet to Dyea and over the Chilkoot Pass to Lake Bennett. From Bennett he carried his survey down the Yukon River to the Yukon-Alaska boundary below Forty Mile. These were the first accurate surveys made of the route through the central Yukon. He then cut the Yukon-Alaska boundary line from the Yukon River south through the Fortymile and Sixty Mile Rivers country, thus settling any dispute as to the national ownership of the rich placer goldfields then being exploited there. He later settled the first disputes as to claim ownership on Bonanza Creek in the Klondike in the fall of 1896. Ogilvie, who was to become the first Commissioner of the Yukon Territory, named a number of prominent peaks after the pioneer prospectors of the Yukon, whom he admired, and a number of streams after geological phenomena observed on them.

The Klondike Gold Rush years of 1896-99 saw hundreds of names added to the maps as thousands of gold-seekers overran the country. The custom of the times allowed the first man who found gold and staked the Discovery claim on any creek (the first or Discovery claim, was double the size of a regular claim) to give it any name he chose. In many cases where the miner was ignorant of this custom the Mining Recorder supplied the name for him.

Other and later mining rushes and stampedes to various parts of the territory added still more names to the maps. Many creeks and lakes were named locally after the trappers, traders and prospectors who made their homes on them. The Geological Survey of Canada has, since Dawson's time, added many names as its geologists mapped the rocks of the region. The Alpine Club of Canada and various institutional mountaineering expeditions have named many of the peaks in the St. Elias Range of the southwestern Yukon. Construction workers of the Alaska Highway and the Canol Pipeline added their share of new names.

The last large group of names was acquired in the 1960-70 period, when the Surveys and Mapping Branch of the Department of Energy, Mines and Resources was preparing its 1:50,000 scale topographical maps. As each sheet is titled by the name of a central feature, any that were without such names were given those of early Yukoners. Gordon McIntyre, Yukon Lands Titles Agent and later member of the Yukon Legislative Assembly was responsible for most of the research. He ensured the perpetuation of the names of many nearly forgotten pioneers.

A continuing class of names is that honouring many Yukoners and other Canadians who died in foreign wars. Individual names have been and are being proposed and adopted with the approval of the Territorial government and the Canada Permanent Committee on Geographical Names (also known as the Canadian Board on Geographical Names or the Geographical Board).

In no way is this book anything but a beginning. There are still many names for which no information has been found. There are still many gaps yet to be filled. Over the years many records have been lost or misplaced and are no longer available. It is my earnest hope that any readers who possess any part of this missing information will share it with the Yukon Archives or with me: it will be received with appreciation. With this help, in time a new and more comprehensive work can be prepared.

R.C. Coutts
Atlin, B.C.

SECOND EDITION

Almost ten years have passed since writing the above. In this time more information has accumulated from various sources. Much from interested people who have read the book and found that they had information to add. A few corrections have been made in light of new evidence. A number of new names have been designated. A great number of native names have and are being saved by the dedicated work of the Native Languages Project, ably headed by John Ritter.

There are still names I am curious about. Perhaps the coming years will reveal the information.

R.C. Coutts
Atlin, B.C.

PUBLISHER'S NOTE

Your comments, suggestions and further information can be posted on our web site: www.yukonplacesandnames.com.

ACKNOWLEDGEMENTS

It is doubtful if any book is solely the work of any one person. Certainly this one is not. Although I have gathered the material together, it would have been a much smaller work without the active help and encouragement of many other people.

My good friend Hugh S. Bostock, PhD, gentleman, scientist and bushman, whose 40 years work with the Geological Survey of Canada in the Yukon Territory makes him an authority which he is quick to disclaim, encouraged me steadily. His expert advice and incisive criticism kept me searching for the right answers.

Mrs. Helen Akrigg, herself an authority on such matters, took an interest at the beginning and sponsored my application for a Canada Council grant.

Brian Speirs, the first Archivist of the Yukon Territory and my second sponsor, has encouraged this work from the start and helped in every way to obtain obscure material as well as providing facilities for working. His successor, Linda Johnson, has continued this interest. Diane Johnston, Assistant Archivist has given much of her own time and thought to finding necessary material.

Ron D'Altroy, Curator of Photography at the Vancouver Public Library (now retired) and an old and valued friend, has contributed much both in ideas and material over the years, for which I thank him.

My gratitude must be expressed to the Explorations Programme of the Canada Council and in particular to Paul-Emile Leblanc, Executive Officer, whose patience with amateur writers seems endless. The grant enabled me to do much of the original research for this work.

Appreciation must be expressed to my friends the rare book dealers, whose advice and assistance in finding almost-unknown material was and is invaluable: particularly to John W. Todd, Jr. of Shorey's in Seattle, David Moon of West Vancouver, Bill Hoffer of Vancouver and sadly, the late R. Hilton Smith of Victoria and Stephen McIntyre of Vancouver. Each one has persistently searched for and found material previously unknown to bibliographers.

My gratitude also goes to the many institutions which gave me access to their northern collections, especially to Ann Yandel of UBC and Andy Johnson of the University of Washington, the BC Provincial and the Public Archives of Canada, the people of the Glenbow-Alberta Institute in Calgary and others too numerous to list here.

The foundation for this work was laid at the offices of the Canada Permanent Committee for Geographical Names in Ottawa with the active encouragement and help of Gordon Delaney, the Executive Secretary and his assistant Frank Stevenson who bore with my many questions and requests for many weeks. This interest and help has been continued by Allan Rayburn, the present Executive Secretary.

Mrs. Shirley Connolly, founder and past-president of the Atlin Historical Society, aided materially from her own personal knowledge of the Yukon and the people in the Ross River country. Mrs. Sue Morhun, also a past-president of the Society, gave me sound professional advice in putting the material into manuscript form.

To all these friends, thank you.

SECOND EDITION

Special mention must be made of another group, especially for this new edition.

The Yukon Native Languages Project, ably headed by John Ritter, one of the foremost authorities on northwestern Canadian native languages and his group of native ladies have given years of time and effort to preserving the languages and native names of the Yukon. Travelling the old native trade and hunting trails of the Territory and re-establishing the original native names, many almost forgotten, they have contributed greatly to keeping the native history of the Territory alive. Too much credit cannot be given to this group. To them, my sincerest appreciation.

LOCATING THE FEATURES LISTED

All features named in this work are listed alphabetically. Their positions are based on the National Topographic series of maps, scale 1:250,000 (1 inch=4 miles), which gives a complete coverage of the Yukon Territory using 45 separate map sheets. They are available at Mac's Fireweed Books on Main St. in Whitehorse (also visit yukonbooks.com) and at a number of other retail locations throughout the Territory. Each of these sheets is known by sheet name and sheet number (e.g. Dawson (116-B), Whitehorse (105-D)).

These maps are plotted in degrees and minutes of latitude and longitude which increase to the north and west from the bottom right hand corner of the sheet. Using these figures the location of any place is easily and quickly obtained. Settlement locations are pin-pointed. The figures given for a mountain are those of its highest point. Those for lakes are at the center of the lake, those for rivers and creeks are given at the mouth of the stream.

In this work a rough description of the location is given after the map sheet number.

ABBREVIATIONS USED IN THE TEXT

BCLS	British Columbia Land Surveyor.
CEF	Canadian Expeditionary Forces. (The Canadian Army overseas during the First World War).
CPCGN	Canada Permanent Committee on Geographical Names.
CIMM	Canadian Institute of Mining and Metallurgy.
CMG	Companion of the Order of St. Michael and St. George (A British Order of Chivalry). A Long Service and Good Conduct Medal awarded to senior civil servants and their equivalents in the Armed Forces.
DFC	Distinguished Flying Cross. Awarded for bravery in action by officers of the British Air Forces.
DFM	Distinguished Flying Medal. Awarded for bravery in action by non-commissioned officers of the British Air Forces.
DLS	Dominion Land Surveyor.
DSM	Distinguished Service Medal. An American decoration for service, both civilian and military.
DSO	Distinguished Service Order. A British award to officers, usually of Field rank, for exceptional bravery and leadership against an enemy.
DTS	Dominion Topographical Surveyor. The most highly qualified degree for Canadian surveyors.
FASAS	Fellow of the American Society for the Advancement of Science.
FRGS	Fellow of the Royal Geographical Society.
FRSC	Fellow of the Royal Society of Canada. (The equivalent of the Royal Society of Great Britain).
G&NHSC	Geological and Natural History Survey of Canada (The forerunner of the Geological Survey of Canada).

GSC	Geological Survey of Canada.
HBC	Governor and Company of Adventurers Trading into Hudson's Bay. As a business title it was more simply called "The Hudson's Bay Company", later shortened to "The Bay".
IODE	Imperial Order of Daughters of the Empire.
KCMG	Knight Commander of the Order of St. Michael and St. George. A British Order of Chivalry awarded for most distinguished service in any field. This conveys Knighthood.
MC	Military Cross. Awarded to officers of the British Armies for bravery in action.
MID	Mentioned in Dispatches. A citation for outstanding conduct during a military operation by any member of the British Forces.
MM	Military Medal. Awarded to non-commissioned officers of the British Army for bravery in action.
MP	Member of Parliament.
NAT&TC	North American Transportation and Trading Company. They built Fort Cudahy at Forty Mile in 1893.
NCO	Non-Commissioned Officers. Corporals, Sergeants, Warrant Officers, etc. in any Police or Armed Forces
NWMP	North West Mounted Police (1873-1904).
NWT	North West Territories. Before June, 1898 the Yukon was part of the NWT.
OBE	Order of the British Empire. A minor British Chivalrous Order, awarded for service in any field.
OMI	Oblates of Mary Immaculate.
QLS	Quebec Land Surveyor.
RCAF	Royal Canadian Air Force.
RCMP	Royal Canadian Mounted Police (1920-present).
RCN	Royal Canadian Navy.
RCNVR	Royal Canadian Naval Volunteer Reserve.
RGS	Royal Geographical Society. A prestigious British Society for the advancement of geographical exploration and study.
RN	Royal Navy.
RNWMP	Royal North West Mounted Police (1904-1920).
T&D	Taylor & Drury.
USC&GS	United States Coast and Geodetic Survey.
USGS	United States Geological Survey.
YOOP	Yukon Order of Pioneers. A society or brotherhood formed by early Yukoners at Forty Mile in 1894, of those who had come into the Yukon before 1887. It is still an active society.

HOW TO NAME A FEATURE IN THE YUKON TERRITORY

It is the privilege of any person or organization to ask that a chosen name be given to any feature in the Yukon Territory. There are definite rules of procedure to be followed to make the name official. A booklet, prepared by the Committee on Geographical Names, which outlines advice and requirements, may be obtained by contacting the office of the Committee, now established in Whitehorse.

Briefly, the requirements for naming a feature are as follows:

1. Names proposed must be for specific geographic features. The Committee does not normally select features for naming.
2. The following information must be supplied for all names or name change proposed:

(a) Location - by latitude and longitude (specify the map you are using), map references, sketch or photograph.

(b) Feature identification - indicate the extent as precisely as possible by colour, arrows or description relative to adjoining features.

(c) If new name(s), also supply

   1. Origin.
   2. Reasons for proposal.
   3. Evidence that the feature is unnamed.

(d) If changing existing name(s), also supply

   1. Alternate name(s).
   2. Reasons for the proposed change(s).

PHOTOS: (top) Yukon River from the Midnight Dome, (top inset) S.S. Klondike on the banks of the Yukon River (bottom) Boat navigating the Yukon River at Dawson City, (bottom inset) Cabin on Wye Lake. Photos: Pat Reece

ABRAHAM CREEK 63°32'N 139°58'W (115-0). A tributary to the Sixty Mile River.

This stream was named after Harry ABRAHAM who mined 27 placer gold claims here from 1913 to 1925 and who had probably prospected in the area much earlier.

ACLAND CREEK 60°18'N 127°30'W (95-D). Flows into the Coal River.

In 1956, G.W. Rowley named this stream in honour of Sgt. Arthur Edward ACLAND, RNWMP, who was in this area around 1910. He was later in charge of the police post at Kluane from 1912 to 1914.

MOUNT ADAMI 4,158' 63°19'N 138°02'W (115-P). Forty-five miles up the Stewart River on the south side.

F.A. Stretch, Warden at Carmacks, named this hill after Frank ADAMI, a long-time Yukoner who had trapped in this area from 1936 to 1957. ADAMI came from a good background, holding three degrees in chemistry and physics from Milwaukee and the Sorbonne, but he preferred the solitary life of a trapper to any other. He died in Vancouver, BC in 1958.

ADAMS CREEK 63°56'N 139°20'W (115-0). A small stream entering Bonanza Creek from the west, a short distance above the mouth.

Originally called ADAMS Gulch, probably by Carlo Tilly who was the first man to stake a claim on it on 31 August 1896, this little stream was staked immediately after Bonanza and at the same time as Eldorado. The first miners found little gold here, showing the chanciness of placer mining. However, two years later in 1898 new miners tried again and found payable gold.

MOUNT ADNEY 64°37'N 138°26'W (116-B). Northwest of North Fork Mountain.

Named after Tappan ADNEY, correspondent for Harpers Weekly and the London Chronicle, covering the Klondike Gold Rush in 1898-99. His book, "Klondike Stampede", written of his experiences during this period, remains one of the best and most factual of those written about the Gold Rush. ADNEY was also an authority on all types of canoes and wrote a definitive book on the subject.

AFE CREEK 62°17'N 135°53'W (105-L). Flows into the Tatchun River.

This stream was named about 1954 after AFE Brown, pioneer packer, trapper and miner in this area for many years. Acknowledged a superior man by his contemporaries, he was well-liked and respected by all who knew him. He died in 1952 at a sawmill owned by his two sons at the mouth of the nearby Tatchun River. This creek had been called by his name by the local people long before he died.

AFE PEAK 5,662' 62°15'N 135°23'W (105-L). At the headwaters of AFE Creek.

AFE Brown's name was further commemorated by giving it to this peak in 1954. (see Afe Creek, Victoria Creek and Mount McDade)

AGHOO CREEK 66°00'N 134°40'W (106-E) A tributary to Nihtal Git Creek.

A Loucheau Indian name meaning "Eggs". The Indians came here in summer to gather the eggs of nesting waterfowl.

AHVEE MOUNTAIN 3,701' 67°10'N 139°47'W (116-O&N). Twenty-eight miles south of Old Crow.

Long known to the people of Old Crow, this is a Vanta Kutchin Indian word meaning "Weasel".

AISHIHIK LAKE 61°25'N 136°15'W (115-H). One hundred miles northwest of Whitehorse.

This is an old Indian name meaning "High Place". Later research into the name meaning says that the word is a Tuchone Indian word referring to a bend or tail in the lake formed by the last bay at the head of the lake.

The lake is 35 miles long and, at an elevation of 3001 feet above sea level, is the highest lake of comparable size in all of Canada. A long-time Indian community of the same name on the north shore was abandoned after 1967.

A hydro-electric power dam was constructed here in the 1970s and, since early 1976, has supplied electricity to the Yukon power grid.

ALASKA HIGHWAY 1523 miles (2454KM) from Mile "0" at Dawson Creek, B.C. to Fairbanks, Alaska, of which 1221 miles (1972KM) are in Canada. A paved road most of the way, together with oil-sealed sections traverse some of the most beautiful scenery in North America.

Since the early 1900s, various groups in Canada and the US had pressed for a highway to Alaska. In 1930, the US government established the Alaska International Highway Commission and in 1931 a similar body was set up by the Canadian government to study the location, financing and construction of such a road.

Finally, two major routes were chosen. Route "A" started from Vancouver, B.C. and went through Prince George, Hazelton, Telegraph Creek and Atlin and on to Whitehorse: 1275 miles approximately. Route "B" went through Prince George, Fort St. James, Dease Lake and Atlin to Whitehorse: 1250 miles approximately. Several other routes were proposed for special or local reasons. The major reason advanced for constructing the road was the advantage of a land link to Alaska in time of war. The major problem was always financing.

In February 1942, the American armed forces, ignoring all previous plans and studies, chose the present and, until then, unconsidered route. The need for an access and service road for the string of airfields being built between Edmonton and Fairbanks to supply Russia with airplanes was immediate; local and future economic needs of the region were of secondary importance. An agreement with the Canadian government was quickly reached.

Surveys were started the same month and by April 1942 construction had begun. Round-the-clock work by 9,000 US Army Engineers saw a usable truck road pushed through by late November. Following the troops were civilian contractors, 77 of them: 62 American and 15 Canadian firms employed 12,000 men to bring the road up to standard by late 1943. In all, 7,000 pieces of equipment were used.

The US government paid all construction costs and the cost of maintenance up to 1 April 1946, when the Canadian section was turned over to the Canadian Army Engineers. The airfields and land communication systems were turned over to the RCAF at the same time. The road was maintained until 1965 by the Canadian Army Engineers and from that date by the Departments of Highways of the Yukon Territory and British Columbia, with federal assistance. The total cost of the highway to 1 April 1946 was never revealed but estimates placed it above $138,000,000.

Officially and originally named the "Alaska Military Highway", the men on the job soon shortened this to "The Alcan". Neither name was popular with the public, which had followed the construction with great interest. On 25 March 1943, Anthony J. Dimond, Congressman from Alaska, proposed the name, "The Alaska Highway", which was officially adopted by both governments on 19 July 1943. (Dimond had been a long-time backer of Route "A").

The speed of construction, the location and the climate all make this project one of the great engineering feats of our time. As shorter and more economical routes are being built closer to the Pacific coast, the highway will gradually lose its overall importance but never its history or impact on the Yukon and central Alaska, where its opening heralded the end of an era.

ALBERT CREEK 60°03'N 128°54'W (105-A). A tributary to the Liard River, crossing the Alaska Highway near Mile 643 (KM1029).

This is a long-known local name after ALBERT Dease, an old-time packer and trapper in the area for many years. As he lisped, many people thought his name was pronounced Deeth or Death.

ALBERT CREEK 61°34'N 137°33'W (115-F). Flows into Sekulmun Lake.

Named after ALBERT Isaac, the son of Chief Isaac. He lived here for many years, hunting and trapping. (see Isaac Creek)

MOUNT ALBERTA 10,985' 60°57'N 140°51'W (115-C). In the Centennial Range of the St. Elias Mountains.

This was named in 1967, in honour of the province of ALBERTA to celebrate Canada's Centennial Year. (see Centennial Range)

ALKI CREEK 64°04'N 138°59'W (116-B). A small stream entering the Klondike River, about twenty miles east of Dawson.

A.E. Elliott, who had come from Seattle to Skagway in the old steamship "ALKI", found gold and staked the Discovery claim here, on 24 November 1897. He named the creek at this time.

ALLAN CREEK 60°30'N 129°45'W (105-A). Flows into the Liard River, forty miles northwest of Watson Lake.

This was a long-used local name after Fred ALLAN who trapped here for many years. A striking character, he resembled Buffalo Bill Cody, was a crack shot with pistol or rifle and preferred an isolated life in the bush. In the early 1900s he and George Adsit (reputed to have been a member of Butch Cassidy's "Hole-in-the-Wall Gang") drove a herd of horses overland from Montana to Teslin Lake.

ALLGOLD CREEK 63°56'N 138°27'W (115-0). A short creek running from King Solomon's Dome to the Klondike River.

Clinton Jones staked and optimistically named this creek on 10 September 1897. He was mistaken. Although it is in the Klondike and between rich placer gold creeks, it produced almost no gold at all.

ALMSTROM CREEK 68°08'N 136°27'W (117-A). A tributary to Cache Creek from the east.

This stream was named in 1973, after Marion Edward ALMSTROM, who came into the Yukon in May 1944 as the first Engineer in charge of Water Surveys in the Yukon area. In 1952 he was appointed the first resident Federal Mining Inspector for the Territory. He died in August 1960.

ALSEK RIVER 60°00'N 137°49'W (115-A). Flows from the Kluane Range through the St. Elias Mountains and into the Pacific Ocean, south of Yakutat Bay.

It is a rough and almost impassable stream. The native name "Alsekh" was reported by the Russian Captain Tebenkov in 1825. Earlier, LaPerouse, the French explorer in 1786 had named it "Riviere du Behring". The New York Times Expedition in 1886 (led by Lt. Frederick Schwatka) had named it the "Jones" River after one of Schwatka's sponsors. The name was laughed to oblivion. The USC&GS called it the "Harrison" River in honour of a US President. The US and Canadian governments, in 1891, officially gave it back its original and present name.

The first white men to explore the river were members of the Frank Leslie Illustrated Newspaper Expedition, Edward James Glave and Jack Dalton who travelled it by canoe from Neskataheen (near Dalton House) to the sea in 1890, the only men ever to do so.

ALVERSON GULCH 64°06'N 135°02'W (106-D). A small tributary to Scougale Creek in the Davidson Range.

Jack ALVERSON, who came into the Yukon in 1899, lived and prospected on this creek. Originally from Oregon, he spent most of his life here and about the upper Stewart River country. In 1910 he and his partner, Grant Hoffman, mined 59 tons of high-grade, silver-lead ore, the first ever mined in the Mayo district. The ore body had been found in 1906 by H.W. McWhorter and was the first such ore found in the Mayo area.

MOUNT ALVERSTONE 14,565' 60°21'N 139°04'W (115-B). In the St. Elias Range, close to the Yukon-Alaska boundary.

This mountain was named in 1908 by the Canadian government after Baron Richard Everard ALVERSTONE, KCMG, Lord Chief Justice of England and the British member of the Canadian-Alaskan Boundary Tribunal of 1903. He cast the vote which established the present boundary between Canada and Alaska, effectively cutting off the Yukon and the northern half of British Columbia from access to the Pacific except through US territory. He was acting on orders from the British government which had been informed secretly by the American President, Theodore Roosevelt, that if the vote went against the US he would send in troops, already in place at Haines, Alaska, to seize all the disputed areas. ALVERSTONE voted as ordered. This threat went unrevealed for many years.

This mountain was first climbed on 28 July 1957 by Robert H. Bates, Peter H. Wood, Nicholas Clifford and Walter A. Wood.

AMERICAN GULCH 63°57'N 139°16'W (115-0). Just one-quarter mile long, this little brook enters Bonanza Creek on the west side, a mile below Eldorado Creek.

It was staked entirely by American prospectors. B.H. Laughlin and his brother Chester made the discovery and staked the first two claims on the 20 August 1897.

On 15 June 1904, a gold nugget was found here which, it was claimed, weighed 450 ounces. This would be by far the largest nugget ever found in the Yukon or Canada, except that a certain amount of quartz was associated with the gold in the nugget and no true weight was ever determined.

AMMERMAN MOUNTAIN 68°3'N 141°00'W (117-B). A high ridge running east-west and centered on the Yukon-Alaska boundary.

A local name after a trapper prospector, George AMMERMAN, who lived on the creek at the base of the mountain in the early 1900s. The name was bestowed in 1911 by the International Boundary Survey crew after this creek.

ANDERSON CREEK 61°34'N 129°25'W (105-H). Joins the Thomas River at the head of the east arm of Frances Lake.

Although this area was travelled from the 1840s and smaller streams named, no one noticed this creek until in 1949, when it was named to honour the memory of First Lt. P.M. ANDERSON, RN, DSC, MID, killed in action during the Second World War.

ANDERSON Lake received its name at the same time.

ANDERSON GLACIER 61°11'N 140°58'W (115-F). Straddles the Yukon-Alaska boundary, in the St. Elias Range.

This was named in 1912-13 by the International Boundary Control Survey party, after P. Chandler ANDERSON (1866-1936), of New York: he was arbiter of the Pecuniary Claims Commission of 1910 and a counsel for the US before the Yukon-Alaska Boundary Tribunal in 1903.

MOUNT ANDERSON 60°13'N 135°09'W (105-D). South of the Wheaton River.

John ANDERSON was a well-known prospector in this area for many years. The hill was given his name when he found the first minerals: gold, silver and others on it in 1910. None of his finds were of economic value at that time.

ANDREW'S LAKE 61°46'N 139°59'W (115-G). South of the Alaska Highway, near Mile 1144 (KM1841).

ANDREW Eklund made this lake his home for many years while he trapped and prospected in the immediate area. He cooked for survey crews on location of the Alaska Highway. The name has been in local use for many years.

ANGEL LAKE 64°49'N 134°39'W (106-D). A very small lake on the Wind River, three miles north of Bond Creek.

Named by L.H. Green in 1970. Around 1960, two prospectors, John Berry O'Neil and John J. O'Neil (not related), crashed here on take-off. Somehow they survived and from the incident the lake got its name.

ANIK ISLAND 66°58'N 137°38'W (116-I). An island in the Porcupine River.

The word ANIK means "brother" in the Inuit (Eskimo) language. It was given to the first northern communications satellite, ANIK 1, which was launched on 9 November 1972. ANIK 2 was put up in April 1973 and ANIK 3 two years later.

Satellites made television and telephone service available throughout Canada's north.

Each satellite carried 12 colour TV channels or 960 one-way telephone calls at the same time. No direct signals were received except through earth stations which were leased to northern communities.

The name was proposed by Gordon McIntyre, MLA.

ANKER CREEK 68°43'N 137°27'W (117-A). A tributary to the Blow River, near the Arctic coast.

This stream was probably named about 1962 by F.G. Young of the Alberta Geological Survey while he was exploring in this area for oil-bearing rock formations.

ANKER Hoidal trapped and prospected for many years on the Arctic slope and was of great service to the geologists mapping the area. (see Mount Hoidal)

ANN GULCH 64°02'N 135°50'W (106-D). A small tributary to Dublin Gulch, in the Mayo area.

Fred Taylor mined longer on Dublin Gulch than anyone else. His wife ANN and their two sons lived near here for several years and the name is used locally.

ANNE CREEK 67°54'N 136°53'W (116-P). A tributary to the Bell River.

Named by the Yukon Government in 1977, to commemorate ANNE Murray, wife of Alexander Hunter Murray. Murray was the HBC man who established Fort Yukon in Alaska in 1847.

ANNE Murray, in the fall of 1847, at LaPierre House, alone except for an Indian companion, gave birth to a daughter, Helen Murray. This girl was the first white child born in the Yukon Territory. (see Helen Creek and LaPierre House)

ANNETT CREEK 68°35'N 137°53'W (117-A). Flows into Anker Creek, near the Arctic coast.

In 1909, William ANNETT (or Annet) and David Lord, two trapper prospectors claimed to have found placer gold here. In 1916 ANNETT enlisted with the George Black contingent of the Yukon Infantry Company and fought during the First World War. (see Lord Creek)

ANTONE CREEK 60°06'N 128°23'W (105-A). A tributary to the Hyland River, ten miles east of Watson Lake.

A local Indian of this name, lived and trapped here for many years.

AQUILA CREEK 66°49'N 137°05'W (116-I). A short tributary to the Eagle River.

This was named during the wilderness study in 1973. The name is Latin for eagle, from the large number of them seen here.

ARCH CREEK 61°30'N 139°44'W (115-G). Flows into the Donjek River, ten miles south of the Alaska Highway.

Placer gold was found here during the rush to Burwash Creek and the Kluane goldfields in May 1904, by Henry Flaherty, Morely Bones and Fred Ater. They named the stream because of a peculiar, arch-like opening in the limestone rocks of the canyon.

MOUNT ARCHIBALD 8,400' 60°47'N 137°52'W (115-A). Fifteen miles west of Haines Junction.

In 1971, this mountain was named after Dr. E.S. ARCHIBALD, sometime director of the Experimental Farm Service of the Department of Agriculture. He was instrumental in setting up the Pine Creek Experimental Farm near here.

ARK MOUNTAIN 60°14'N 136°10'W (115-A). On the southwest side of Kusawa Lake.

Many years ago, local Indians hunting sheep on the mountain found the remains of an old log cabin, built by prospectors far above the tree line. Newly exposed to missionary religious teachings and unable to find any reason for anyone to carry logs this high, they thought the structure to be the remains of Noah's ARK.

Dr. E. Kindle, GSC, who explored the mountain in 1950 was told this story and confirmed the local name.

ARKANSAS CREEK 63°45'N 138°31'W (115-O). A tributary to Dominion Creek, one mile below Jensen Creek.

The Discovery claim was staked here on 19 February 1898 by P.E. Fuboman and his partner.

ARKELL CREEK 60°48'N 135°43'W (105-D). Flows into Ibex Creek and to the Takhini River.

In 1890, E.J. Glave and Jack Dalton of the first Frank Leslie Illustrated Newspaper Expedition, after separating from the other two members of the party at Lake Kusawa, travelled in this area and named this creek and also Lake Kusawa after the owner of a patent medicine company. ARKELL had organized this expedition to cash in on the publicity value of the recent news of rich gold finds at Forty Mile. In 1891 he sent Glave and Dalton back again to explore more of the country.

It was from these two journeys that Dalton conceived the idea of the Dalton Trail to the Yukon. (see Dalton Trail)

An interesting sequel to these expeditions was that in 1897 when news of the fabulous wealth of the Klondike reached the outside world, ARKELL instituted legal claims to the whole of the Klondike, based on these travels. His brother-in-law offered A.B. Schanz, one of the four members of the expedition, $50,000 for any rights he might have to such a claim. So great was the euphoria engendered by the Klondike riches that Schanz turned the offer down. Needless to say the lawsuit came to nothing. (see Alsek River and Dalton Trail)

LAKE ARKELL (see Kusawa Lake).

MOUNT ARKELL 7,246' 60°36'N 135°37'W (105-D). At the head of Arkell Creek, twenty miles southwest of Whitehorse.

This was named in the 1920s in conjunction with the creek.

MOUNT ARMSTRONG 7,083' 63°12'N 133°15'W (105-N). The highest peak in the Russell Range.

This was named in 1954 under the auspices of the Hon. George Black, MP for the Yukon, after Lt. Col. Neville Alexander Drummond ARMSTRONG, OBE, FRGS, '98er, prospector, miner, geographer, big-game hunter and conservationist, soldier and gentleman.

Born in England in 1874, ARMSTRONG at the age of 17 spent three years in Texas and New Mexico as a day labourer. In 1898, he came to the Klondike via St. Michaels as assistant manager of the Yukon Goldfields Company. He acquired rich claims for the company on Bonanza Creek and Cheechako Hill and became manager of the company. In 1901, he made a deal with Duncan Gillies (or Gillis), the discoverer, for a placer concession on Russell Creek on the MacMillan River. On 3 August 1901, together with his crew of six, he took the first steamboat, the Prospector, up the MacMillan River to Russell Creek. For this journey he was made a Fellow of the Royal Geographical Society.

In 1904 and 1905, he was appointed Game Warden for the MacMillan River country. Until 1914 he spent almost every summer and several winters on Russell Creek, searching for the elusive gold but with little success. In 1914, ARMSTRONG joined the Canadian Expeditionary Forces in France. Given the rank of Major, he trained scouts and snipers and was awarded the Order of the British Empire for his outstanding services. Returning to Russell Creek in 1920, he worked until 1926 before giving up the quest. In 1928 he left for England, never to return.

In 1939, at the age of 65, he joined the British Army and organized a sniping school. He served in France in early 1940, missing Dunkirk. Transferring to the Canadian First Division he was later retired because of his age. The British Army, with better judgement, promoted him to Lieutenant Colonel and placed him in command of the Royal Marines Small Arms School.

He died in November 1954. For most of 30 years he was a part of the Yukon, believing in its bounty, studying its animals and features and gaining the respect of all who knew him. His two books: "After Big Game in the Upper Yukon" and "Yukon Yesterdays: Thirty Years of Adventure in the Klondike" are a window on Yukon backcountry adventure. (see Russell, George, Jessica and Marion Creeks and Mount Gillis)

ARMSTRONG 63°03'N 133°24'W (105-N).

This was a small trading post established in 1919 by Alex Coward and Arthur Zimmerman of Fort Selkirk. It was about one half mile downstream from ARMSTRONG Landing. They were in business here until the 1930s.

ARMSTRONG LANDING 63°05'N 13°25'W (105-N). At the mouth of Russell Creek.

Neville ARMSTRONG built a landing place here with storage cabins in 1901 and later, to service his operations nearby. No one lived here permanently and it fell into disuse after 1926 when he abandoned operations.

ARTHUR LAING PEAK 69°11'N 140°56'W (117-C). In the British Mountains.

The suggestion of James Smith, Commissioner of the Yukon Territory, to commemorate the late Senator ARTHUR LAING, once Minister of Indian Affairs and Northern Development in a Liberal government cabinet.

MOUNT ARTHUR WHEELER 61°11'N 140°09'W (115-F). Above the Steele Glacier, in the St. Elias Range.

A peak named by the Alpine Club of Canada in memory of their first President, ARTHUR Oliver WHEELER (1906-10). Born in Kilkenny, Ireland on 1 May 1860, he came to Canada in 1876. He became a surveyor and a founder of the Alpine Club in 1906. He died in 1945.

ART LEWIS GLACIER 60°00'N 139°00'W (115-B). On the Yukon-Alaska boundary.

This small glacier was named jointly by the US and Canadian governments in 1922, in memory of ARTHUR LEWIS, a member of the Canadian Boundary Survey parties in 1912 and 1917. He was killed in action in France while serving with the 72nd Highlanders of Canada during the First World War.

ASKIN LAKE 61°56'N 133°14'W (105-F). Twenty-five miles west of Ross River.

In 1951, this little lake was chosen to honour the memory of Gunner C.D. ASKIN, Royal Canadian Artillery, MID. He was killed in action during the Second World War.

MOUNT ATHERTON 62°02'N 133°54'W (105-K). Seventeen miles southwest of Faro, in the Pelly mountains.

This hill was named about 1970 after Charles T. ATHERTON, long-time Yukoner at Whitehorse and a Territorial Councillor in the mid-1930s.

ATLAS CREEK 61°14'N 139°12'W (115-F). A short tributary to the Duke River from the south.

Named in 1972, by the Yukon Scenic and Wilderness Study Group because a huge, two storey high boulder is wedged between the walls of its gorge.

ATLIN LAKE 60°00'N 133°50'W (105-C). Straddles the Yukon-B.C. boundary, twenty miles east of Carcross.

With its surrounding mountains, ATLIN LAKE is one of the most beautiful in North America. It is 70 miles long and, so far, unpolluted. The Tlingit Indians who came here for centuries from the Taku River region called it "Ahklen" or "Aht-lah" meaning "Big Water". Dr. George Mercer Dawson, G&NHSC, officially adopted the Indian name in 1887.

Probably the first white man to see the lake was Michael Byrne, an explorer working for the Western Union Telegraph Co., who is now believed to have reached the south end of the lake from the Taku River in 1867.

In August 1898, Fritz Miller and Kenneth MacLaren of Juneau found rich placer goldfields on the east side of the lake, second in importance only to the Klondike itself. Of the many people bound for the Klondike via the White and Chilkoot Passes, 10,000 to 15,000 were diverted to this discovery. The White Pass and Yukon Railway, under construction at the time, lost 80% of its workers almost overnight as they deserted, some with their tools. Gold has been mined here ever since.

MOUNT AUGUSTA 14,070' 60°18'N 140°27'W (115-C). One of the boundary marker mountains in the St. Elias Range.

Named in 1891 by Professor Israel C. Russell, USGS, after his wife J. AUGUSTA Olmstead Russell. Russell was the first scientist to explore the topography and geology of the St. Elias region. His expedition was jointly sponsored by the USGS and the National Geographical Society in 1890-91. AUGUSTA Glacier was named at the same time. (see Russell Col)

AUSSIE CREEK 64°02'N 137°56'W (116-A). Flows into the Klondike River from the north.

It was originally named Australia Creek in 1897 by Australian miners, of whom there were many in the stampede to the Klondike. The name was changed by W.H. Miller, GSC, in 1935, to avoid confusion with the earlier named creek of the same name flowing into the Indian River, in the south Klondike.

MOUNT AUSTON 64°39'N 138°31'W (116-B). In the south Wernecke Mountains, twelve miles west of Worm Lake.

This mountain was named about 1968 by G.W. Rowley after the late Robert AUSTON, long-time prospector and big-game guide, who discovered and tried to develop copper deposits at nearby Worm Lake.

AUSTRALIA CREEK 63°37'N 138°42'W (115-O). A tributary to the Indian River in the south Klondike.

Although Robert Henderson was the first recorded prospector on this stream, it was very likely named by other prospectors around 1891-94.

AXEMAN CREEK 64°29'N 138°27'W (116-B). A tributary to the North Klondike River.

In 1968, Dr. Dirk Tempelman-Kluit, GSC, named this creek because of the very old blazed trail he found on it.

AZURE LAKE 64°29'N 138°36'W (116-B). A mile east of the Blackstone River.

Named by Dr. Dirk Tempelman-Kluit, GSC, in 1968 because of its intense blue colour.

BABBAGE RIVER 69°14'N 138°27'W (117-D). Flows north into the Beaufort Sea, near Herschel Island.

One of the earliest named features in the Yukon Territory. Found and named by Sir John Franklin, RN, during his second Arctic expedition in 1826. Charles BABBAGE (1792-1871) was a noted British mathematician and a founder of the Astronomical Society.

The Inuit (Eskimo) called it "Cook-Keaktok" meaning "Rocky River".

BABICHE MOUNTAIN 60°18'N 124°21'W (95-C). In the far southeastern corner of the territory, in a bend of the LaBiche River.

This feature was probably named by or for Bobby LaBiche, a MacKenzie River Indian from Fort Simpson and Fort Liard in the NWT, whose trapping area centered here for many years.

BABICHE is a northern word (from French-Canadian voyageurs) used to describe raw or untanned leather from moose, caribou or deer hides. It is used to string snowshoes and to bind tools as it shrinks when drying.

MOUNT BACH 61°08'N 136°31'W (115-H). An isolated peak east of the Hutchi Lakes, at the head of the Nordenskiold River.

This was named in 1897, after Frank BACH who helped Jack Dalton make the Dalton Trail through here to the Yukon River.

BACK CREEK 62°03'N 137°04'W (115-I). A tributary to Victoria Creek, ten miles southeast of Mount Nansen.

Captain Henry Seymour BACK and his son Frank prospected this stream and named it in 1910. (see Seymour Creek, Discovery Creek and Mount Nansen)

BACKE GLACIER 61°13'N 140°19'W (115-F). On the east side of Mount Wood, in the St. Elias Range.

In 1971, this glacier was named to honour a pioneer, John BACKE (or Bakke) who lived and mined for many years in the Mayo district. Moving to Haines Junction in 1945, he built the first lodge here. He died in 1970.

BACKHOUSE RIVER 69°35'N 140°32'W (117-C). A small river entering the Beaufort Sea east of Clarence Lagoon.

Named in 1826, by Sir John Franklin, RN, on his second Arctic Expedition, after his friend John BACKHOUSE, the Under Secretary of State for Foreign Affairs for Great Britain at the time.

MOUNT BADHAM 12,625' 60°51'N 139°52'W (115-B). At the head of the Donjek Glacier, in the St. Elias Range.

This was named in 1919, to honour the memory of Francis Molyneaux BADHAM, a member of various International Boundary Survey parties. Enlisting in the Canadian Army in 1914, one of the first, he was killed in action in France in 1915.

MOUNT BAIRD 60°20'N 140°31'W (115-C). A high peak, five miles northwest of Mount Augusta.

Named by Professor Israel C. Russell, USGS, in 1890, after Professor Spencer Fullerton BAIRD, Secretary of the Smithsonian Institution.

MOUNT BAIRD 5,487' 65°20'N 133°49'W (106-F). Northwest of Mount Augusta.

Named by James Smith, Commissioner of the Yukon Territory, in 1973 after Andrew BAIRD. Born in Ballarat, Australia into a farming family in 1876. In 1898, at age 22, he joined the Klondike Stampede and packed his supplies over the White Pass. He staked a claim on Sulphur Creek. The stream was not the richest in the Klondike but supplied a steady income. Believing in its potential he bought 10 other claims on the creek as others left for the Tanana and Nome rushes. In 1909 he associated with A.N.C. Treadgold who was consolidating large areas of placer ground on Dominion, Sulphur, Quartz and Gold Run Creeks, to be mined by large scale methods. He became Chief Accountant with Treadgold and each of the succeeding companies, and eventually General Manager of the Yukon Consolidated Gold Company, until they ceased dredging operations in 1966. He retired to Vancouver, B.C. and died in 1976, just a few days short of his 100th birthday. His book "Sixty Years in The Klondike", is well worth reading.

BAKER CREEK 64°00'N 139°38'W (115-O). A small tributary to the Yukon River from the east side, eight miles above Dawson.

J.A. BAKER named this stream in 1897-98. He found little on it but prospected for many years in the Livingstone Creek and Boswell River districts.

BAKER LAKE 60°12'N 128°28'W (105-A). Twelve miles northeast of Watson Lake.

This was named after Jack W. BAKER, the first weather observer and radio-wireless operator for the Yukon Southern Transport Ltd. at Watson Lake. BAKER was an all-round bushman and, in 1941 before the Alaska Highway was built, he and his wife and daughters were the only white inhabitants of the area that today is the site of the Watson Lake Airport.

MOUNT BAKER 62°34'N 140°09'W (115-J). On the west side of the White River, three miles north of Ten Mile Creek.

William J. Peters and Alfred H. Brooks, USGS, named this peak while on their expedition to the White River and Tanana River basin in June 1898. They named it after one of their four packers, H.B. BAKER.

BALLARAT CREEK 64°17'N 139°39'W (116-B). A tributary to the Chandindu River.

W.F. Woodward named this stream after the famous goldfields in southwestern Australia when he found enough gold here to stake a Discovery claim on 9 March 1898. The Dawson Mining Recorder allowed another Discovery to be recorded on 14 October 1899 by J.A. Kirkman.

At the time this took place a person staking a claim had forty days to record it at the Mining Recorder's office for that district. Owing to the lack of maps of the area and to the distances involved it sometimes happened that two men found gold on different parts of the same stream at the same time. In such a case the Mining Recorder had the option to allow both Discovery claims. In another case, if all claims on a stream were abandoned, the next man to stake could file a Discovery claim. Discovery claims were twice the size of regular claims. This happened on Quartz and Dominion Creeks in the Klondike and at several other places in the Yukon. (see Touleary Creek)

BALLARD CREEK 63°56'N 136°28'W (115-P). A tributary to the North McQuesten River.

A prospector-trapper of this name made his home here from the early 1900s to the 1930s.

MOUNT BARK 61°05'N 137°30'W (115-H). Fifteen miles south of Sekulmun Lake.

This mountain was named in 1958 to honour the name of 0-04450 Sub. Lt. Wilfred BARK, RCN, MID. He was born in Toronto, Ontario, on 1 March 1922 and enlisted in the Royal Canadian Navy on 13 January 1942 at Montreal. He served in Canada and at sea and was missing, presumed dead, on 22 February 1943.

BARKER CREEK 63°11'N 138°54'W (115-0). A tributary to the Stewart River, twenty miles above its mouth.

This was named on the 8 November 1898 by F.M. BARKER who staked the lower half of the Discovery claim that day. Little gold was found and all claims were soon abandoned. In 1903 Louis Marret found good prospects and staked a new Discovery claim. There was another and later stampede on this creek in 1906 but it never lived up to its early promise.

MOUNT BARKER 60°23'N 137°13'W (115-A). Five miles west of Beloud Post.

Edward Herman BARKER was a dredgemaster in the Klondike and Mayo districts and in Siberia. He and his partner, Irvine Ray, mined on Haggart Creek in the 1930s and on Shorty Creek around 1946. This mountain was named in 1973.

BARLOW 63°37'N 137°38'W (115-P). At the junction of Clear Creek and the Stewart River.

A small settlement was started here in 1903 when placer mining began on Clear Creek and its tributaries. A steamboat landing, roadhouse and trading post to supply the miners were built. It was abandoned sometime in the 1920s.

BARLOW CITY 63°45'N 137°38'W (115-P). At the junction of Barlow and Clear Creeks.

A small settlement, connected to BARLOW by a rough trail, was built here in 1903 with a trading post and roadhouse to service miners on the creek. It too was abandoned in the 1920s. The government has officially designated this site as BARLOW (locality).

MOUNT BARLOW 65°21'N 141°00'W (116-G). On the Yukon-Alaska boundary.

This feature was named in 1912 by D.D. Cairnes, GSC, after his assistant, F.J. BARLOW, who helped him map the geology along this portion of the Yukon-Alaska boundary that year.

BARNEY CREEK 63°59'N 135°10'W (105-M). A small stream flowing into the Keno Ladue River, north of Keno Hill.

This creek was one of the first to be named in this part of the country when BARNEY Hill found gold on it in 1890.

BARNEY LAKE 60°00'N 127°24'W (95-D). On the Yukon-B.C. boundary, ten miles west of the Coal River.

Kenneth MacMillan trapped for many years in this area. He made his camp on this lake and named it after his son, BARNEY, who was born here.

BARR CREEK 63°04'N 132°48'W (105-N). A tributary to the North MacMillan River.

This creek was the home of John BARR and was known by his name since 1900. His cabin was at the mouth of the stream. BARR came into the country in 1898 and ranged this area for a great many years, trapping and prospecting. Tall, rugged and a supreme bushman, he was known as the "King of the MacMillan Country" by both whites and Indians. Courteous and ever helpful, he was liked and respected by all.

BARWELL LAKE 62°39'N 133°05'W (105-K). Thirty-five miles north of Faro, near the Tay River.

A young Englishman, Charles S.W. BARWELL, became a Dominion Land Surveyor. Coming into the Klondike in the spring of 1897 he worked for the government for several years in many parts of the territory, mostly on claim and route surveys. A friend of his gave the lake its name.

BATTLE CREEK 62°42'N 138°18'W (115-J). A tributary to the Selwyn River.

Pontius Servus Larson and Charles J. Brown found gold here and named the creek on 28 September 1915. They had just heard the news of heavy fighting in France, involving Canadian troops.

BAULTOFF CREEK 62°10'N 141°00'W (115-J). A tributary to Beaver Creek.

W.M. BAULTOFF came into the Yukon in 1898 and prospected in the Klondike and western regions for many years. He found lode-gold (vein) prospects here in 1903-04. His find led to a minor rush in which other vein deposits were discovered, as well as placer gold on some nearby streams.

BAULTOFF Mountain, above the creek was probably named by D.D. Cairnes, GSC, while mapping the geology of the boundary area in 1911-12.

BAWN BOY GULCH 64°02'N 135°47'W (106-D). A very small tributary to Dublin Gulch.

Rich silver-lead ore was found here by Robert Fisher in 1916. He gave his Discovery claim an old Celtic name meaning "cowherd" or "cowboy". The name was locally corrupted to "Bum Boy" and was so used for many years in the literature and on mining maps. (see Fisher Creek)

BEAR CREEK 64°02'N 139°15'W (116-B). A small stream entering the Klondike River, about six miles east of Dawson.

On 24 September 1896, shortly after George Carmack found gold on Bonanza Creek, Salmo Manberg, too late to find a claim on either Bonanza or Eldorado Creeks, prospected this little stream, found gold and staked a Discovery claim that day. He and his partners, William Corley and Frank Johnson, who staked Nos. 1 and 2 below Discovery, called the creek by this name because of the number of black bears who found them and their camp.

The creek gave up considerable wealth although it was not nearly as rich as Bonanza or Eldorado. A settlement was later established at the mouth of the creek by Joe Boyle, who was mining on Bear Creak as early as 1898. Yukon Consolidated Gold Corporation Ltd. eventually had their headquarters at Bear Creek, but they did not get organized until the late 1920s and took over Bear Creek when they consolidated Joe Boyle's company, along with several others in 1933. They then started building dredges and operating the ones that had belonged to the companies they took over. YCGC shut down all operations and abandoned the site in 1966.

Parks Canada took over the site in the 1970s and today uses the old YCGC camp to display methods of mining in the Klondike and as a museum of mining machinery.

BEAR RIVER 64°55'N 134°43'W (106-D). A tributary to the Wind River.

This is a translation of an old Loucheaux Indian name meaning "Bear Killed One of Us Here".

BEARFEED CREEK 62°10'N 135°05'W (105-L). A tributary to the Little Salmon River.

In 1925, W.E. Cockfield, GSC, gave the creek this name because of the large number of bears attracted to the stream by the extensive berry patches on its banks.

MOUNT BEATON 60°01'N 137°02'W (115-A). An isolated peak seven miles south of Dalton Post.

J.N. Wallace, DLS, named this peak after P. BEATON, a member of his International Boundary Survey crew in 1908.

BEAUFORT SEA (117-D).

The Beaufort Sea is that part of the Arctic Ocean touching the northern shore of Alaska and the Yukon. It is bounded by Cape Barrow on the west and Prince Patrick Island on the east.

It received its name in 1826 when Sir John Franklin, RN, named it after his friend, Captain (later Admiral) Sir Francis BEAUFORT, RN (1774-1857), at that time hydrographer to the British Admiralty. He is best remembered for the scale of wind velocities which he invented, still in general use by most sailors. Several other features on the Arctic Slope in Alaska are also named for him.

BEAUVETTE HILL 63°57'N 136°06'W (105-M). The easternmost of the five summits of Keno Hill.

Louis BEAUVETTE (often spelled Bouvette or Bovette) discovered rich silver-lead ore on this hill in 1919. (see Mount Bouvette and Keno Hill, also Carson Creek)

BEAVER CITY 64°29'N 135°17'W (106-D). At the junction of Carpenter and Settlemier Creeks.

This small settlement was established here in 1923 when silver-lead deposits were found in the vicinity. The name was given because travellers to the area came up the Beaver River. It was a distribution and supply point for the miners in the area. The ore bodies found were not rich enough to support economic production and the area was abandoned by 1925 and soon all traces vanished.

Mining interest and activity in the area began again in the late 1970s and early 1980s. (see Carpenter and Settlemier Creeks)

BEAVER CREEK 65°47'N 135°13'W (106-E). A tributary to the Wind River.

This stream was named by HBC men before 1875. Perhaps because of large numbers of beaver trapped on it.

BEAVER CREEK 62°27'N 140°13'W (115-J). A tributary to Snag Creek.

The whole stream was called "Snag Creek" until 1902, when this part was renamed BEAVER, leaving the lower part with the original name.

The BEAVER CREEK area was first prospected by Frederick W. Best, Peter Nelson and William James between 1909 and 1914. Nelson and James went on to discover the rich placer goldfields of the Chisana, Alaska district, just over the boundary, in 1913. This creek was used as a supply route and winter trail between the steamboat landing on the White River and the Chisana diggings.

James B. Hendryx, the western novelist, used this creek as the setting for his series of Yukon short stories and novels concerning Corporal Downey, RNWMP, Black John Smith, Cushing's Fort and Halfaday Creek, which are still read and enjoyed.

The small settlement where the stream crosses the Alaska Highway at Mile 1196 (KM1914) was started around 1955 and had a Post Office in 1958. Canada Customs and other businesses have enlarged the community since then. This place is also the scene of the contact point of the northern and southern construction crews building the Alaska Highway. On 20 October 1942 bulldozer operator Cpl. Refine Sims Jr. of Philadelphia and the 18th US Army Engineers were working south on the section from Fairbanks. He met his opposite number, Pte. Alfred Jalufka of Kennedy, Texas and the 97th US Army Engineers, who were working north from Whitehorse. (see Contact Creek)

BECKER CREEK 60°14'N 135°10'W (105-D). A tributary to the Wheaton River, fifteen miles west of Carcross.

Theodore BECKER was an active prospector for many years in this district and found good mineral showings near this creek in 1906, when he named it. The mineral finds proved uneconomic at the time but much mining development has taken place since in the 1980s.

BELIVEAU CREEK 63°48'N 135°29'W (105-M). A tributary to Duncan Creek, on the southeast side of Mount Beliveau.

A discovery of good placer gold was made on this stream, and the Discovery claim was staked, on 7 January 1902 by Ernest BELIVEAU of Quebec, an active prospector who was connected with many of the early finds in this district.

Mount BELIVEAU was also later named for him.

BELL CREEK 61°20'N 135°18'W (105-E). Flows into Lake Laberge on the west side, five miles from the foot of the lake.

A Discovery claim was staked here on 8 September 1900 by P.W. BELL and his partner, Martin Seel. Little or no actual mining was ever carried out on the creek.

MOUNT BELL 6,328' 60°10'N 135°11'W (105-D). Seventeen miles west of Carcross.

D.D. Cairnes, GSC, named this feature after his assistant, W.A. BELL of Queens University, Kingston, Ontario. BELL had done much of the surveying when Cairnes mapped the geology of the Wheaton River district in the summer of 1909.

Dr. Walter Andrew BELL, BSc (Queens), MA (Cambridge), PhD (Yale), joined the GSC in 1909 and enlisted in the Canadian Army 1916-19. After the First World War he continued his education and his work with the GSC. He was appointed Chief Paleontologist in 1938 and Director of the GSC from 1949 to 1953. He was awarded the Gold Medal of the Professional Institute of Public Services of Canada, the Inco Medal of the CIMM and the Honorary Degree of LLD from St. Xavier University. He died in 1969.

BELL RIVER 67°17'N 137°47'W (116-P). Flows from the MacDougall Pass to the Porcupine River.

John BELL Chief Trader of the HBC, explored this river in 1839 seeking new sources of furs. He was in charge of Fort Good Hope on the MacKenzie River at the time and was married to a daughter of Peter Warren Dease, a famous Arctic explorer of the HBC.

This stream was originally known as the "West Rat River" and sometimes as "Bell's River". R.G. McConnell, GSC, while on his geological mapping expedition of 1887-88, mapped it as the BELL River to avoid confusion with the East Rat River flowing to the MacKenzie River from the same source on the Continental Divide. The eastern branch of the BELL is still called the Rat River.

This isolated river was the main trade route into the Yukon Territory for many years, servicing Fort Yukon from 1847 and Rampart House from 1867-1890 when the HBC abandoned the route as uneconomic. Shortly after this time, the company gave up all its business in the Territory.

BELOUD CREEK 60°25'N 137°27'W (115-A). Flows into Victoria Creek, about eleven miles south of Louise Lake.

B. BELOUD found placer gold here in 1938 and mined until 1939. He found many nuggets of native copper, some weighing as much as 28 pounds.

BELOUD POST 60°22'N 137°04'W (115-A). Thirty-four miles from Haines Junction, at the south end of Dezadeash Lake.

In 1938, B.BELOUD made a camp here to explore and mine placer gold. He also began to carry on limited trading.

BENNETT CREEK 63°43'N 136°03'W (115-P). A tributary to Minto Creek from the north.

On 25 May 1903, Charles E. BENNETT found placer gold and staked the Discovery claim on this stream.

LAKE BENNETT 60°05'N 134°52'W (105-D). Straddles the Yukon-B.C. boundary, below Carcross.

This is the "Kusooa Lake" of the Tagish Indians and the "Boat Lake" of the early miners, the place where they stopped after the back-breaking toil of the Chilkoot Pass. Cutting the spruce trees on the shores of the lake, they labouriously hand-sawed planking and built their boats for the long voyage down the Yukon River to the goldfields. Dr. Aurel Krause of the Bremen Geographical Society led an expedition through the Chilkat Pass in 1881 and gave the name "East Kussooa Lake".

Lt. Frederick Schwatka, US Army, on his expedition in 1883 from Dyea over the Chilkoot Pass and down the length of the Yukon River blithely ignored all previous native, miners and explorers names. He made the first, rough survey of the river's course and named most of the features after superior officers, contemporary and prominent academics, and patrons of exploration. Many of his names never received official recognition.

He named LAKE BENNETT after James Gordon BENNETT, editor of the New York Herald and a supporter of American exploration. It became one of the best known names in the north because of its position and part in the Stampede to the Klondike in 1897-99. The scene here during that period was one of intense activity as tens of thousands of goldseekers funneled through the Chilkoot Pass and White Pass, stopping here to organize themselves and build boats for the remainder of the journey to the Klondike. In the winter of 1897-98 the largest tent city in the world was at the head of the lake. Standing now on the Carcross bridge, it is hard to imagine that over 7,000 watercraft of all shapes and sizes passed here during an eighteen hour period on 29 and 30 May 1898. Many more would follow.

A town was built, as sawmills and boatyards sprang up on these shores. Steamboats, their boilers and engines hauled with heart-breaking effort over the passes, were constructed here in a matter of weeks and, until the White Pass and Yukon Railroad was completed to Whitehorse in July 1900, they transported most of the passengers and freight to the territory.

BERNEY CREEK 60°10'N 135°20'W (105-D). Flows into the Wheaton River near Carbon Hill.

This was named around 1906 after Adam BIRNIE (correct spelling), one of a group of English prospectors who were known as "The Tally Ho Boys". (see Tally Ho Mountain)

BERTHA CREEK 63°47'N 139°30'W (115-O). A tributary to the Indian River.

On 11 August 1898, James E. Fairbairn and George B. Perry found placer gold and staked the Discovery claim, naming the stream. A stampede from Dawson saw the whole creek and its main tributaries staked in a few days. Little gold was found and the creek was soon abandoned. In 1902, Fred E. Envoldsen and his partner recorded a new Discovery claim and a new staking rush ensued. They renamed the stream "Gladstone Creek" but the Mining Recorder refused the name, retaining the original.

MOUNT BIG ALEX 64°29'N 138°03'W (116-B). Northeast of Mount Chisholm.

Named around 1973, to commemorate one of the most outstanding figures of the Klondike Gold Rush, Alexander (BIG ALEX) MacDonald.

He was born in Antigonish, Nova Scotia in November 1854, he went to school and mined there until 1880. For the next 13 years he mined in Colorado, early on becoming a Mine Superintendent. The depression of 1893 broke him, along with most of the miners in the country. He went to Alaska following the stories of gold. After working for a year at the Mexican Mine in Douglas, Alaska, he went over the Chilkoot Pass in April 1895. He was mining on the headwaters of Fortymile River when he got word of Carmack's find on Bonanza Creek.

A bear of a man, he was slow of speech and movement but his expert knowledge of mining, along with his phenomenal memory for facts and figures and his appetite for mining deals built him the largest fortune in the Klondike in just three short years between 1896 and 1899. At his peak he was estimated to worth in excess of $20,000,000.

Arriving in what was to become Dawson on 22 September 1896, he located claim No. 89 above on Bonanza Creek and No. 11 below on Hunker Creek. Grasping the potential of the district well before most of the men there, he acted quickly to acquire interests in as many claims as possible before development work could disclose their unbelievable riches. His methods were simple: as little cash down as would be acceptable, and a further sum to be paid after the spring clean-up when the gravel mined during the winter could be sluiced and the gold recovered. After making such a deal he then found miners who had been unsuccessful in locating good claims of their own or who were short of money. To these he offered a percentage partnership, or a "lay", as they called such an arrangement. They were to mine the claim, or a portion of it and in the spring would return to him an agreed percentage of the gold they recovered. In this way and by staking claims, he acquired interests and claims on every gold-bearing stream in the Klondike.

At the same time he quickly bought land in Dawson City at the first low prices. His ability to persuade others to invest their money and labour with him enabled him to build the MacDonald Hotel, the Pioneer Drug Store Block, the Post Office Building and many other business establishments in the town. These he immediately rented to others.

The spring clean-up of 1897 vindicated his judgement and made him a multimillionaire within weeks. His estimates of the amount of gold in the creeks was proven correct. The value of his holdings, both mining and business, appreciated by hundreds of percent overnight.

Through it all he remained the same man. He continued to buy and acquire more claims. He contributed major financing to build the Dawson electric plant, the telephone company, an iron works and a brewery among others. He gave $40,000, a large fortune at the time, to build the Roman Catholic Church. He was the largest supporter of the hospital and never refused financial help to any civic cause or needy friends. He was entertained by the highest circles in New York and London, where he met and married his wife.

The depopulation of the Klondike in late 1899 and 1900, caused by the discovery of the rich Nome goldfields, started his downfall. Miners became unavailable to work his claims and further, the richest ground on Bonanza and Eldorado Creeks was nearly worked out. His returns dropped and he had to buy extensions of time. His unfaltering belief in the Klondike would not let him sell any of his holdings and kept him acquiring others. By 1900 he was unable to meet some of his commitments and his financial pyramid began to crumble. The population of Dawson had halved and his businesses began to lose money. His efforts to consolidate came too late and by 1904 he had lost almost the whole of his fortune.

He repaid every debt. Nearly penniless he returned to the simple life of the prospector on the creeks. His wife and son were supported by the income of a small insurance policy he had earlier purchased at the insistence of Belinda Mulroney. (see Grand Forks)

On 8 January 1909, the King of the Klondike died of a heart attack while chopping wood at his cabin on Slough Creek, a tributary of Clear Creek. There were three men with him when he died, one a cousin of his named Angus Chisholm, who brought the body to Dawson by dog team. (see Clear Creek)

BIG CAMPBELL CREEK 61°46'N 131°07'W (105-G). A tributary to the Pelly River at Pelly Banks.

This stream was named shortly after 1887 by prospectors who could not distinguish it from Campbell Creek, as they join into a common stream a few yards from the Pelly River.

BIG CREEK 62°37'N 137°00'W (115-I). Enters the Yukon River four miles below Minto.

This stream, quite a large one, entered the Yukon River behind an island which has since been eroded and so was missed by William Ogilvie on his survey in 1887.

A soldier named McMartin entered the Yukon with the Yukon Field Force in 1898, served at Fort Selkirk and took his discharge from the army there in 1899. When he took up the first homestead at the mouth of the stream he asked the local Indians for its name. Their reply was that it was a "BIG CREEK"; by which they meant that it was too large for a creek and was really a river. McMartin filed his application for his homestead under this name, which remains.

BIG CREEK 62°53'N 140°11'W (115-J). A tributary to the Indian River.

A staking rush took place on this creek in June 1898 from Dawson and the whole creek was staked and named.

There are five BIG CREEKS in the Yukon.

BIG GOLD CREEK 64°01'N 140°42'W (116-C). Flows into the Sixty Mile River.

This was originally called "Gold Creek" in 1891 during the rush to the newly found Sixty Mile River goldfields, the second major discovery in the Yukon. Although tributaries of this stream produced good gold, little was found on the main stream itself until 1905, when John Stockton found the pay-streak. The stream was then immediately restaked and renamed "BIG GOLD CREEK".

BIG HORN CREEK 61°09'N 139°25'W (115-F). A tributary to the Donjek River.

Edward Benson, with W.R. and W.B. Lamb, named this creek when they found and mined gold on it in August 1914.

BIG KALZAS LAKE 63°15'N 134°35'W (105-M). Between the Stewart and MacMillan Rivers.

It is highly probable that this is the lake named "Gauche Lake" by Robert Campbell in 1849-50. It is shown as such on the earliest map of the territory. Gauche was one of Campbell's Indian employees. He was an able and reliable man and was noted, even by Campbell, for his clairvoyant powers.

This is one of the lakes which supplied fish for Fort Selkirk.

BIG LAKE 64°03'N 138°30'W (116-B). South of the Mischenko Lakes.

One of the lakes used to form the water storage system which fed the "Big Ditch" of the Yukon Consolidated Gold Corporation. (see Mischenko, Trana and Tom O'Hara Lakes)

BIG SALMON 62°53'N 134°55'W (105-E). At the mouth of Big Salmon River.

This is an abandoned settlement on the Yukon. Before the white man came there was an ancient Indian fishing village at this place. By 1898 it was a steamboat landing, a woodcutters camp and a supply point for the people up the Big Salmon River. For many years it was a station on the Yukon Telegraph Line.

BIG SALMON LAKE 61°16'N 133°17'W (105-F). Five miles northwest of Quiet Lake, on the Big Salmon River.

This was originally named "Island Lake" by John McCormack, prospector, in 1887. The name was forgotten and changed to the present one sometime around 1898.

BIG SALMON RIVER 61°53'N 134°55'W (105-E). A major tributary to the Yukon River.

In 1881, a party of four prospectors including George G. Langtry and Patrick McGlinchy of Juneau, ascended this river 200 miles above its mouth. They were the first white men to explore the stream. Gold prospects were found along the whole length of the river and two of the party won a fair amount of fine gold (gold dust) from the river bars.

In 1883, Lt. Frederick Schwatka, US Army, rafting down the Yukon River, was told by his Chilkat interpreter that the Indian name meant "BIG SALMON". The Tagish or local Indian name was "Ta-Tlin-Hini". Schwatka called it the "d'Abbadie" after M. Antoine d'Abbadie, Membre D'Institut and noted French explorer.

Dr. George Mercer Dawson, G&NHSC, when reviewing his own notes of the locality and William Ogilvie's survey of the river, disallowed the name and retained the original as used by the natives and the miners. Dawson was given much information on this river by John McCormack, a New Brunswick prospector, who had, with three partners, prospected the river in 1887 and had named several features including Quiet Lake.

Dr. Hugh S. Bostock, GSC, while mapping the area in 1935 applied the name "d'Abbadie" to a small branch of the North Fork of the BIG SALMON River.

BIG SITDOWN CREEK 65°41'N 141°00'W (116-F). Flows into the Kandik River in Alaska.

In 1910, an International Boundary Survey crew was camp-bound by weather for several days, giving the creek its name.

BIG THING CREEK 60°03'N 134°34'W (105-D) Flows into Windy Arm, on Tagish Lake.

In 1905, a large, wide vein of gold and silver bearing ore was found at the headwaters of this creek. The finder was extremely proud of his discovery. Payable in the first years, it has been worked unprofitably several times since.

MOUNT BILLINGS 6,909' 61°11'N 128°54'W (105-H). In the Logan Mountains, southeast of Frances Lake.

Probably named in 1887, by Dr. George Mercer Dawson, G&NHSC, after Elkanah BILLINGS (1820-1876), paleontologist with the G&NHSC.

MOUNT BISEL 61°37'N 137°07'W (115-H). A small hill northeast of the head of Aishihik Lake.

This was named in 1897, probably by J.J. McArthur, GSC, after a member of Jack Dalton's crew.

MOUNT BLACK 61°13'N 134°04'W (105-E). At the headwaters of the South Big Salmon River, in the Livingstone Creek area.

George BLACK was born in Woodstock, New Brunswick in 1872. He qualified as a lawyer but soon was involved in the Klondike Gold Rush. He came to the Yukon in 1897. He had little success in the Klondike area and tried other places. In 1898 he and his partner found good gold on Livingstone Creek. However, in 1901 he was forced to get to Dawson by working as a deckhand on a riverboat.

In Dawson he again engaged in the practice of criminal law. He also became active in politics. He served three terms on the Yukon Council as a member from the Klondike Riding and then represented South Dawson (1905-1912).

In February 1912, he was appointed Commissioner of the Yukon Territory. He served with distinction, his term being marked by progressive reforms in the civil service, increased road building and better labour and mining laws. He and C.A. Thomas, Manager of the Yukon Gold Company, drove the first automobile from Whitehorse to Dawson in December 1912.

He was given leave of absence in 1916 to enlist for service in the First World War. He formed the Yukon Infantry Company and raised 226 men whom he led to England in January 1917. They were re-formed into the 17th Canadian Machine Gun Company and served with distinction. BLACK was severely wounded in the Battle of Amiens in France during August 1917.

Returning to the Yukon, he was elected in 1921 to sit in Parliament as member from the Yukon. He represented the Conservative party. He sat continuously until forced to retire due to ill health caused by his war wounds. His wife, Martha Louise Black, ran in his stead and was elected. He recovered and was again elected in 1940, serving two terms as Speaker of the House of Commons. On his retirement in 1949 he returned to Dawson and his law practice. In August 1951 he was appointed a member for life of the King's Privy Council for Canada, by Prime Minister Louis St. Laurent . He entered politics once more in the election of 1953, losing to J. Aubrey Simmons, a liberal. He died in Vancouver, B.C. on 23 September 1965 at the age of 94.

George BLACK, BA, LLB, PC, was a capable, unassuming, well-liked man. It would be hard to find a more worthy Canadian to honour with a permanent landmark memorial.

The mountain was mapped by H.S. Bostock, GSC, in 1935 and is the highest point in the Big Salmon Range. He also suggested the name, as he was a long time friend of George BLACK and thoroughly acquainted with his superior qualities. (see Livingstone Creek)

BLACK HILLS CREEK 63°15'N 138°41'W (115-O). A tributary to the Stewart River.

One of the earliest miner's names in the Territory, this creek was apparently named about 1883-85 by miners who had been in the Gold Rush to the Black Hills of South Dakota in the late 1870s. Although prospected earlier, payable gold was not found here until July 1898 when a stampede took place and the whole creek was staked in a few days. (see Rosebud Creek)

BLACK MIKE CREEK 64°26'N 138°15'W (116-B). Flows to the North Klondike River.

Named around 1983 to remember a Yukon character, the legendary "BLACK MIKE" Winage of Dawson. A noted raconteur, he could spin a tale about anything in the Territory. He was kind and would always help those in need.

BLACKSTONE RIVER 65°51'N 137°15'W (116-H). A tributary to the Peel River.

Indians many years ago named this river because of the deep, extensive seams of coal (lignite) exposed on both sides of a canyon in the stream.

BLANCHARD RIVER 60°02'N 136°53'W (115-A). Crosses the Yukon-B.C. boundary and joins the Tatshenshini River, near Dalton Post.

This was originally called the "Kleheela" River by the NWMP who were here in 1898. They learned the name from the local Indians. It was renamed about 1915 after G. BLANCHARD Dodge, DLS, who was born in Halifax, Nova Scotia, in 1874 and educated at Dalhousie University. He served with the Topographical Survey of Canada from 1900 to 1932. He was in charge of survey parties that delineated much of the Yukon-B.C. boundary. He died in Ottawa in 1945.

BLOOMFIELD LAKE 69°13'N 138°37'W (117-D). A small lake near Phillips Bay, on the Arctic Coast.

This lake was named in 1958 to honour the memory of B-67396 Pte. George Page BLOOMFIELD, MID. Born in Toronto, Ontario on 24 August 1914, he enlisted in the Canadian Army at Toronto on 5 March 1940 and served in Canada, Iceland, Great Britain and France. He was killed in action at Dieppe, France on 19 August 1942.

BLUEBERRY CREEK 63°05'N 139°11'W (115-O). A small tributary to Thistle Creek.

During the Klondike Gold Rush there were many smaller rushes and stampedes to other areas in the Yukon. One of these was a stampede to Thistle Creek in late 1898. A syndicate of Swedes from Minnesota, who called themselves the "Monitors", staked, named and unsuccessfully worked on this creek that year. (see Monitor Creek and Thistle Creek)

MOUNT BOMPAS 10,027' 61°24'N 140°36'W (115-F). West of Mount Constantine, in the St. Elias Range.

This mountain was named in 1918 to perpetuate the name of the most remarkable churchman in Yukon history, the Right Reverend William Carpenter BOMPAS, DD, first Bishop of Athabaska (1874-1884), first Bishop of the MacKenzie River (1884-1891) and first Bishop of Selkirk, Yukon (1891-1906). He was born in London, England in 1834 and he died, still serving at Carcross in 1906.

His father, Charles Carpenter BOMPAS, Sergeant-at-Law and eminent advocate before the British Bar, was said to have been the original of Charles Dickens Sergeant Buzfuz in the "Pickwick Papers".

William BOMPAS first entered the Yukon in 1873, visiting the Indians at LaPierre House from the MacKenzie River. In 1874 he went to Fort Yukon to encourage and enlarge his Anglican Church missionary services to the natives. He spent 1891-1892 at Rampart House on the Porcupine River. When he heard of the needs of the miners at Fortymile district he set up a mission there. (see Buxton Mission). He established missions at Fort Selkirk and at Carcross and in 1897 he erected the original St. Paul's Church in Dawson. His greatest efforts were always for the native people and his school for native children at Carcross survived into the 1960s.

He served for forty-three years in the MacKenzie and Yukon, returning only once to England in all that time. (see Buxton Mission)

BONANZA CREEK 64°03'N 139°25'W (115-B). A tributary to the Klondike River, about three miles above Dawson.

This is one of the richest and most famous gold-bearing streams ever found in the world. The name is a synonym for immediate and vast wealth. The word BONANZA comes from the Spanish miners and conquistadors to denote rich ore deposits.

On 16 August 1896, George Washington Carmack, Skookum Jim Mason and Tagish (later Dawson) Charlie found rich, coarse gold in the gravels of this stream when they were returning from an inspection of Robert Henderson's diggings on Gold Bottom Creek. On 17 August 1896, George Carmack staked the Discovery claim, wrote the name "BONANZA" on a piece of bark and nailed it to his Discovery post.

On 22 August, on a hillside opposite claim No. 17 below Discovery, a miner's meeting was held by twenty five men, all those who had staked claims on the creek to that time. They agreed to a rough survey to avoid further confusion in claim staking; they elected one of their number, David McKay, to be Mining Recorder and they confirmed the name of the creek as BONANZA. It had previously been called "Rabbit Creek" by the miners and "Tha-Tat-Dik" meaning "Muffler Creek" by the local Indians.

This is the stream that started a controversy which has never been settled to this day. Did Carmack on this creek, or Henderson on Gold Bottom Creek first discover the Klondike Gold? Henderson, after 1901 and backed by newspaper and government officials claimed the honour for the rest of his life. He was finally awarded a pension, a government position as Mining Expert in the Yukon and was proclaimed the Discoverer by the Canadian government. Carmack refused to become embroiled in the matter and claimed only that he had simply discovered gold on BONANZA CREEK. His claim was actively forwarded by the predominant American presence in the Yukon and elsewhere. The Canadian government in 1962 erected a bronze plaque on Carmack's Discovery claim, giving the honours equally to Carmack, Skookum Jim and Tagish Charlie. Oddly enough, it has never been established just who was present at the discovery. Kate Carmack, George's wife and a boy Patsy Henderson, both Tagish Indians, claimed have to first found the gold. No matter who found the gold, one thing is certain; the discovery on BONANZA CREEK touched off the Klondike Stampede.

BONANZA CREEK was phenomenally productive for a length of nearly twelve miles. Counting Eldorado Creek, a tributary, extremely rich gold deposits were mined for nearly seventeen miles. A remarkable fact of this discovery was that few of the original claims there were staked by experienced miners. The creek had been cursorily prospected by a number of prospectors as early as 1883 and passed by. (see Fort Reliance). At the time of Carmack's find nearly all the miners in the Yukon were busy on the productive creeks at the head of the Fortymile River and at the Sixty Mile River diggings. As a result, when Carmack made the announcement of his find at Fortymile, only the local tradesmen and the lay-abouts had the first news. With newly arrived prospectors he met when travelling up and down the river, these comprised the men who staked BONANZA and Eldorado. Many of them were inexperienced and when the true miners arrived on the scene and evaluated the potential they quickly bought claims from the Cheechakos (newcomers) at low prices.

The first mining on the ground was done by hand; pick, shovel and fire were used to thaw and gouge out the frozen gold-bearing gravels that lay above bedrock. This was the period from 1897-1900 that was the heyday of the Klondike. The suddenly rich, free-wheeling, big spending miners made Dawson the "Paris of the North", where gold dust could purchase anything.

Then, as steam-thawing and machinery became available, larger and poorer quantities of gravel were worked, still yielding large profits. Finally, large capital was interested and millions of dollars were invested in large-scale water supply for hydraulicking (flumes and ditches stretching in places for over fifty miles), dredges and large scale hydraulic equipment. In this period which is still continuing, nearly all the gravel of the valley bottoms was processed. Huge quantities carrying gold values as low as 40 cents per cubic yard were handled, still at a profit. In 1966 the last large dredge shut down. The price of gold ($35.00 an ounce) was not enough to pay a profit, since the rise in the price of gold in 1972 work has gone on and low grade gravels on these streams are now being worked at a profit.

It is impossible to arrive at the correct figure for the total value of the gold won from the Klondike but the estimated figure for the first sixty-eight years is well over $200,000,000. Most of this was mined when gold was worth only $20.00 an ounce.

From 1897 to 1905, as the whole creek was being mined, a number of reports were made of finding older, earlier workings. (see Little Blanche Creek)

BOND CREEK 64°48'N 134°41'W (106-D). A tributary to the Wind River.

James H. BOND, American, big-game hunter and naturalist, of Portland, Oregon, spent fifty-seven days in the upper Beaver and Wind Rivers country in the late summer of 1947. Louis Brown of Mayo outfitted and guided him on his travels and named this stream after him. Bond later wrote an interesting book on his experiences called "From Out of the Yukon".

BONNET PLUME RIVER 65°54'N 134°57'W (106-E). A large tributary to the Peel River.

Andrew Flett, "BONNET PLUME", was a Loucheaux Indian Chief. He had worked for many years as an interpreter for the HBC. He and his band made their home on this river. During the Klondike Gold Rush many of the stampeders from Edmonton made their way through this part of the country. BONNET PLUME gave assistance to many of these unfortunates caught by winter on the trail to Dawson. They named the river after him.

The Loucheaux themselves called it the "Black Sands River", from the amount of black magnetite sand (iron ore) found in its bed.

BONNEVILLE LAKES 60°36'N 135°18'W (105-D). Three small lakes west of Fish Lake, southwest of Whitehorse.

In 1958, these lakes were honoured with the name of A-61080 Lt. Cpl. Hector BONNEVILLE, MM. He was born in Ottawa on 5 June 1912 and enlisted in the Canadian Army at Windsor, Ontario on 10 August 1942. He served in Canada, Great Britain and the Central Mediterranean Theater. He was killed in action during the attack on the Gothic Line in Italy on 31 August 1944.

BORDEN CREEK 63°31'N 140°28'W (115-N). A small tributary to Matson Creek, in the Sixty Mile River area.

This creek was named when it was first staked in 1912. The discoverer named it after Sir Robert BORDEN who was Prime Minister of Canada at the time.

BORONITE CITY 62°23'N 136°37'W (115-I). A short-lived settlement at the mouth of Williams Creek, on the Yukon River.

A settlement was established here in 1907 to service the many prospectors on the new hardrock copper finds on Williams and adjacent creeks. The WP&YR laid up their steamboat Whitehorse here for the winter of 1907-08. About twenty people lived here, running a store, hotel and blacksmith shop. No commercial copper deposits were found at the time and the settlement was abandoned by 1909.

BORTHWICK LAKE 61°28'N 137°27'W (115-H). Between Aishihik and Sekulmun Lakes.

In 1956, this lake was named to perpetuate the memory of A-10567 Pte. George Ross BORTHWICK, MID, who was born on 18 June 1923 at Thedford, Ontario. He enlisted in the Canadian Army at Windsor, Ontario on 6 January 1943. He served in Canada, Great Britain and Northwest Europe and was killed in action on 29 July 1944.

MOUNT BOSTOCK 5,882' 63°46'N 136°43'W (115-P). At the south end of East Ridge, the highest point in this locality.

Hugh S. BOSTOCK, BSc (RMC), MSc (McGill), PhD (Wisconsin) was born in Vancouver in 1901. He engaged with the GSC in 1924 and was the Senior Geologist in the Yukon Territory from 1931 to 1956. During this period he mapped much of the central Yukon and did much to further mineral exploration and development during that time. His many reports and papers are still in use. He was awarded the Massey Medal of the RGSC for his outstanding work.

This point overlooks the major areas where he did most of his work, as he himself pointed out. He died in Ottawa in February, 1994.

A fitting obituary to this exceptional man: "Gentlemen, scientist, bushman and a good friend". The name was proposed by his friend, R.C. Coutts, in June 1994.

BOSWELL RIVER 61°03'N 134°13'W (105-E). A tributary to the Teslin River.

The river was named by miners in 1887 after the two BOSWELL brothers, Thomas and George of Peterborough, Ontario. They were the first to prospect the Teslin River. The BOSWELLs were among the first prospectors in the Yukon watershed; records show that Thomas came in over the Chilkoot Pass in the spring of 1882 and George came in either then or the following year. They were active men and among the first to find the rich, fine bar gold on the Stewart River at Chapman's Bar. A major tributary of the Stewart River was given their name at the time. (see Nadaleen River)

The two men ranged widely across the Yukon and Alaska for years, always in the forefront of the pioneers. Thomas lost a leg to a grizzly bear in Alaska in 1891 but he and his brother still joined in the Klondike Stampede.

BOSWELL MOUNTAIN 61°11'N 134°15'W (105-E). On the north side of the Teslin River, in the Seminov Hills.

Named some time after the turn of the century for the BOSWELL brothers, Thomas and George who prospected this area in the early 1880s. (see Nadaleen River)

BOSSUYT LAKE 66°39'N 135°14'W (106-L). East of the Road River.

Charles BOSSUYT, of Quebec, was a Yukon Councillor for North Dawson in 1912-15. Years later, he had a butcher shop on 2nd avenue in Dawson, near the Dawson Hardware Store. His name was used as the title on the new topographical map of the area, printed in 1973. The name was proposed by Gordon McIntyre, MLA.

BOUCHER CREEK 64°01'N 140°20'W (116-C). Flows north into the Sixty Mile River.

Felix BOUCHER, of Quebec, had prospected the Sixtymile country in 1891 when the first gold was discovered. At that time this stream was staked and called "Larsen Creek". Larsen worked it with fair results until he was called away in 1896 by news of far richer ground in the Klondike. The creek was abandoned.

In July 1902, Felix BOUCHER and his partner, James Huot, returned, prospected and staked a new Discovery claim. The Mining Recorder renamed the stream after BOUCHER. (see Huot Gulch)

BOULDER CREEK 63°58'N 139°21'W (115-O). A tributary to Bonanza Creek, about six miles from the Klondike River.

A Discovery claim was staked and recorded here by F.J. Steele on 19 August 1897, although the creek may have been staked and abandoned earlier.

BOUTELLIER CREEK 60°59'N 138°13'W (115-B). A tributary to Christmas Creek, southwest of Kluane Lake.

Charles BOUTELLIER of Quebec, prospected and mined on this creek in 1903 when it received its name. He spent many years in the Yukon, prospecting, trapping and cutting firewood for riverboats. In 1914, he owned and operated a roadhouse at Lower Laberge. Many years later he lived on the A.C. Trail on the hill above Dawson and mined on what was known as the "Potato Patch" group of claims on the hill above the Klondike River, near Thomas Gulch, from which he got his water for mining. He had a family of three girls and three boys. One of his daughters is Margaret Fry, who (in 2003) is 91 years old, and still lives in Whitehorse.

MOUNT BOUVETTE 65°17'N 138°37'W (116-G). South of the Ogilvie River.

In 1973, the name of this feature was used by the Topographical Surveys Branch as a title for their new map sheet of this area. It has been long used as a local name. Louis BOUVETTE (Beauvette, Bovette) was a pioneer prospector in the district, finding the first of the rich silver-lead ore deposits in 1919 on Keno Hill while hunting mountain sheep. (see Beauvette and Keno Hills)

BOVE ISLAND 60°07'N 134°31'W (105-D). The island in Tagish Lake, at the mouth of Windy Arm.

In 1883, Lt. Frederick Schwatka, US Army, renamed Tagish Lake as "BOVE LAKE" after Lt. BOVE of the Italian Navy, who had served with the Austro-Hungarian Expedition of 1872-74.

Dr. George Mercer Dawson, G&NHSC, in 1887, gave the lake back its original name but left BOVE's name on this island.

BOW CREEK 62°18'N 137°12'W (115-I). A tributary to Seymour Creek, near Mount Freegold.

P.F. Guder of Carmacks assisted the GSC in this area in the summer of 1930. While travelling this stream he commented on its shape's almost a perfect arc, hence its name.

Previously Captain H.S. Back had named the stream "Rogers Creek" after one of his men in the summer of 1917. They never worked the creek and the name had been forgotten. (see Back, Guder, Nansen and Seymour Creeks)

BRABAZON GLACIER 61°21'N 140°38'W (115-F). A tail from the huge Klutlan Glacier, west of Mount Bompas.

Alfred James BRABAZON, DLS, was in charge of surveys for the International Boundary Commission from 1895-1906 and again in 1909. This glacier was named in his memory in 1925.

BRADEN'S CANYON 62°50'N 136°52'W (115-I). On the Pelly River, about fifteen miles below Pelly Crossing.

A trapper of this name settled here in 1899 on the old winter trail from Whitehorse to Dawson. A small settlement remained here until the 1950s.

BRAEBURN 61°31'N 135°50'W (105-E). On the west side of the Whitehorse to Dawson (Klondike) highway, fifty-six miles north of the Alaska Highway.

A roadhouse was established here on the old winter trail from Whitehorse to Dawson. A small settlement remained here until the 1950s.

MOUNT BRAGG 65°39'N 140°18'W (116-F). West of the Porcupine River.

T.A. BRAGG was the Principal of the Dawson Public School during 1904-05. In 1973 his name was chosen to title the new topographical map of the area.

BRAINE CREEK 64°22'N 134°59'W (106-D). A tributary to the Beaver River, in the Wernecke Mountains.

Named in 1898, after Frank BRAINE who lived in this area at the time. Mount BRAINE at the head of the creek was named later in the century. (see Lansing)

BRAINE PASS 64°33'N 134°50'W (106-D). Passes through the MacKenzie Mountains to the Wind River.

This pass, discovered by Frank BRAINE, was named by Charles Camsell, GSC, after BRAINE gave him valuable information about it and the surrounding country in 1904.

MOUNT BRATNOBER 6,313' 60°44'N 136°40'W (115-A). In the bend of the Dezadeash River, ten miles southwest of Champagne.

This mountain was named in July 1897 by J.J. McArthur, DLS, a Canadian government surveyor who made a cursory survey of the Dalton Trail that year. He was assisted by Jack Dalton and Henry BRATNOBER, who was one of Dalton's axemen at the time.

Henry BRATNOBER, of San Francisco, played more than an ordinary part in the Yukon. He was an accredited riverboat captain and had prospected and mined widely in the western United States. He took part in the Klondike Rush, was a partner with Dalton during 1901-04 prospecting in the Alsek and White River regions, built and captained the riverboat "Ella" in 1905 and was operating it on the Tanana River in 1910. He was an agent and "mining expert" for the Rothschilds for many years in their mining ventures in the North.

BREFALT CREEK 63°55'N 135°30'W (105-M). A small creek flowing into Flat Creek, from Galena Hill near Elsa.

This little stream was named in the late 1920s, after Charles BREFALT, a Swedish prospector, who first found high-grade lead-silver ore here.

MOUNT BRENNER 64°28'N 138°46'W (116-B). Five miles west of Tombstone Mountain, in the north Klondike district.

Named after Otto BRENNER of London, Ontario, a pioneer Yukoner and an active and successful prospector and miner.

BREWER CREEK 63°11'N 139°00'W (115-O). A tributary to Barker Creek.

In 1898, a prospector named BREWER had staked and named this creek but abandoned his claim. In June 1906, Charles M. Graham staked a new Discovery claim here when he found workable gold. Again abandoned, on 10 January 1915, Otis Franklin Jenkins and William Stevens again staked a new Discovery claim. No one recovered much gold.

BREWER LAKE 60°41'N 133°27'W (105-G). Twelve miles north of Johnson's Crossing.

Joseph BREWER, pioneer prospector and trapper, made his home on this lake for many years.

BREWERY CREEK 64°02'N 138°01'W (116-B). A tributary to the South Klondike River.

Until 1965, this stream was known as "O'Brien Creek". It had been named in 1897-98. The name was changed to avoid conflict with a similar name in the White River district which had been named much later.

Thomas W. O'Brien came to the Yukon in 1886 and mined in the Fortymile diggings. He gained business interests in Forty Mile and in Circle City, Alaska. He was an early staker in the Klondike and is said to have carried the first news of the Bonanza find to Circle City. He and J.M. Wilson of the Alaska Commercial Company arrived there on 15 December 1896 and their tidings started a stampede to Dawson which left Circle City virtually deserted. He was one of the founders of the Yukon Order of Pioneers at Forty Mile on 1 December 1894.

Becoming prominent in the business and political life of Dawson and the Territory, he built the first brewery in 1898 and, in the same year was instrumental, with "Big Alex" MacDonald, in establishing the first electrical plant and telephone system in Dawson. He owned the first newspaper, the Yukon Midnight Sun, a pro-government paper. He was the promoter and financier of the Klondike Mines Railway, which ran from Dawson to Sulphur Springs and he sought unsuccessfully for federal assistance to extend it to Fort McLeod in British Columbia.

He served several terms as a Yukon Councillor in the early 1900s. The Liberal Party in the Yukon was known for a number of years as the "Steam Beers" because of O'Brien's prominence in their affairs.

Thomas O'Brien died in Dawson on 24 August 1916.

MOUNT BRIMSTON 65°33'N 139°06'W (116-G). In the Nahoni Range, north of the Ogilvie River.

In 1973, the Topographical Surveys Branch named this feature after George BRIMSTON, former Klondiker and for many years Sheriff of the Yukon. He was also a past-president of the Yukon Order of Pioneers. (see Brimstone Gulch)

BRIMSTONE GULCH 63°44'N 138°51'W (115-O). Leads into Sulphur Creek, in the south Klondike district.

This short creek was staked and named in late 1897 by George Brimston. The name was a play on his own and the name of Sulphur Creek. By November 1898 he was working his claim and had built a roadhouse at the mouth of this gulch. He worked this ground for a number of years before moving to Dawson, when he became Sheriff. (see Mount Brimston)

BRITANNIA CREEK 62°52'N 138°41'W (115-J). A tributary to the Yukon River.

This creek was named by E.L.C. de la Pole and C.M. Printz who staked the Discovery claim on 18 April 1911.

MOUNT BRITISH COLUMBIA 10,200' 60°57'N 140°57'W (115-C). Near the Yukon-Alaska boundary, in the western St. Elias Mountains.

This is one of the group of mountains named to celebrate Canada's Centennial Year in 1967. (see Centennial Range)

BRITISH MOUNTAINS 69°00'N 140°30'W (117-C). The range of mountains which cross the Yukon-Alaska boundary, forty miles south of the Arctic coast.

These mountains were named by Sir John Franklin, RN, on his second Arctic Expedition in 1826, in honour of his native land.

BRITTON RIDGE 5,286' 62°21'N 138°51'W (115-J). The high ridge between the Nisling and Klotassin Rivers.

This ridge was named in 1973 after J.C. BRITTON, a pioneer prospector and miner in this region for many years.

MOUNT BROOKE 10,791' 61°30'N 140°57'W (115-F). Near the Yukon-Alaska boundary, north of the Klutan Glacier, in the St. Elias Range.

This peak was dedicated in 1918 to the memory of 8186 Pte. William BROOKE. He was born on 15 August 1893 at Huntingdon, Quebec and enlisted in the 2nd Battalion CEF on 13 September 1914, one of the very first. He was taken prisoner at Ypres in Belgium on 24 April 1915 and died in a prisoner of war camp in Germany on 13 March 1917.

BROOKS ARM 61°28'N 139°01'W (115-G). A large bay on the north end of Kluane Lake.

This bay received its name in 1945 from Hugh S. Bostock, GSC, when he was mapping the geology of this region that year. Formerly called "Little Arm", he changed it to commemorate Alfred Hulse BROOKS (1871-1924), who served the USGS in Alaska from 1898-1923. BROOKS travelled this way on an expedition from Pyramid Harbour to Eagle, Alaska in 1899 and wrote the first geological report about the area. He was appointed Chief of the USGS in Alaska in 1903 and later was appointed Chief Alaskan Geologist. He was the Chief Geologist for the American Expeditionary Forces in the First World War. He contributed greatly and widely to the knowledge and mapping of Alaskan geology.

BROOKS CREEK and BROOKS VALLEY are named after him.

BROOKS BROOK 60°25'N 133°12'W (105-C). A small stream flowing into Teslin Lake, near Mile 829 (KM1326) on the Alaska Highway.

This little stream was named in 1942 by black troops of the US Army Engineers. They constructed this section of the highway and named the stream after their company officer, Lt. BROOKS.

BROTEN CREEK 61°43'N 129°08'W (105-H). Three miles east of Tustles Lake.

A locally used name after Martin BROTEN who trapped and prospected this area for a long time.

BROWN LAKE 60°19'N 124°39'W (95-C). In the southeast corner of the Yukon Territory.

This lake commemorates the name of V-19206 Leading Seaman David Henry BROWN, MID, and was designated in 1963. He was born 30 April 1926 at Perth, Ontario and enlisted in the RCNVR on 20 November 1940 at Windsor, Ontario. He served in Canada and was missing, presumed killed in action on the high seas on 7 May 1944.

MOUNT BROWN 60°01'N 135°03'W (105-D). On the east side of Munroe Lake.

This hill was probably used as a survey point station by Arthur St. Cyr, DLS, in 1901 while surveying the Yukon-B.C. boundary and was named for one of his crew.

BROWNS CREEK 64°20'N 140°53'W (116-C). A tributary to the Fortymile River.

In late 1886 or early 1887, "Shoemaker" BROWN found and mined gold on this stream, giving it his name. When the rush to the district started in the summer of 1887 he sold his claim for $140.00 and a Winchester rifle "because the country is getting too damn crowded".

In the spring of 1893, J.A. Howard and Frank Montgomery rafted logs down the Fortymile River from Sam Patch's Bar to BROWNS CREEK. They built and ran a roadhouse to service the traffic between Fortymile and the new diggings in the Sixty Mile River country as the trail between the two ran beside this stream. They called it BROWNS CREEK Roadhouse.

The Fortymile country lay dormant after 1896, most miners being in the Klondike. By 1906 the old goldfields were again being prospected and in September of that year George L. Gates staked a Discovery claim on the creek. The Mining Recorder thought that the claim was on Bear Creek (now Bruin Creek) and decided to change the name, as there were too many Bear Creeks in the country. He named it "Gates Creek" and the name was allowed to stand, although it was referred to by both names on different maps.

In December 1958, the Geographical Board rectified the error and restored the name BROWNS CREEK to the stream.

BRUCE LAKE 61°49'N 132°06'W (105-F). Two miles west of Hoole Canyon, on the Pelly River.

Named in 1944, by L.O.R. Dozais, GSC, after his assistant in the field, V. BRUCE, BSc, of Ottawa.

MOUNT BRYDE 60°06'N 133°11'W (106-C). Twenty miles west of Teslin.

This mountain and the lake at its foot were probably named by a GSC mapping party in 1935. Making his home on the lake, Andrew (or Carl) BRYDE trapped here many winters. He was born in Norway and served on a family whaler, coming to San Francisco about 1914. He made his way to Juneau and Atlin and settled in Teslin where he worked at Taylor and Drury's trading post from 1924-1951.

BRYANT CREEK 64°01'N 139°32'W (116-B). Flows into the Yukon River, six miles above Dawson.

J. H. Howell of Seattle, found gold in the gravels of this stream and staked a Discovery claim on 8 September 1897. When recording it he named it after his schoolmate, three time presidential candidate and noted orator, William Jennings Bryan. The "t" was added in error by the Mining Recorder.

BUCKLAND HILLS 69°17'N 139°40'W (117-D). The first range of hills on the Arctic coast, facing Herschel Island.

Originally named the BUCKLAND Range in 1826 by Sir John Franklin, RN, after his friend Professor William BUCKLAND (1784-1865), an English geologist and clergyman, Dean of Westminster in 1845.

BUFFALO MOUNTAIN 5,650' 61°54'N 136°46'W (115-H). Thirty miles northeast of Aishihik Lake.

This hill was named by C.W. Rowley, as some of the last buffalo in the Yukon ranged here one winter. Buffalo have, since then, been re-introduced to the area.

BULL CREEK 61°32'N 140°22'W (115-F). A tributary to St. Claire Creek, east of the Klutlan Glacier.

Named in the early 1900s, by Tom Dickinson, '98er, ex-NWMP and noted big-game guide in the area around Kluane and the White River region. He lived and hunted here for many years. He had killed a number of very fine bull caribou near this stream.

BULLION CITY 60°57'N 138°36'W (115-B). At the mouth of Bullion Creek, on the Slim's River.

This was a short-lived camp built to service the miners in the rush to Bullion Creek. A post office was opened in 1905. The name was changed to "Kluane" in 1906 but the settlement lasted only a few more years.

BULLION CREEK 60°58'N 138°36'W (115-B). A tributary to the Slim's River, five miles from Kluane Lake.

On 28 September 1903, Frank Altemose, Joseph W. Smith, Fred Ater and Morely Bones found rich placer gold on this creek. J.W. Smith made the discovery. They took out 40 ounces of gold in a few hours but never again found as rich a pocket. This discovery started a major rush to the district which continued to the fall of 1905. As many as 8,000 to 10,000 people took part. A wagon road was constructed from Whitehorse to Kluane which later formed part of the route of the Alaska Highway. (see Burwash Creek)

BUM BOY GULCH see Bawn Boy Gulch.

MOUNT BUNOZ 65°29'N 137°12'W (116-H). Between the Blackstone and Hart Rivers.

Bishop BUNOZ was the first Roman Catholic Bishop of the Yukon.

MOUNT BURGESS 60°03'N 139°38'W (116-J). In the Ogilvie Mountains near the Miner River.

William Ogilvie, DLS, named this peak in April 1888 after A.M. BURGESS, the Deputy Minister of the Interior from 1883-1897 and who had been of great assistance in organizing Ogilvie's and Dawson's expedition to the Yukon in 1887-88.

BURKE CREEK 60°52'N 130°36'W (105-B). A tributary to the Liard River, south of Wasson Lake.

In February 1936, G.A. Jeckell, Controller of the Yukon Territory and Livingstone Wernecke of the Treadwell Yukon Mining Company, requested this name. Captain E.J.A. (Paddy) BURKE, formerly of the Royal Flying Corps, died near here.

On 11 October 1930, while flying in to a mining property, he crashed his airplane on the frozen Liard River. Being uninjured but unable to repair the airplane, he and his two companions, Emil Kading and Robert Martin, decided to walk north on the Liard River to Junkers Lake where they had earlier established a food and fuel cache. Deep snow and unseasonably cold weather, together with a lack of snowshoes made travel extremely difficult. BURKE died of exhaustion and exposure on 20 November, the first pilot to die in the Yukon.

Pilot Everett Wasson found the party after an extensive search. (see Wasson and Junkers Lakes)

The oddest part of the story is that although BURKE's name has been given to a creek in the vicinity near where he landed, the exact creek has not yet been located. Here is an official name with no location.

BURKE is buried in Atlin, B.C.

BURNHAM CREEK 63°44'N 138°32'W (115-O). A tributary to Dominion Creek, from the east.

On 26 January 1898, John Hafler staked the Discovery claim on this creek. He was probably one of the group which included Major Frederick R. BURNHAM, DSO, a noted American scout and frontiersman. BURNHAM distinguished himself in the American west and in the Matabele Wars in Southern Africa. He came into the Klondike in 1897 and was active in this area. After leaving the Yukon he returned to South Africa as Chief of Scouts for the British Forces and served with great distinction.

BURWASH CREEK 61°30'N 139°17'W (115-F). Flows into the Kluane River, near Kluane Lake.

Named on the 28 May 1904, by the well-known team of prospectors, Frank Altemose, Joseph W. Smith, Fred Ater and Morely Bones. On that day they discovered the rich gold placers of this creek and named the stream after their friend, the Mining Recorder at Silver City, Lachlin Taylor BURWASH. The pay streak on the stream was sporadic, and consistent deposits were not found until 1909. The creek produced steadily thereafter for many years.

BURWASH (1874-1940) was born in Coburg, Ontario the son of the Rev. J. Burwash, Chancellor of Victoria College in Toronto in 1896. He came to the Yukon in 1897 as a prospector for the NAT&TC but soon was appointed Mining Recorder at Stewart City in 1900, at Silver City in 1903 and was later named Government Mining Engineer and Mines Inspector for the Territory. He served in the First World War in the 1st Pioneer Battalion CEF, from 1915-19, rising to the rank of Major. In later years he explored much of Arctic Canada for the Department of the Interior. (see Bullion Creek)

BURWASH LANDING 61°21'N 139°00'W (115-G). On the northwestern shore of Kluane Lake, near Mile 1095 (KM1762) of the Alaska Highway.

This small settlement began in 1904, shortly after the discovery of gold on Burwash Creek by the brothers Eugene and Louis Jacquot, who were from Alsace-Lorraine in France. It was a supply center, serviced by boat, for the miners on the various creeks in the district. The brothers named it after their friend Lachlin Taylor BURWASH. It later became the supply point for the Gold Rush to the Chisana River placer fields in Alaska during 1913-15.

The Jacquots, who originally were miners, homesteaded here and after the First World War and for many years, became outstanding big-game guides and outfitters. On some GSC maps around 1917 the settlement was called "Jacquot". (see Burwash Creek)

MOUNT BUSH 60°19'N 135°05'W (105-D). The ridge between Perkins and Schnabel Creeks.

This was probably named in 1898-99 after Charles J. BUSH, pioneer prospector in the Wheaton River region and a partner of William Schnabel. They discovered and owned the Nevada Mines property on this ridge.

BUTLER GULCH 63°58'N 140°33'W (115-N). A tributary to Boucher Creek, in the Sixtymile district.

This was named by a man named BUTLER who staked the Discovery claim in July 1902 during the stampede to the new discoveries on Boucher Creek. His full name is not known.

BUTTLE CREEK 62°12'N 133°17'W (105-K). Flows into the Pelly River near Faro.

Roy E. BUTTLE was a trapper, prospector and trader who lived on this stream for many years from the early 1900s to the 1920s and had a trading post at Ross River in the 1930s.

BUXTON MISSION 64°26'N 140°33'W (116-C). About one-half mile above the town of Forty Mile, on the Yukon River.

In 1887, Bishop Bompas of the Anglican Church, in response to requests from miners and natives, sent the Rev. J.W. Ellington to Forty Mile to start an Anglican mission. The sum of one hundred pounds sterling had been contributed for this purpose by T. Fowell BUXTON of Easneye, Ware, England.

Ellington, a young man and the son of missionaries, was evidently humourless and quite incompatible with the rough and ready miners. They found him an easy butt for their practical jokes, many of them crude. His health and mind gave way and he soon returned to Winnipeg.

The mission was unoccupied until Bishop Bompas reopened it in 1892. Its main purpose was always the education of Indian children. He stayed here until 1896 when Forty Mile was almost abandoned because of the Klondike discovery. He moved to Dawson City in early 1897 and built the first church there, St. Paul's.

An attempt was made by Bompas to change the name of Forty Mile to BUXTON but the miners refused to use the name. The mission is separated from the town by a deep ravine, flooded at high water and crossed by a footbridge, which led some to describe it as being on an island in the Yukon River. (see Fortymile and Mount Bompas)

CABIN CREEK 60°15'N 129°08'W (105-A). A tributary to the Liard River, just below the Frances River.

In 1949, the Board on Geographical Names recorded this name, as the cabin and grave of a trapper named Stewart are at the mouth of the stream. (see Stewart Lake)

CABIN CREEK 60°44'N 130°16'W (105-B). A tributary to the upper Liard River.

In the winter of 1874-75, miners from the Cassiar found and mined gold on this stream, the first payable gold deposit found in the Yukon Territory. They built cabins here, which were later found, giving the stream its name. (see Sayyea and Scurvy Creeks)

CACHE LAKE 61°13'N 139°04'W (115-F). At the headwaters of Halfbreed Creek.

This small lake was named in the summer of 1973 by personnel of the Yukon Wilderness and Scenic Study Group, who left supplies here.

CADZOW LAKE 67°34'N 138°58'W (116-N). On the south side of the Porcupine River, twenty-five miles east of Old Crow.

In 1897, Daniel CADZOW, a Scot, left Edmonton for the Klondike. He took the MacKenzie-Peel-Rat Rivers route and reached Dawson in the summer of 1899, only to find that the Klondike Rush was over. Soon afterward he returned to the northern rivers and settled at Rampart House. He set up as a small trader in 1903 or 1904. After the smallpox epidemic of 1911-12 the post was burned and abandoned and CADZOW moved with the Indians and built anew at Old Crow. He married an Indian woman. His trading post, supplied by water from Dawson, was the only base of supplies in the northern Yukon for many years. His family is still in the North.

The Loucheaux Indian inhabitants of the place call this lake "Red Sands Lake".

CAESAR LAKES 61°26'N 127°54'W (95-E). At the headwaters of the Coal River.

On 20 August 1968, Dr. H. Gabrielse, GSC, gave this name to these small lakes for an Indian family of this name who had lived here for many years.

MOUNT CAIRNES 9,150' 60°52'N 138°17'W (115-B). In the Kluane Range, fifteen miles south of Kluane Lake.

This mountain was named in the 1920s for D.D. CAIRNES, GSC, (1879-1917), noted pioneer Yukon Geologist who explored and mapped much of this area. His explorations added enormously to the knowledge of the Yukon's geology.

CAIRNES graduated from Queen's University in Kingston, Ontario. He worked in the Yukon from 1905-1917 when he died in Ottawa at the age of 37.

MOUNT CAIRNES 64°27'N 138°19'W (116-B). In the Ogilvie Mountains, at the headwaters of the North Klondike River.

This peak was named in July 1968 by Dr. Dirk Tempelman-Kluit, GSC, while mapping this area. He greatly admired the work done previously by D.D. CAIRNES, GSC.

There is also a Mount Cairnes in British Columbia, named for the same man.

CALAMITES CREEK 65°59'N 134°35'W (106-E). A tributary to the Peel River.

Around 1944, Dr. Stelck, GSC, found many of these fossil plants in the rocks of this stream. It was returned to its original Indian name, "Nihtal Git Creek", in 1977.

CALDER CREEK 63°47'N 139°07'W (115-O). A small tributary to Quartz Creek, in the Klondike.

This was named by the first discoverer of gold on the creek, Alex CALDER, who staked on 21 October 1897, starting a staking rush to Quartz Creek. He was a partner of "Big Alex" MacDonald. From Cape Breton, Nova Scotia, he came into the Yukon in 1896 and was one of the first lucky men to stake a claim on Eldorado Creek. He died on 30 March 1900 at Fort Selkirk.

No payable gold was ever found on this creek except at its junction with Quartz Creek, on CALDER'S claim.

CALEDONIA CREEK 62°41'N 140°05'W (115-J). A tributary to the Donjek River.

On 1 November 1913, David Edwards and his partner Burnett Middleton discovered placer gold on this stream, staked the Discovery claim and probably named it after their native Scotland.

CALICO LAKE 64°49'N 138°22'W (116-B). South of Chapman Lake.

Around the turn of the century, Indians from Fort MacPherson in the NWT and others from Dawson met near here for trading purposes. They set up camps here called "CALICO City", from the cloth they used for tents.

CALIFORNIA CREEK 64°01'N 140°21'W (116-C). A tributary to the Sixty Mile River.

This creek was named in 1892, when coarse gold was first found in the Sixtymile district. In 1905, a Klondiker named Leonard found payable gold on one of the small tributaries which he named after himself. In June 1905, further finds caused a small stampede and the whole stream was named "Leonard Creek". The name reverted to CALIFORNIA CREEK when the excitement died down and most of the miners abandoned the stream.

CAMERON GULCH 64°06'N 135°03'W (106-D). A small brook running into Scougale Creek, in the Davidson Range.

This was named before 1910, by a prospector named CAMERON. He found and mined gold in this little valley. This is probably the same CAMERON who died one winter in his cabin on the banks of the Stewart River below Russell Creek. His body lay in the cabin for six years before the river changed course and swept both away.

CAMPBELL CREEK 61°46'N 131°07'W (105-G). Joins Big Campbell Creek, just above its junction with the Pelly River.

Robert CAMPBELL, HBC, the first explorer of the central Yukon, travelled this creek on his famous journey of exploration in July 1840, when he discovered the Pelly River. Dr. George Mercer Dawson, G&NHSC, named this stream when he retraced Campbell's route while on his first geological expedition to the Yukon in 1887.

Robert Campbell was born in Perthshire, Scotland on 21 February 1808, the son of a sheep farmer. At the age of 22 he was hired by the HBC as a sub-manager of their experimental farm at Fort Garry, in what is now Manitoba.

In 1833, he left the farm and was sent to Fort Resolution in the NWT, where he traded for the next four years. 1838 saw Campbell starting the series of explorations for which he became noted. The first journey was from Fort Halkett on the Liard River to Dease Lake, B.C. where he and his Indian companions nearly starved to death the following winter. In early 1840 he ascended the Liard River up to the Frances River on to Frances Lake then, by way of the Finlayson River and Lake, to the Pelly River by CAMPBELL Creek, where he established Pelly Banks Post a little later, in 1846. He named all the features mentioned after leaving the Liard River.

In 1843, he descended the Pelly River to its junction with the Yukon (the upper part of which he named the "Lewes"). In 1848 he again made this journey and built Fort Selkirk where the two rivers meet. This first post was moved to the west bank of the Yukon the following year due to flooding problems. It was raided and pillaged by the Chilkat Indians from the coast in 1852. His post was interfering with their trade with the interior Indians.

Due to this catastrophe, CAMPBELL made, in the winter of 1852-53, one of the longest snowshoe journeys on record; from Fort Simpson on the MacKenzie River to Crow Wing, Minnesota on the Mississippi River, about 3,300 miles, between 30 November 1852 and 13 March 1853. (This record stood for 24 years until exceeded by Chief Factor J.S. Camsell of Fort Simpson who retraced CAMPBELL's route plus the additional 180 miles from Fort Liard to Fort Simpson).

Although he was promoted to command the Peace River and Athabaska country, CAMPBELL was never allowed to return to the Yukon. After 41 years service with the HBC he was abruptly and mysteriously dismissed in 1871. He died on 9 May 1894 and was buried in Winnipeg.

A man named Theakson first prospected this creek and the area in 1878-79. (see Mount Campbell, Frances Lake, River, Fort Selkirk and all Pelly references)

MOUNT CAMPBELL 8,200' 64°24'N 138°41'W (116-B). Thirty-three miles northeast of Dawson, on the headwaters of the Tombstone River.

This name has been changed to "Tombstone Mountain".

CAMPBELL GULCH 63°57'N 139°26'W (115-O). A tributary to Boulder Creek.

This little valley was named on 7 September 1897 when Alexander CAMPBELL staked claim No. 6.

CAMPBELL RANGE 61°20'N 130°30'W (105-H). The range of mountains on the west side of Frances Lake.

These mountains were named in 1887 by Dr. George Mercer Dawson, G&NHSC, after Chief Factor Robert CAMPBELL of the HBC. (see Campbell Creek)

CAMPING CREEK 69°16'N 139°45'W (117-D). A tributary to Timber Creek.

This name is an English translation of a Loucheaux Indian word meanings "Tents Set Together Creek". This little stream is situated in the midst of many small lakes and ponds in the richest muskrat trapping area in the world.

CANADIAN CREEK 62°49'N 138°43'W (115-J). Flows to Brittania Creek.

Joseph Britton and Charles J. Brown found enough gold here to stake a Discovery claim on 21 April 1911. (see Britton Ridge)

CANALASKA MOUNTAIN 2,200' 67°22'N 141°00'W (116-N). On the Yukon-Alaska boundary.

This composite name was given by J.H. Turner, USC&GS, in 1890. It has previously been called "Boundary Mountain".

THE CANOL ROAD AND PIPELINE

This road, 513 miles long, was built to provide access for the construction of a war-time emergency oil pipeline from the oil fields at Fort Norman, NWT, on the lower MacKenzie River, to Whitehorse. It ran from Johnson's Crossing past Quiet Lake to Ross River and through the MacMillan Pass to Fort Norman. From Johnson's Crossing, the pipeline was built along the Alaska Highway to a refinery at Whitehorse. The gasoline from the Whitehorse refinery was to power the aircraft being flown to Russia and to provide for military needs in Alaska, which was expecting a Japanese invasion at the time. Later, it could help to mount air strikes against Japan.

The line laid was four inches in diameter and supplied about 3,000 barrels of oil per day. The project started in April 1942 and was carried through to completion in April 1944, when the first oil flowed through the line. The road was officially opened to traffic in September 1944 but it and the pipeline were abandoned shortly after the war.

The total cost of the CANOL project was $134,000,000, which included the road, the pipeline, the refinery and the cost of drilling 26 oil wells at Fort Norman.

In recent years the Yukon government has gradually opened portions of the road until now it is a good summer road in use by tourists and mining exploration companies searching the region for minerals.

CANTLIE LAKE 60°40'N 134°50'W (105-D). Eight miles southeast of Whitehorse.

In 1948, this lake was honoured with the name of Lt. Col. Stuart Stephen Tufnell CANTLIE, MID, CEM. He was born in Winnipeg, Manitoba on 5 October 1907 and enlisted on 4 September 1939 at Montreal. He served in Canada, Great Britain and northwest Europe with the Black Watch (The Royal Highland Regiment of Canada) and died of wounds received in action in France on 25 July 1944.

CANYON 60°52'N 137°03'W (115-A). Mile 996 (KM1604) on the Alaska Highway, on the east side of the Aishihik River.

During the stampede to the Kluane Lake goldfields in 1903, a wagon road was built from Whitehorse to Kluane Lake. A roadhouse and stores were built here and the small community existed until 1935. It gained its name from the stream beside it, called CANYON Creek until in the 1940s when it was changed to the Aishihik River. The original bridge across the stream was built by Gilbert Skelly and Sam McGee (of Robert Service fame). Tourist services were opened here after the opening of the Alaska Highway

CANYON CITY 61°49'N 140°46'W (115-F). On the White River, ten miles east of the Yukon-Alaska boundary.

A long-abandoned mining settlement that was started here in 1905 as a supply center and winter quarters for the prospectors who were developing the new copper finds in the vicinity. It was the head of water transportation and became active when the rich placer goldfields of the Chisana were found in 1913, which attracted thousands to the area. Much prospecting was done in the area after Solomon Albert found promising deposits of native (pure) copper near here in May 1905.

After roads were built in Alaska to serve the Chisana and the deposits themselves were declining, this village lost its reason for being and was abandoned in the 1920s.

CANYON CITY 60°40'N 135°03'W (115-D). On the east side of the Yukon River, at the head of Miles Canyon.

This settlement grew up in the summer and fall of 1897 due to the need to portage goods around the dangerous waters of Miles Canyon and the Whitehorse Rapids. Between 1897-1899 numerous people drowned and large quantities of supplies were lost in trying to ferry boats through these waters.

In the winter of 1897-98, two tramways were built around these obstructions. The one on the west bank was built by John Hepburn and was six and one half miles long. The one on the east bank was built by Norman MacAuley. The toll on both was three cents per pound and $25.00 per boat. (Most boats were usually taken through the canyon and rapids by professional pilots for less). Goods were transported by the tramway by horse-drawn cars which carried about a ton.

MacAuley bought out Hepburn and concentrated his operations on the east bank of the river. Here he built offices, freight sheds and a hotel to serve the travellers. Others built stores and dwellings.

The settlement thrived until July 1900 when the WP&YR arrived in what became Whitehorse. CANYON CITY was quickly abandoned and the businessmen moved their operations to Whitehorse.

CANYON MOUNTAIN 60°40'N 134°54'W (105-D). Four miles east of Miles Canyon and opposite Whitehorse.

This long, low ridge was named by the earliest miners travelling down the river in the 1880s. It was a good landmark to warn of the approach to the dangerous waterway.

Local people now call it Grey Mountain, because of its colour.

CARBON HILL 60°10'N 135°16'W (105-D). On the south side of the Wheaton River.

In 1893, well before the Klondike Gold Rush, two prospectors from Juneau, Frank Corwin and Thomas Rickman, investigated this area and found veins with rich gold, copper and silver-antimony ore in a number of locations.

They found the black silver-antimony ore on this hill. Returning to Juneau in the fall they both died within a short time and the exact location of their finds was lost. (There were no maps of this area at that time.) In August 1906 H.E. Porter (see Porter Creek) rediscovered their old workings and named the hill from the colour of the ore. (see Mount Hodnett and Gold Hill)

CARCROSS 60°10'N 135°42'W (105-D). At the junction of Bennett and Tagish Lakes.

This location was first known as Caribou Crossing from the time of the earliest miners to come across the Chilkoot Pass, because of the large herds of caribou which crossed the narrows here twice a year on their annual migration. A major way point on the route to the Yukon goldfields and later to Atlin, B.C., the townsite was pre-empted by the WP&YR in September 1898. The largest sawmill on the Yukon was near here, owned by Mike King, who also built boats and scows from early 1897. The Caribou Hotel, built in 1898, is still in operation, the oldest hotel in continuous operation in the Yukon Territory.

In 1903, Bishop Bompas, who had established a school here for Indian children in 1901, petitioned the Dominion government to change the name of the community to CARCROSS because of the confusion in mail services due to the duplication of names in Alaska and British Columbia as well as in the Klondike. The post office made the change official the following year but the good Bishop had to fight longer with the WP&YR, which retained the name of the station until 1916.

Numerous Yukon pioneers are buried here including Bishop Bompas, Kate Carmack, Skookum Jim Mason and Tagish Charlie.

CARCROSS DESERT 60°10'N 135°42'W (105-D). Just north of Carcross.

Affectionately known as the smallest desert in the world. This area was originally covered by a large glacial lake. As the glaciers retreated, causing lower water levels, sandy lake bottom material was left behind. Strong prevailing winds from Lake Bennett have constantly worked this sand, making it difficult for vegetation to become established. Species of plants that have survived include lodgepole pine and kinnikinnick.

CARIBOU CITY 63°50'N 138°45'W (115-O). At the junction of Caribou and Dominion Creeks, in the Klondike.

A settlement sprang up here in early 1897 as a supply point and stopping place for the many miners on the adjacent creeks. Several hotels provided accommodations and amusement to the local miners, among them the Gold Run, the Driard and the Caribou Hotels. A post office was opened in November 1899 but after 1905 the settlement and the post office became known as "Dominion".

The place died out during the First World War due to the end of pick and shovel mining and the outflow of young able bodied men, heading off to war.

CARIBOU CREEK 61°19'N 133°20'W (105-F). Flows into Big Salmon Lake.

This was one of the earliest named streams in the Territory. Named by John McCormack of New Brunswick and his partners while prospecting it for gold in the summer of 1887.

CARIBOU CREEK 63°58'N 139°40'W (115-O). A tributary to the Yukon River from the east.

By 1898, this creek had been called Davis Creek but, the name being forgotten, it was later called by this name.

CARLICK CREEK 60°04'N 130°50'W (105-B). A tributary to the Rancheria River.

The hunting and trapping area of an Indian family of this name, many of whose relatives live in Atlin, B.C. and other northern communities.

CARLSON CREEK 63°40'N 136°22'W (115-P). A tributary to Bear Creek.

Louis Beauvette and Charles Johnson staked the first placer gold claim on this creek on 10 March 1911 and named it for a friend.

CARMACKS 62°05'N 136°17'W (115-I). A settlement on the Yukon River, at the mouth of the Nordenskiold River.

George Washington CARMACK was born at Port Costa, California on 24 September 1860 after his parents had crossed the continent by ox-team and Conestoga wagon. In 1885 he went north to Juneau and in April of the same year joined a party of seven miners and went over the Chilkoot Pass to prospect the Stewart and other Yukon rivers.

He met and liked the Tagish Indians of the region and, to a certain extent, adopted their lifestyle. About this time he became associated with Skookum Jim Mason and his sister Kate. In 1887 they worked for William Ogilvie, DLS, packing his supplies over the Chilkoot Pass and travelling with him from Dyea to Forty Mile. In the next few years they hunted and prospected the Big Salmon River, the Hootalinqua (Teslin) and the Stewart River.

In 1893, CARMACK found a seam of coal near Five Finger Rapids and another near Tantalus Butte. He built a cabin here while he tried to develop the coal and carried on a certain amount of fur trading with the local Indians. Arthur Harper backed his coal ventures and owned a 50 percent interest in them. This was the beginning of present day CARMACKS.

The settlement grew and became a riverboat stop during the Gold Rush and later a supply point for various mining operations in the district. After the building of the Whitehorse to Dawson Highway it expanded again.

CARMACK, Skookum Jim and Tagish Charlie went on to uncover the golden wealth of Bonanza Creek in August 1896. CARMACK died on 5 June 1922 in Vancouver, B.C. a relatively wealthy man. Contrary to the many stories purporting him to be a renegade white man, he was well educated and intelligent. His cabin at Carmacks contained an organ which he played, and many volumes of classical literature. He subscribed to Scientific American and other literary journals and was in a way a romantic poet. In all the controversy regarding the discovery of gold in the Klondike he was the only principal who did not attack the stories or characters of the others.

CARMACK CREEK 63°55'N 139°09'W (115-O). The north fork of Bonanza Creek.

This small section of the famous Bonanza Creek is the only feature in the Klondike to perpetuate the name of the discoverer. Very little gold has been found here.

Until recent years this stream was known as "CARMACK'S FORK".

CARMACKS-FREEGOLD ROAD

This road was built by the N.A. Timmins mining interests in 1949 to explore and develop the LaForma Gold Mine on Mount Freegold. It was quickly extended by prospectors and the Territorial government to other parts of this mineral rich district.

CARPENTER CREEK 64°23'N 135°12'W (106-D). Flows into Beaver Creek.

Jack CARPENTER was an enterprising prospector who found the first rich, silver-lead ore in this district. The find sparked a sizeable rush to the area from 1920-23, but as the minerals found were not economically viable at that time, the rush petered out and the country was deserted again. In the 1980s interest again revived in the area.

The big ridge to the northwest of the creek was later named "CARPENTER RIDGE".

MOUNT CARTER 4,751' 65°40'N 137°03'W (116-H). Between the Blackstone and Hart Rivers.

In 1973, this mountain was named after Special Constable Sam CARTER, RCMP, a member of the lost Fitzgerald police patrol in 1911. (see Dempster Highway)

CASCADE CREEK 63°38'N 134°46'W (105-M). Flows into the southeast end of Mayo Lake.

Gold was first discovered here by Thomas Heney about August 1903. He was one of a party of four Australians who first prospected the area at that time and found rich placer gold on this and several adjacent creeks. (see Ledge and Steep Creeks)

CASINO CREEK 62°38'N 138°51'W (115-J). A tributary to Dip Creek, in the Dawson Range.

This stream was named on, or shortly before 28 November 1915 by two prospectors, Jack O'Hara and Frank Farnan, who discovered placer gold and named the creek after their favorite card game.

CASSIAR BAR 61°48'N 135°00'W (105-E). One of a group of gravel bars in the Yukon River, six miles above the Big Salmon River and opposite the mouth of Fyfe Creek.

This series of gravel bars was the first and richest found on the Lewes (Yukon) River. Found in the summer of 1884 by Thomas Boswell, Howard Franklin and Michael Hess, it produced the first considerable amount of gold taken out of the upper Yukon region.

In 1886, over $30.00 (about two ounces) per man per day was taken from here by many of the miners. The deposits, being shallow, were soon depleted but they gave encouragement to further prospecting in the territory. The miners who found the bar named it after the place they had just come from, the CASSIAR country, in northern British Columbia.

CASSIAR MOUNTAINS 60°00'N 131°00'W (105-B). On the north side of the Alaska Highway, between Mile 690 (KM1110) and Mile 760 (KM1223).

This word is a corruption of the Indian word "Kaska" which was applied to two tribes occupying the country to the east of the Stikine River in northern British Columbia.

CATHEDRAL CREEK 65°12'N 141°00'W (116-F). Runs across the Yukon-Alaska boundary into Hardluck Creek in Alaska.

In 1909, surveyors on the International Boundary Survey named this creek because of the beautiful, cathedral-like mountains along its course.

CATHEDRAL ROCKS 66°07'N 138°48'W (116-J). On the east side of the Miner River.

In May 1888, William Ogilvie, DLS, passed down the Miner River and thought this feature interesting enough to name. He described it as a large rock exposure extending for half a mile. It rises 300 to 400 feet from the river and as it is weathered into resemblances of ancient buildings, he gave it this name.

CATTLE CREEK 61°35'N 136°02'W (115-H). Flows east to the Nordenskiold River.

This creek crosses the old Dalton Trail and it is believed that cattle herds being driven from Haines to Dawson were watered and rested here. The name was suggested by H.S. Bostock, GSC.

CENTENNIAL RANGE 60°58'N 140°39'W (115-C). In the northwest corner of the St. Elias Range.

This group of thirteen peaks was first selected in 1967 (although the idea was first advanced in 1965) to become the locale for perhaps the most unusual project in Canada's Centennial Year.

It was organized mainly by David R. Fisher of the Alpine Club of Canada, David Judd, Executive Assistant to the Commissioner of the Yukon Territory and Monty Alford of the Water Resources Board at Whitehorse and a co-ordinator of the Polar Shelf Project. The proposal was accepted by the Centennial Committee and was named the Yukon Alpine Centennial Expedition.

As 1967 also marked the Alaska Purchase Centennial it was decided to have a team of four Americans and four Canadians climb the highest unclimbed peak on the Yukon-Alaska boundary. This peak, situated two miles north of Mount Vancouver, was to be named "Good Neighbour Peak". This was the first part of the project to be carried out on 25 June 1967.

The second and much more ambitious part of the project was the attempted ascent of the thirteen Centennial Peaks in a two week period. None had been climbed before.

Thirteen teams of four climbers each were organized and, with support personnel, more than 250 people took part in the effort. It was the largest project of its kind ever attempted in North America.

The attempt was nearly a total success. Nine peaks were scaled for the first time and climbers came within feet of conquering the others. The nine ascents were all made in the period 13-24 July 1967.

CHADBURN LAKE 60°39'N 134°57'W (105-D). One mile east of Miles Canyon.

This little lake was used in October 1948 to perpetuate the name of a Canadian hero, Wing Commander Lloyd Vernon CHADBURN, DSO and Bar, DFC. He was born on 21 August 1919 in Montreal, Quebec and enlisted in the RCAF on 16 April 1940 at Toronto, Ontario. He served in Canada and overseas, and died of wounds suffered in action on 19 June 1944.

MOUNT CHAMBERS 5,301' 65°10'N 138°48'W (116-G). South of the Ogilvie River.

In 1973, the Topographical Surveys Branch named this hill for Harlow "Shorty" CHAMBERS, who built the first trading post at Champagne and served as postmaster there for many years.

CHAMPAGNE 60°47'N 136°29'W (115-A). At the junction of the Dalton Trail and the Dezadeash River, near Mile 974 (KM1658) on the Alaska Highway.

This small settlement, nearly abandoned now, was the center of activity of the area for many years until the Alaska Highway was built. There are several different stories concerning the origin of the name.

CHAMPAGNE was originally a camping spot on the Dalton Trail to Rink Rapids. The Klondike Gold Rush brought a great increase in travel and a demand for more horses for a longer part of the year. Jack Dalton wintered stock here as well as at Dalton Post, further south.

In 1897, Gordon Bounds was taking a herd of 40 cattle to Dawson. He was probably working for Dalton at the time. When this point was reached, the worst of the trail was over and it is said that they opened a case of French champagne from the freight they were carrying to Dawson and celebrated the end of their hardships.

The place assumed some importance in 1902 when Harlow "Shorty" Chambers built his roadhouse and trading post. It became a supply center the next year when the rush to the Bullion Creek finds started and gained again from the rush to the Burwash Creek diggings in 1904. During these days it was usually called CHAMPAGNE Landing and, sometimes, Champlain or Champlain's Landing. Chambers' family still owned and ran the roadhouse when it burned in March 1962.

Since the end of placer gold mining in this district and the end of highway construction, the settlement has gradually shrunk to its present small size.

CHANDINDU RIVER 64°15'N 139°43'W (116-B). A tributary to the Yukon River, twelve miles below Dawson.

This river name was recorded by Lt. Frederick Schwatka, US Army, in 1883. It is an Indian name for which he did not bother to find a translation. The early miners called it the "Twelve Mile River" because of its distance from Dawson. After 1900 large ditches were dug by the Yukon Gold Company from its headwaters to supply the hydraulic mining operations on the Klondike Creeks.

CHANG MOUNTAIN see MOUNT SELOUS.

CHAPPIE LAKE 65°47'N 134°56'W (106-E). Near the Bonnet Plume River, below its junction with the Peel River.

Ernest CHAPMAN was a trapper, prospector and trader for many years in this area. His home and trading post were on this lake in the 1930s-40s. He was killed in an airplane crash at Dawson on 31 January 1941.

CHARLIE'S RIVER see Kandik River.

CHEECHAKO HILL 63°56'N 139°20'W (115-O). On the west side of Bonanza Creek, between Grand Forks and Adams Creek.

Oliver B. Millet, from Lunenburg, Nova Scotia, while working a lay (lease) on Eldorado Creek, formed a theory regarding an ancient and different stream channel crossing Bonanza Creek. Acting upon his idea, he prospected the hill above Tagish Charlie's claim in the winter of 1897-98. On 14 April 1898, he struck the White Channel gravels and their riches. The Bonanza and Eldorado miners, watching his efforts that winter, called the hill CHEECHAKO HILL, for only a green newcomer would look for gold on a hilltop. Millet, sick with scurvy and nearly penniless, took out $20,000 in gold from a small part of his claim (which was only 100 feet square) and then sold it for $60,000. The new owner took a further $500,000 from the ground. The scoffers still worked for wages on the claims below.

The remainder of the hill, also staked mainly by newly arrived Cheechakos, was almost as rich and many fortunes were dug from the hill's gravels.

MOUNT CHESTER HENDERSON 64°30'N 138°08'W (116-B). Southwest of Mount Robert Henderson.

Named after Chester HENDERSON, the grandson of Robert Henderson of Klondike fame. His hunting area was centered on this hill. As a big-game guide he gave great support to scientific parties of various kinds in this area.

CHIEF GULCH 63°52'N 139°15'W (115-O). The last tributary to Eldorado Creek.

CHIEF ISAAC and men of his Moosehide Band of Indians were in at the beginning of the Klondike Discovery. Contrary to public belief, Indians had every right to stake, record and mine in any part of the territory. Several of them staked claims on Bonanza and other creeks. CHIEF ISAAC found gold and staked the Discovery claim on this short stream on 4 December 1896. He and his people were the first to trade with McQuesten when he built Fort Reliance.

An able man and a good leader, he was well respected by all. The stream was originally named Chief Isaac Creek. (see Mount Chief Isaac)

MOUNT CHIEF ISAAC 5,280' 65°27'N 139°25'W (116-G). North of the Ogilvie River.

The mountain was named in 1973 after CHIEF ISAAC, Chief of the Moosehide Band of Indians who lived at the site of Dawson before and after the Gold Rush. Much mentioned in the literature of the time, he was helpful and friendly to the early miners. The Moosehide Band received its name from the scar left by a large landslide on the Midnight Dome above Dawson, which resembles a large moosehide stretched to dry.

CHI DANAADAA CREEK 66°44'N 135°24'W (106-L). A tributary to Road River.

On the old Indian trail from the MacKenzie River to the Yukon interior. An old Loucheaux Indian word referring to the red colour of the rocks on the mountain above the creek.

CHI ITREE LAKE & CREEK 66°43'N 134°30'W (106-L). A tributary to the Peel River.

A camping place on the old Indian trail from the MacKenzie to the Yukon interior. The word is Loucheaux Indian meaning "Crying Head".

CHI NAHIL MOUNTAIN 66°45'N 136°00'W (106-I). A peak east of Mount Cronin, in the Richardson Mountains.

A landmark on the old Indian trail from the MacKenzie River to the Yukon interior. A Loucheaux Indian word meaning "Rock Hanging Down", referring to the shape of the mountain.

The creek takes its name from the mountain.

CHINAIDLAI CREEK 67°46'N 139°13'W (116-0). Branch of a stream running into Johnson Creek.

A stream where the Indians placed fish traps. The name is a Loucheaux Indian word which in translation refers to the strange flow of current in the creek.

On some maps this stream bears the name "Little Flett Creek", perhaps after one of the Flett family in the country.

MOUNT CHISHOLM 64°22'N 138°13'W (116-B). North of Antimony Mountain.

Named in 1973, after Tom CHISHOLM, a Scottish bushman and prospector here in the 1920s-30s. He also mined in the North Klondike area.

CHITINA GLACIER 61°01'N 141°00'W (115-F). Crosses the Yukon-Alaska boundary, in the St. Elias Mountains.

The glacier was named in 1912 by the an International Boundary Survey team, from its closeness to the Copper River in Alaska. The name "Chitina" is an Indian word meaning "Copper", as reported by Dall in 1870. There are variations in spelling such as Chettyna, Chitennah, Chechitna, etc.

CHOHO HILL 67°27'N 138°42'W (116-O). A long, low ridge ten miles southeast of Cadzow Lake.

Long known locally, this is a Vanta Kutchin Indian word meaning "Egg".

CHRISTAL CREEK 63°57'N 135°31'W (105-M). A small tributary to the South McQuesten River.

Charles CHRISTAL found and staked the first gold found here on 14 November 1902.

CHRISTIE PASS 63°04'N 129°41'W (105-P). The pass through the Selwyn Mountains, connecting the Gravel River in the NWT to the headwaters of the Ross River.

James Murdoch "Jim" CHRISTIE was born on 22 October 1874 in Perth, Scotland. He came to the prairies as a young man and, in early 1898, left Carman, Manitoba to take the Edmonton Trail to the Klondike. He found and used this pass on the way. He prospected the NWT and Yukon for years, mainly interested in a vast stretch of territory centering on the Rogue River.

In 1907, Joseph Keele, GSC, whom CHRISTIE assisted in his geological survey of this area, named the pass and the mountain after him.

It was near here, in late October 1909, that a huge grizzly bear attacked him. With his skull and jaw fractured, his right arm broken and his right thigh terribly bitten, this courageous man made his way, in sub-zero temperatures, seven miles to a temporary camp. His partner, George Crissfield, tended his wounds with the only medicine they had, some scotch whisky. Crissfield obtained the help of some nearby Indians and their dogs and after four long and terrible days, over rugged mountain country, got CHRISTIE to the small settlement of Lansing, on the Stewart River. There the trader J.E. Ferrell, who had some medical knowledge, tended his injuries and set his arm and jaw. He and his wife nursed CHRISTIE for two months. On New Years Day he was taken by dog-sled to Dawson, a journey of seventeen days. Later he went to Victoria, B.C. where his jaw was re-set and his other injuries given further attention. He was back prospecting in the summer of 1910.

CHRISTIE went to Ottawa and enlisted as a private in the famous Princess Patricia's Canadian Light Infantry on 24 August 1914, one of the very first. He served with outstanding distinction throughout the First World War. He fought in France and was first mentioned in dispatches and then won the DCM. He was commissioned in the field and won the Military Cross and further allied decorations.

His courage, integrity and good humour were appreciated by all who knew him. As a bushman he was almost without an equal; he once took a party from Dawson to Edmonton by a new route in a remarkably short time, in the dead of winter.

In later life, bothered by his old wounds, he retired with his wife to Saltspring Island, B.C. where he died.

MOUNT CHRISTIE 63°01'N 129°41'W (105-P) On the southside of Christie Pass.

This peak was named by Joseph Keele, GSC, in 1909, when he named CHRISTIE PASS.

CHRISTMAS CREEK 61°04'N 138°21'W (115-G). A tributary to Kluane Lake, in Christmas Bay.

The Rev. John Pringle was an outstanding figure of the Klondike with his down-to-earth brand of Presbyterianism. He did not believe in turning the other cheek but had a helping hand for every unfortunate. He was active in community life and was a Member of the Yukon Council. He was an active prospector when he had time and he and Richard Fullerton found gold and staked the Discovery claim on this creek on Christmas Day 1903. He served as a Chaplain in the Canadian Army during the First World War. He was what has been termed "a muscular Christian".

CHRISTMAS CREEK 63°31'N 140°31'W (115-N). A tributary to Matson Creek, in the Sixty Mile River district.

This creek was discovered (i.e. gold was found) on Christmas Day 1911. There is no record of the name of the finder.

CHUNGKLEE LAKE 67°51'N 139°13'W (116-O). Between the forks of Johnson and Little Flat Creeks.

This is a Vanta Kutchin Indian word meaning "Open Place".

CHUNGKUCH LAKE 67° 57'N 138° 55'W (116-O&N) Near the headwaters of Johnson Creek.

This is an old Vanta Kutchin Indian name meaning "No Timber".

CHURCHWARD HILL 2,875' 65°34'N 138°12'W (116-G). West of the Ogilvie River.

This peak was named in 1973, after Guy S. CHURCHWARD, Dawson's first tinsmith in 1898. He later moved to Mayo in the 1920s. He invented and produced the Yukon Airtight Heater stove, which because of its light weight became a boon to prospectors and settlers.

CLAIRE CREEK 61°59'N 135°25'W (105-E). A short creek connecting Claire Lake (later named) with the Yukon River.

This was probably named by or for Thomas CLAIRE, a prospector well-known in this district for many years after 1900.

CLARENCE LAGOON 69°37'N 140°50'W (117-C). On the Arctic coast, about five miles east of the Yukon-Alaska boundary.

This almost enclosed, shallow bay was named by Sir John Franklin, RN, in 1826 after Prince William Henry, Duke of CLARENCE, and afterward King William IV of Great Britain. The CLARENCE River was named at the same time.

CLARK LAKES 64°08'N 134°56'W (106-D). Four small lakes on Scougale Creek.

These were named in 1950, to honour the memory of C-19545 Gunner Arthur Raymond CLARK, MID. He was born in Brockville, Ontario, on 17 December 1919. He enlisted in the Canadian Army on 4 September 1939, one of the first, at Ottawa, Ontario. He served in Canada, Great Britain and northwest Europe and was killed in action on 31 July 1944.

CLEAR CREEK 63°37'N 137°38'W (115-P). A tributary to the Stewart River, about ten miles below the McQuesten River.

This stream was known and named by miners in the 1880s but it was not until 1900 that payable gold was found on it.

It was near here that "Big Alex" MacDonald, the so-called "King of the Klondike", died of a heart attack on 8 January 1909. (see Mount Big Alex)

MOUNT CLEMENT 68°26'N 139°24'W (117-A). East of Timber Creek.

Named in 1973, by the Topographical Surveys Branch after W.H.P. CLEMENT, who was the legal adviser and Registrar of Land and Titles in Dawson from 1898-1900.

CLINTON CREEK 64°24'N 140°36'W (116-C). A tributary to the Fortymile River, three miles above its mouth.

CLINTON Felcht first prospected this stream in late 1886 or early 1887. Having prospected in Africa, his friends nicknamed him "The African Hunter". He died of heart disease on 16 August 1897, the first white man to die in Dawson.

No payable gold was ever found on the creek but it later gave its name to a thriving settlement and an asbestos mine.

CLINTON CREEK 64°24'N 140°36'W (116-C). Located on Clinton Creek, four miles above its mouth.

In 1957, Arthur Anderson, an Indian trapper at Dawson, found the large and valuable asbestos deposits which were worked here. He was born in Forty Mile in 1912. This town was built in 1967 to house the employees of the Cassiar Asbestos Corp. Ltd.

This was, at the time, the most northerly open-pit mine in Canada and the mill had the largest eccentric jaw crusher ever made at that time. The mine began production in October 1967 and closed in July 1978. The housing and equipment were all sold off, leaving only the memory of a village.

MOUNT CLOSE 68°20'N 137°25'W (117-A). Thirteen miles northwest of Bonnet Lake, in the Richardson Mountains.

Named in 1973, after Robert CLOSE. He was born in Mayo and was killed in a training accident at Penhold, Alberta, in 1957, while serving in the RCAF.

CLOSELEIGH

In September 1899, the WP&YR proposed this name for the settlement which would be constructed around their railroad terminus at the foot of the Whitehorse Rapids, on the west bank of the Yukon River. The only settlement at that time was on the east bank of the river and was already known as Whitehorse.

W.B. CLOSE, of Close Brothers, financiers of London, England, had raised the majority of the capital to build the railway. The name was used from September 1899 to April 1900 when the WP&YR bowed to public pressure and changed the name to Whitehorse. The east bank settlement had been abandoned by then. (see Whitehorse)

CLOUTIER CREEK 61°42'N 132°09'W (105-F). A small creek flowing to the Ketza River, in the St. Cyr Range.

This stream perpetuates the memory and name of D-61181 Fusilier Gerard Ludger CLOUTIER, MID, who was born 1 January 1917 in Montreal, Quebec. He served in Canada, Iceland, Great Britain and France. He was killed in action at Dieppe, France, on 19 August 1942.

CLUETT CREEK 61°16'N 138°47'W (115-G). Flows into the west side of Kluane Lake, at Destruction Bay.

Albert CLUETT was born in Dorsetshire in England in 1875. He came to Canada in 1895 and joined in the stampede to the Klondike in 1897.

He met the Jacquot brothers on the trail to the Klondike goldfields on Christmas Day, 1903 and helped them build their trading post at Burwash Landing the following spring.

He worked there for many years when he was not prospecting or trapping. He cooked in a US Army Engineers camp nearby during the construction of the Alaska Highway and was instrumental in having the memorial plaque erected at Destruction Bay.

In 1954, when conflict arose over the name of a water feature in the area, his name was suggested. Everyone knew Bert but few knew or could spell his last name. He was away prospecting at the time and could not be reached, so another name was adopted. However, in 1957 it was decided to name this stream in Bert's territory and after some investigation it was called Klewitt Creek. In 1959, Dr. J.E. Muller, GSC, saw Bert and found the correct spelling. In 1960 the name was officially changed to CLUETT CREEK.

Bert died at Burwash on 15 December 1972, a cheerful, friendly and energetic little man.

MOUNT CLUETT 65°36'N 138°46'W (116-G). East of the Whitestone River.

This hill was named in September 1973, after Hubert CLUETT. This was the same man as above except that a different government department checked the name and came up with this variation. Also, Bert was never in this part of the country.

CLUM CREEK 64°04'N 137°28'W (116-A). A tributary to the Klondike River.

This creek was named in 1897 by four brothers who first prospected the stream. They were Peter, Charles, Joseph and Phillip CLUM (or Coulombe) from Massachusetts. They went on after the Klondike to mine in Alaska.

COAL CREEK 64°29'N 140°26'W (116-C). Flows to the Yukon River, about six miles below the Fortymile River.

This creek was named by William Ogilvie, DLS, in 1887-88 for the coal seams previously found there by prospectors, which he examined.

The first workable coal deposits were found here by Henry Seimer in 1900. By 1904, English financiers had formed a company to mine the coal and produce thermal electricity for the large gold dredges in the Klondike. They built a plant here and a thirty-eight mile power line to Dawson. They also built a twelve mile long, narrow gauge railway along the creek from the mine to the Yukon River to supply coal to the riverboats.

The company ceased operations when cheaper hydro-electric power was made available in Dawson.

COAL GULCH 63°40'N 139°15'W (116-O). Flows into Ruby Creek.

The McKinnon brothers, Archibald and Donald, who were trying to develop huge tonnage of low-grade gold ore in the Indian River conglomerates near here (see McKinnon Creek), attempted to develop the coal seams on this gulch as a source of cheap power. Their gold property failing to produce, they also shut down work on the coal, although they had worked both from 1910-1915.

COAL LAKE 60°30'N 135°10'W (105-D). Fifteen miles southwest of Whitehorse, at the foot of Mount Granger.

Several seams of anthracite coal from three to ten feet in thickness are located in this area. They were developed for some years after 1905 to supply the copper mines at Whitehorse.

The lake was given its name in 1900, by R.G. McConnell, GSC, when he mapped the area.

COARSE GOLD PUP 63°50'N 138°47'W (115-O). A very short valley entering Eldorado Creek from Cheechako Hill.

J.J. Rutledge staked the first claim here on 23 September 1897 and optimistically named it at that time. Payable gold was recovered.

COBALT HILL 63°59'N 134°57'W (105-M). Just east of Keno Hill.

This hill was named by Jim MacDonald when he found rich silver-lead ore here in 1922. He named it after COBALT, Ontario, a silver mining camp which flourished from 1905-1927. He had prospected and mined there before coming to the Yukon.

MOUNT COCKFIELD 62°39'N 138°28'W (115-J). In the Selwyn River area of the Dawson Range.

This peak was named in 1915 after William E. COCKFIELD, GSC, by D.D. Cairnes, GSC. He was a long-time member of the GSC and especially active in the Yukon. In 1915, he started as an assistant packer with Cairnes on a geological survey party in this area. He became senior assistant to Cairnes and later, in charge of his own operations, mapped and explored many parts of the Yukon.

COFFEE CREEK 62°55'N 139°03'W (115-J). A tributary to the Yukon River from the west.

"COFFEE JACK" was an Indian trapper well-known in this country at the turn of the century. Noted for his dry humour, he was once accused of allowing his dogs to rob a white trapper's supplies. The trapper informed Jack that at the next offense he would poison Jack's dogs. Jack replied "in that case I might shoot you and tell the mountie that I thought you were a moose!".

The creek was mined for gold intermittently over the years giving reasonable returns but no bonanzas.

COFFEE CREEK POST 62°55'N 139°05'W (115-J). At the mouth of Coffee Creek.

Jim Derry ran a small trading post here in the 1920s and 1930s and serve local miners and trappers.

COGHLAN LAKE 61°33'N 135°29'W (105-E). Ten miles north of Lake Laberge, on the old winter trail to Dawson.

Charles COGHLAN lived and trapped here for many years. He came to the Klondike in 1898 and remained. He accompanied F.C. Selous, the famed African white hunter and naturalist on his big-game hunting expedition to the upper MacMillan River in 1904. (see Mount Selous)

MOUNT COLEMAN 61°10'N 140°08'W (115-G). At the head of the Steele Glacier, in the St. Elias Range.

This was named by the Alpine Club of Canada after Arthur Philomen COLEMAN (1852-1939), geologist and past-president of the club.

MOUNT COLLEY 65°05'N 133°13'W (106-F). West of the head of the Snake River.

Named by the Topographical Surveys Branch in 1973, after Howard "Harry" COLLEY, a well-known and successful prospector in the Dawson and Mayo districts from 1920-1955.

COLORADO CREEK 63°56'N 139°00'W (115-O). One of the larger tributaries of Hunker Creek, from the west.

This creek was staked and named by Max Scanzon on 26 May 1898. He, like many other Klondikers, had mined in COLORADO.

COLUMBUS GLACIER 60°24'N 140°52'W (115-C). On the Yukon-Alaska boundary, west of the Seward Glacier in the St. Elias Range.

This glacier was named by H.R.H. Prince Luigi Amedeo, Duke of Abruzzi, on 31 July 1897, for Christopher COLUMBUS. Prince Luigi led the Italian expedition which first climbed Mount St. Elias.

CONE HILL 64°24'N 140°35'W (116-C). On the south side of the Fortymile River, three miles upstream from the Yukon River.

This cone-shaped hill was named by Lt. Frederick Schwatka, US Army, on his trip down the Yukon River in 1883. Although the hill is still known locally by this name, it has been officially abandoned by the Board on Geographical Names because there is another Cone Hill and a Cone Mountain in the Territory, both named much later.

CONGDON CREEK 61°09'N 138°33'W (115-G). Flows into the southwest end of Kluane Lake.

This stream was probably named after Fredrick Tennyson CONGDON by a miner whom he had grubstaked in February 1904.

F.T. CONGDON, a lawyer from Nova Scotia, came to the Yukon in early 1898 as a legal adviser to the Commissioner of the Yukon Territory. This post he held until 1901. He quickly became the leader of the Liberal party in the Yukon and was appointed Commissioner of the Yukon Territory in March 1903, a post he held until May 1905. He established a newspaper, the Yukon World, as a party mouthpiece. His tenure was marked by political graft and extreme political patronage, even in a day when this was common everywhere. In 1908 he was elected to Parliament, losing the seat in the next election in 1911. He left the Yukon and engaged in law practice in Vancouver, B.C. He died in Ottawa on 13 March 1932.

CONEY LAKE 68°51'N 136°52'W (117-A). West of the Blow River, ten miles South of the Arctic coast.

A local name owing to the number of Inconnu fish that are here and netted in large numbers. The colloquial name for Inconnu is CONEY.

MOUNT CONNOLLY 7,018' 62°32'N 132°21'W (105-K). Thirty-five miles northeast of Faro.

Thomas Osborne CONNOLLY was born in Prince Albert, Saskatchewan, on 4 July 1918. He was a born bushman. In his late teens he and his life-long friend John Dewhurst went to Goldfields and then to Yellowknife, NWT, where they earned a living mining and freighting. They went further north and spent two years trapping in the Nahanni country, and on to the Pelly River district.

He enlisted in the Royal Canadian Naval Fishermen's Reserve in 1942 and soon was sent overseas on combined operations. He took part in the invasion of France, landing with 3rd Division Canadian troops on the beach on D-Day. He was engaged in numerous other landings and was discharged in March 1945.

Returning to the Yukon, he took over the Taylor and Drury trading post at Ross River for a year and then set up his own store. Until 1964 he combined this with outfitting and guiding big-game hunters to the area. Then he moved his family to Atlin, B.C. and continued to guide in the Taku River region until his death on 31 July 1975.

His fearlessness, combined with his mastery of the bush and his outgoing personality made him a true example of the northern pioneer.

CONNOLLY LAKE 62°32'N 132°10'W (105-K). Four miles east of Mount Connolly.

Both this lake and the mountain to the west were known locally by this name for a number of years prior to the official designation in 1978.

CONRAD 60°04'N 134°33'W (105-D) On the west side of Windy Arm, on Tagish Lake, about eight miles southeast of Carcross.

On 13 July 1899, Ira Petty and W.R. Young had found and staked the silver-gold deposits that were to spark an intensive mining era in this section of the Yukon.

By 1905, Colonel John Howard CONRAD, an American mining promoter, had acquired control of most of the newly discovered gold-silver-lead deposits on the west side of Windy Arm. He organized this settlement as an intended supply base for his operations. By 1909, it was a thriving town, with stores, hotels, churches and a District Mining Recorder. Steamboats ran schedules between here and Carcross.

The ore in the various mines; the Big Thing, Montana, Joe Petty, Aurora, Venus, all under CONRAD Consolidated Mines Ltd., were being actively developed but extensive work showed an erratic nature to the ore bodies. By 1914, with a drop in the world price of silver, the mines closed down and the town was abandoned. Several attempts to reopen the mines since then have met with limited success.

White Mountain, across the lake on the east side of Windy Arm, was locally called Mount CONRAD at that time but the name was not officially allowed due to the earlier designation. (see White Range)

THE CONSERVATIVE TRAIL (115-F)

According to Hugh S. Bostock, GSC, the Liberal Trail was a part of the original winter road between Dawson and Mayo. When placer mining developed on the creeks to the north, the government was urged to build a new trail that would serve more miners. In one of the elections, the Conservative candidate supported the financing of this new trail, while the Liberal candidate advocated maintaining the trail as it was. The Conservatives won and the new trail was built. It ran from Minto Lake, along Bear Creek, across the McQuesten River and up Vancouver Creek to Clear Creek, at which point it merged with the old trail. Thus, the two trails were locally known as the "Conservative" and "Liberal" Trails.

The trails are now abandoned as mail routes but the names are still in use and the trails appear clearly in aerial photographs. (see Thoroughfare Creek)

MOUNT CONSTANTINE 10,295' 61°25'N 140°34'W (115-F). Overlooking the huge Klutan Glacier, in the St. Elias Range.

This beautiful peak was named in July 1900 by J.J. McArthur, DLS, of the International Boundary Survey.

Charles CONSTANTINE was born in Bradford, Yorkshire, England in 1849. A short, neat man with a piercing eye and a commanding presence, he joined the army at an early age. He took part in the Red River Expedition of 1870, became Chief of the Provincial Police of Manitoba and held a commission in the Winnipeg Light Infantry (The Little Black Devils). He saw action in the Northwest Rebellion in 1885 and then enlisted in the NWMP with the rank of Inspector.

In 1894, there were no government officials of any kind in what was to become the Yukon Territory. The only law was the Miner's Meeting. When attended by the usual working miners and prospectors it was a most democratic procedure. However, as the flow of gold and the population both increased, the settlements became filled with the usual frontier scum and parasites. When a Miner's Meeting was called, these people attended while most of the miners were out at work on the creeks. The verdicts of such meetings became more and more biased and frivolous.

In early 1894, Bishop Bompas and Captain J.J. Healy (who had organized the NAT&TC and built Fort Cudahy at Forty Mile) had C.H. Hamilton (Healy's manager) write a letter to the Canadian Government requesting police to bring law, justice and order to the territory

In June 1894, Inspector CONSTANTINE with Staff Sergeant Brown of the NWMP arrived at Forty Mile and after an inspection of conditions in the region, returned to Ottawa and recommended that a Force of NWMP and a Customs Agent be established at Forty Mile. S/Sgt Brown remained behind to represent the government.

CONSTANTINE returned to Forty Mile on 24 July 1895 on the NAT&TC's riverboat "Porteous B. Weare", from St. Michaels with 20 NCO's and Constables, Inspector D'Arcy Strickland, Asst. Surgeon Willis and W. Davis, Collector of Customs for the Yukon. CONSTANTINE was appointed Magistrate, Mining Recorder, Coroner, Land and Timber Agent and all other necessary government posts not specified. His powers were wide and his instructions were to govern by the spirit, rather than the exact letter of the law. They built Fort CONSTANTINE just below Fort Cudahy on the west bank of the Yukon River, the most northern military post of the British Empire at the time.

In August 1896, when the Klondike gold was found, CONSTANTINE decided to use the local miners' name for the river and district and he settled on "Klondyke" as being nearest their pronunciation of the Indian name. In all the excitement and pressure on him he never lost control and his handling of such a potentially explosive situation, almost alone, still excites admiration.

In 1901, he was given command of the Athabaska District, NWT and from 1905-1907 was engaged in building a road from Fort St. John, B.C. to the headwaters of the Skeena River. The road was never completed and the hardships he suffered on this project left him weakened physically.

Superintendent Charles CONSTANTINE died in Long Beach, California, while on leave, on 5 May 1912.

CONTACT CREEK 60°00'N 127°44'W (95-D). Crosses the Yukon-B.C. boundary at Mile 588.1 (KM947) of the Alaska Highway.

On 24 September 1942, bulldozers working their way south from Watson Lake met those working north from Fort Nelson, B.C. This meeting of the road construction crews of the US Army Engineers marked the breakthrough of the Alaska Highway from Dawson Creek, B.C. to Whitehorse and the first road access to the Yukon Territory. (see Beaver Creek)

MOUNT CONYBEARE 2,062' 69°29'N 140°07'W (117-C). Ten miles south of the Arctic coast.

This feature was named in 1826, by Sir John Franklin while on his second Arctic expedition. He named it for William Daniel CONYBEARE (1787-1857), a prominent English clergyman and noted amateur geologist.

COOK LAKE 62°09'N 130°54'W (105-J). Fifteen miles northwest of the Pelly Lakes.

This lake was named in September 1971, after Lesley "Les" COOK, a bush pilot and trader. He had a cabin on this lake and a trading post at Sheldon Lake. The trading post was run for a short while by his brother Jim, who was killed by a gun trap he had set for bears.

COOK scouted the route of the Alaska Highway between Watson Lake and Teslin in 1942 for the US Army Engineers and flew supplies to their survey camps. He was later posthumously, awarded the US Air Medal for several emergency flights he made at this time.

His Norseman aircraft crashed in Whitehorse at the corner of 2nd Ave. and Elliott St. in early December 1942, killing himself and two mechanics, Kenneth McLean and Donald Dixon.

MOUNT COOK 13,760' 60°11'N 130°57'W (115-B). A boundary peak in the St. Elias Range.

This splendid peak was named by W.H. Dall, Assistant of the US Coast Survey (later the USC&GS) in 1874 after Captain James COOK, RN (1728-1779), the famous English navigator and explorer who carried out much of the first mapping and exploration of the Alaska coast.

MOUNT COOK 61°56'N 132°55'W (105-F). About fifteen miles southwest of Ross River.

In 1951, this mountain was chosen to honour the memory of J-6276 Squadron Leader Robert Geoffrey COOK, DFC, who was born in Toronto, Ontario on 5 February 1921. He enlisted in the RCAF at Toronto on 20 September 1940. He served in Canada and overseas and was missing, presumed killed in action on 4 December 1943.

The mountain had previously been mapped and named "Priest Mountain" in the spring of the same year by a GSC party in the region. The population of the region being almost nil, they had been completely surprised one day when a priest, in clerical garb, riding a motorcycle, went by. The Board on Geographical Names disallowed their name but some local people still use it.

COOKING ROCKS CREEK 66°34'N 134°15'W (106-L). A tributary to the Peel River.

A stopping place on the old Indian Trail from the MacKenzie to the Yukon interior. The Loucheaux Indians found this place to be a good source of rocks or boulders of the proper type for cooking purposes. The rocks were heated and then placed in a container holding water and the meat to be cooked.

MOUNT COOPER 61°11'N 136°20'W (115-H). At the headwaters of the Nordenskiold River.

Named in 1898, after George COOPER, probably by J.B. Tyrrell, GSC, whom he assisted in this area at the time.

CORBETT HILL 2,511' 66°21'N 136°43'W (116-I). West of the Eagle River.

In 1973, this feature was named to commemorate K-73831 Sapper Herbert Logan CORBETT, 2nd Tunnelling Company, Royal Canadian Engineers. He was killed in a blasting accident while constructing underground fortifications at Gibraltar, on the 28 November 1942. He had been a placer miner in Dawson and Atlin, B.C. before the War.

MOUNT CORCORAN 2,514' 62°48'N 137°28'W (115-I). Two miles northwest of Fort Selkirk.

This hill was named in November 1971, after Rgt. No. 42 Gunner J. CORCORAN, Royal Canadian Artillery. He was a member of the Yukon Field Force. He died while on duty at Fort Selkirk and was buried there on 27 September 1898. (see Mounts Evans, Hansen, Watson and Walters)

MOUNT CORP 65°22'N 133°13'W (106-F). East of the Snake River, in the Canyon Range.

This mountain was named by Hugh S. Bostock, GSC, in 1973 after Ernest J. CORP. He came to the Klondike in 1897-98 via the MacKenzie River, the Gravel River, Bonnet Plume Pass and the Stewart River. He was a successful miner in the Klondike and later prospected for silver on Keno Hill. He was elected for several years a member of the Yukon Council for the Mayo Riding.

CORWIN VALLEY 60°17'N 134°58'W (105-D). The valley of the Wheaton River, from Lake Bennett north to Annie Lake.

Frank CORWIN, a pioneer Yukoner and his partner, Tom Rickman, camped in this valley and prospected the area in 1893. They found several rich looking veins of gold and silver-antimony ores. They returned to Juneau in the fall where they both died within a few months. Although they had staked claims on their finds, others whom they had told were unable to locate them. Some were found in 1906 by later prospectors. (see Carbon Hill and Gold Hill)

MOUNT COUDERT 60°32'N 136°03'W (115-A). On the northeast side of Kusawa Lake.

This hill was named in 1966, in memory of Bishop John Louis COUDERT, the first Roman Catholic Bishop of Whitehorse. He had served in the north for 45 years. He died in November 1965 while attending a Vatican Council in Rome. His body was brought back and buried in Whitehorse.

COWARD CREEK 62°39'N 134°04'W (105-L). A small tributary to the Tay River.

Alec COWARD came in the Klondike Rush and remained to trap and trade. He and his partner Arthur Zimmerlee ran a trading post at Armstrong on the MacMillan River between 1905-10. COWARD then set up a trading post at Fort Selkirk where he traded, trapped and prospected until the 1950s. His wife, who had been a missionary teacher at Fort Selkirk since 1916, did not care for her husband's surname and always referred to herself, Mrs. "Cowaret" after their marriage in 1929.

COWLEY 60°31'N 134°54'W (105-D). A way station and stop on the WP&YR, twenty-one miles south of Whitehorse.

This was a construction camp and way station during the construction of the WP&YR in 1899-1900. It was named after COWLEY Lambert, an English financier who was one of the major supporters of the railroad and a director of the company. The little lake nearby was named at the same time.

CRAIG CREEK 69°37'N 140°55'W (117-C). Flows into Clarence Lagoon on the Arctic coast.

This stream was named in 1912, by the International Boundary Survey party for J.D. CRAIG, DLS, who was in charge of the Canadian team. (see Mount Craig)

MOUNT CRAIG 13'250' 61°16'N 140°53'W (115-F). In the Icefield Ranges of the St. Elias Mountains.

John Davidson CRAIG, BSc, DLS (1875-1936), a surveyor, joined the International Boundary Commission in 1905. In the following years he surveyed the Yukon-Alaska boundary from Mount St. Elias to the Beaufort Sea. From 1910 he was Chief of Canadian survey parties until the task was finished in 1914. He was a member of the International Boundary Commission from 1925-31 and Director General of Surveys for the Department of the Interior from 1924-31.

CRATER CREEK 61°04'N 133°05'W (105-F). Flows into the west side of Quiet Lake.

This was probably named in 1887, by John McCormack and his three companions when they became the first men to find and prospect Quiet Lake. It was so named because of a peculiar circular basin or valley nearby.

CRAWFORDSVILLE 61°34'N 134°52'W (105-E). On the east bank of the Yukon River, at the mouth of the Teslin River.

A short-lived but active settlement was built here in early 1898 and abandoned the following year. Captain Jack CRAWFORD, a famous American army scout, Indian fighter, poet and miner, was the Assistant General manager of the Klondike, Yukon and Copper River Company. He hired large numbers of men and brought in much equipment to start a dredging operation on the Teslin River. Owing to various physical problems and a shortage of cash, the operation failed. Captain Jack went on to other ventures in the Yukon.

MOUNT CREEDEN 7,000' 61°16'N 137°15'W (115-H). On the west side of Aishihik Lake, six miles north of the Three Guardsmen Mountains.

This mountain received its name in 1966, to perpetuate the memory of J-15353 Pilot Officer James Waldron CREEDEN, DFM. He was born on 4 February 1922 at Brantford, Ontario. Enlisting in the RCAF at Hamilton, Ontario, he served in Canada and overseas. He was killed during air operations on 16 May 1942.

CRIPPLE GULCH 64°00'N 139°21'W (116-B). A short brook flowing into Bonanza Creek from the east, three miles from the Klondike River.

On 5 November 1897, William Dugan staked the Discovery claim here and named the place after CRIPPLE Creek, Colorado, one of the richest gold mining camps in the USA. The hill above the gulch carried extremely rich gold in the White Channel gravels and was very productive. He had named the stream "Cripple Creek".

MOUNT CRONIN 66°47'N 136°10'W (116-I). East of the Rock River, in the Richardson Mountains.

In 1973, this mountain was chosen to honour the name of Lt. Alfred CRONIN, born 24 March 1884 in Liverpool, England. He was working in the Yukon at Whitehorse and went to Victoria, B.C. where he enlisted in the 57th Battalion CEF on 28 October 1915. He served in Canada and Great Britain, and was killed in action in France on 27 September 1918.

MOUNT CRONKHITE 65°32'N 137°38'W (116-H). West of the Blackstone River.

Supt. Howard Hooper CRONKHITE, RCMP, served in the Yukon from 1912-1935 and from 1942-1946. This peak was named for him in 1973.

CROSBY CREEK 62°51'N 137°06'W (115-I). A tributary to the Pelly River.

This creek was named in the early 1900s, after George CROSBY who was a trapper and long-time prospector in this area. CROSBY came to the Yukon in 1898 and was a partner of John Barr for many years. They lived in cabins twenty miles apart but worked together. (see Barr Creek)

CROUCHER CREEK 60°47'N 135°05'W (105-D). Enters the Yukon River three miles below Whitehorse from the east side.

This creek was named in 1949, as a memorial to J-26857 Flight Lt. Gordon CROUCHER, MID, who was born 2 January 1916 at Montreal, Quebec. He enlisted there on 7 June 1942 and served in Canada and overseas. He was missing, presumed killed in action, on 29 July 1944.

CUB LAKE 60°47'N 135°27'W (105-D). The smaller of two lakes, five miles south of Takhini.

This was named in November 1973. The CUBS and Boy Scouts had camped here for a number of years. (see Scout Lake)

CUESTA CREEK 68°45'N 136°54'W (117-A). A tributary to Rapid Creek.

In the summer of 1970, F.G. Young, GSC, named this creek after an uncommon geological formation found near its mouth. CUESTA is a Spanish term meaning, roughly, a hill. The term is used mostly by geologists in the American southwest to describe a hill in which the rock bedding is normal to the gentler sloping side of the hill rather than parallel to it as is usually the case.

CYR CREEK 61°19'N 138°34'W (115-G). Flows into Gladstone Creek.

This stream was named about 1903, after Michael CYR of Quebec, who mined here. He was a well-known trapper and prospector in the Yukon for many years.

D'ABBADIE RIVER (see Big Salmon River).

D'ABBADIE CREEK 61°46'N 134°22'W (105-E). A tributary to the North Big Salmon River. (see Big Salmon River).

MOUNT D'ABBADIE 61°43'N 134°06'W (105-E). Lies at the head of D'Abbadie Creek.

Named because of its position at the headwaters of the creek. (see Big Salmon River)

DAIL CREEK 60°16'N 135°05'W (105-D). A small tributary to the Wheaton River, from Gold Hill.

In the summer of 1906, a stampede of prospectors was caused by the finds of rich, lode-gold ores (veins) on Gold Hill. George DAIL, a Klondiker, was one of the first to locate claims on this creek. He was a successful prospector and miner and was widely known in the Yukon for a long time.

DAIL PEAK 60°01'N 134°40'W (105-D). A prominent ridge on the southwest side of Windy Arm, on Tagish Lake.

George DAIL was one of the pioneer prospectors in this area. He found and staked the first mineral claims here in 1905 when the hill received its name from fellow prospectors. (see Conrad)

DALAYEE LAKE 60°20'N 133°38'W (105-C). South of Squanga Lake.

A Tagish or Tlingit name meaning "Plentiful Fish". The lake contains whitefish, pike and trout.

DALTON CREEK 60°19'N 137°17'W (115-A). Flows into Alder Creek, ten miles southwest of Dezadeash Lake.

This creek was named in May or June 1898 after Jack DALTON, famous Yukon and Alaskan pioneer.

DALTON POST or HOUSE 60°07'N 137°02'W (115-A). About eighteen miles south of Dezadeash Lake and two miles west of the Haines Highway.

Jack DALTON established a trading post and base camp here in 1893 or 1894 to trade with the interior Indians. The climate being so good, he wintered his pack-horses nearby for many years. A NWMP Post was built here in 1897 and closed in 1904.

DALTON RANGE 60°29'N 137°10'W (115-A). A short range of mountains facing the west side of Dezadeash Lake.

These hills were probably named by J.J. McArthur, DLS, when he mapped the DALTON Trail in 1897, after Jack DALTON, One of the most colourful of the Yukon and Alaskan pioneers.

THE DALTON TRAIL

This trail, from Haines, Alaska to Carmacks on the Yukon River, was a major route to the Klondike goldfields. It also was the best route over which horses, cattle, sheep and other animals could be brought into the interior.

The route was originally an ancient Chilkat Indian "Grease Trail" or trade route to the interior. The Chilkats carried fish oil, or grease, along with other trade goods (except guns). The route was, like the Chilkoot Pass, jealously guarded, as it was so lucrative to the Chilkats. It was this trail they used when they ravaged Robert Campbell's post at Fort Selkirk.

In 1869, Professor George Davidson, senior officer of the USC&GS in Alaska, persuaded the Chilkat Chief Koh-klux to draw a map of the trail. (see Fort Selkirk)

In 1882, Dr. Aurel Krause of the Bremen Geographical Society was the first white man known to enter the country by this route, which he mapped to the Tatshenshini River.

In 1890, the Frank Leslie Illustrated Newspaper Expedition, led by E. Hazard Wells and E.J. Glave, with A.B. Schanz and Jack DALTON, went to Kusawa Lake where the party split in two. Wells and Schanz went into the Tanana country while Glave and DALTON explored the Alsek River country and descended it to the sea by canoe, the only men to do it so far. DALTON and Glave returned the following year and brought the first horses in to the Yukon to what became DALTON POST.

Jack DALTON was born in the Oklahoma Territory in 1855. He ran away from home at age fifteen, some say because of a shooting scrape in which he was forced to kill a man. He roamed the American west in its most lawless period until, another shooting is hinted, he reached Juneau in 1887.

In 1891, he and Glave re-explored the trail country and after Glave left that fall, DALTON remained in the country. He had seen the potential and started to improve the trail and established posts on it. He both proposed to trade with the Indians in the interior and to freight supplies from Pyramid Harbor to the Yukon River for the ever increasing mining population. He also saw that the trail was the only feasible way to move sizeable herds of livestock into the goldfields. By 1895 he had found and laid out the best trail and built posts. The first recorded herd of cattle to be taken in over the trail was the one driven by Willis Thorpe, his two sons, "Long Shorty" Brooks (Bigelow), George Bounds (a butcher) and two other men in the summer of 1896. It is not certain if they were working for DALTON or paid him toll to pass. The herd consisted of about forty steer which carried packs of freight. They were driven to Carmacks and rafted downriver to Dawson, arriving in early September 1896.

There are unconfirmed reports that a small herd was taken over the trail in 1895. (see Shorty Creek)

The trail was quickly and roughly mapped by J.J. McArthur, DLS, in 1897. In the winter of 1897-98, following reports of starvation conditions in the Klondike, the American government gathered reindeer and Lapland herders from Scandinavia and sent a herd over this trail to relieve the miners. By the time they arrived (less than half the herd survived the journey) the famine had been averted and the remainder of the herd was sent on into Alaska.

The only man to control a major route into the Yukon and Klondike, DALTON ran pack trains and drove livestock to the miners. He allowed others to use his trail on payment of a toll and backed his authority with his reputation and gun.

One group who refused to pay the toll was accompanied by DALTON for the whole journey, who kept them well away from his route and in rough country. They lost most of their stock. No one else tried to travel the trail without payment.

In 1897, he brought in an additional 250 head of fine Oregon horses and started the DALTON Pony Express, to give rapid service to passengers and mail between Pyramid Harbor and Fort Selkirk. He could not compete with the riverboats and the venture soon ended.

After the gold fever died down DALTON continued his packing and freighting until the more economical riverboats and the WP&YR took away his business. He stayed in the country for many years, engaging in mining activities in the White River and nearby Alaska country. He helped survey the route of the Alaska and Copper River Railroads.

Retiring in the late 1920s, he spent many more years in Seaside, Oregon and died in January 1945 in San Francisco.

Gold seekers using the DALTON Trail prospected along the way and found good gold on Shorty Creek. Either DALTON himself, or men working for him found gold on this stream. Over the years he prospected and invested in many mining propositions in this part of the country with some success.

DALZIEL CREEK 60°29'N 127°09'W (95-D). A tributary to the Rock River, sixty miles northeast of Watson Lake.

This was named after George Campbell Ford DALZIEL, trapper, bushman, bush pilot and big-game guide. At age 18 he came to the Yukon from North Vancouver, B.C. and spent the first winter alone, trapping on the upper Coal River in the southeast Yukon. Soon acquiring an airplane, he quickly became a superb bush pilot. He scouted the location of the Alaska Highway in this area for the US Army Engineers and was instrumental in finding several downed aircraft that had been lost while being ferried from Edmonton to Alaska to Russia during the Second World War.

A pioneer in Watson Lake and the surrounding country, DALZIEL was noted for his ability to survive anywhere, in any season, alone. He died in Watson Lake on 26 December 1982.

DANGER CREEK 62°02'N 132°39'W (105-P). Flows into the Pelly River, two miles below the Lapie River.

In the summer of 1905, Charles Sheldon, noted amateur naturalist and big-game hunter, named this stream after his horse "Old Danger". The horse was the first one ever seen in the upper Pelly region. Some older maps carried the name "Old Danger Creek".

DAN MAN CREEK 62°58'N 139°17'W (115-J). A small creek flowing into the Yukon River, four miles above Kirkman Creek.

This was known for many years as the home and territory of Daniel MAN, a well-known trapper and prospector.

MOUNT DAOUST 62°04'N 136°06'W (115-I). About five miles southeast of Carmacks.

This was named about 1905, after an operator on the Yukon Telegraph Line who was stationed at Carmacks.

DARCY CREEK 67°25'N 140°57'W 116-N). Flows to the Porcupine River.

Named after DARCY Arden, surveyor and trapper, who lived here from 1910 to the 1930s.

DAUGHNEY LAKE 60°09'N 130°55'W (105-B). On the Swift River, near Mile 726 (KM1169) on the Alaska Highway.

In 1947, this lake was given the name of an outstanding Canadian soldier, Major Ralph Herman DAUGHNEY, DSO. He was born on 30 November 1908 at Dalhousie Junction, New Brunswick and was commissioned in the Canadian Army on 5 September 1940, at Woodstock, New Brunswick. He served in Canada, Great Britain and northwest Europe and was killed in action on 20 August 1944.

DAVIDSON CREEK 63°46'N 135°27'W (105-M). Flows into Duncan Creek near Mayo Lake.

About 1901, Jake DAVIDSON was one of the four men who staked the first claims on Duncan Creek. Shortly afterward he found gold on this stream. He later went to the silver and gold rushes in Cobalt and Porcupine in northern Ontario. (see Duncan and Galena Creeks)

DAVIS CREEK 64°04'N 141°00'W (116-C). A tributary to Poker Creek in Alaska.

This creek was named in 1891, by the man who discovered and mined gold on it in 1888 during the rush to the Fortymile goldfields.

DAVIS LAKE 66°11'N 136°25'W (116-I). One-half mile south of Moose Lake.

This quiet lake was named in 1973, to honour the name of Pte. Harry Henry DAVIS, K-76942, who died a prisoner of war in Holland on 15 January 1945. He was born in Dawson on 9 January 1921, enlisted at Whitehorse and served in Canada, Great Britain and Northwest Europe in the Lake Superior Regiment.

DAWSON (CITY) 64°04'N 139°26'W (116-B). At the junction of the Klondike and Yukon Rivers.

DAWSON CITY, the so-called "Paris of the North", was the capital of the Yukon Territory from 1897-1951.

This was originally the site of an Indian fishing camp for untold years before the white man ever saw the territory, as the Klondike River was one of the best salmon streams in the country.

George Carmack camped here with Skookum Jim and Tagish Charlie, fishing for salmon, in early August 1896, before they made their journey of discovery up Rabbit (Bonanza) Creek.

Joseph Ladue, who operated the trading post and small sawmill at Ogilvie (Sixtymile), had for years been a booster of the gold-mining possibilities of the district on the east side of the Yukon River and had grubstaked Robert Henderson who was and had been, with others, prospecting the tributaries of the Indian River. While Carmack and his friends found the riches of Bonanza Creek and started the great Gold Rush, Henderson and three companions were digging on Gold Bottom Creek with indifferent to poor results. Henderson went down the Indian River to Ogilvie for more supplies and, in early August, showed Ladue a small amount of gold dust from his workings. Ladue, confirmed in his belief of the value of the Klondike district, decided to move some lumber and supplies downriver to the mouth of the Klondike River, stake a townsite and establish a small trading post.

Seldom has a decision been more fortuitous. He arrived on the scene on 28 August to hear for the first time of the Bonanza strike and to find the area alive with excited men. He immediately staked out a 160 acre townsite on the only available ground (the Dawson Flats) and, on 1 September, started to build his store, the first building in Dawson. He sent some of his men back to Ogilvie to bring up his sawmill, which ran day and night for the next two years. He built a small log building and opened the "Pioneer", the first saloon in town. He sold lots in his townsite and bought rich claims from the cheechako stakers who did not foresee their value. In January 1897, William Ogilvie, DLS, surveyed the townsite and Ladue and his partner, Arthur Harper, had it officially named after Dr. George Mercer DAWSON (1849-1901), Director of the Geological and Natural History Survey of Canada from 1895-1901, explorer, scientist and extraordinary human being.

Called "The Little Doctor" by all who knew him, he was born in Pictou, Nova Scotia on 1 August 1849, a son of Sir John William Dawson, naturalist, geologist and the first Principal of McGill University. A severe illness at the age of twelve made him a hunchback and stunted his growth, leaving him in poor health for the remainder of his life. Tutored at home he had an abounding interest in the natural sciences and carried this into his studies at McGill and at the Royal School of Mines in London, England, where he graduated at the head of his class.

In 1873, he was appointed Geologist and Botanist to the British North American International Boundary Commission. His report on the geology and mineral resources along the 49th Parallel from the Lake-of-the-Woods to the Pacific Ocean is still a Canadian classic and resulted in his appointment to the G&NHSC in 1875.

Although crippled and frail, he carried out some of the most strenuous surveys ever attempted in Canada, and his yearly reports are incredible for both the quality and the sheer quantity of the work accomplished. He reported exhaustively on everything and everyone he encountered. In 1887, with William Ogilvie, DLS, of the Department of the Interior, he organized and headed the first geological and lateral survey conducted in the Yukon Territory. It was typical of DAWSON that he chose the hardest route for himself. He came from Wrangell, Alaska up the Stikine River, the Dease River, the Liard and Frances Rivers and into Frances Lake. From there he went down the Pelly River to the Yukon, up that stream and over the Chilkoot Pass to Dyea on the Pacific. His report encompassed almost everything known about the Yukon at that time.

He was an authority on ethnology, archaeology and botany as well as geology and was later to be called "The Father of Canadian Anthropology". His collections in these fields, made on his surveys, laid the base of the ethnological collection of the National Museum of Canada. He published dozens of papers, many of them still standard reference.

Appointed Director of the Geological Survey of Canada in 1895, he enhanced and continued the works of his towering predecessors Logan and Selwyn. His honours include the CMG, LLD's from both Queen's and McGill Universities, FRS, President and Charter Member of the RSC, the Patron's Gold Medal of the RGS and FASAS.

He died unexpectedly, after a one-day illness of acute bronchitis, in Ottawa on 2 March 1901.

Dawson City's heyday was from 1897 to late 1899 and most of the literature concerning it was written about this period. The exhaustion of the richest, hand worked placer gold deposits, and the news of more fabulous finds in the beach sands at Nome, Alaska depleted the population in 1899. The equally rich finds at Tanana (Fairbanks, Alaska) in 1903 also took many people away from the Klondike.

By 1900, many wives and families had arrived. The machine methods of mining attracted a more skilled and settled people and Dawson became a quieter and more stable town.

The population in late 1898 was estimated at greater than 5,000 but the town was a service and social center for more than 30,000 in the immediate area. In January 1902, Dawson was incorporated to city status but with the drop in population a petition to rescind the charter was accepted and it was cancelled in 1904. The town then had no mayor and affairs were managed by the Office of the Commissioner of the Yukon Territory.

The town always had a rich and varied social life, the more so because of its isolation, especially during the eight winter months. However, as the placers were worked out and little new gold gravels were found, the population steadily declined. The final blow was the cessation of dredging activities by the Yukon Consolidated Gold Corporation in 1966. Owing to the development of the Clinton Creek asbestos mine at Fortymile and to an increase in the tourist trade, Dawson's population climbed to about 800-900 persons. The mine closed in 1978 but the rising price of gold kept things stable and Dawson has held its own.

During the 1960s-80s, various governments finally realized the importance of the town as an historic site and moved to save and restore many of the old buildings. The work continues to this day.

"DAWSON" CHARLIE CREEK 60°14'N 135°10'W (105-D). A tributary to the Wheaton River, flowing from Gold Hill.

After August 1896, Tagish Charlie, nephew of Skookum Jim and Kate Carmack, became known as "DAWSON" CHARLIE. He and Skookum Jim prospected widely in the southern Yukon and grubstaked other Indian friends and relatives. This area was close to his home at Carcross and in 1903 he staked claims on mineral showings on this stream.

Charlie became a wealthy man from his Klondike claim on Bonanza Creek. On 2 July 1904, a special Act of Parliament was passed enfranchising him "with all the rights and privileges of a white citizen". He could vote, sue or be sued, buy and drink liquor and hold office.

Returning home from a celebration on 26 January 1908, he fell from the WP&YR bridge at Carcross and was drowned. (see Bonanza and Fourth of July Creeks)

DAWSON RANGE 62°40'N 139°00'W (115-I). The range of mountains stretching for nearly forty miles west of the Yukon River, north of its junction with the Pelly River.

These hills were named well before the turn of the century after Dr. George Mercer DAWSON, G&NHSC.

The area came into prominence about 1969 with the discovery of potentially vast deposits of copper-molybdenite ore. They were found to be uneconomic at that time but changing technology may arouse interest in them in the future.

DEADMANS CREEK 64°20'N 133°04'W (105-C). A small creek flowing into Teslin Lake, crossing the Alaska Highway near Mile 816 (KM1314).

Although officially named at the time of highway construction, the local people point out that the creek has always been named from the hill from which it runs and which is so-called because it resembles a prostrate man.

DEADWOOD CREEK 64°06'N 139°28'W (116-B). A tributary to the Yukon River, from the west, at Dog Island three miles below Dawson.

B.B.S. Phillips, who had probably mined in the Black Hills of South Dakota, named this creek when he discovered gold here on 24 September 1897.

MOUNT DECOELI 60°50'N 137°53'W (115-A). A prominent peak about four miles west of Mile 1030 (KM1658) on the Alaska Highway.

This mountain was named in 1950, after E.J. DECOELI, a member of the International Boundary Commission survey party in 1913.

DeCOURCY LAKE 61°29'N 137°08'W (115-H). Five miles east of central Aishihik Lake.

This three mile long lake was named in 1956, to honour the memory of J-17641 Squadron leader Thomas Joseph DeCOURCY, DFC. He was born 2 August 1921 at Mitchell, Ontario. He enlisted in the RCAF on 7 October 1940 at Windsor, Ontario. He was serving overseas when he was killed accidentally on 7 June 1945.

DEMPSTER HIGHWAY

The Yukon's newest highway, it was begun in 1959 as Yukon Territorial Road No. 11. Later it was called the Flat Creek Road when it reached that far, then as it lengthened, it was called the Eagle Plain Road and lastly, the Aklavik Road.

Leaving the Klondike Highway at Mile 26, east of Dawson, the road follows the Klondike River valley. There it turns north through the Ogilvie Mountains to the Blackstone River, crosses the Ogilvie River and on to the Eagle River which it follows until it turns east through the MacKenzie Mountains to Fort MacPherson and on to Inuvik.

The Yukon Order of Pioneers, founded in Forty Mile in 1894 and active in honouring early Yukoners, proposed that the highway be named after Inspector W.J.D. DEMPSTER, RNWMP.

The route of the highway follows roughly the track of the NWMP patrols from Dawson to Fort MacPherson, started in 1905. These patrols were always done in the winter with dog teams.

Inspector F.J. Fitzgerald, Constables G.F. Kinney, Taylor and Special Constable Sam Carter left Fort MacPherson on 21 December 1910, on the return journey of this annual patrol. They went astray while trying to find the trail between Little Wind River and the Hart River. Running short of food, they decided to return to Fort MacPherson but owing to exhaustion and starvation they were unable to reach it. Kinney and Taylor died about 35 miles from Fort MacPherson while Fitzgerald and Carter died about 25 miles out.

On 20 February 1911, when the patrol had not arrived in Dawson, Inspector Snyder, the officer in charge, being concerned, ordered Cpl. DEMPSTER with Const. J.F. Fyfe, ex-Const. F. Turner and Charles Stewart, an Indian guide, to search for the missing party. Leaving Dawson on the 28 February they covered the route in record time, despite storms and bad weather which cost them valuable time. On 12 March they found a snow covered trail on the Little Wind River, followed it with great difficulty and found the bodies of Fitzgerald and his companions. In a country of hardy men DEMPSTER and his party earned respect for this journey.

William John Duncan "Jack" DEMPSTER, RNWMP Rgt. No. 3193 was born in Wales in 1876. He joined the Force in 1897 and went to the Yukon the same year. By 1911 he was famous as a bushman and a musher. He went on to render outstanding service to the Yukon for a total of 37 years. He retired in 1934 with the rank of Inspector, to Vancouver, B.C. where he died on 25 October 1964. (see Mounts Turner, Carter and Mount Fyfe)

MOUNT DEMPSTER 65°08'N 136°05'W (116-H). North of the Little Wind River.

This mountain, near the trail he travelled many times, was named in 1973 to further honour Inspector W.J.D. DEMPSTER, RCMP.

DENNIS GLACIER 60°54'N 140°23'W (115-C). A small tongue of the Walsh Glacier, just east of the Centennial Range, in the far northwest of the St. Elias Mountains.

This glacier was named in 1920, after T.C. DENNIS, DLS, the assistant in charge of the International Boundary Survey party in 1910 and who commanded the party in 1912.

MOUNT DENNIS 67°42'N 136°37'W (116-P). On the headwaters of the Bell River, near MacDougall Pass.

This hill was named by William Ogilvie, DLS, in May 1888, after a friend Col. John Stoughton DENNIS who was, or had been Surveyor General of Dominion Lands and Deputy Minister of the Interior at the time.

DESTRUCTION BAY 61°15'N 138°48'W (115-G). On the west side of Kluane Lake.

The first settlement here was a US Army Engineers highway construction camp in 1942. Shortly after construction high winds destroyed most of the buildings, hence the name.

The memorial plaque erected here to commemorate this event was the result of efforts of Herbert Cluett, a long-time pioneer who was annoyed at the false tales told tourists about the loss of life and boats here during the Klondike Gold Rush. (see Cluett Creek)

THE DETOUR 62°44'N 134°42'W (105-L). The long, fifteen mile "S" bend in the Pelly River, starting just below the Earn River and ending at Harvey Creek.

This stretch of river was named by miners in the early 1880s, perhaps even earlier by HBC men in the 1850s. It was so-called because this sudden change in direction seemed to take them many miles out of their way.

DEVILHOLE CREEK 60°17'N 136°18'W (115-A). Flows into the west side of Kusawa Lake.

In 1950, Dr. E.D. Kindle, GSC, reported that the creek was named by the Indians of the area. They said sheep that were shot on the mountainsides disappeared into mysterious holes in the mountain and could not be found.

MOUNT DEVILLE 65°13'N 140°24'W (116-F). On the headwaters of the Tatonduk River, in the Ogilvie Mountains.

William Ogilvie, DLS, named this mountain in March 1888, while making his survey of the Yukon-Alaska boundary.

Edouard Gaston DEVILLE (1849-1924), OLS, DLS, DTS, was Surveyor General of Canada from 1885-1924.

MOUNT DEWDNEY 66°03'N 139°12'W (116-J). On the upper Miner River, in the Ogilvie Mountains.

William Ogilvie, DLS, named this mountain in March 1888, after his good friend, the Hon. Edgar DEWDNEY.

DEWDNEY, born in Devonshire, England, and educated as a civil engineer came to British Columbia in 1859 as a surveyor. When rich gold placer deposits were found in the Similkameen district he was given the contract to build a road from Fort Hope, the head of navigation on the Fraser River, to the Similkameen. Started in 1860, it was completed in 1863 and was called the "DEWDNEY Trail". When new gold finds were made farther east he extended his road to Wild Horse Creek in the Big Bend country of the Columbia River in 1865. These roads opened the interior of British Columbia to the coast and lessened the American influence in the interior of the province.

He was elected to the provincial legislature in 1868-69. He represented Yale, B.C. in the House of Commons in Ottawa from 1872-79, when he was appointed Lieutenant Governor of the North West Territories as well as remaining Indian Commissioner. During this time he is credited with averting major Indian uprisings during the Riel Rebellion by his just treatment of the larger tribes. He served Sir John A. MacDonald as Minister of the Interior and Superintendent of Indian Affairs from 1888-1892. In 1892 he was appointed Lieutenant Governor of British Columbia and served until 1897. He died on 8 August 1916 at Victoria, B.C.

de WETTE 60°22'N 134°49'W (105-D). At the north end of Lewes (Lewis) Lake.

Auguste de Wette was an early supporter and shareholder of the WP&YR. This section point was named after him in 1899.

DEZADEASH LAKE 60°28'N 136°59'W (115-A). A beautiful fifteen mile long lake, about twenty-five miles south of Haines Junction.

One of the earliest known features in this part of the Yukon, this lake was described to George Davidson, senior officer of the US Geodetic Survey in Alaska, in 1869 by Koh-klux, the great Chief of the Chilkat Indians. They called it "Dasar-dee-Ash" or "Dasa-dee-Arsh", meaning "Lake of the Big Winds". Another source says that this is a Tlingit Indian word that refers to platforms that were built at the foot of the lake from which to spear fish.

DIAMAIN LAKE 62°55'N 136°19'W (115-I). Ten miles northeast of Pelly Crossing.

In 1935, Hugh S. Bostock, GSC, was looking for the name of this lake while mapping the area. Mrs. Ira Van Bibber told him the Indian name was DIAMAIN. The generic term "main" itself means "lake" so the presently used name is redundant.

DICKSON CREEK 61°07'N 138°56'W (115-G). A tributary to the Duke River.

Thomas A. DICKSON (1856-1952), was one of four brothers, all ex-NWMP. He was with the Tagish Lake Detachment in 1898. Leaving the force, he became the first big-game guide in the Yukon. In 1916 he was the Game Warden at Kluane Lake and had his homestead on this creek. Many of his descendants are still in the Yukon. (see Bull Creek)

DICKSON HILL 60°12'N 135°01'W (105-D). Just south of the Wheaton River.

Ole DICKSON staked one of the first copper discoveries in the Whitehorse area, the Rabbit's Foot claim, on 7 July 1899. He prospected actively in these parts for many years.

DIIKEE CREEK 65°57'N 135°00'W (106-E). A tributary to the Peel River.

This word is a translation of the Loucheaux Indian word meaning "Long, Sharp Mountain".

MOUNT DINES 65°37'N 140°38'W (116-F). North of the Nation River.

John Dawson DINES was born in Dawson City. He served overseas during the Second World War and was later Mining Recorder at Dawson and Yellowknife, NWT. He moved up to Land Administrator at Ottawa with the Department of Indian and Northern affairs and died there in 1973.

DION CREEK 64°02'N 139°23'W (116-B). A small creek entering the Yukon River from the east, about two miles above Dawson.

This creek was named after H. DION, the leader of a prospecting party from Quebec. They found some gold here in October 1897.

DIP CREEK 62°32'N 139°23'W (115-J). A tributary to the Klotassin River.

Gold was discovered here by Jens Rude and the creek named on 12 August 1915. (see Jens and Rude Creeks)

DISCOVERY CREEK 62°04'N 137°14'W (115-I). A tributary to Nansen Creek, from the west.

Captain H.S. Back made the first discovery of gold in the area on this creek in August 1899, at the point where it joins Nansen Creek. No work was done at the time but he returned to the region in 1907 with a large prospecting party. On 13 June 1910, his son Frank H. Back, with Tom Bee, staked the first claims on both Nansen Creek and this stream. (see Mount Nansen and Back and Seymour Creeks)

DISCOVERY PUP 64°03'N 139°37'W (116-B). A tributary to Swede Creek from the north.

Daniel Donovan found gold and staked the Discovery claim here in 1911. (see Donovan Creek)

DISTINCTA PEAK 65°01'N 138°17'W (116-G). Southeast of Mount Chambers.

In the summer of 1975, graduate student Gerald J. Hilchie and his assistant Felix Sperling, both of the University of Alaska, came into the Yukon. They were collecting butterflies for scientific information. On the sides of this mountain they found large numbers of Buloria DISTINCTA, one of the rarest of North American butterflies.

DIXIE CREEK 61°02'N 137°51'W (115-H). A small tributary to McKinley Creek, in the Alsek district.

P. Harvey Hebb created a great deal of excitement in August, 1906 when he thought he had found diamonds in the blue clays on this stream. He had not.

The creek had been named in July 1903, when it was first staked for placer gold during the stampede to the Ruby Creek finds in the Shakwak Valley. (see Monte Cristo Gulch)

DOGHEAD POINT 61°21'N 138°47'W (115-G). A point on Kluane Lake on the west side of Talbot Arm.

In the summer of 1945, Hugh S. Bostock, GSC, gave this name because of the remarkable similarity to a husky dog's head.

DOGPACK LAKE 61°42'N 139°12'W (115-G). A small lake about twelve miles north of Brooks Arm, on Kluane Lake.

The name has been used for many years by the local Indians who used pack dogs to take supplies in to the lake for their winter trapping.

DOLLIS CREEK 60°02'N 137°10'W (115-A). A tributary to the Tatshenshini River.

This stream was named in the early years of the century by J.N. Wallace, DLS, after a stream near his home in a northern suburb of London, England.

The name was forgotten over the years and the creek was given another name in 1927. (see Squaw Creek)

DOLLY CREEK 62°04'N 137°13'W (115-I). A short brook flowing into upper Nansen Creek.

About 1910, George Mack, one of the original discoverers of gold here, named the stream after his daughter DOLLY (Mack) Golter, who lived here with him.

DOLORES CREEK 64°53'N 133°21'W (106-C). Fifteen miles east of Fairchild Lake, in the Bonnet Plume Range.

Louis Brown, long-time trapper and big-game guide in this area, named this creek in 1964 after his wife and partner, DOLORES Cline Brown. He had found rich copper mineralization here in 1951. Bonnet Plume Copper Mines Ltd. was organized to finance its exploration. It was never proved to be economic.

Mrs. Brown wrote a most interesting book about their guiding and living experiences, entitled "Yukon Trophy Trails".

DOMINION CREEK 63°37'N 138°42'W (115-O). Flows into the Indian River from the north.

One of the richest and most famous of the Klondike creeks. There is good evidence that "Hootch Albert" Fortier found gold here in late 1896 but did nothing about it until the spring of 1897. He staked the lower Discovery claim in late May 1897 but did not record it. Instead, he allowed John E. Brannin to stake it on 12 June while he recorded No. 1 above. At the same time Frank Biederman was prospecting the upper part of the stream and thinking he was the first to find gold on it, staked a Discovery claim on 28 lay. The Mining Recorder allowed both discoveries and accepted the name DOMINION, proposed by Fortier.

Albert Fortier came into the Yukon in 1887 from Quebec and, as his nickname implies, was noted in the Fortymile country for the ability to make alcohol out of just about anything.

This stream was the locale for many of the charges of corruption against the Yukon administration in 1898. The action of Commissioner James Walsh in reserving alternate claims on the creek as a government reserve aroused great bitterness among the miners. His action in opening the claims to public staking shortly afterwards aroused an even greater outcry when it was found that friends and relatives of government officials had staked claims the day before the general public was informed that the creek was open for staking. These, and other complaints, soon led to Walsh's recall to Ottawa and to the appointment of William Ogilvie, whose integrity was accepted by all. A commission of inquiry was appointed and, owing to its stretched out delays and to the distances involved, the matter more or less died out with few if any being punished for wrongdoing.

The major settlement on the creek was at its junction with Caribou Creek and was called Caribou City until 1905. From that date it was known as DOMINION. The settlement died out during the First World War.

DONJEK CITY 62°40'N 140°05'W (115-J). On the west side of the White River, one mile below Caledonia Creek.

A roadhouse was built here in 1913, on the trail from Stewart to the Chisana goldfields. Freight could be brought this far up river by small steamboats. Some gold was found on creeks nearby and a small settlement grew here for a number of years to service the miners. The place was abandoned in the 1920s.

DONJEK RIVER 62°39'N 140°00'W (115-J). A major tributary to the White River.

This large river was apparently named by Charles Willard Hayes in 1891, while on his expedition for the American Geographical Society. He took the name from the Indian word "Donyak" or "Donchek", it being the name of a type of pea-vine which grows profusely in the valley. It is very nutritious and makes excellent winter feed for game and stock animals.

DONAHUE CREEK 63°07'N 139°31'W (115-D). Flows into the Yukon River a short distance below Thistle Creek.

A prospector named DONAHUE found a gold-bearing quartz vein on this creek. He staked the find and named the creek in October 1900.

DONOVAN CREEK 63°32'N 139°56'W (115-O). Flows into Abraham Creek in the Sixtymile district.

This name has been used locally since 1911, after Daniel DONOVAN who found the first gold and staked the first claim at Discovery Pup in that year.

MOUNT DOOSHKA 7,156' 61°20'N 127°10'W (95-E). Near the Yukon-NWT boundary, close to the head of Coal River.

This name was submitted in 1971, under the auspices of the Commissioner of the Yukon Territory, James Smith. It was adopted in 1972.

DOOSHKA is the Kutchin Indian word for "Love", as noted in a once popular song entitled "Squaws Along the Yukon". One line says "DOOSHKA, DOOSHKA, DOOSHKA", which means "I Love You".

DOUGLAS CREEK 60°53'N 138°38'W (115-B). A tributary to the Slim's River, about ten miles above Kluane Lake.

Gold was found and this creek named by J. Kay in March 1904 during the rush to the Kluane Lake goldfields.

DRAPEAU CREEK 64°00'N 136°53'W (115-P). A short tributary to Hobo Creek.

Gerrard Charles DRAPEAU staked the Discovery claim here on 22 December 1902. He prospected and mined in the Mayo district for many years.

DRIFTWOOD RIVER 67°34'N 138°30'W (116-O). A tributary to the Porcupine River.

This name derives from the Loucheaux Indian word meaning "Big Firewood Creek".

DRURY SPIRE 62°20'N 134°26'W (116-O). At the south end of Drury Lake.

Hugh S. Bostock, GSC, proposed this name to honour William S. DRURY of Lincolnshire, England. Coming to the Yukon in early 1898, DRURY met Isaac Taylor while working on the Discovery claim on Pine Creek at Atlin, B.C. They became partners and, over the years, built a thriving merchandising business all over the Yukon. (see Tadru Lake)

DRY CREEK 62°20'N 140°23'W (115-K). A tributary to the White River, near Snag, Yukon.

Prospectors working on this creek about 1913 gave it this name because it froze to the bottom in winter. This is not remarkable as it runs through Snag, which holds the record for the coldest temperature ever officially recorded in Canada (-63°C or -81.4°F on February 3, 1947).

DRY CREEK 62°10'N 140°41'W (115-K). At the junction of Dry Creek and the White River.

A small settlement was located here for a few years after 1913 and served as a transfer point for men and supplies going to the Chisana goldfields.

DUBLIN GULCH 64°03'N 135°48'W (106-D). A small valley off Haggart Creek, in the Mayo district.

This is one of the best known and famous names in the Mayo area. Thomas Haggart, one of the area's first and long time prospectors, found coarse gold here in 1889. In 1896 he built the first cabin on the gulch and named it. When the influx of Klondikers invaded the country, Haggart and others decided to record their claims to protect them against claim jumpers. John J. Suttles recorded claim No. 1 and continued to work it until 1910. (see Suttle Gulch)

DUKE RIVER 61°26'N 139°06'W (115-G). Flows into the Kluane River, a few miles above Kluane Lake.

George DUKE was one of the first prospectors in the Kluane Lake country before 1900. This river was named at that time for him.

DULLMITT LAKE 61°00'N 137°11'W (115-A). West of the Aishihik River.

A Tuchone Indian word meaning, roughly, "Lake on a Hill Where Many Trout are Caught".

DUNCAN CREEK 63°46'N 135°31'W (105-M). A tributary to the Mayo River, just above Mayo Lake.

In 1898 three Norwegians, Gustavus Gustavesen and his two sons, alone in this part of the Yukon, discovered rich placer gold in the canyon on this creek. Because they wished to keep their find a secret and because the Mining Recorder was so far away, they did not stake or record any claims on their find. They went to great lengths to prevent anyone else from finding out about it, so much so that they were known as "The Mysterious Three". By September 1901 it was estimated that they had recovered more than $30,000 in gold from the creek.

A party of four Scottish Klondikers began prospecting in the area that summer and found the Gustavesen workings. The four, Duncan Patterson, Colin Hamilton, Allen McIntosh and Jake Davidson, found that the find was not recorded and promptly jumped the Gustavesen claims, while the Gustavesens were downriver for supplies. They staked on 12 September 1901 and named the creek after DUNCAN Patterson. The remainder of the creek was quickly staked by others.

The Gustavesens eventually left the country. The creek was one of the richest found in the Yukon, outside the Klondike. (see Gustavus Range)

DUSTY RIVER 60°40'N 137°57'W (115-A). A tributary to the Kaskawulsh River.

E.D. Kindle, GSC, named this stream in 1951. He wrote, "Great clouds of white dust that are visible for miles are whipped up along this river almost every day during the summer months. The dust is derived from the fine silts that are deposited daily over wide river flats as a result of the daily rise and fall of the river waters which are melt waters of the north lobe of the Lowell Glacier".

EAGLE CREEK 64°47'N 141°00'W (116-G). A tributary to the Yukon River, north of Fortymile.

E.C. Barnard, USGS, gave this creek its name in 1898 because the bluffs near its mouth (which is in Alaska) are a favourite nesting place for the bald eagles in the area.

EAGLES NEST BLUFF 2,445' 62°01'N 135°48'W (105-L). On the north bank of the Yukon River, five miles below the mouth of the Little Salmon River.

This was formerly called Eagle Rock by the early miners and riverboat men from the Indian name of the same meaning.

It was here that the worst riverboat disaster in Yukon history took place. On 25 September 1906, the riverboat Columbian was destroyed by an explosion and fire which killed six men and wrecked the ship. A crew member, shooting at some wildfowl, accidentally hit a shipment of gunpowder and explosives placed on the forward deck, setting it off. The efforts of the survivors to help the injured were heroic. A monument in the Whitehorse Cemetery is the only record of this disaster.

EAGLE RIVER 67°18'N 137°08'W (116-P). This large stream flows into the Porcupine River from the south, a few miles below Lapierre House.

John Bell, Chief Factor at Fort MacPherson, was probably the first white man to see this river and record the Indian name when he first crossed into the Yukon in 1839.

This lonely river was, in January and February 1932, the scene of the first aircraft assisted manhunt in Canada. From a Fort-like cabin on the Rat River, NWT, Albert Johnson, the "Mad Trapper of Rat River", for 48 days, in temperatures averaging -40 F., fought a series of four gun battles with the RCMP. He crossed the continental divide and but for the use of an airplane piloted by the famous bush pilot "Wop" May, might have escaped. He shot and killed Constable Edgar "Spike" Millen (see Mount Millen) and wounded two other constables. He was killed on 17 February in a small ravine about fifteen miles upstream from the mouth of this river.

Much private investigation has been pursued to find out his true identity and motives but much mystery still surrounds the story. (see "The Mad Trapper of Rat River" by Dick North)

EAR LAKE 60°41'N 135°02'W (105-D). A small lake on the west side of the Yukon River, at the foot of Miles Canyon.

Originally the site of a construction camp of the WP&YR.

This pleasant little lake became a favourite camping spot for the people of Whitehorse. It was the scene of the worst mass murder in Yukon history when Alexander Gagoff, a Cossack, shot and killed the section foreman and three workers of the WP&YR here on 30 September 1915. He was hanged in the Whitehorse jail on 10 March 1916.

EARN RIVER 62°44'N 134°42'W (105-L). Enters the Pelly River near the start of the Detour.

Robert Campbell of the HBC, the famous explorer of the Yukon and Pelly Rivers, named this stream after a river of the same name near his home in Perthshire, Scotland. The date was the summer of 1840 when he made his momentous journey down the Pelly to the Yukon.

EDIGII HILL 66°19'N 134°59'W (106-L). At the headwaters of Vitrih Creek.

This is a Loucheaux Indian word meaning "Hill Where the Caribou Breed".

EDMONTON CREEK 63°47'N 134°49'W (105-M). Flows into the southeast side of Mayo Lake.

On 13 June 1904, gold was discovered here by P. Beliveau and his partner, Desutel. Beliveau had come to the Yukon via the Edmonton Trail. Before his discovery the creek had been known locally as "Fan" or "Old Fan" Creek.

EHNJUU CHOO CREEK 66°14'N 136°35'W (116-I). A tributary to the Eagle River.

This is a Loucheaux Indian word meaning "A Big Stand of Timber", a rarity in this country.

EIKLAND MOUNTAIN 4,773 62°14'N 140°50'W (115-K). Five miles west of Mile 1185 (KM1908) on the Alaska Highway.

In 1967, the name of this mountain, then known as "Niggerhead Mountain", was changed to commemorate Peter EIKLAND, a long time prospector in the area. The change was made by the Board on Geographic Names, owing to complaints that the original name might give offense to certain travellers.

The original name was probably given by stampeders on their way to the Chisana goldfields in 1913-14. It describes the large clumps of blackened grass growing on muskeg swamps which make walking extremely difficult. They are unstable and if a person trying to step from one to another slips, he or she, is precipitated into the mud of the swamp. The name is a very old one, common across northern Canada. Earlier they were given the name "Tetes des Femmes" by the French-Canadian voyageurs of the HBC. (see Enger Lakes)

EINARSON LAKE 63°55'N 131°35'W (105-O). A small lake on Einarson Creek, a tributary of the Rogue river.

This name, both for the lake and the creek, was given in 1946 to immortalize a hero, J-17276 Flight Lt. Johann Walter EINARSON, DFC, DFM, RCAF. He was born in Wynyard, Saskatchewan on 20 November 1920 and enlisted in the RCAF on 10 February 1941 at Saskatoon. He served in Canada and overseas and was missing, presumed killed in action, on 25 February 1944.

ELDORADO CREEK 63°55'N 139°19'W (115-O). The main tributary to Bonanza Creek.

In late August 1896, a party of five, Anton Stander, Frank Kellar, Jamee Clements, Jay "Old Man" Whipple and Frank Phiscator, who had just staked Nos. 32 to 36 above on Bonanza Creek, decided to prospect this stream on their way back to the Klondike River. Clements and Kellar had panned gold here on their way up Bonanza in late August. A number of others had passed it up and a story persists that someone blazed a tree at the mouth of the creek and wrote "Reserved for Swedes and Cheechakos".

They discovered rich gold on No.3 claim. Whipple claimed Discovery and named the creek after himself. They staked their claims on 1 September. Another party of four arrived on 5 September and found dissension among the original five over claim ownership. They reached agreement and that evening Knut Halstead, a Fortymiler, suggested the name ELDORADO. Whipple's name was overruled because he was trying to hog too many claims and had also jumped claims in the Fortymile district.

Because of a rule newly passed by Inspector Constantine NWMP (also Mining Recorder), limiting the number of Discovery claims on a creek and the number of claims to be held by any one man in a district, further claim jumping took place. F.W. Cobb, a famous Harvard University football star, jumped Frank Phiscator's No. 2 claim on 6 September but Constantine disallowed his claim. He later claimed to have discovered and named ELDORADO CREEK.

It has been claimed by various authorities that ELDORADO Creek was the richest placer gold stream ever found anywhere in the world. The first 40 claims, about three and one half miles on the creek produced well over half a million dollars each, with gold then valued at $20.00 an ounce. Some of the claims gave up over a million and a half dollars over their length of 500 feet. Gold is still being taken from the gravels of this small stream, over 100 years later. (see Fort Reliance)

ELLEN CREEK 66°42'N 137°57'W (116-I). A small tributary to the Porcupine River.

A local name after an Indian woman "Ellentsie" who lived and was buried at the mouth of the stream, many years ago.

ELLIOTT CREEK 64°36'N 135°48'W (106-D). A tributary to the Beaver River, in the Wernecke Mountains.

This stream was named in 1945 after Fredrick ELLIOTT who prospected in this area in the 1920s. He was associated with Charles Settlemier, another well-known prospector. ELLIOTT Ridge, north of the creek was named later. (see Settlemier Creek)

ELMER CREEK 63°32'N 130°37'W (105-O). Flows to the Hess River.

Known locally for ELMER Middlecoff who mined in this area with his father for many years.

ELSA 63°55'N 135°29'W (105-M).

This small village on Galena Hill in the Mayo district, was established in 1929 to house miners at the newly discovered Calumet silver-lead mine.

The village received its name from the original claim staked in 1924 by Charles Brefalt who had named it after his niece in Sweden.

Production at the mine did not start until 1937. A post office was opened in 1949. Shortly afterward the first oil exploration winter road in the country, the "Wind River Trail" was built from here to drilling sites in the Bell River area, 300 miles north. (see Wind River Trail and Brefalt Creek)

EMERALD LAKE 60° 16' N 134° 45' W (105-D)

Located in the Watson River valley, nine kilometers north of Carcross, this very colourful lake drains underground into Spirit Lake, which then drains into the Watson River. On government maps it is called Blue Lake, and it has also been called Turquoise Lake and Rainbow Lake due to the intense colours that have made it the most photographed lake in the Yukon.

ENGER LAKES 62°16'N 140°42'W (115-K). Four small lakes near Mile 1185 (KM1908) on the Alaska Highway.

These lakes were named during the rush to the Chisana goldfields in 1913 as the "Niggerhead Lakes" by those unfortunate enough to have to backpack their supplies over them. The Territorial government in 1967 requested the name be changed and Harry ENGER's name was proposed. He was a long-time prospector in the area. (see Eikland Mountain)

ENGINEER CREEK 64°22'N 138°18'W (116-G). A tributary to the Ogilvie River.

This replaced the name Big Creek in 1971 at the request of Commissioner James Smith. It was renamed to commemorate the work of the Department of Public Works engineers in the district during the location of the Dempster Highway.

ENSLEY CREEK 63°54'N 139°43'W (115-O). A tributary to the Yukon River, below the Indian River.

The lower Discovery claim here was staked on 29 November 1897 by S. ENSLEY.

ERICKSON GULCH 63°56'N 135°20'W (105-M). A small tributary to Christal Creek, on Galena Hill in the Mayo district.

L.B. ERICKSON, a pioneer miner in the Mayo area, made one of his first discoveries of silver-lead ore in this gulch.

MOUNT ERICKSON 62°02'N 138°41'W (115-J). East of Onion Creek.

This name was proposed by James Smith, Commissioner of the Yukon Territory to commemorate John ERICKSON, a pioneer of Whitehorse owned and ran the Regina Hotel for over 50 years.

ERVIN CREEK 64°27'N 135°15'W (106-D). Flows into Carpenter Creek, in the Wernecke Mountains.

E. ERVIN found silver-lead ore on the banks of this creek in 1923 during the rush to the Grey Copper Hill finds. (see Grey Copper Hill and Settlemier Creek)

ESAU HILL 65°42'N 136°51'W (116-H). Eight miles southwest of Pothole Lake and north of the Hart River.

ESAU was an Indian guide whose report to Inspector Snyder at Dawson resulted in Cpl. Dempster being sent to search for the lost Fitzgerald Patrol in 1911. (see Dempster Highway)

ESCAPE REEF 69°00'N 137°15'W (117-A). A long, low, narrow island or reef, about three miles east of Shingle point in MacKenzie Bay, on the Arctic coast.

In 1826, Sir John Franklin, RN, named this reef after a touchy meeting with a band of unfriendly Eskimos (Inuit) at Shingle Point. (see Pillage Point)

ETHEL LAKE 63°21'N 136°06'W (105-M). About twelve miles east of Stewart Crossing.

J.J. McArthur, DLS, named this large lake after his daughter in 1898 when he was surveying in the vicinity. He was one of the first government surveyors in the territory and was active in surveying routes and claim surveys in the early days of the Klondike.

ETTRAIN CREEK 65°27'N 141°00'W (116-F). A tributary to the Nation River.

Thomas Riggs, American member of the International Boundary Survey team, named this creek in 1910. An Indian family of this name lived in the vicinity, their name was "Yetran". The word was said to mean "mosquito" in the local dialect.

EUREKA CREEK 63°38'N 138°49'W (115-O). A tributary to the Indian River, from the south.

Gold was found here and a Discovery claim staked on 28 August 1897 by J.G. Brown from EUREKA, California. His discovery did not lead to payable gold until February 1905 when a newer and richer discovery led to a stampede in which the whole creek and its tributaries were staked.

EUREKA LANDING 61°15'N 134°36'W (105-E). On the Teslin River.

This was a riverboat landing and supply point for the miners of the Livingstone Creek area, to which a wagon road was built in the summer of 1902. It was abandoned when a shorter route was established from Mason Landing.

MOUNT EVANS 4,232' 62°57'N 137°04'W (115-I). Fifteen miles northeast of Fort Selkirk.

Lt. Col. T.D.B. EVANS was the first commander of the Yukon Field Force (1898-1900). EVANS marched his party of 280 men and 6 women from Telegraph Creek on the Stikine River, to the head of Teslin Lake in the spring of 1898. They built boats and sailed and rowed to Fort Selkirk. There they built quarters and half the detachment remained there while the other half went on to Dawson to assist the NWMP.

Three of his men died and were buried at Fort Selkirk. Lt. Col. EVANS went on to command a battalion of Mounted Rifles in the Boer War in South Africa where he earned the Order of the Bath for his services. In March 1907 he was promoted to full Colonel and given command of Military Disrict No. 10 with headquarters in Winnipeg. He died of overwork and exhaustion in August 1908.

This mountain was given his name in 1971. Four others, Corcoran, Hansen, Walters and Watson were named at the same time after the men of his command who had died while on service in the Yukon.

EVERETT CREEK 60°51'N 130°35'W (105-B). Flows from near Watson Lake, southwest to the Liard River.

This stream was named after EVERETT Wasson, a pioneer bush pilot of the Yukon and northern B.C. This stream is near the scene of the first airborne search and rescue mission in the Yukon. He found and rescued the "Paddy" Burke party who were stranded here in October and November 1930. The name change was requested in 1936 (the creek was then named Quartz Creek). Wasson's name has never been officially applied to this stream, so it is still Quartz Creek on all maps. (see Burke Creek and Wasson Lake)

EXAMINER GULCH 64°02'N 139°23'W (115-B). The first small valley on the right side of Bonanza Creek, above its mouth.

This small valley was given the name of W.R. Hearst's newspaper, the San Francisco EXAMINER, by W.H. Campbell, a former employee. He discovered gold and staked the first claim on the gulch on 28 October 1897.

EXCELSIOR CREEK 62°53'N 138°58'W (115-J). A tributary to the Yukon River, just above Coffee Creek.

This stream was named in July 1898 by Mrs. Martha Munger Black, MP. She was one of the most noted women in Yukon history. Camping here while on her way to Dawson, at the height of the Gold Rush, she met a group of New Zealand miners prospecting the stream. They had found gold and their leader, William J. Beaven, asked Mrs. Black to name the stream. They then staked claims for all, including Mrs. Black. Her claim was later profitable. She went on to great prominence in the life of the Yukon. (see Mount Martha Black)

MOUNT FAIRBORN 65°07'N 139°53'W (116-G). Nineteen miles east of Sheep Mountain.

In 1973, this mountain was named after James FAIRBORN who was a pioneer transportation man and agent for the WP&YR at several locations for many years.

FALSE TEETH CREEK 62°12'N 137°49'W (115-I). A tributary to the Klaza River.

In the summer of 1937, W.H. Miller and H.S. Bostock, GSC, were camped here. Their packer, J.V. White, an exceptionally athletic man of 43, left his false teeth here when they moved camp to a high ridge seven miles to the west. Arising early the next morning he discovered his loss. He ran down to the camp here and returned in time for breakfast.

FANGO LAKE 63°40'N 131°42'W (115-O). A small lake which drains into Old Cabin Creek and the Rogue River.

This was named by Dr. Aro Aho, President of Dynasty Exploration Co., Ltd., about 1971. It is a Spanish word meaning "swamp".

FARO 62°14'N 133°20'W (105-K). Twenty-five miles west of the junction of the Ross and Pelly Rivers.

The newest town in the Yukon was built in 1969 to house the people from the nearby Anvil Mine. This a large, open pit mine producing lead, zinc and silver. On 13 June 1969 a forest fire destroyed most of the town but it was rebuilt within three months.

The game of FARO is an old and simple gambling game played throughout the early west. It was probably applied to the town by Dr. Aro Aho after the name of the first claims staked on the ore body.

FAT CREEK 60°11'N 132°54'W (105-C). Flows into Fat Lake and then into Teslin Lake, on the west side.

Arthur St. Cyr, DLS, in 1897, recorded the local name of this stream as "Hall River", probably after Hall Williams, an ex-HBC man who trapped around Teslin Lake in the 1890s and early 1900s.

By 1903, the stream was being called the "North River" on maps of the area. In 1931 the GSC, when mapping the geology of the region, reported that local people were calling it "Flat Creek" and so they marked it. Somehow, when their maps appeared the name showed as FAT Creek and so it remains. (see Hall Creek)

FAULKNER GULCH 64°00'N 135°12'W (105-D). A tributary to the Keno Ladue River.

All that is known of this place is that it is named after an early miner, J. Falconer.

FENWICK CREEK 60°11'N 135°19'W (105-D). Flows into the Wheaton River.

In 1910, one of the Yukon's early geologists, D.D. Cairnes, GSC, gave this creek his wife's maiden name when he was mapping the geology of the region.

MOUNT FERRELL 64°05'N 133°12'W (106-C). Just south of the Nadaleen River.

James E. FERRELL was a Yukon Councillor for the Dawson District from 1922-1928. He earlier ran a trading post at Lansing from 1908-1915. This hill was named for him in 1973. (see Christie Pass)

FIDO CREEK 63°28'N 132°32'W (105-N). A tributary to the Rogue River, from the north.

This creek was named in 1973 by Dr. Aro Aho, President of Dynasty Exploration Co., Ltd., after Norman Niddery's lead sled dog. The name was a common one for dogs and comes from the Latin "Fidus" meaning "Faithful". (see Niddery Lake)

FIELD CREEK 63°48'N 135°41'W (105-M). A tributary to the Mayo River, from the north.

Fred FIELD, of Gordon Landing, went out hunting before the close of navigation in the late fall of 1902 and did not return when he was expected. In February 1903 he was reported lost and search parties went out. On 25 May 1903 his body, surrounded by his belongings, was found on a raft in the ice on the Stewart River near Lansing Creek. He had apparently died of exposure and starvation. He had presumably got lost on land and was floating down the river, hoping to find a settlement before the river froze. His body was untouched by animals and was perfectly preserved.

A terse and chilling report to this effect was made by the NWMP constable in the district and was the epitaph of a hardy Klondiker, one of the first men to prospect the Mayo region. It is believed that FIELD found gold and staked the first claim on this creek.

FIELD LAKE 62°40'N 131°03'W (105-J). One of the four lakes near the junction of the Ross and Prevost Rivers.

This was named in 1907 by Joseph Keele, GSC, after Poole FIELD, who ran the trading post at nearby Ross River.

FIELD was born at Fort Garry, Manitoba, where his father was the HBC trader. He had worked his way west, across the territories and eventually was caught up in the Klondike Stampede. He spent some time in the NWMP. He and his partner, Clement Lewis, liked the Pelly and Ross River country and bought out Tom Smith's trading post at Ross River in 1905. They named it "Nahanni House".

A third associate, Martin Jorgenson, was one of the mystery men of the Nahanni country. In 1910, he went in to the Nahanni in search of the rich placer gold supposed to be there and later sent a message to FIELD by some wandering Indians; it said that he had found rich diggings and requested his assistance and supplies. The message had taken two years to deliver. FIELD made the journey and found Jorgenson's skeleton, minus the skull, his cabin burned and no gold or any sign of workings. FIELD was convinced enough by his partner's story to return many times to the Nahanni in later years.

FINLAYSON LAKE 61°41'N 130°38'W (105-G). At the height of land, between Frances Lake and the Pelly River.

This lake and river were named by Robert Campbell of the HBC in July 1840, while he was on his famous journey of exploration of the central Yukon. He named it after Chief Factor Duncan FINLAYSON, his friend and sponsor, who later became a Director of the HBC. The stream and lake were on the main supply route: Fort Liard, Fort Frances, Fort Pelly Banks and to Fort Selkirk.

Placer gold was mined from the bars at the mouth of the river in 1875, the miners taking $8-$9 per day. This was among the first gold deposits mined in the Yukon Territory.

FIRESTONE CREEK 63°21'N 137°05'W (115-P). A fork of Lake Creek, in the Mayo district.

This stream was named in 1946 by Hugh S. Bostock, GSC. His description is quoted: "The following day September 1st (1946) we reached a good campsite on the creek that enters Lake Creek above its canyon from the east. This was a good campsite and situated on a low terrace of fine gravel with clumps of spruce on it and looking south over a meadow. The presence of large stones, often eroded and discoloured by burning, were evidence of its occupation in the past by Indians. I referred to it as "FIRESTONE CREEK"".

FIRTH RIVER 69°33'N 139°32'W (117-D). A large river which flows into the Beaufort Sea, southwest of Herschel Island.

This was first named "Mountain Indian River" by Sir John Franklin, RN, in July 1826. He encamped on the Arctic shore just east of the river and met a group of Eskimos (Inuit) who told him that once a year each spring, a band of Indians came down the river from the interior to trade with them.

In 1890, J.H. Turner, USC&GS, renamed the river after John FIRTH, HBC Agent at Rampart House, who had accompanied him to the Arctic coast that year.

FIRTH (who came from the Orkney Islands north of Scotland) lived in the country as an HBC Factor for over 50 years. A Klondiker who met FIRTH at Fort MacPherson in 1898 was much impressed: "He looked like a man of granite square, broad and powerful and there was a formidable quietness about him which had a compelling effect on the Indians and Eskimos. They felt that his cool, grey-blue eyes were looking right into their thoughts, and minded their manners accordingly."

John FIRTH had a large family and one of his grandsons was elected twice as Member of Parliament for the Northwest Territories.

Gold was found on High Cache Creek, a small tributary of the river, in 1908 by Jujira Wada, a famous Japanese traveller and prospector and his partner, Ben Smith. This led to a small stampede to the area. There have been several revivals of interest in the area and staking rushes about every fifteen years but no payable gold has ever been found. (see High Cache Creek)

FISHER CREEK 61°02'N 138°38'W (115-G). A small creek flowing into Sheep Creek, from the west.

Two brothers, Bruce and A.C. FISHER, were early and continuing prospectors in the Kluane country. They found gold and named this creek during the stampede of 1903-04 to the Bullion Creek finds.

The grave of A.C. FISHER had to be removed from the right-of-way of the Alaska Highway in 1943 and was placed just south of the marker on Soldier's Summit.

FISHER CREEK 63°52'N 135°18'W (105-M). A tributary to Duncan Creek.

Named for Robert "Bobby" FISHER, one of the best prospectors in the Mayo area. From about 1910 on he discovered the "Hector" vein on Galena Hill, the "Bumboy" (Bawn Boy) Gulch tin deposits in the Dublin Gulch area and the "Olive" gold vein in the same area.

FISHER CREEK 64°12'N 136°11'W (116-A). A tributary to the North McQuesten River.

In September 1898, two unknown prospectors started a fake stampede to this area. So many people took part and staked claims that a man named FISHER was appointed Mining Recorder for the district.

The excitement died quickly and almost everyone left the creek. FISHER remained here alone all winter. In Dawson it was reported that he was dead and the fact was accepted officially. His relatives claimed and received his effects and life insurance. All were surprised when he arrived in Stewart in the spring of 1899 and handed in his records.

FISHING BRANCH 66°27'N 138°35'W (116-J). Flows into the Porcupine River.

On 28 May 1888, William Ogilvie, DLS, on his way to Fort MacPherson, stopped here. His reports state that at the mouth of the stream there were old racks for drying fish, that had been erected by the Indians. They called it "Spawning Place Creek" from the immense number of grayling found here. Ogilvie adopted their meaning.

MOUNT FITTON 68°29'N 138°02'W (117-A). In the Richardson Mountains, near the Arctic coast.

This peak was named in 1826 by Sir John Franklin, RN, after William Henry FITTON, MD (1780-1861), who in 1852 was President of the Geological Society of Great Britain. It was originally named "FITTON Peak".

FIVE FINGER RAPIDS 62°16'N 136°21'W (115-I). In the Yukon River, about twenty miles north of Carmacks.

Four columns of rock separate the Yukon River into five channels of which only the easterly one is passable by riverboats. They were named by one of the earliest miners, W.B. Moore of Tombstone, Arizona, in 1882.

Lt. Frederick Schwatka, US Army, on his excursion in 1883 changed the name to Rink Rapids but the name was never accepted and later Dr. George Mercer Dawson, G&NHSC, gave the name to a minor rapid a little lower down the river. (see Rink Rapids)

FLAT CREEK 63°57'N 138°37'W (115-O). Flows into the Klondike River, from the south.

William Ogilvie, DLS, gave the creek this name in 1896, recognizing how it enters the Klondike River through a large flat valley.

It was said that this creek was the mythical "Too Much Gold Creek" of the early Indians. They told the miners that there was a creek far up the Klondike in which the gold was so plentiful that they would have to add gravel in order to sluice it.

FLET CREEK 63°59'N 136°20'W (115-P). A tributary to the North McQuesten River.

Robert G. FLETT was a well-known trapper and prospector in this area in the early 1900s. He was subject to fits of insanity and frightened others in the district who complained to the authorities. In 1907, two RNWMP constables were sent to apprehend him. He evaded them easily and they eventually returned to Dawson empty-handed. (The Mounties didn't always get their man!)

In the winter of 1907-08, a group of miners captured him and he was taken to Dawson by dog team and placed in a mental hospital. The name was misspelled by the map makers.

FLUME CREEK 63°30'N 140°02'W (115-N). Flows southeast into Ten Mile Creek.

Named about 1912 when work was started on a water project in the Sixtymile District. A flume was constructed to carry water from the headwaters of the Sixty Mile River to placer workings on the lower reaches of the stream. The flume ran along this creek.

MOUNT FOLLE 60°18'N 135°03'W (105-D). On the north side of the Wheaton River, at the Big Bend.

John "Jack" A. FOLLE was a Klondiker and pioneer prospector in the Wheaton River area with his partner W.F. Schnabel. In 1905, he staked claims on ore showings he found on this hill and worked prospects in the region for many years.

FORCIER RIVER (see Indian River).

FORREST CREEK 65°05'N 135°57'W (106-E). A tributary to the Little Wind River.

This was named around 1905 when Constable A.E. FORREST, RNWMP, began making his annual Dawson to Fort MacPherson patrols. He was noted as one of the greatest travellers of the time. He once carried the mail by dog sled from Fort MacPherson to Dawson in 19 days, a distance of over 500 miles, in January and February. The mouth of this creek was one of his overnight camping spots.

He enlisted in Joe Boyle's Yukon Motor Machine Gun Battery in November 1914 and was made Sergeant Major in France in 1917.

MOUNT FORREST 5,041' 62°13'N 139°20'W (115-J). In the Nisling Range.

The name was proposed by James Smith, Commissioner of the Yukon Territory after Emil FORREST, a pioneer who piloted small riverboats in the Yukon River side streams. He grubstaked prospectors who made mineral discoveries in the Beaver River and Mount Freegold areas.

FORT CONSTANTINE 64°26'N 140°32'W (116-C). On the north side of the Fortymile River, at its junction with the Yukon River, north of Fort Cudahy.

This was the first NWMP post in the Yukon Territory from 1895-1897. It contained all the law and government in the Territory and Inspector Charles CONSTANTINE was just that.

Fort CONSTANTINE was abandoned in 1898 when the growth of Dawson and the abandonment of the Fortymile mining district required the relocation of NWMP headquarters to Dawson. (see Mount Constantine)

FORT CUDAHY 64°25'N 140°32'W (116-C). On the north side of the Fortymile River, at its junction with the Yukon River, directly across the Fortymile River from the settlement of Forty Mile and adjoined by Fort Constantine on the north.

Captain John Jerome Healy was a soldier, Indian fighter, trader and early Alaskan and Yukon pioneer. Engaging in the whiskey trade in Montana and what is now Alberta in the 1870s, he built and operated Fort Whoop-Up in Alberta until dispossessed by the newly formed NWMP. He had at one time been Sheriff of Cocteau County, Montana (Fort Benton). He arrived in Alaska in 1882 and operated the first trading post at Dyea, years before the Gold Rush.

He was a firm believer in the potential of the interior country and, in 1893, with the backing of his old partners, the Cudahy meat-packing family of Chicago, formed the North American Trading and Transportation Company and began establishing trading posts along the Yukon

River. The post at Forty Mile was named after John CUDAHY, a Chicago merchant and a Director of the NAT&TC.

The first post office in the Yukon territory was opened here in October 1894 and used American postage stamps.

This Fort too was forced to close down in 1898 as business moved to the larger center of Dawson.

FORT FRANCES 61°17'N 129°16'W (105-H). On the north side of Frances Lake, at the junction of the East and West Arms.

In 1840, a rough building called "Glenlyon House" was built here by Robert Campbell of the HBC. Trading with the Indians did not start until December 1842, when the post was enlarged and named FORT FRANCES, after Lady FRANCES Simpson, wife of the Governor of the HBC. It was the first trading post in the Yukon Territory. The post prospered as long as Campbell ran it, but in the late 1840s, while he was establishing Fort Pelly Banks and Fort Selkirk, his assistant allowed it to deteriorate and did little trade. By 1851 the post was vacant for periods while personnel were at Fort Pelly Banks. When Campbell came this way in October 1852 after the loss of Fort Selkirk, he found that the natives had burned and destroyed the post. After twelve years the HBC had no posts left in the Yukon.

The post was revived by the HBC for a short time in the early 1900s and rebuilt on the south side of the narrows. It was later sold and operated at various times by independent traders, and again by the HBC from the 1930s until the Alaska Highway was built. The local Indians then moved to Lower Post and Watson Lake and no business remained. In these later years the post was called simply "Frances Lake", the name used on present day maps. (see Frances River)

FORT NELSON (see Stewart River).

FORT RELIANCE 64°09'N 139°29'W (116-B). Eight miles north of Dawson, on the east bank of the Yukon River.

This was the first trading post built in the Yukon after the HBC withdrawal. On 20 August 1874, Jack McQuesten and Alfred Mayo, assisted by a young man named Frank Barnfeld (Clarence Andrews, the distinguished Alaskan historian insisted that the name was Bernstein), arrived here on the small steamboat "Yukon" and began erecting the post. As was common in the west in those days they called it a Fort. Although their intention was mainly to exploit the Indian fur trade, these men were also prospectors and were highly optimistic about the mineral potential of the country.

Their trading was successful. Mayo stayed at his regular job, running the steamboats for the Alaska Commercial Company and in the spring of 1875 Arthur Harper joined McQuesten at the post. The first miners to winter in the Territory were here in the winter of 1882-83. Eleven in number, they were led by E.M. Carr who later became a General in the US National Guard and Commissioner at Fairbanks in 1906. This party prospected in the Klondike area that winter and camped on Eldorado Creek; they found gold showings but none rich enough to impress them or bring them back in the spring.

FORT RELIANCE was the center of trade on the upper Yukon River between the years 1874-1886. It was the Mile "O" of the Yukon River, all distances along the River were calculated from this point (e.g. the Fortymile and Sixty Mile Rivers).

In 1886, many miners had invaded the Territory and good gold was being mined on the Stewart River bars so, in the spring of that year, FORT RELIANCE was abandoned in favour of the new post at the mouth of the Stewart River. The abandoned buildings were soon removed for boiler wood by the riverboats.

FORT SELKIRK 62°47'N 137°23'W (115-I). On the west side of the Yukon River, just above its confluence with the Pelly River.

This spot was selected by Robert Campbell, HBC, in 1848 to control the fur trade of the central Yukon. On 1 June that year he built the first post on the east bank of the Yukon River, on the point between it and the Pelly River. He named it after Thomas Douglas, fifth Earl of SELKIRK (1771-1820) and also after the post of the HBC at Fort Selkirk in Manitoba. This post was abandoned in April 1852 because of flooding problems and the next and present post was built across the Yukon River at this site.

FORT SELKIRK broke the trading monopoly of the Chilkat Indians of the coast with the interior Indians. They determined to rectify this situation and, on 19 August 1852, led by their Chief Koh-klux, they attacked and pillaged the post. They were careful not to hurt any of the white men there, but took or destroyed almost all the trade goods, supplies and furnishings. Campbell sent some of his people to Fort Yukon and took the rest to Fort Pelly Banks while he continued on to Fort Simpson. The local natives later burned the Fort buildings to recover the iron fittings to make tools.

Robert Campbell then made his famous journey that winter. He went over 3,000 miles on snowshoes on his way to Lachine, Quebec seeking permission to re-establish the post. His request was denied and, except for Rampart House and sometimes Lapierre House, the HBC left the Yukon for nearly fifty years. Campbell never saw the Yukon Territory again.

On 1 September 1889, Arthur Harper, who had split up with Ladue, landed on the site of the original Fort (on the east bank) with his wife and several children. He had a large stock of trade goods and started a post here, independent of the Alaska Commercial Company. It was known locally as "Campbell's Fort". He hired "Buffalo" Pitts to assist him and Pitts was still here when the Gold Rush was on.

Bishop Bompas built a mission on the west bank in 1892 and put the Rev. T.H. Canham in charge. Canham was later needed elsewhere and the mission closed in 1895.

The place assumed some importance in late 1898 when it became the headquarters of the Yukon Field Force of the Canadian Army. There was a vague intention by Sir Wilfrid Laurier's Liberal government to make FORT SELKIRK the capital of the Yukon Territory. Owing to the loss of population caused by the Nome Gold Rush in 1899 and to the Yukon Field Force being recalled because of the South African War, nothing came of the idea. The Yukon Field Force left three of its number behind, buried at the Fort. Nearby Mountains are named in their memory as well as one for their commanding officer. (see Mounts Evans, Corcoran, Hansen, Walters and Watson)

Independent traders and missionaries kept the place alive for many years. In 1938 the HBC returned but remained only until 1950. With the halting of riverboat traffic due to the completion of the Alaska Highway and an all-weather road from Whitehorse to Dawson and Mayo, by 1950 the settlement lost all reason for being and, with exception of one family, was abandoned. (see Mount Pitts and Pelly P.O.)

FORT SIFTON (see Tagish).

FORTYMILE RIVER 64°26'N 140°32'W (116-C). A large tributary to the Yukon River, about forty-eight miles below Dawson.

Originally called the "Shitando" or "Chittondeg" by the Tena Indians, meaning "Creek of the Leaves", this is also probably the river that Robert Campbell, on his way to Fort Yukon in 1851, called "Ayonie's River" after the Chief of the Indians he found there. Even before gold was found on it in 1886, the miners called it the FORTYMILE River, from its location that distance below Fort Reliance, their only supply point. Lt. Frederick Schwatka, US Army, in 1883 named it the "Cone Hill" River from the isolated hill a short distance above its mouth but the name was not accepted.

Arthur Harper, the pioneer prospector of the central Yukon, found gold showings on the lower part of the river a short time after 1875 but did not pursue them after being told stories of dangerous canyons and rapids upstream by the local natives. Acting on his advice, George McCue and Dick Poplin, in the summer of 1886, found the first payable gold on a gravel bar (Discovery Bar) at the mouth of Moose Creek (on the Alaska side). This again was fine or flour gold and, as usual in river bars, was of limited extent. Shortly afterward Howard Franklin and Harry Madison on 7 September 1886 found the first coarse gold in the Yukon watershed at Franklin Gulch, about eighty five miles up the FORTYMILE RIVER and well into American territory.

Coarse gold was the goal of all miners and this find established the credibility of the Yukon Territory as a major mining district. The real rush to the Yukon started at this time.

Michael "Mickey" O'Brien found coarse gold on a nearby creek, also a tributary of the Fortymile, a short time after Franklin and Madison, which reinforced the impact of the first discovery.

Harper, McQuesten and Mayo realized the importance of the finds. Harper immediately went from the Stewart River post to the mouth of the Fortymile and in June 1887 started the erection of a trading post there for the Alaska Commercial Company. It quickly grew into a thriving town as more of the Fortymile creeks gave up their gold and by 1893 it was serving several thousand miners in the region.

The settlement was almost completely abandoned in weeks after 17 August 1896, with the discovery of the Bonanza gold and never regained any importance. (see Buxton)

49 GULCH 64°02'N 139°22'W (116-B). A tributary to Bonanza Creek from the west, five miles from the Klondike River.

The Discovery claim was located on 29 May 1897 by Louis Hansen. He named it because the mouth of the gulch was on claim No. 49 below Discovery on Bonanza Creek.

MOUNT FOSTER 61°09'N 140°03'W (115-F). East of the Steele Glacier, in the St. Elias Range.

This was named in 1970 by the Alpine Club of Canada after Col. William Wasborough FOSTER (1875-1954), a past-president (1920-24) of the club.

FOURTH OF JULY CREEK 61°07'N 138°02'W (115-G). A tributary to the Jarvis River, in the Kluane region.

On 4 July 1903, gold was found and the Discovery claim was staked by "Dawson" Charlie of Carcross (better known as "Tagish" Charlie). "Dawson" Charlie, with George Carmack and Skookum Jim Mason, had found the rich gold of Bonanza Creek in 1896 which started the Klondike Gold Rush.

This 1903 find was the first payable gold found in the Kluane district. It started a large rush to the region which lasted for the next few years.

MOUNT FOWLIE 65°47'N 139°11'W (116-G). On the east side of the East Porcupine River.

Gavin FOWLIE came in to the Yukon in 1898 and was prominent in the life and politics of Dawson. He was a Yukon Councillor from 1920-23.

FOX CREEK 60°11'N 132°48'W (105-C). A tributary to Teslin Lake, from the east.

This creek and Fox Point were named many years ago by the Teslin Indians. A legend of theirs tells of a supernatural warning to the tribe against returning to this area. It told of great disasters to come, on a point in the lake where they would see a fox. Disregarding the warning, the tribe returned and a fox entered their camp. Shortly afterwards the Tahltan Indians attacked and destroyed their camp, killing everyone except one young woman who escaped to tell the story.

FOX LAKE 60°39'N 134°04'W (105-D). Twelve miles northeast of Marsh Lake.

In 1943, Major FOX of the US Air Force made a forced landing on this lake and it has been the local name since.

FOXY CREEK 64°39'N 138°22'W (116-B). Flows north into the east Blackstone River.

Named in 1968 to commemorate the famous musical "FOXY", stayed in Dawson during its Festival in 1962 and starring Bert Lahr, in the newly rebuilt Palace Grand Theatre.

FRANCES LAKE 61°23'N 129°35'W (105-H), and FRANCES RIVER 60°16'N 129°11'W (105-A). The lake is about ninety miles north of Watson Lake, between the Campbell and Logan Mountains. The river is a tributary to the Liard River.

In the summer of 1840, Robert Campbell of the HBC made his famous journey of exploration from Dease Lake into the central Yukon, the first white man to do so. He ascended the Liard River to the Frances River, then to Frances Lake and on to the Pelly River.

The local Indians called the Frances River the "Too-Tsho-Tooa" meaning "Big Lake River". Campbell named both river and lake after Lady FRANCES Simpson, wife of Sir George Simpson, for nearly forty years the Governor of the Hudson's Bay Company.

For a number of years this river and lake were part of the HBC's route to the central Yukon but it was finally abandoned because of the loss of life in the dangerous rapids, both here and especially on the Liard River.

FRANKLIN LAKE 60°41'N 135°18'W (105-D). The southernmost of the two small Jackson lakes.

This local name has been used here since the early 1900s when a copper mining company camped and operated in the area.

MOUNT FRANK RAE 64°28'N 138°33'W (116-B). At the headwaters of the Tombstone River.

This mountain was named in 1968 by Dr. Dirk Tempelman-Kluit, GSC, after FRANK RAE, a pioneer trapper and hunter in the area in the early days. It is the highest mountain in the Tombstone River region.

FRASER CREEK 60°19'N 137°20'W (115-A). A tributary to Alder Creek and Mush Lake.

Gold was found here and the Discovery claim staked by J.W. Smith and Fred Altemose in the summer of 1903. They named the creek after Assistant Surgeon S.M. FRASER of the NWMP who was also Mining Recorder and Customs Officer at Dalton Post in 1901-03. (see Bullion and Burwash Creeks)

FRASER FALLS 63°31'N 135°09'W (105-M). On the Stewart River, ten miles above Gordon Landing.

The Falls were named in 1885 when the first prospectors, a party of FRASER, Chapman, Thomas Boswell and others, were exploring the upper reaches of the Stewart River.

Robert Levac operated a trading post here for some time in the 1920s-30s.

FREDERICK LAKE 60°23'N 136°39'W (115-A). Between Kusawa and Dezadeash Lakes.

This lake was named by the English explorer, Edward James Glave in 1890 when, with Jack Dalton, he made the first entry into this part of the country. He made camp at the head of the lake and named it FREDERICK after his brother who had died a few years earlier.

MOUNT FREEGOLD 4,772' 62°17'N 137°07'W (115-I). Thirty miles northwest of Carmacks.

Lode gold (vein) was discovered here and the mountain named in June 1930 by P.F. "Fritz" Guder on his Augusta claim. A rush immediately developed in the area, resulting in many other mineral discoveries. (see Guder Creek)

FRENCH GULCH 63°54'N 139°18'W (115-O). A small tributary to Eldorado Creek.

In December 1896, George Lamarre of Quebec, found rich gold on this gulch and, because of his origin, named it FRENCH GULCH. Claim No. 17 on Eldorado Creek, at the mouth of this gulch, was reported to be the richest claim ever found in the Klondike, yielding nearly 100,000 ounces of gold over its' length of 500 feet.

FRENCH HILL 63°54'N 139°19'W (115-O). On the west side of Eldorado Creek, above French Gulch.

One of the Famous "Hill" or Bench" deposits of the fabulously rich White Channel gravels whose existence went unsuspected for the first year and a half of the Gold Rush.

On 20 October 1897, William "Cariboo Bill" Dettering, an old Cariboo miner from Illinois, and his partner Joseph Staley, staked the second bench claim. They were acting on a theory formed by Dettering and sank a shaft on the hill. It was reported that they recovered 11 ounces of gold from the first pan of gravel taken from bedrock. They took out $13,000 and sold the claim (100 by 100 feet square) in July 1898 for $40,000. J.N. Demers staked a bench claim on 9 September 1897 but did not work it until Dettering and Staley made their find. He then found rich gold at bedrock on his claim. (see Cheechako Hill)

MOUNT FRENCH 64°19'N 138°15'W (116-B). Northwest of Mount Walker.

Robert FRENCH and his partner Walker found and staked the Antimony claim here, the first find in the area.

FRESNO CREEK 64°16'N 139°48'W (116-B). A tributary to the Yukon River from the west, twenty five miles below Dawson.

F.R. Chandler found some gold here on 14 April 1898. He staked a claim and probably named the stream after the city of the same name in California.

FRIDAY GULCH 63°47'N 138°54'W (115-O). A tributary to Sulphur Creek, from the northeast.

The Discovery claim was staked and the creek named on 2 September 1897 by A. Gifford and William J. Chesley.

FRISCO CREEK 63°13'N 139°30'W (115-O). A tributary to Thistle Creek.

Gold was found and a Discovery claim staked on 10 November 1897 by a California miner.

FRYING PAN CREEK 62°00'N 140°55'W (115-F). Flows from Hump Mountain to Tchawsahmon Creek.

In the winter of 1912-13, William E James, Peter Nelson and Frederick Best discovered good placer gold on this stream. One of them used a frying pan to wash the first colours (fine gold) from the gravel. They claimed to have good values but an inrush of water to their workings forced them to stop. In the spring of 1913 James and Nelson prospected further west, over the Yukon-Alaska boundary. There they found the rich and famous Chisana goldfields.

On 23 August 1913, Paul Jacobs recorded a new Discovery claim on this creek and at this time the Gold Commissioner, for some reason, changed the name to "Pan" Creek. In 1915 it was again changed to FRYING PAN CREEK, which it remains.

FULLER LAKE 62°59'N 130°13'W (105-J). At the headwaters of the South MacMillan River.

This lake was named on 1 April 1943 by Herman Peterson, of Atlin, B.C., a northern bush pilot well-known for many years in the Yukon and northern B.C. He landed Keith FULLER, surveyor, who was laying out the Canol Pipeline, here on that day. To keep his log in order he asked FULLER what name to call it. Fuller told him to choose any name he wished.

MOUNT FYFE 4,793 65°17'N 136°52'W (116-H). On the east side of the Hart River.

Near the route of the Dawson-MacPherson Patrol, this mountain was named in 1973 after Rgt. No. 4937 Constable J.F. FYFE, RNWMP. He was one of Cpl. Dempster's party who searched for and found the lost Fitzgerald Patrol in February and March 1911.

FYSH CREEK 64°09'N 139°11'W (116-B). Flows into Lepine Creek, fifteen miles northeast of Dawson.

This stream was named by miners around 1905 after a popular public official in the Gold Commissioners office in Dawson, Frederick A.H. FYSH of London, Ontario.

FYSH, a young accountant and his brother-in-law Charles Williams made one of the most incredible and least known journeys of the Klondike Gold Rush. In the fall of 1897 they were prospecting on the northwest coast of Alaska with little success. After the first snowfall their companions decided to return to St. Michaels for the winter. FYSH and Williams however, decided to go overland to Fort Yukon and Dawson.

In the dead of an Alaskan winter, with only a small toboggan to haul their supplies and a map torn from a high school atlas to guide them, this amazing pair crossed nearly six hundred miles of almost unknown country, including several unmapped mountain ranges. They reached Dawson in early January 1898.

FYSH secured a position in the Gold Commissioner's office which he kept until he moved his family to the Okanagan Valley in B.C. in September 1909. He was a modest man who was very well liked and especially respected by the prospectors who understood and admired his hardihood.

MOUNT GALE 65°29'N 139°35'W (116-G). East of the Porcupine River.

E.I. GALE was the Principal of the Dawson Public School from 1918-1921.

GALENA 63°47'N 139°46'W (115-O). On the west side of the Yukon River, opposite Indian River.

This is the site of a small trading post, built in the 1930s by Wy Spees to serve travellers and nearby miners. It burned down in April 1954 and was never rebuilt.

GALENA CREEK 63°55'N 135°35'W (105-M). Flows into Flat Creek, about three miles west of Elsa.

In 1913, Henry W. McWhorter, Jack Alverson, Mark Evans and Grant Hoffman, in a loose association, staked a vein of silver-lead ore on this creek. It had been found in 1903 by Jake Davidson who staked and abandoned it. Before he left the country he told McWhorter about it.

The part of the creek upon which they mined, they called "Gambler's Gulch". They labouriously mined the vein and made a profit. This led to a staking rush which led to further finds and the development of Keno Hill.

This party also named Galena Hill at the same time they named the creek. (see Duncan Creek)

GAMBLER'S GULCH (see Morrison Creek.)

GARDEN CREEK 60°07'N 128°21'W (105-A). Flows into the Hyland River, east of Watson Lake.

A prospector-trapper kept a good garden for many years on the banks of this stream. In the early years both people and gardens were rare in this part of the Yukon.

GATES CREEK (see Browns Creek).

GAUCHE LAKE (see Big Kalzas Lake).

GAUVIN GULCH 63°55'N 139°17'W (115-O). A short creek flowing into Bonanza Creek.

Alfred and Wilfred GAUVIN of St. Simon, Quebec, came into the Yukon in 1895. On 20 May 1897 they found this small but rich valley and made their fortunes.

GAY CREEK 63°14'N 139°05'W (115-C). Flows into the Stewart River from the north, about twelve miles above its mouth.

Around 1886-87, Emil Meriguet (known in the Yukon as Emil GAY), prospected and named this stream. It was later known locally as "Three Kings Creek", after three partners who worked it successfully for some time. (see Gay Gulch)

GAY GULCH 63°52'N 139°15'W (115-O). A very short gulch off Eldorado Creek on the east, four miles from the mouth.

Emil GAY (Meriguet) discovered the wealth of this tiny valley on 4 January 1897 when he staked the first claim and named it. An old-time Yukoner, he had come into the country in 1886 and became wealthy from this and other Klondike claims and mining ventures. He returned to France, his birthplace, when he retired.

His Discovery claim on this gulch yielded over $3,000 to the running foot for a distance of 500 feet.

In 1962, GAY's grandson, Henri Meriguet, of Annecy, France, came to the Yukon during the Dawson Festival, hitchhiking across Canada. He wished to visit the claim that had made his grandfather wealthy and to see the wonderful country he had talked about. Sadly, on his return trip he was murdered and his body buried in a gravel pit near Mile 693 (KM1123) on the Alaska Highway. His suspected murderer, Karoli Marsi, hung himself in the Don Jail in Toronto, Ontario, in August 1967.

GEM CREEK 63°57'N 136°49'W (115-P). A tributary to Sprague Creek.

In the late 1930s, George Retter, Jack Alverstone and Cecil Poli found and mined placer gold on this creek.

GEORGE CREEK 63°10'N 133°28'W (105-N). A tributary to Russell Creek.

This was named in 1901 by Major Neville A.D. Armstrong after his partner, GEORGE Leith of England. They worked the Gillis or Armstrong Concession for placer gold on Russell Creek in 1901-02. (see Mount Armstrong and Jessica Creek)

GERMAN CREEK 64°18'N 139°18'W (116-B). A tributary to the Chandindu River.

Gold was discovered here in 1898 by two brothers, Conrad and George Hammierr who came from Germany. It was never productive.

GHECHUK CREEK 63°28'N 136°15'W (115-P). A short creek flowing into the Stewart River, east of Stewart Crossing.

The name was recorded in 1957. It was named after Billy "GHECHUK" Malcolm, whose Indian name means "Porcupine".

MOUNT GIBBEN 6,500' 64°43'N 139°11'W (116-B). Forty-five miles north of Dawson, at the head of Fifteen Mile Creek.

The highest mountain in the area, it was named for the Honourable Justice J.E. GIBBEN, former Commissioner of the Yukon Territory and Judge of the Territorial Court. In 1970 the name was officially adopted. (see Mount Ina)

MOUNT GIBSON 61°14'N 140°05'W (115-F). On the southeast side of the Steele Glacier, in the St. Elias Range.

This was named in 1970 by the Alpine Club of Canada after a past-president of the club, E. Rex GIBSON (1892-1957). The summit was first achieved by Walter A. Wood and Hans Fuhrer on 20 July 1935.

GILLESPIE LAKE 64°44'N 134°00'W (106-C). At the head of Bear River.

On 19 August 1945, Herman Peterson, a well-known bush pilot, landed four prospectors on this lake and named it. The prospectors were from Mayo and were searching for coal in the area. The party was led by Frank GILLESPIE of Mayo.

At high water the lake overflows into both the Bear River and the Bonnet Plume River. Normally it flows to the Bear River.

MOUNT GILLIAM 64°17'N 134°55'W (105-D). On the north end of Gray Ridge, ten miles northwest of Carcross.

This name was reported by W.E. Cockfield, GSC, about 1920. Marc M. GILLIAM was a Cornish miner and a pioneer prospector and mine superintendent locally for many years. The mountain had borne his name for a long time locally before it was made official.

MOUNT GILLILAND 4,715' 60°13'N 127°21'W (95-D). Northwest of the junction of the Coal and Rock Rivers.

Named for Frank GILLILAND who prospected this area from 1943 to his death in 1954, well-respected by his friends.

GILLIS LAKES 66°26'N 134°44'W (106-L). A large group of small lakes, west of the Peel River.

In 1973, these lakes were named after A.J. GILLIS, Speaker of the Yukon Council from 1912-15. He represented South Dawson on the Council.

MOUNT GILLIS 5,418' 62°51'N 133°21'W (105-K). An isolated peak east of Stokes Lake, north of the Tay River.

Duncan GILLIS of Nova Scotia came to the Yukon in 1892. While on a holiday at home he heard the news of the Klondike find. He returned to the Yukon via the Edmonton Trail and the Gravel (Keele) River. He descended the MacMillan River, mistaking it for the Hess. It was on this journey that he discovered the placer gold of Russell Creek. (see Mount Armstrong)

GIROUARD HILL 1,672' 68°10'N 138°17'W (117-A). Ten miles west of Bonnet Lake.

This hill was named in 1973 after J.E. GIROUARD, Registrar of Land Titles in the Yukon (and appointed Member of the Yukon Council for the same period) from 1898-1908.

GLACIER CITY 64°01'N 140°44'W (116-C). On Glacier Creek, one mile above the mouth of the Sixty Mile River.

This settlement was established in 1905. It had a trading post, laundry, RNWMP post, church, blacksmith shop and a roadhouse called the Glacier City Hotel. A post office called GLACIER was opened on 1 August 1910. The name was changed in December 1911 to GLACIER CITY. The RNWMP post was closed in 1906. The village was sometimes called "Sixtymile". It was abandoned in the 1920s.

GLACIER CREEK 64°01'N 140°43'W (116-C). A tributary to Big Gold Creek, in the Sixtymile district.

Gold found on this creek in 1891 started the rush to the Sixtymile district. The creek received its name because glacial ice had to be removed on its upper reaches in order to work the gold-bearing gravels underneath.

MOUNT GLADMAN 64°42'N 140°49'W (116-C). Near the Yukon-Alaska boundary and the Yukon River.

William Ogilvie, DLS, had four assistants with him in 1887-88 when he established the first part of the Yukon-Alaska boundary, from the Yukon River south to the Sixty Mile River country.

In March 1888, he named this mountain after one of them, Charles GLADMAN of Peterborough, Ontario. It was first called GLADMAN Peak. GLADMAN accompanied Ogilvie on many other surveys in other parts of Canada. He died in Peterborough, Ontario in July 1947.

He also accompanied Warburton Pike, the English explorer of the Frances Lake country, to Lower Post in 1893 but had to leave him there as Ogilvie wanted him for another task.

GLADSTONE CREEK (see Bertha Creek).

GLADSTONE CREEK 61°19'N 138°40'W (115-G). Flows into Kluane Lake.

Although this creek was named during the original stampede to the Bullion Creek country of the Kluane district in 1903, it was not until 1911 that T.T. Murray and Axel Swanson found the first payable gold on it. (see Swanson Creek)

GLENBOYLE 63°58'N 138°43'W (115-O). At the junction of the Klondike and North Klondike Rivers.

A small settlement which was formed to be the headquarters of Joe Boyle's Canadian Klondike Dredging Company in 1904.

Boyle was a fabulous character and one of the major figures of the Klondike Gold Rush. He came to the Klondike in 1898, travelling with his companion, Joe Slavin, an Australian heavyweight boxing champion. Putting his ingenuity and persuasive tongue to work, he amassed claim concessions on Dominion Creek and the Klondike River. By 1904 he had formed his company and had his first dredge working in 1905. He formed a Machine Gun Company in the First World War and took them to France. His adventures during the war outdid many lurid novels. Several books have been written about him, one of the best being "Joe Boyle, King of the Klondike" by William Rodney.

GLENLYON HOUSE 61°17'N 129°17'N (105-H). On the point between the east and west arms of Frances Lake.

The first trading post in the Yukon was built here. Robert Campbell of the HBC, in the summer of 1840 left some of his crew here to construct a small building while he continued his expedition to the Pelly River.

He decided to make this a permanent trading post and named it after GLENLYON HOUSE, the seat of the Campbell clan, in Perthshire, Scotland. In 1842 he changed the name of the post to Fort Frances.

The post was destroyed by fire in the spring of 1852. (see Fort Frances)

GLENLYON PEAK 7,184' 62°32'N 134°29'W (105-L). The most northerly peak in the Glenlyon Range.

A.C. Tuttle, topographer, gave this peak the name Mount Hodder in 1946-7, after the creek flowing at its base. This was soon changed to honour Robert Campbell instead, but the name Hodder still appears on some older maps. (see Hodder Creek)

GODDARD POINT 61°21'N 135°14'W (105-E). A point on the northeast side of Lake Laberge.

This place was named in 1899 after the little steamboat "A.J. GODDARD", which was named after her builder, captain and owner. The hull was built in San Francisco and with the engine, was hauled over the White Pass in the winter of 1897-98 and assembled at Lake Bennett. It was 40 feet long and displaced 15 tons. It was the first steamboat to make the run from Lake Bennett to Dawson. She left Lake Bennett on 29 May 1898, ran Miles Canyon and the Whitehorse Rapids and arrived in Dawson on 21 June.

The boat was wrecked in a storm near this point in September 1899 with the loss of the Captain (not Goddard), the fireman, cook and a waiter. Their bodies were not recovered until 3 May 1902. The boat was never raised and its remains may still be seen in calm weather.

GOLD BOTTOM CREEK 63°58'N 138°58'W (115-O). The west branch of Hunker Creek.

Robert Douglas Henderson, born in Pictou County, Nova Scotia, came to the Yukon over the Chilkoot Pass in June 1894. Grubstaked by Joe Ladue, the trader at Ogilvie (Sixtymile) and by some small earnings gained on Quartz Creeks, he spent the next two years prospecting the tributaries of the Indian River.

In April 1896, he crossed the divide between Quartz Creek and the west branch of what was to be Hunker Creek. On this stream he found low gold values but better than he had seen elsewhere. In his imagination he saw the bedrock of this creek-paved with gold nuggets and named it GOLD BOTTOM. Needing supplies and wishing to explore a little more of the country, he went down Hunker Creek to the Klondike River where, at its mouth, he found George Carmack and his party who were fishing for salmon.

He extolled his new find to Carmack and invited him to visit his creek. However, he stipulated that he did not wish Carmack's Indian relatives and friends to stake claims. (Contrary to popularly held belief, Indians of the Yukon Territory have always held the right to stake and own mineral claims.)

Henderson continued on to Ogilvie and obtained supplies. He returned to GOLD BOTTOM by way of Quartz Creek, where he induced eighteen miners working there to accompany him to his new find. Arriving at GOLD BOTTOM, fourteen of the men, unimpressed with Henderson's find after testing the gravels, returned immediately to Quartz Creek. Henderson, with the remaining three (one man had turned back), set to work on his claim. In three months they recovered only $720.00 worth of gold.

In early August George Carmack, Skookum Jim and Tagish Charlie travelled up Rabbit Creek (later Bonanza) to visit Henderson. On the way they found encouraging showings of gold.

On GOLD BOTTOM they examined Henderson's showings and were not greatly impressed. Carmack staked a claim beside Henderson's. They then returned to the mouth of the Klondike along Rabbit Creek. It was on this journey that they found the rich, coarse gold on the stream that Carmack now renamed Bonanza. Skookum Jim remained on the claim, Tagish Charlie stayed at the fishing camp at the mouth of the Klondike River and Carmack went to Forty Mile to obtain more supplies and to record his claim with Inspector Constantine. (Some accounts claim that he and Tagish Charlie took saw logs to Forty Mile to sell for supplies). No one went back to GOLD BOTTOM to tell Henderson.

The rush started and Andrew Hunker, after staking on upper Bonanza, looked east. With his partner, Charles M. Johnson, he went up Hunker Creek from the Klondike River. Panning as they went they soon discovered rich gold showings and staked a Discovery claim and two others on 6 September 1896. They went back to Forty Mile and recorded their claims and named the stream Hunker Creek. On their return Hunker went farther up the creek and found Henderson and his three companions at work. They had heard and seen nothing. He persuaded them to come downstream to his discovery. When Henderson saw Hunker's showings he and his companions immediately staked beside them. Henderson staked No.3 above Discovery. Henderson then set out for Forty Mile where he tried to record a Discovery claim on GOLD BOTTOM. This was disallowed by Constantine as being part of Hunker Creek. Faced with a choice he recorded No. 3 above rather than his original claim. On his way down he had also staked No. 12 on Bear Creek. This also was not allowed as rules had been made confining a staker to one claim in a mining district. In September 1897 Henderson sold No. 3 above to Big Alex MacDonald for $3,000, a very respectable sum in those days. MacDonald recovered over $800,000 from the claim. Timothy Crowley staked Henderson's original claim on Gold Bottom Creek on 18 September 1896, He sold it to Big Alex MacDonald in December 1897. MacDonald also bought out two of Henderson's partners claims on Hunker Creek about the same time. There is no record of any appreciable amount of gold ever being recovered from GOLD BOTTOM Creek.

GOLD HILL 63°55'N 139°22'W (115-0). The hill on the west side of Bonanza Creek, at its junction with Eldorado Creek.

On the 3rd July 1897, according to O. Finnie the government historian, G.A. Lancaster located a bench claim at claim No. 2 on Eldorado Creek. (A bench claim is the first claim uphill from a creek claim which only occupies the bottom of a valley). The claim was part of what was later called GOLD HILL. A Dr. P.D. Carper who had possibly grubstaked Lancaster, gave the hill its name. Lancaster's was the first claim staked on it and produced the first gold mined from the White Channel gravels.

On 23 July 1897, Nathan Kresky (he later changed it to Kresge) and Nils Peterson staked the Discovery hill claim. (A hill claim was one hundred feet square and was not connected with any creek claim). In ten days, using a rocker and re-circulated water, they won $6,375 from a piece of ground 11 by 17 feet and 3 feet deep. This is a little better than $300.00 per cubic yard, rich indeed! Nils Peterson moved a little farther up the hill, sank a shaft 63 feet deep to bedrock and found far richer gold at the bottom. The hill was well named.

By 14 September every possible claim on the hill had been staked. This find led to the discovery of similar deposits on the neighbouring hills a few days later. (see Cheechako and French Hills)

GOLD HILL 60°17'N 135°09'W (105-D). On the north side of the Wheaton River, seventeen miles northwest of Carcross.

In 1893, Frank Corwin and Thomas Rickman of Juneau prospected this area and found extremely rich gold in a quartz vein on this hill. Both men died shortly after their return to Juneau and as the area was unmapped at the time, the exact location of their find was lost.

Many others searched for the vein and, although some of their claim posts were found, it was not until 25 June 1906, that David Hodnett and Jack Stagar found and staked the Gold Reef claim, believing that they had found the lost lode. Within ninety days over seven hundred claims had been staked surrounding them. (see Mount Hodnett, Carbon Hill and Corwin Valley)

GOLDEN HORN MOUNTAIN 5,610' 60°33'N 135°03'W (105-D). The solitary peak twelve miles south of Whitehorse.

Used as a landmark to warn of the approach to Miles Canyon by miners boating down the Yukon River. This beautiful hill was named by the earliest miners to see it in 1881 or 1882.

GOLD RUN CREEK 63°41'N 138°35'W (115-D). A tributary to Dominion Creek.

Robert Henderson, in June or July 1896, prospected here and found showings of gold that ran 3 to 5 cents per pan. He named the stream but did not think it worth while to develop. He returned to Gold Bottom.

A Discovery claim was staked here in March 1898 and the creek has since yielded much profitable gold.

MOUNT GOOD 6,556' 64°20'N 134°26'W (106-D). In the Wernecke Mountains, north of the Beaver River.

In 1973, this peak was named to honour the memory of J-88030 Pilot Officer Ralph Edward GOOD who was born at Carcross on 1 May 1919. He enlisted in the RCAF in Vancouver B.C. on 24 August 1942 and served in Canada and overseas. He was killed during air operations over Germany on 19 August 1944.

GOODE CREEK 60°33'N 133°52'W (105-C). Flows northeast into Jackfish Lake.

Bob GOODE and his two brothers trapped in this area for many years.

GOOD NEIGHBOUR PEAK 15,700' 60°22'N 139°42'W (115-B). Two miles north of Mount Vancouver.

This peak is supposed to be the second highest in the Yukon, Mount St. Elias being the highest. It was climbed as part of the Canadian Centennial Celebration in 1967 by eight members of the Yukon Alpine Centennial Expedition, four American and four Canadian climbers. Monty Alford of the Water Resources Branch, Department of Northern Affairs, Whitehorse, was Canadian co-leader and Vin Hoeman the American co-leader of the climbing party. They made the ascent on 25 June 1967. (see Centennial Range)

GORDON LANDING 63°38'N 135°27'W (105-M). A former settlement on the Stewart River above Mayo, near the mouth of Janet Creek.

This little settlement was established about 1902 to serve the new placer goldfields on Duncan Creek. A trader of this name built the post. Roads were pushed out to Duncan, Highet and Haggart Creeks. The place was abandoned as Mayo and Keno assumed importance.

GORING CREEK 64°03'N 138°53'W (116-B). A tributary to the Klondike River.

Theodore GORING staked the Discovery claim and named this creek in early 1897.

MOUNT GOULTER 62°07'N 136°23'W (115-I). Southwest of Mount Monson.

Frank GOULTER was born in England on 21 January 1877. He served for eight years in the Royal Field Artillery including service in the Boer War. He came to Canada and joined the NWMP in 1903. He came to the Yukon in 1904 and served until 1908. He married and lived at Carmacks where he cut wood for riverboats and later operated fox and mink fur farms at Carmacks. He died there on 27 May 1981, aged 104 years. He was the last surviving member of the NWMP.

GRAFE CREEK 61°48'N 140°02'W (115-G). Crosses the Alaska Highway near Mile 1145 (KM1855).

Willis R. GRAFE was an engineering aide with the US Public Roads Administration on location and construction of the Alaska Highway from Kluane Lake west to White River during the period April to November 1942.

On 13 August 1942, the survey line crossed this creek where they were camped. Since it was his twenty-second birthday his crew insisted on naming the creek after him.

GRAND FORKS 63°55'N 139°19'W (115-O).

This was the largest settlement in the Yukon after Dawson City. Forming naturally at the junction of Bonanza and Eldorado Creeks, one day's journey from Dawson, the settlement began to grow in early 1897. Grand Forks official name was "Bonanza Town Site". Belinda Mulroney built the first roadhouse, the Magnet Hotel, in September 1897, two miles downstream from Grand Forks, at Magnet Gulch. Surrounded by the richest gravels in the world, the town expanded. Hotels, stores and services of all kinds flourished. By 1903 the population was over 3,000 and the town was incorporated with Peter Coutts, of Grey North, Ontario, as the first Mayor. As long as the gravels were rich enough to sustain hand work the town prospered but as these dwindled so did the business and the population.

By 1921 dredging operations encompassing the whole valley had destroyed the town and dug up the gravel underneath.

It was the last remaining chartered town in the Yukon until the charter was surrendered on 9 December 1905.

GRAND VALLEY CREEK 63°15'N 138°19'W (115-O). A tributary to Rosebud Creek.

This stream was probably named in the early 1890s. The Grand Valley Roadhouse was built in 1898-99.

MOUNT GRANGER 6,675' 60°31'N 135°16'W (105-D). Sixteen miles southwest of Whitehorse.

William P. GRANGER came from Kentucky to the Yukon in 1895. He was one of the first to find and develop the copper deposits at Whitehorse and the gold-quartz ores of the Wheaton Valley country.

He was killed by carbon monoxide poisoning in a prospect shaft at the Copper King Mine at Whitehorse on 10 May 1907. This hill was named after him shortly afterward.

GRANVILLE 63°40'N 138°37'W (115-O). On Sulphur Creek, just above its junction with Dominion Creek.

The GRANVILLE Mining Company was established in 1911. It was the first large attempt by English capital to consolidate the Klondike placer deposits and to mine them by large scale mechanical means. A.N.C. Treadgold, an Oxford Don and one of the most colourful figures of the Klondike for many years, was the leading figure in this enterprise.

The company was named after Lord GRANVILLE who was a major backer of the enterprise and the British Secretary of State for the Colonies in the late 19th century. This settlement, started by Treadgold and named by him, was the headquarters of his operations for many years beginning in 1903. It was later utilized by the Yukon Consolidated Gold Corporation. It was abandoned when the last operating dredge shut down in 1966. (see Treadgold Creek)

MOUNT GRAY 6,085' 60°09'N 134°51'W (105-D). Six miles west of Carcross, on the north shore of Lake Bennett.

Named by William Ogilvie, DLS, in 1887 or possibly earlier by miners travelling through. The name is not identified.

GRAY RIDGE 60°19'N 134°55'W (105-D).

This ridge, starting at Mount Gray and as far north as Needle Mountain was named much later than Mount Gray and is an extension of that name.

GREAVES CREEK 66°29'N 137°40'W (116-I). A tributary to Canoe Creek.

Robert Bruce GREAVES was a well-known figure in early Dawson as the proprietor of the Red Feather Saloon. Later, he was in business in Mayo. This creek was named after him in 1973.

GREEN GULCH 63°04'N 139°26'W (115-O). A tributary to Thistle Creek.

Gold was first found here and the creek named in October 1898. The finder named the creek after the Mining Recorder at Stewart River, a man named GREEN.

MOUNT GREEN 6,669' 61°44'N 132°27'W (105-F). In the St. Cyr Range.

In 1951, this mountain was named to honour the memory of Lt. A.D. GREEN, MID, of the Canadian Army, who was killed in action during the Second World War.

GREW CREEK 62°05'N 132°52'W (105-K). Flows into the Peel River from the south.

This name was known before 1905. James "Jim" GREW was an old HBC man who lived and trapped this area for a long time. He was about 70 years of age when he died here, alone, in 1906.

GREY COPPER HILL 5,254' 64°25'N 135°15'W (106-D). East of Carpenter Creek, in the Wernecke Mountains.

This was named by Robert Fisher, a pioneer prospector who found rich tetrahedrite (a silver-copper mineral of a rich grey colour) float (loose pieces of rock in the soil) here in the autumn of 1923. This led to a stampede to the area in the winter of 1923-24. Several hundred men took part in this rush, with hundreds of claims being staked.

GREY HUNTER PEAK 7,265' 63°08'N 135°38'W (105-M). In the McArthur Range.

This peak was named by Hugh S. Bostock, GSC, in 1940, from its dark, grey, forbidding appearance.

GREY MOUNTAIN (see Canyon Mountain).

GRIBBLES GULCH 60°18'N 137°00'W (115-A). Flows into Klukshu Lake.

In 1949, H. Gabrielse was an assistant to E.D. Kindle, GSC, mapping this district. Alex Van Bibber was in charge of the pack horses for the party. He found Gabrielse's name too hard to pronounce and settled on "GRIBBLES". The name stuck with the others in the party and they named this brook to memorialize it.

GROUSE CREEK 60°03'N 132°51'W (105-C). A tributary to Fat Creek, from the west.

This stream was named "McCleary Creek" by the GSC in 1946-47 after the trader and Justice of the Peace at Teslin, Robert McCleery. The Forest Warden at Teslin protested that the common name for the creek was GROUSE Creek, that no one used McCleary, that the name was misspelled and that McCleery should he commemorated by a mountain north of Teslin. (see Mount McCleery)

GUDER CREEK 62°19'N 137°12'W (115-I). A tributary to Seymour Creek, in the Mount Freegold area.

Paul Fritz "Fred" GUDER was born in June 1895 in Middle Waldenburgh, Silesia, Germany. As a young man he took a ship to Panama and walked across the isthmus. Working his way north by ship, he arrived in the Yukon in 1912, walking from Skagway to Whitehorse. He worked for a number of years for the noted Captain H.S. Back in the Mount Nansen region and independently for many more years in the Mount Freegold district which he pioneered and named. He made many mineral discoveries.

This creek was named in 1929 by his friend "Happy" Lepage of Carmacks. Fred had found silver-lead ore and was living on the creek at that time.

Among other exploits, Fred once spent a winter alone, trapping in the Nahanni Valley. In the winter of 1918-19 he came and went, hauling supplies from Ross River with a hand sled up the Pelly River and across the mountains. Still actively prospecting in his late 70s, this quiet, hardworking man was liked and respected by all who knew him.

He died in Whitehorse on 20 June 1981.

GUKAN CREEK 66°37'N 134°19'W (106-L). A tributary to the Peel River.

A Loucheaux Indian word meaning "Burning Place Creek". This probably refers to burning lignite beds on the upper reaches of the stream.

GULL LAKE 62°16'N 129°51'W (105-I). Northeast of the Pelly Lakes, near Mount Pike.

This small lake was named in 1893 by Warburton Pike the English sportsman, explorer, and later, trader at Dease Lake in 1898-99. He found enormous numbers of black-headed gulls (Arctic Tern) breeding here. (see Narchilla Brook)

GUSTAVUS RANGE 63°52'N 135°08'W (105-M). The range of hills that lie north of Mayo Lake.

These mountains were named in 1904 by Joseph Keele, GSC, while he was mapping the geology of the region. Known as "The Mysterious Three", GUSTAVUS Gustavusen, a Norwegian and his two sons found and-mined the first gold in the district on Duncan Creek in 1898.

Contemporary accounts spell the name Gustavusen, although others spell it Gustavus, Gustavessen and Gustavuson. (see Duncan Creek)

GWAATLIT HILL 67°00'N 135°10'W (106-L). On the Yukon-NWT boundary, on the west side of the Peel River.

This is a Loucheaux Indian word meaning "Soft, Sliding Surface", probably referring to talus slopes on the mountainside.

GWACHOO CREEK 66°37'N 134°41'W (106-L). A small creek running into the Trail River.

A Loucheaux Indian word with the meaning "Big Creek and Big Slough".

GWINEE EDITLUK CREEK 66°36'N 134°43'W (106-L).

The translation of this name is uncertain but the Loucheaux Indians of the region call it "Dog Team Creek".

GWITSHIH DIINEE LAKE 66°47'N 134°43'W (106-L). East of the Peel River.

A Loucheaux Indian word meaning "Sharp Tail Lake", from the numbers of these ducks found there.

HAECKEL HILL 60°46'N 135°17'W (105-D). Eight miles northwest of Whitehorse.

This hill was named "HAECKEL Butte" by Lt. Frederick Schwatka, US Army, while on his excursion down the Yukon River in 1883, after Professor Ernst Heinrich HAECKEL, a distinguished German naturalist of Jena.

Because HAECKEL was a noted scientist and also because the mountain had no previous name, Dr. George Mercer Dawson, G&NHSC, allowed the name to stand in 1887.

HAGGART CREEK 63°54'N 136 01'W (115-P). A tributary to the South McQuesten River.

Thomas Nelson prospected this stream in 1895 and in 1896 found good gold in the canyon about four miles upstream from the mouth. At that time it was called "Nelson Creek". At the same time Nelson built a cabin on the creek and one on Dublin Gulch. No claims were recorded in the area at the time.

Thomas Nelson, with Thomas Haggart, Peter Haggart and Warren Hiatt, all unsuccessful in the Klondike, returned to the area in 1898. Enroute from Dawson they quarrelled and the party split in two. Peter HAGGART and Warren Hiatt reached Nelson Creek first and staked a Discovery claim. When they recorded their claims they renamed the stream after Peter HAGGART. (see Highet Creek)

HAINES JUNCTION 60°45'N 137°30'W (115-A). Situated at the junction of the Haines and Alaska Highways.

Begun in 1942, and starting at Mile 1016 on the Alaska Highway, a road was built south and west to Haines, Alaska on the Pacific coast. It was a wartime measure to increase the shipment of materials and supplies from the US to Alaska. It was constructed by the US Army Engineers and follows the old Dalton Trail quite closely.

The first buildings at the junction were the Army Engineers barracks and shops. Because of its location the settlement continues to grow.

The settlement was named after its terminal, Haines, Alaska, a town which was originally located in 1879 by the famous pioneer missionary S. Hall Young, as the site of a Presbyterian Mission. It was given the name of the first Secretary of the Committee of Home Missions, Mrs. Francine E. HAINES.

MOUNT HALDANE 6,015' 63°52'N 135°50'W (105-M). About fifteen miles west of Mayo Lake.

This was named around 1920 for an early prospector who lived and mined on HALDANE Creek at the foot of the mountain. Up to that time, the hill had been called "Lookout Mountain".

HALL CREEK 60°30'N 133°41'W (105-C). Flows into the west end of Squanga Lake.

This name seems to have been applied for no particular reason in the 1940s. HALL Williams was an old HBC man who lived on Teslin Lake about the turn of the century, trapping for a living. Fat Creek, on the west side of Teslin Lake was originally named "HALL River" into the 1900s. Also just south of Fat Creek, in B.C. there is a HALL Lake named after the same man.

HANCOCK HILLS 61°10'N 135°00'W (105-E). On the east side of Lake Laberge.

These were named by Lt. Frederick Schwatka, US Army, in 1883 after one of his superiors, General Winfield Scott HANCOCK (1824-1886).

MOUNT HANSEN 3,127' 62°47'N 137°15'W (115-I). A low hill, two miles east of Fort Selkirk.

This hill was named in 1971 after Corporal G. HANSEN, Rgt. No. 63 of the Royal Regiment of Canadian Infantry, a member of the Yukon Field Force. He died while serving at Fort Selkirk on 18 February 1899. (see Mounts Evans, Corcoran, Walters and Watson)

HAPPY VALLEY 60°01'N 133°31'W (105-C). A large valley crossing the Yukon-B.C. boundary, between Atlin and Teslin Lakes.

On 12 May 1899, George White-Fraser, DTS, was setting survey monuments on the Yukon-B.C. boundary between Teslin and Bennett Lakes. This valley, with its chain of small lakes, was so pleasant after the rugged, mountainous terrain he had just encountered that he rested his crew and horses here and gave the valley its name. (see White Range)

MOUNT HARBOTTLE 65°49'N 138°20'W (116-G). South of the Whitestone River.

This peak was named in 1973 after Francis E. HARBOTTLE. He was a member of the NWMP in the Yukon from 1901-05 and afterward served with the Canadian Customs Service.

HARDLUCK CREEK 65°05'N 141°00'W (116-K). A tributary to Harrington Creek.

An International Boundary Survey team lost some of its supplies here in 1910. The name originally applied to the whole stream, including Harrington Creek. This name no longer applies as it was renamed in 1965 to Harrington Creek. The part of Harrington Creek which is now called HARDLUCK is all in Alaska. (see Harrington Creek)

HARDLUCK CREEK 61°43'N 139°52'W (115-G). Crosses the Alaska Highway near Mile 1136 (KM1840).

Willis R. Grafe, an assistant engineer with the US Public Roads Administration was surveying location of the Alaska Highway here in August 1942. His crew ran out of food for several days owing to an error by the pilot of an airplane who landed them on the wrong lake. They went hungry until one of the party shot a mountain sheep.

This name is not yet officially recognized but is used locally. (see Grafe Creek)

MOUNT HARE 4,073' 66°38'N 136°12'W (116-I). In the Richardson Mountains.

This mountain was named for a soldier of this name who was killed during the Second World War. Sadly, nothing more about him is known.

MOUNT HARPER 6,149' 64°41'N 139°57'W (116-B). A high peak in the Ogilvie Mountains, north of Dawson.

This mountain was named in 1887-88 by William Ogilvie, DLS, while he was surveying the International Boundary. He named it after one of the first pioneers and the first recorded prospector in the Yukon.

Arthur "Cariboo" HARPER was born in County Antrim, Ireland in 1835. As a young man he mined in California and moved north in search of gold, always in the advance guard of the searchers. From the Fraser River goldfields he went on to the Cariboo and then opened the Omineca diggings of northern B.C. In 1872, along with Frederick Hart and others, he went down the Liard River and the MacKenzie, crossed the Rocky Mountains to the Porcupine River and arrived at Fort Yukon on 15 August 1873, about the same time as McQuesten, Mayo and their party.

In the fall and winter of 1873-74, HARPER, Fred Hart and George Fitch went up to the headwaters of the White River, following an Indian tale of gold. They found prospects of placer gold and also of copper deposits but nothing that they could mine at a profit. They were the first white men to explore the stream and the first to prospect in the Yukon watershed.

HARPER alternated prospecting with trading and for many years, in a loose association, ran the Alaska Commercial Company's posts at Fort Reliance, Sixtymile (Ogilvie), Stewart River, Fort Selkirk and other locations. He married an Indian woman and had several children.

Although he pioneered most of the major goldfields that were found in the Yukon and his experience and advice led other men to fortune, he never found the riches he sought. He left the Yukon in 1897, with modest means, broken in health from his privations and hardships, and died of tuberculosis in Yuma, Arizona, in November 1898. (see Dawson City)

HARRINGTON CREEK 65°05'N 141°00'W (116-F). A tributary to Pleasant and Hardluck Creeks, in Alaska.

Originating in the Yukon, this stream flows about nine miles into Alaska to join Pleasant Creek which in turn joins Hardluck Creek. Named in 1910-11 by the International Boundary Survey, the whole creek had been named Hardluck Creek. The name Harrington was used in 1910 for the lower stream. In 1965 the two governments agreed on this appelation. (see Hardluck Creek)

HARRISON CREEK 60°55'N 136°14'W (115-A). A small tributary to Cranberry Creek, which in turn flows into the Mendenhall River.

This brook was named in 1951 to perpetuate the memory of Cpl. E. HARRISON, MID, killed in action with the Canadian Army during the Second World War.

MOUNT HARRISON 61°05'N 140°05'W (115-G). Near the Steele Glacier.

This peak was named in memory of HARRISON Wood, a member of the National Geographical Society Expedition of 1935. They explored the upper Steele Glacier and made the first ascent of Mount Steele on 15 August 1935.

HART RIVER 65°51'N 136°23'W (116-H). Flows north to the Peel River, from the Wernecke Mountains.

This stream was named in the 1880s by miners, after Howard Hamilton HART of Montana. He came to the Yukon in 1884 over the Chilkoot Pass, one of the earliest prospectors in the Yukon. He was an active man and was constantly pushing farther afield than most. He prospected and mined gold on most of the tributaries of the Yukon River. In the early fall of 1886, acting on advice from Arthur Harper, he discovered and mined gold on Hamilton Bar on the Fortymile River.

From 1896-1898, he had a lay (lease) on "Dawson" Charlie's No. 1 above claim on Bonanza Creek, from which he took a fortune. Most of it was lost when the steamer Islander was wrecked near Juneau, Alaska, in 1906. He died in Dawson in 1908 after falling into the freezing waters of Bonanza Creek. He sometimes called himself Howard Hamilton.

HARVEY GULCH 63°46'N 136°13'W (115-P). A short creek flowing into Highet Creek, from Scheelite Dome.

This was locally named for HARVEY Ray, a prospector-trapper who lived here in the 1930s.

HASSELBERG CREEK 60°38'N 129°56'W (105-A). A tributary to the upper Liard River.

This stream was named in 1959 after Frederick HASSELBERG, who prospected and trapped in the upper Liard country for many years after 1910. His cabin is at the mouth of the creek.

When first mapped the name was spelled, incorrectly, Heigelberg.

HASSELL LAKE 60°10'N 132°08'W (105-C). A small lake ten miles north of Morely Lake.

This lake and creek were named in the summer of 1951 to honour the name of Sgt. D.B.L. HASSELL, MID, of the Canadian Army who was killed in action during the Second World War.

The creek name later reverted to Caribou Creek.

HATCH'S ISLAND 64°02'N 139°27'W (116-B). A large island, one and a half miles long, in the Yukon River, a mile and a half above Dawson.

George A. HATCH bought this island in 1901. He cut off the cottonwood trees and sold them for firewood in Dawson. In 1902, he planted potatoes on the ground he had cleared and by 1909 he was producing more than 60 tons per year as well as large crops of oats and other grains and vegetables. He also raised hogs and chickens. He was probably the most successful farmer in the Yukon. He died at his home in Morrill, Maine in 1917.

HAUNKA CREEK 60°14'N 133°54'W (105-C). Flows into Little Atlin Lake.

In both Tagish and Tlingit Indian languages this word means "Cottonwood" from the numbers of poplar trees which grow there.

HAWKING CREEK 60°04'N 134°50'W (105-D). A tributary to Lake Bennett, immediately north of Dundald Siding on the WP&YR.

A Discovery claim staked by an enthusiastic amateur, John C. Phelps, on 18 May 1901 caused this creek to be named. No signs of gold were ever found on it.

HAWTHORNE CREEK 63°45'N 130°34'W (105-O). Flows southwest to the Hess River.

Named after Jack HAWTHORNE a well-known prospector in the area from 1920-1980.

HAYDEN LAKE 61°02'N 138°08'W (115-G). Ten miles east of the south end of Kluane Lake.

Named after Jack HAYDEN, Klondiker, trapper and noted guide who lived and worked in this area from the earliest years. An American, HAYDEN was a colourful character who had driven stagecoaches in Texas and mined in the Klondike. He married an Indian woman and lived here for many years.

HAYES CREEK 62°43'N 138°14'W (115-J). A tributary to the Selwyn River.

This stream was named for Dr. Charles Willard HAYES, USC&GS, who made the first map of this area in his exploration report for the American Geographical Society in 1891. HAYES was later made Director of the United States Geological Survey.

HAYES PEAK 60°24'N 133°18'W (105-C). On the west side of Teslin Lake, seven miles south of Johnson's Crossing.

This beautiful, lone hill was named by Arthur St. Cyr, DLS, in 1897, when he was searching for and surveying a possible route from Telegraph Creek to the head of Teslin Lake and on to the goldfields. It was named after Dr. Charles Willard HAYES, USC&GS. HAYES, together with Mark Russell and Lt. Frederick Schwatka, US Army, in 1891 came this way while travelling from the Taku River to the upper White River country. HAYES later published the first notes on the geology and topography of this region. St. Cyr also named a river entering Teslin Lake at the south end for HAYES.

HAYSTACK MOUNTAIN 3,751' 63°39'N 139°10'W (115-O). On the headwaters of Ruby Creek, south of the Indian River.

The mountain was named about 1897 by the first miners in the Klondike because of its shape. It is notable as the site of one of the most unusual funerals in the Klondike.

One June in the early 1920s Carl Hafstead died. He had mined on Quartz Creek and had looked at this mountain from his claim for all the years he was there. He had expressed the desire to be buried on the summit of this hill and left instructions in his will to that end, including money for a barrel of beer for his pall-bearers and mourners.

Upon his death a simple service was held in a roadhouse at the base of the mountain, conducted by one of his fellow miners. A party of 30 miners then set off carrying the coffin and a barrel of beer. It was a twelve mile journey and a climb of 1000 feet by wagon and on foot, on a hot day. An advance party of miners went ahead and dug and blasted a grave on top of the hill overlooking the Indian River and Quartz Creek valleys. By late evening the burial party had arrived and Carl was laid to rest in his favourite place.

HAZARD CREEK 61°16'N 140°11'W (115-G). A small creek flowing into the Steele Glacier, from the west side.

I. Peace HAZARD was a sponsor and member of the American Geographical Society Expedition of 1935 which was the first to explore the upper reaches of the phenomenal Steele Glacier. This stream was given his name in 1966.

HEADLESS CREEK 61°48'N 134°41'W (105-E). A tributary to the Big Salmon River, immediately above Illusion Creek.

Not a murder mystery! This stream was given its name in the summer of 1934 by Hugh S. Bostock, GSC. When mapping the area he found that glaciation had turned the headwaters of this stream into nearby Lokken Creek, leaving this creek headless, or shorter.

HEIGELBERG CREEK (see Hasselberg Creek).

HELEN CREEK 67°56'N 136°52'W (116-P). Flows east to the Bell River.

Named after the first white child to be born in the Yukon Territory, HELEN Murray. She was born in the early winter of 1847 at Lapierre House. She was the daughter of Anne and Alexander Hunter Murray of the HBC. (see Lapierre House and Anne Creek)

HELL RIVER (see Rackla River).

HENDERSON CREEK 63°21'N 139°27'W (115-O). A large creek entering the Yukon River, about two and one-half miles below the Stewart River.

Robert HENDERSON, of Klondike fame, with John Collins and Underwood, found gold and staked the Discovery claim on 9 June 1897. They wrote on the No. 1 post "This creek shall be known as HENDERSON Creek".

A stampede of considerable proportions took place but little payable gold was found. HENDERSON was so convinced of the stream's potential that he staked a 160 acre townsite on the west side of the Yukon River, opposite the mouth of the creek. Nothing came of it.

HERSCHEL ISLAND 69°35'N 139°05'W (117-D). The only major island on the Arctic coast of the Yukon Territory.

The most northerly place in the Yukon, this historic island was first sighted and named by Sir John Franklin, RN, in 1826 (he did not land there). He gave it the name of Sir William HERSCHEL (1738-1822), the famous English astronomer.

The "USS Thetis" surveyed the island in 1889 and named many of its features. This was also the year that the first whaler wintered at the island. It was the only safe winter anchorage from Point Barrow to the MacKenzie Delta. As the riches of the Beaufort Sea whaling grounds became known, more whalers wintered here. Being remote from authority of any kind, they began a period of unlicensed debauchery and murder. As many as 100 ships lay here at one time and took full advantage of the unsophisticated Eskimo (Inuit) population. It was the only time and place in the history of Western Canada that complete and unbridled lawlessness ran amok.

In 1896, the Canadian Church Missionary Society learned of conditions on the island and Isaac O. Stringer (later Bishop of the Yukon), a fearless and indomitable man, was sent to erect a mission and attempt to alleviate the lot of the natives. He pressed Ottawa for help but it was not until 1903 that the NWMP set up a detachment here. By that time the whaling industry had recessed and conditions on the island had improved.

The island continued to be a trading center and a little whaling by both natives and whites was carried on. In 1925 a post office (run by the RCMP) was opened. As trade decreased and the population shrank, the settlement dwindled. In September 1938 the post office was closed. By 1968 all activity had ceased and no one remained.

HESS RIVER 63°33'N 133°56'W (105-N). A major tributary to the Stewart River.

Michael HESS was one of the earliest miners in both the Yukon and Alaska. He entered the Yukon over the Chilkoot Pass in 1884 and prospected most of the major Yukon River tributaries. He was one of the discoverers of the Cassiar Bar in the Yukon River, the first rich diggings found in the territory. It is probable that he prospected this stream before 1886 and it was given his name because he was the first man on it. Although well-known and often mentioned in the literature of the time, little is known of the man himself. He died and was buried at Forty Mile in 1892.

The range of mountains between the HESS and Rogue Rivers was named for him at a later date.

HESTER CREEK 63°59'N 139°02'W (115-O). Flows into Hunker Creek from the southwest, two miles above Last Chance Creek.

John Huntington staked the Discovery claim here on 28 October 1897. It is not known for whom it was named, although a man named HESTER was a partner in a very rich claim on Monte Cristo Gulch in 1899.

MOUNT HICKSON 61°11'N 140°03'W (115-G). Beside Mount Gibson, in the St. Elias Range.

This was named in 1970 by the Alpine Club of Canada after J.W.A. HICKSON (1873-1956), a past-president (1924-1926) of the club.

MOUNT HIGGENS 2,973' 66°09'N 136°33'W (116-I). At the head of Eagle River.

In 1973, this hill was named in remembrance of K-49920 Trooper Struan Alexander HIGGENS who was born 12 July 1918 in Vancouver, B.C. He enlisted at Dawson and served in Canada, Great Britain and Northwest Europe. He was reported missing in action and presumed killed on 9 August 1944, in France.

HIGH CACHE CREEK 69°09'N 140°09'W (117-C). A tributary to the Firth River, about seventy-five miles from its mouth.

Jujira Wada found placer gold on the Firth River at this point on 1 March 1908 and named this stream. He found an old cache here. A cache is a small, log building, usually built on high posts to keep animals out and used to store dry supplies.

Wada was an exceptional musher (dog team driver) and made many extraordinary journeys to the far corners of the Yukon and Alaska. He took part in all the major and many minor gold rushes and stampedes in both regions from 1898-1925. He went from Fairbanks, Alaska (before it had that name, it was called "Tanana"), to Dawson with the news of a new, rich (and mainly imaginary) gold strike. About 1000 men followed him back and when they assessed the new camp, held a miners meeting at which they discussed hanging him. As it transpired they really did not mean it and by summer gold was being found in large quantities. He once mushed, in 1923, from central northern Alaska to Herschel Island, down the MacKenzie River and on to Winnipeg, Manitoba, a distance of 2,500 miles.

His find here sparked a stampede but results were uneconomic. About every ten to fifteen years since, another stampede takes place to the same prospects and with the same results. The creek was renamed during one of these staking rushes in 1937 when, owing to poor maps and lapse of time, this name had been forgotten. The name since then is "Sheep Creek". (see Firth River)

HIGHET CREEK 63°43'N 139°04'W (115-P). Flows into the Minto River.

Warren HIATT discovered the first gold here in May 1903. When he was recording his claim his name was spelled phonetically by the Mining Recorder. It was the richest creek in the Mayo area, by 1915 over $500,000 had been won from it. Native bismuth, a mineralogical rarity was common in its gravels.

William Ogilvie, DLS, when President of the Yukon Basin Gold Dredging Co. in 1908, called it "Hyatt Creek".

MOUNT HINTON 6,755' 63°52'N 135°08'W (105-M). Six miles north of Mayo Lake, in the Gustavus Range.

This hill was named in 1904 after Thomas HINTON, a well-liked Mining Recorder at Dawson and Mayo in the early 1900s.

HOBO CREEK 63°56'N 136°57'W (115-P). Flows into the Little Klondike River.

This small stream was named on 13 November 1897 by the noted Captain H.S. Back, when he prospected this country. (see Back, Nansen and Seymour Creeks)

HODDER CREEK 62°34'N 134°21'W (105-L). Flows into the Pelly River, from the Glenlyon Range.

HODDER, a "ne'er do well" who existed on a little trapping and charity of the local Indians. They were kind to him because they considered him mad. He died here, at the mouth of the creek in the winter of 1940, when he drunkenly locked himself out of his cabin in sub-zero weather and froze to death.

The mountain at the head of the creek was given his name but when his circumstances became known the name was quickly changed to Glenlyon Peak.

HODGSON GLACIER 61°10'N 140°19'W (115-G). A western branch of the Steele Glacier, in the St. Elias Range.

In 1966, Col. Walter A. Wood named this feature in memory of his wife, Foresta HODGSON Wood, a member of nine expeditions to the St. Elias Range between 1935-1951.

On 27 July 1951, Foresta Wood left the Seward Glacier in a Norseman airplane with the pilot and her daughter Valerie. They were never seen again. The name "Foresta" was approved for a peak in the St. Elias Range in Alaska in 1957.

MOUNT HODNETT 6,540' 60°19'N 135°12'W (105-D). Between the Wheaton and Watson Rivers.

This hill was named in 1906 after David HODNETT, the discoverer of lode gold in this area that same year. Hodnett Lakes were also named for him at a later date. (see Gold Hill)

MOUNT HOFFMAN 64°29'N 136°20'W (116-A). In the south Wernecke Mountains.

Fred HOFFMAN was a pioneer prospector and trapper in this area and a partner of Frank Rae. (see Rae Creek)

HOGAN LAKE 66°22'N 134°02'W (109-L). Between the Caribou and Peel Rivers.

This was named in 1973 for Eugene A. HOGAN who was a Yukon Councillor for the Klondike District, 1912-15.

MOUNT HOGE 61°14'N 139°24'W (115-G). In the Donjek Range, west of Kluane Lake.

This peak was named in 1945 by George Jeckell, Comptroller of the Yukon Territory and Hugh S. Bostock, GSC, after Brigadier General William A. HOGE, US Army. HOGE was the Officer Commanding the Northern Command of the US Army Engineers during the construction of the Yukon Section of the Alaska Highway, March to August 1942. It was his drive and leadership which led to this section of the highway being built in so short a time.

A native of Booneville, Missouri and a career soldier, he was awarded the DSM in the First World War.

A creek flowing from the mountain was also given his name at a later date.

MOUNT HOGG, 6,774' 61°21'N 132°14'W (105-F). East of the McConnell River.

This mountain was named in 1951 to perpetuate the name of an other Canadian hero, Squadron Leader J. E. HOGG, DFC, of the RCAF who was killed in action during the Second World War.

HOIDAL MOUNTAIN 2,969' 68°17'N 137°50'W (117-A). Seven miles north of Bonnet Lake.

Anker HOIDAL was a noted northern prospector who headquartered in Dawson and Aklavik. He spent many years from 1920-1960 prospecting the Arctic slope of the Yukon Territory. This mountain was named for him in 1973. (see Anker Creek)

HOLLENBECK CREEK 64°07'N 138°30'W (116-B). A tributary to the North Klondike River.

Named for Anthony HOLLENBECK who operated a roadhouse and logged in this area for many years.

HOLMANS LAKE 60°21'N 134°20'W (105-D). A small lake, three miles northwest of Tagish.

Although not officially named until after his death in 1952, this lake was the home of HOLMAN Good. He settled here shortly after the Klondike Rush and remained, trapping and prospecting for many years. HOLMON is the correct spelling of his name.

HOMESTAKE GULCH 63°55'N 139°15'W (115-O). Flows into upper Bonanza Creek, two miles from Grand Forks.

James H. Sullivan staked the Discovery claim here on 28 June 1897 and was working the claim when it was "jumped" (staked unethically by another person) on 13 July. He was able to confirm his ownership and carried on, earning a homestake.

A "homestake" is the term used among miners to denote enough money to go home, as opposed to a "grubstake" which is enough money to go prospecting.

HOOCHEKOO BLUFF 62°27'N 136°39'W (115-I). On the Lewes (Yukon) River, just below Tatchun.

This cliff was a landmark of the riverboat pilots. In former days the name was spelled "Hutshiku".

HOOLE RIVER 61°45'N 131°43'W (105-G). A tributary to the Pelly River.

Francis HOOLE, half Iroquois and half French-Canadian, was a life-long employee of the HBC and, for a number of years interpreter for Robert Campbell and his companions on their journeys of exploration in northern B.C. and the Yukon.

This river and the major rapids on the Pelly River, HOOLE Canyon, were named for him by Campbell in the summer of 1843 when they made their first trip down the Pelly River.

HOOTALINQUA 61°35'N 134°54'W (105-E).

This spot was from ancient times an Indian fishing camp. Situated at the junction of the Teslin (earlier called the HOOTALINQUA) River and the Yukon River it soon became, in the early days, a steamboat landing and supply point for the miners in the Teslin River country. A roadhouse here catered to the travellers on the river. The settlement, except for a telegraph operator, was nearly abandoned by 1910.

The name was sometimes spelled "Hootalinka".

HOPE GULCH 63°35'N 135°12'W (105-M). A tributary to Lightning Creek, from Keno Hill.

The Rev. George Pringle, the noted Klondike minister and an active prospector, staked the first claim and named this small stream on 3 March 1902.

There is a "Faith Gulch" next to the west and a "Charity Gulch" immediately to the east.

HORNET CREEK 68°45'N 136°35'W (117-A). Flows into Rapid Creek, a tributary to the Blow River, near the Arctic coast.

In 1972, F.G. Young, GSC, was working on this stream when his party ran into trouble due to the excessive numbers of these pesky flying insects.

HORSFALL CREEK 62°54'N 134°59'W (105-L). A tributary to the MacMillan River.

Joseph S. HORSFALL (or, as he sometimes signed, HOSFALL) was an Englishman who came into the country during the Klondike Gold Rush, overland from Edmonton. The country and the life suited him so well that he married one of Jack McQuesten's daughters and stayed. He earned a living trapping and prospecting. He accompanied F.C. Selous, Charles Sheldon and other noted big-game hunters into the MacMillan River country and in their writings, was well spoken of by them. He spent a good deal of his time searching for the Lost McHenry Gold Mine, a legendary stream supposedly located at the headwaters of the Pelly River. Remarkably, he was a poor bushman and was often lost. The HORSFALLs started a farm on the east bank of the Yukon River about five miles below Fort Selkirk and grew good vegetable crops for several years. He died on or near this stream about 1935.

No account of HORSFALL would be complete without particular mention of his wife. In almost every written account which mentions her, she is invariably spoken of in superlatives. She was educated at the mission school at Fort MacPherson and at 20 she married HORSFALL. She evidently inherited the best characteristics of both her Indian mother and her New Englander father. She could hunt and shoot, handle boats and canoes, trap, and build cabins as well as most men, in addition she was as well educated, well spoken, modest and graceful as any woman might aspire to be. Her knowledge of woodcraft and animal life was superior to that of most people. She did all the traditional tasks of Indian women, tanning skins, catching and drying fish, making clothes, doing beadwork-and she was an excellent cook. The HORSFALLs had four daughters, the two youngest of whom were born in the middle of winters, when Mrs. HORSFALL was alone with her other children in their cabin on the Pelly River. Her husband was away on his trapline, so Mrs. HORSFALL kept the cabin warm, looked after her little daughters and gave birth, entirely unaided, with the temperature outside far below zero. She was liked, admired and respected by everyone who knew her.

HORTON CREEK 61°49'N 132°01'W (105-F). A small creek joining the Pelly River from the south, just above Hoole Canyon.

Named in 1909 after an early prospector who lived here.

HOTSPRING CREEK 63°01'N 135°51'W (105-M). A tributary to Woodburn Creek, in the McArthur Range.

One of the few, true hotsprings is located at the headwaters of this creek.

MOUNT HOUGH 61°24'N 137°59'W (115-H). North of Isaac Creek.

This hill was named in 1974 by James Smith, Commissioner of the Yukon Territory. He named it in remembrance of William HOUGH who was Superintendent of the Dominion Experimental Farm near Haines Junction in the 1950s. He was drowned in a boating accident in a nearby lake.

HOUGHTON LAKE 61°22'N 137°20'W (115-H). A small lake about six miles west of Aishihik Lake.

In 1956, this lake was chosen to honour the memory of Pte. Donald HOUGHTON of the Canadian Army, who was killed in action during the Second World War.

HOWARD LAKE 60°14'N 136°49'W (115-A). At the head of the Takhanne River.

In March 1898, ex-Lt. Adair, US Cavalry, came from Haines, Alaska and arrived at the new gold finds on Shorty Creek, just north of Dalton Post. He had a crew of 36 men and large amounts of equipment and supplies. His party, run on military lines, was sworn to secrecy, so much so that other prospectors and the NWMP called them "The Mysterious 36". It was thought that Adair was backed by the Standard Oil Company and eastern Canadian capital. They built large camps on Shorty Creek and prospected widely in the region for both placer gold and lode minerals. HOWARD S. Scott was Adair's second in command and highly regarded by the local NWMP. It is thought that this lake was named for him by his prospectors.

MOUNT HUBBARD 15,015' 60°19'N 139°04'W (115-B). In the St. Elias Range.

In 1890, Professor Isaac C. Russell, USC&GS, named this high peak in honour of Gardiner Green HUBBARD (1822-1897), Massachusetts lawyer and educator, Regent of the Smithsonian Institution and founder and first President of the National Geographical Society, which offices he held from 1888 until his death. Interested in the exploration of Alaska, he helped to organize Russell's 1890 and 1891 expeditions, which were sponsored jointly by the National Geographical Society and the USGS.

In 1960, because of continued support of exploration in the St. Elias region by the National Geographical Society, the Canadian government also gave his name to a large glacier on the northwest side of the mountain.

The mountain was first climbed on 28 July 1951 by Col. Walter A. Wood, Peter Wood, Robert Bates and Nicholas R. Clifford. (see Hodgson Glacier)

HUBBARD GLACIER 60°21'N 139°23'W (115-B). Flows along the bases of Mounts Alverstone and Hubbard.

This is the longest glacier in North America, being sixty-six miles from its source to its end in the sea at Disenchantment Bay.

MOUNT HULEY 65°55'N 138°40'W (116-G). On the east side of the East Porcupine River.

In 1973, this mountain was named after Peter HULEY who spent 50 years in the Dawson area. Known as the "Charlie Chaplin " of the Yukon, he had been a silent film comedian who was exact in his imitation of Charlie Chaplin.

HULSE LAKE 61°32'N 127°52'W (95-D). West of the Coal River.

In 1969, James A. Harquail, President of Fort Reliance Minerals Ltd., requested that the name of this small lake be changed to perpetuate the name of John HULSE. He was a geophysicist who spent the last three months of his life in this area and was killed here in an airplane crash on 2 September 1968. The name was formerly "Quartz Lake". (see Roy Lake)

MOUNT HUNDERE 60°35'N 128°52'W (105-A). East of the Campbell Highway, near KM60, north of Watson Lake.

This name was proposed by Dr. Aro Aho, President of the Francis River Syndicate. After Jake HUNDERE, who found a spectacular mineral deposit here in 1962. It was so rich that HUNDERE originally called the mountain Jewel Box Hill. In the 1990s a large mine was developed here by Curragh Resources Ltd. called the "SA-DENE-HES Mine".

HUNGRY CREEK 65°36'N 135°28'W (106-E). A tributary to the Wind River, from the west.

This creek was named in the winter of 1897-98 by stampeders from Edmonton who were caught here by winter with short supplies.

HUNKER CREEK 64°02'N 139°13'W (116-B). Flows into the Klondike River, from King Solomon's Dome.

Andrew "Old Man" HUNKER was a native of Wittenberg, Germany and an old Cariboo miner who had come into the Yukon in 1886 or 1887. He was working on the upper Fortymile diggings when he heard the news of Carmack's find. When he and his partner, Charles Mathew Johnson, a Swedish farmer and logger from Ohio, reached Bonanza Creek they were in time to find ground open to staking. HUNKER staked No. 31 below Discovery and Johnson staked No. 43 below, a few days after the discovery. Not bothering to go to Forty Mile to record their claims immediately, they decided to prospect some of the creeks farther up the Klondike River. (miners had 60 days to record their claims after staking).

They reached this creek around 1 September 1896 and spent four days prospecting upstream, finding better colours (fine gold) as they went. About twelve miles from the mouth they found a location which gave them $22.75 in gold in two hours panning. This was extremely rich. HUNKER and Johnson staked the Discovery claim, then HUNKER staked No. 1 below and Johnson No. 1 above. They then prospected further upstream and, seeing muddy water coming down the north fork, followed it up and found Robert Henderson and his three companions at work. Telling them about his find he returned downstream. Henderson and his friends followed the next day. When they saw and investigated Hunker's find they immediately staked claims next to them. They never returned to their claims on Gold Bottom Creek. It is doubtful that they knew of the finds on Bonanza and Eldorado until Hunker met them. Of the four, Henderson, Munson and Swanson sold their claims the following year to Big Alex MacDonald. Dalton alone kept his claim and worked it, winning himself a fortune. (see Gold Bottom Creek)

HUNKER married a Swedish woman whom he had financed to run a roadhouse near his claim. A man of sober habits, he was never ostentatious and remained active in mining and prospecting. In 1907 he was in Fort McPherson, NWT, after spending some time investigating reports of gold-quartz deposits on the upper Peel River discovered by H.F. Waugh, whom he had backed. (see Waugh Creek)

HUNKER Creek was one of the richest placer gold creeks in the world. It ranked next to Bonanza and Eldorado Creeks in the amount of gold recovered per foot of creek.

MOUNT HUNT 61°29'N 129°16'W (105-H). On the east side of Frances Lake, in the Logan Range.

This mountain was originally named "Mount Logan" by Dr. George Mercer Dawson, G&NHSC, in 1887, after Sir William Edmond Logan (1798-1875), founder and Director of the Geological and Natural History Survey of Canada.

In 1916, the name was changed as it was in conflict with the later named Mount Logan in the St. Elias Range, a more appropriate mountain being the highest in Canada and the second highest in North America.

This mountain was then re-named after Thomas Sterry HUNT (1826-1892), a chemist with the Geological and Natural History Survey of Canada.

HUOT GULCH 63°59'N 140°29'W (115-N). A short stream running into Boucher Creek, in the Sixtymile District.

On 12 August 1902, W.M. Richardson, I.A. Jackson and James HUOT filed locations on the Discovery claim and others on what they named HUOT Gulch, a tributary of Boucher Creek on which they had just previously also made the Discovery. James HUOT was a son of Napoleon HUOT of Quebec, an early staker in the Klondike. (see Boucher Creek)

HUTSHI LAKES 61°08'N 136°35'W (115-H). On the Nordenskiold River, southeast of Aishihik Lake.

These lakes are on the Dalton Trail and were the last lakes before reaching the Yukon River at Carmacks.

This is an Indian word meaning "Last Lakes".

HYATT CREEK (see Highet Creek).

HYLAND RIVER 60°00'N 128°10'W (105-A). A major tributary to the Liard River, at Lower Post, B.C.

Robert HYLAND, an Englishman, shipped around Cape Horn in the 1860s and was one of the first men in the rush to the Stikine River and Dease Lake (Cassiar) goldfields. He was always in the vanguard and though primarily a trader, was an adventurous prospector. He was the first man to ascend the river which bears his name, in the summer of 1874 or perhaps as early as 1873. Near Stewart Lake he found and staked the first lode mineral claim in the Yukon Territory. He had found a deposit of silver-lead ore. He lived the remainder of his life in this area, owning and operating trading posts at Spatzi River, Dease Lake, Cassiar and Lower Post. He was always in competition with the HBC and other traders. At one time he printed his own money which was accepted by the Indians and miners.

In 1834, Peter McLeod of the HBC was the first white man to see this stream which he had named the "MacPherson River" but by 1873 the name had been forgotten.

The Indians of this region were afraid to go to the headwaters of HYLAND River as they believed that something evil lived there. One of their legends tells of a party of hunters who ascended the river and while passing through a canyon, met with a sudden darkness during which an evil monster rose from the depths of the river and dragged the unlucky hunters into a whirlpool. The Indians disliked the rivers in the district and turned back whenever they saw the bones of huge animals (fossil remains) on the bars or banks of the stream.

ICE CHEST MOUNTAIN 3,895' 63°31'N 137°35'W (115-P). Five miles south of McQuesten.

Hugh S. Bostock, GSC, named this mountain in the summer of 1949 to preserve the name of ICE CHEST Reef, a bad rock in the channel of the Stewart River just to the west. Named by early steamboat captains and pilots, the rock had caused a number of accidents.

IKE BROOK 60°34'N 133°54'W (105-C). A tributary to Michie Creek.

This little stream was named in 1952 after an old-time trapper who lived here in a cabin at its mouth.

ILLES BROOK (see Money Creek).

ILLUSION CREEK 61°50'N 134°40'W (105-E). A tributary to the Big Salmon River.

This stream was named in the summer of 1934 by Hugh S. Bostock, GSC, when some of his party missed a rendezvous, mistaking this creek for Lokken Creek.

MOUNT INA 5,261' 64°26'N 139°34'W (116-B). Thirty miles north of Dawson, in the Ogilvie Mountains.

This peak was named in 1970 after the wife of the Hon. Justice H.E. Gibben a long-time Yukoner, Justice of the Territorial Court and one-time Commissioner of the Yukon Territory. (see Mount Gibben)

INDEPENDENCE CREEK 63°31'N 137°49'W (115-P). A tributary to the Stewart River.

Fine gold (dust) was found here about 4 July 1893 by Hugh and A.H. Day. They were among the first miners to enter the Yukon, coming over the Chilkoot pass in the spring of 1884. They were successful miners on the Stewart River bars.

Later, in the summer of 1896, Jack McQuesten and Dick Poplin (another old-timer who had been here since 1883) found coarse gold on this creek but the find was overshadowed by the Klondike discoveries.

INDEPENDENCE CREEK 63°59'N 139°01'W (116-O). Flows into Hunker Creek, between Hester and Colorado Creeks.

Sam Abramson was optimistic when he found enough gold here to stake a Discovery claim and name the stream on 6 December 1897.

INDIAN RIVER 63°47'N 139°44'W (116-O). Flows into the Yukon River.

This river and the Klondike River enclose what is now known as the Klondike area. All the richest placer gold creeks are between these two streams.

The earliest travellers on the Yukon River noted an Indian community at the mouth of the stream from which it received its name. As was the case in those times, the Indians moved from here and settled closer to the trading posts as they were established.

When Robert Campbell, HBC, made his first journey from Fort Selkirk to Fort Yukon in 1851, it was probably this river that he named the "Forcier" after one of his French-Canadian voyageurs, Baptiste Forcier. Between that time and the influx of prospectors in the 1890s the name had been forgotten. (see Forcier River)

INGERSOLL ISLANDS 62°41'N 137°11'W (115-I). Ten miles above Fort Selkirk, in the Yukon River.

This group of small islands was named by Lt. Frederick Schwatka, US Army, in 1883 after Col. INGERSOLL, US Army, of Washington, D.C.

MOUNT INGRAM 7,080' 60°44'N 135°37'W (105-D). Twenty miles west of Whitehorse, south of the Ibex River.

This peak was named in August 1897 by J. J. McArthur, DLS. He was making a hurried trip over the Dalton Trail for the Department of the Interior and mapping roughly as he went.

On the banks of the Takhini River he found a grave, with a headboard inscribed with the name INGRAM. This man and his partner had come up the Yukon from its mouth and after a few years of prospecting, they headed upstream for the coast. They were told to take the right hand stream at the first fork above the Pelly River but mistakenly ended up on the Takhini. Ten miles of rapids were evidently too much for them. INGRAM's body was buried by a Tlingit trader, William Dickenson.

INGS RIVER 61°04'N 131°00'W (105-G). Joins the upper Liard River from the north, in the St. Cyr Range.

The river was named in 1947 in memory of Wing Commander R.R. INGS, RCAF, who was killed in action during the Second World War.

INNISSIAQ HILL 69°22'N 139°31'W (117-D). On the bank of the Firth River, near the Arctic coast.

This is an Eskimo (Inuit) word meaning "The Useful Flintstone". In earlier times they came here to gather chert (flint rock) to make stone tools and weapons.

In the summer of 1956, Dr. R.S. McNeish, an archaeologist with the National Museum of Canada, found the remnants of nine prehistoric cultures near this place. The lower remains may be some of the oldest found on the continent, up to 10,000 years of age. This find filled in several gaps in the knowledge of Canadian prehistory. Dr. McNeish noted the old Eskimo name for the hill at that time.

IRON CREEK 60°51'N 133°19'W (105-C). A tributary to Sidney Creek, about ten miles west of the Canol Road.

Gold was found here and the creek staked and named "Willow Creek" in June 1905 by W. Mooreside, Joe Brewer, Jim Thompson and Charles Anderson. When recording the claim, the Mining Recorder, R.C. Miller, changed the name to IRON Creek, as he said that there were too many Willow Creeks in the country already. Many attempts were made to mine the creek profitably up to 1936 but with little success as the gold deposits were too erratic.

IRONS CREEK 60°00'N 127°53'W (95-D). A tributary to the Liard River.

This creek was the trapping grounds of the IRONS family of Indians who worked here for many years.

IRVINE CREEK 60°36'N 131°36'W (105-B). A large stream which flows into the east side of Wolf Lake.

Formerly known as Murray Creek, this name was changed in 1947. W.T. IRVINE lived here in the 1920s and 30s trapping and prospecting. His cabin was near the mouth of the stream. He made the first sketch map of the area to assist the GSC.

ISAAC CREEK 61°28'N 137°34'W (115-H). Flows into the west side of Sekulmun Lake.

This creek was named many years ago after Chief ISAAC of the Aishihik Band of Tuchone Indians. Chief ISAAC guided the first white men, Jack Dalton and E.J. Glave when they entered this part of the country in 1890 and 1891.

A small, short-lived settlement was established at the mouth of this stream in 1913 during the stampede to the Chisana goldfields in Alaska. The settlement was on the winter trail and catered to the miners passing through. It disappeared a few years later.

ITSI LAKES 62°50'N 130°12'W (105-J). At the headwaters of the Ross River.

This is an old Indian word meaning "Wind". Some years ago the small range of mountains north of the lake were given the same name.

IYON RIVER (see Pelly and Teslin Rivers).

JACKSON POINT 61°03'N 138°30'W (115-6). On the shore of Kluane Lake, near Mile 1063 (KM1722) of the Alaska Highway.

This point was named in 1960 after Rex JACKSON, the first Forestry Engineer in the Yukon Territory.

JACQUOT ISLAND 61°20'N 138°46'W (115-G). The largest island in Kluane Lake, opposite Mile 1086 (KM1759) on the Alaska Highway.

This island was named in 1945 by Hugh S. Bostock, GSC, after two brothers, Eugene and Louis JACQUOT of Alsace-Lorraine, France. They came over the Chilkoot Pass in 1898. They were not successful in the Klondike but decided to stay and trap in the Yukon.

Taking part in the rush to the Burwash Creek finds, they instead established a trading post and a settlement at Burwash Landing in 1903. Here they remained, trading, homesteading, guiding and successfully mining on Burwash Creek in 1909. (see Burwash Landing)

JAEGER LAKE 64°37'N 138°19'W (116-B). South of Lone Moose Lake.

Many long-tailed JAEGERS inhabit this lake. It may be a breeding place. They usually are seen on the Arctic coast.

JAKE'S CORNER 60°20'N 133°58'W (105-C). At Mile 865.5 (KM1402) on the Alaska Highway.

In 1942, US Army Engineers set up a camp here under the command of Captain Jacoby (or Jacobsen) to build this section of the Alaska Highway and a cut-off to Tagish and Carcross for the Canol Pipeline. In 1949-50, a highway south to Atlin, B.C. was also built from this location.

JAMES TRAIL 62°20'N 140°35'W (115-K). The road from Snag Junction to Snag.

William James was one of the first prospectors in this area and laid out the trail which the government later followed to make this road. He spent most of his life in this district. (see Beaver Creek)

JANET LAKE 63°41'N 135°31'W (105-M). Twelve miles northeast of Mayo Landing.

In 1898, J.J. McArthur, DLS, was surveying in the area and named this lake after his daughter.

JARVIS CREEK 63°42'N 136°09'W (115-P). A tributary to Minto Creek at its mouth.

Archie McIntyre staked the Discovery claim and named this creek when he found placer gold here on 14 May 1903.

JARVIS RIVER 60°46'N 138°09'W (115-B). A tributary to the Kaskawulsh River.

The river was named by the first prospectors in the area about 1899-1900 after Major Arthur Murray JARVIS, Inspector in the NWMP. He had established the police post and customs on the Dalton Trail in the first days of the Gold Rush.

MOUNT JECKELL 6,400' 64°19'N 138°50'W (116-B). Twenty-five miles northeast of Dawson, in the Ogilvie Mountains.

This mountain was named about 1957 to commemorate George Allan JECKELL. He was a school teacher who was appointed Comptroller of the Yukon Territory from 30 June 1932 to 18 September 1947. During the Depression the government did away with the office of Commissioner of the Yukon Territory in an attempt to reduce expenses in the Territorial government. JECKELL proved to be an outstanding administrator and performed an exceptional job.

JENS CREEK 62°40'N 138°40'W (115-K). A small brook on Rude Creek.

When JENS Rude discovered gold on Rude Creek in March 1915 he and his partner built their cabin at the mouth of this small stream. The other miners called it JENS Creek. However, the gold on it was found by Otto F. Kastner and John A Ross, who staked it and officially named it on 16 September 1915. (see Rude and Dip Creeks)

JESSICA CREEK 63°08'N 133°25'W (105-N). Enters Russell Creek from the east, one mile above Limestone Creek.

Major Neville A.D. Armstrong, who worked for many years in this area, named this stream after the wife of his partner, Mrs. George Leith of England. The Leiths spent 18 months on Russell Creek with Armstrong and his wife in 1904-05. (see Russell Creek, George Creek and Mount Armstrong)

MOUNT JESUS 64°02'N 132°59'W (106-C). Three miles southwest of Ortell Lake.

A landmark on the Stewart River from the time of the earliest miners, it was named and known from 1885. It is a beautiful, solitary peak. William Ogilvie, DLS, described it as a very high peak that resembled Mount Hood in Oregon. Somehow, around 1900 the name disappeared from all the maps, a curious happening, as it had been so well-known up to that time.

MOUNT JETTÉ 8,460' 60°00'N 139°03'W (115-C). On the corner of the International Boundary where the Yukon, Alaska and British Columbia meet.

Named in 1905, after Sir Louis JETTÉ, KCMG, Lt. Governor of Quebec and Member of the Canadian-Alaskan Boundary Tribunal in 1903.

JOHN LAKE 62°49'N 130°22'W (105-J). On the upper Ross River.

In 1909, when Joseph Keele, GSC, was mapping the geology of this area he named this little lake after his favourite sled dog, JOHN.

JOHNSON CREEK 66°59'N 138°09'W (116-J). A small stream flowing into Pine Creek.

Named by Otto Heist, in 1958, after Andrew JOHNSON, a trapper from Fort Yukon who married a woman from Old Crow and settled in this extremely isolated country for many years. He died at Fort Yukon about 1955.

JOHNSON CREEK 63°49'N 136°27'W (115-P). Enters the McQuesten River, just below Ortell's Crossing.

In 1894, the two Garrison brothers found gold on this creek but did not mine it. In the autumn of 1898, F. JOHNSON, who had been unlucky in the Klondike and had prospected this stream previously, returned and staked a discovery claim, naming the creek.

MOUNT JOHNSON 61°12'N 131°29'W (105-G). Southeast of McNeil Lake.

This hill was named by Dr. George Mercer Dawson, G&NHSC, after D. JOHNSON who was a member of his expedition to the Yukon in 1887-88.

JOHNSONS CROSSING 60°29'N 133°18'W (105-C). Near the Teslin River crossing of the Alaska Highway.

During 1942, the Teslin River was bridged here to carry the Alaska Highway and the Canol Pipeline. An army construction camp first occupied the site. The US Army Engineers built the bridge and named the camp after their Commanding Officer, Col. Frank M.S. JOHNSON, 93rd Engineers.

Local people claim that the crossing was named after George JOHNSON a Chief of the Teslin Indian band who ferried the army men across the river at this point, when the bridge was being built.

JOHOBO LAKE 60°29'N 137°35'W (115-A). Southwest of Louise Lake.

The JOHOBO Mining Co. explored a copper deposit here between 1956-1972. The mine remains have been incorporated into the history of Kluane National Park.

JONES RIDGE 65°06'N 140°59'W (116-F). Crosses the Yukon-Alaska boundary.

Around 1914, D.D. Cairnes, GSC, named this ridge after Charles JONES, who had been a member of his Geological Survey parties in this area for a number of years.

MOUNT JOY 7,333' 63°45'N 132°54'W (105-N). The highest peak in the Lansing Range.

While mapping the geology of this region in 1909, Joseph Keele, GSC, named this peak after Sergeant G.B. JOY, Rgt. No. 3045 of the RNWMP.

MOUNT JOYAL 3,055' 66°37'N 136°48'W (116-I). East of the Eagle River.

This mountain was chosen in 1973 to honour 2140278 Pte. Felix JOYAL who was born in Merril, Wisconsin on 13 January 1887. He enlisted in Victoria, B.C. on 2 July 1918 and succumbed to the dreaded "Spanish Flu" (influenza), which was epidemic around the world at that time, on 19 October 1918, before leaving Canada for overseas.

JUBILEE MOUNTAIN 5,950' 60°12'N 134°07'W (105-D). On the east side of Tagish Lake.

Dr. George Mercer Dawson, G&NHSC, named this prominent hill in 1887 in honour of Queen Victoria's Jubilee. In that year she had reigned on the throne of the British Empire for 50 years.

JUBILEE PEAKS (see Mounts King George and Queen Mary).

JUDAS CREEK 60°25'N 134°14'W (105-D). Flows into the east side of Marsh Lake.

A stampede took place here in August 1911 from Whitehorse, to stake claims near a find made earlier by Benjamin Miller. Some of the stampeders wanted to call it "All-In" Creek because they were exhausted when they reached it. When they found there was very little or no gold on the creek they gave it this name.

This name is wrongly attributed, by some, to highway construction crews in 1942.

JUNGLE CREEK 65°29'N 141°00'W (116-F). Flows across the Yukon-Alaska boundary to the Nation River.

The International Boundary Survey party of 1910 named this creek because of the exceptionally luxuriant growth of vegetation in its valley, which made travel exceedingly difficult.

JUNKERS LAKE 61°02'N 131°21'W (105-G). At the headwaters of the Liard River.

This lake was named in the summer of 1930 by bush pilot Captain E.J.A. "Paddy" Burke and mechanic Emil Kading. They set up a food and fuel cache here to service prospecting activity in the area, from Atlin, B.C. They were flying a low-wing JUNKERS aircraft, serial CF-AMX.

On 11 October 1930, Burke, Kading and prospector Robert Martin left Lower Post, B.C., to return to Atlin. Blinded by a blizzard, they were forced down on the ice of the Liard River a short distance north of the present upper Liard River bridge. They damaged the aircraft on the second landing. They set out on foot, without snowshoes, to reach this lake with its store of food and fuel. Burke died of exhaustion and exposure after 27 days. Martin and Kading were rescued on 6 December by Everett Wasson and one of the Yukon's best bushmen, Joe Walsh.

This was the first air search and rescue ever carried out in the Yukon. (see Wasson Lake and Burke Creek)

KALZAS LAKE 62°57'N 135°37'W (105-L). On the Little Kalzas River.

This lake was named by Robert Campbell of the HBC, or one of his men, about 1849-52 while establishing Fort Selkirk. It was named after one of his Indian employees. Fish, needed for the Fort, were plentiful here. The lake is noted on the earliest map of the Territory. It is now called "Little KALZAS Lake". (see Big Kalzas Lake)

KANDIK RIVER 65°50'N 141°00'W (116-F). Crosses the Yukon-Alaska boundary and flows into the Yukon River.

This is an Indian name, recorded by Lt. Frederick Schwatka, US Army, on his 1883 excursion. He did not report the translation. It was called "Charlie's River" by the miners and traders, after the Chief of the Indian band who had a village at the mouth of the stream.

Later research has revealed that this is a Han Indian word meaning "Willow Creek".

KASKAWULSH RIVER 60°39'N 137°49'W (115-B). The east fork of the Alsek River.

The river names in this area have been much confused and mistaken since the first exploration. This name was first recorded by E.J. Glave in 1891. Later it was applied to what is now the Dezadeash River and at one time was applied to the whole upper Alsek River. For many years this stream was locally called the "O'Connor" River, after a rather mysterious Captain M.J. O'Connor, who prospected and mined in this part of the country it was said, even before Glave and Dalton explored it. A river in Alaska further west is also named for him.

KATHLEEN LAKES 64°14'N 134°11'W (109-D). Empties into the Rackla River.

These lakes were named on 4 July 1945 by Bernard J. Woodruff, DTS, of the Geodetic Survey of Canada, after KATHLEEN Emery, wife of the CPA pilot with their survey party. The name was originally applied only to the largest of the three lakes.

These are not to be confused with the Kathleen Lakes west of the Haines Highway.

KATRINA CREEK 62°54'N 140°14'W (115-J). A tributary to the White River.

Although the origin of this name has been lost, this creek was known by this name to the miners long before the Klondike Gold Rush.

KAY POINT 69°18'N 138°23'W (117-D). At Phillips Bay, on the Arctic coast.

This point was named by Sir John Franklin, RN, in 1826 while on his second expedition, after an esteemed nephew.

MOUNT KEARNEY 3,923' 66°22'N 135°50'W (106-L). On the headwaters of the Trail River, in the Richardson Mountains.

This was named in 1973 after Thomas J. KEARNEY, who was a Yukon Councillor for the Bonanza District, 1907-09.

KEELE PEAK 63°26'N 130°19'W (105-O). In the Hess Mountains, north of the Canol Road.

Joseph KEELE was a noted northern explorer-geologist who was hired in 1898 by the GSC as a topographical surveyor. He spent much of his time from 1901 on in the Yukon and NWT. He mapped much previously unexplored country and added greatly to the knowledge of these areas. He was an expert bushman, canoeman and, above all, a scientist. His traverse from the Pelly River, up the Ross River, over Christie Pass and down the Gravel River to the MacKenzie River in the winter of 1907-08 is among the great Canadian exploration sagas.

He died of throat cancer in 1923, at the height of his career. This large mountain was named in his honour by R.G. McConnell, GSC, whose assistant he was that season. Keele Creek and Lake were named much later.

KEELE RANGE 66°50'N 141°00'W (116-J). The range of mountains crossing the Yukon-Alaska boundary, south of the Porcupine River.

D.D. Cairnes, GSC, named this range in 1911 in honour of his compatriot Joseph KEELE.

KELLY CREEK 62°16'N 136°01'W (115-I). A tributary to the Tatchun River.

Most probably named after Gerry KELLY, a trapper and prospector for many years in this area. He married Rose Horsfall, a grand-daughter of Jack McQuesten. For a number of years, he was an operator on the Yukon Telegraph at the Stewart River station and for a winter, at Armstrong Landing.

KELLY CREEK 63°53'N 135°19'W (105-M). Flows into Fisher Creek, in the Mayo district.

Named after Phillip KELLY who was Mining Recorder for the Mayo District about 1919.

MOUNT KELVIN 60°40'N 136°32'W (115-A). Eight miles south of Champagne.

This mountain was named before 1909 after William Thomson, Lord KELVIN, the celebrated British mathematician and physicist.

KENNEBEC CREEK 62°47'N 140°06'W (115-J). A tributary to the White River.

The KENNEBEC is a river in the state of Maine and the name was an Indian one, known long before the Revolutionary War. The river was famous during much of the nineteenth century for its immense stands of white pine and the evolution of modern lumbering methods.

This name was carried west by lumbermen and used again in Quebec and Ontario in the late 1880s-90s. This stream was likely named by one of these lumberjacks turned miner during the rush to the upper White River copper deposits in 1903.

MOUNT KENNEDY 13,905' 60°20'N 138°58'W (115-B). Four miles east of Mount Alverstone, in the St. Elias Range.

Named for the late President of the United States of America, John Fitzgerald KENNEDY, at the request of Prime Minister Lester B. Pearson of Canada. It was the anniversary of the assassination of President KENNEDY. The feature was chosen by Dr. Bradford Washburn, a world famous mountaineer and a friend of the President.

It was first climbed on 24 March 1965. Senator Robert Kennedy, the President's brother, was one of the three climbers to attain the summit.

KENO HILL 6,065' 63°57'N 135°11'W (105-M). Twelve miles north of Mayo Lake.

KENO is a simple gambling game. It was popular throughout the early west in saloons and gambling houses.

In July 1918, Louis Beauvette (or Bovette) found high-grade silver-lead ore on the hill. It was called Sheep Hill at the time. He staked his first claim, the Roulette in July 1919. Alfred Kirk Schellinger staked the KENO claim. The camp went forward immediately as Livingstone Wernecke, manager of the Treadwell-Yukon Mining Co. took charge. The name of the hill was changed that summer to KENO HILL. Wernecke operated several mines on the hill from 1919 to his death in 1941. The town prospered. Ore was shipped by riverboat to Whitehorse, then by WP&YR to Skagway and on by steamer to the smelter at Tacoma, Washington. After Wernecke's death the mines were shut down. A new company was formed in 1947 and reopened several of the mines but emphasis had shifted to Elsa and the town never regained its prominence. The population fell to about 50 and remains small. Known today as Keno City. (see Wernecke)

KENO LADUE RIVER 63°54'N 134°02'W (105-M). Flows from north of Keno Hill to the Stewart River.

Before 1897, this stream was known as Ladue Creek, after Joseph Ladue, a pioneer Yukoner who had prospected its lower reaches in the 1880s. Later on it was given its present name to avoid confusion with the River and Creek of the same name in the Sixtymile district. (see Ogilvie, Ladue River and Dawson)

KENTUCKY CREEK 64°18'N 139°21'W (116-B). A tributary to Twelve Mile Creek.

A stampede from Dawson, sparked by rumors of a gold find on the creek, took place in early October 1898. The first man to stake a claim named it after his home state.

KETZA RIVER 61°53'N 132°15'W (105-F). Enters the Pelly River about ten miles upstream from Ross River.

This river was named by Robert Campbell of the HBC on his initial journey down the Pelly River in 1843. He named it after his Iroquois canoeman and companion, KITZA. The name was subsequently misspelled by mapmakers.

KILLERMUN LAKE 61°10'N 137°41'W (115-H). In the Ruby Range, the lake empties into the West Aishihik River.

Recorded in 1962, this name is an old Indian word meaning "Flint Rock". It is believed that the ancient Indians obtained a type of chert (flint) here to make tools and weapons.

KIMBERLEY CREEK 60°51'N 138°04'W (115-B). A tributary to the Jarvis River.

During the rush to the Alsek goldfields in January 1904, Tom Laird discovered gold on this creek and named it.

MOUNT KING 65°14'N 140°18'W (116-F). At the head of Tatonduc River, near Mount Deville.

In March 1888, William Ogilvie, DLS, named this peak after William Frederick KING (1854-1916), DLS, DTS, Chief Astronomer of Canada from 1890-1905, Director of the Dominion Observatory from 1905-1916 and member of the International Boundary Commission (Canada-US) 1892-1916.

MOUNT KING GEORGE 12,250' 60°32'N 139°47'W (115-B). Twenty-five miles north of Mount Vancouver, in the St. Elias Range.

In the period February to May 1935, a National Geographical Society Yukon Expedition explored the central part of the St. Elias Range. They named this peak in honour of the Silver Jubilee year of KING GEORGE V of Great Britain. They named the twin peaks, about twelve miles to the north, after Queen Mary. They called the two Jubilee Peaks.

The party, led by Bradford Washburn, was the first to cross the St. Elias Range on foot from the Yukon to Alaska. They were assisted by Jack Haydon of Carcross whose dog-team moved most of their supplies.

KING PEAK 16,971' 60°35'N 140°39'W (115-C). Ten miles west of Mount Logan.

This was named about 1918 after Dr. W.F. KING, one-time International Boundary Survey Commissioner. The peak was first climbed on 6 July 1966. (see Mount King)

KING POINT 69°06'N 137°59'W (117-D). Fifteen miles southeast of Phillips Bay, on the Arctic coast.

This point was named by Sir John Franklin, RN, in 1826, after Captain Phillip P. KING, RN (1793-1856), who made the first survey of the coast of Australia.

Roald Amundsen, the famous Arctic explorer, wintered here in 1905-06 in the ship "Gjoa", studying and collecting Arctic bird life.

KING SOLOMON'S DOME 4,048' 63°52'N 138°57'W (115-O). The highest and most central hill in the Klondike district.

From it radiate the six richest creeks in one of the richest placer goldfields ever found in the world. Before 1896 prospectors in the area called it simply, The Dome, because of its shape. When the riches of the surrounding ground became apparent the present fanciful name was applied, in reference to KING SOLOMON's riches and to his mythical lost gold mines. From its summit the whole of the Klondike country and more can be seen.

MOUNT KINNEY 5,674' 65°03'N 137°04'W (116-H). East of the Hart River.

Constable G.F. KINNEY, RNWMP, died on the Peel River thirty-five miles from Fort MacPherson, a member of the lost Fitzgerald Patrol in 1911. This mountain lies just east of their route to Fort MacPherson and was named in his memory in May 1973. (see Dempster Highway)

KIPLING MOUNTAIN (see Mount Sheldon).

KIRKLAND CREEK 61°45'N 136°02'W (115-H). The west branch of the Nordenskiold River.

J.B. Tyrrell, GSC, named this creek in 1898 while mapping the geology of the area. He named it "Wright Creek" after Professor R. Ramsay Wright of the University of Toronto. The creek was abandoned and the name forgotten. In 1915, a new discovery was made and the original staker renamed it.

KIRKMAN CREEK 62°59'N 139°23'W (115-J). Flows into the Yukon River, about fifteen miles above the White River.

On 13 October 1898, Grant and Albert KIRKMAN of Tulare, California, discovered the first gold here. Their claim did not pay and the creek was soon abandoned. However, in April 1914, a new discovery was staked by Joseph C. Britton and William Heas. They found the paystreak and prospered. The creek was a good producer for many years and a small settlement grew up at its mouth. (see Touleary Creek and Britton Ridge)

KIWI LAKE 63°13'N 134°37'W (106-E). Southwest of Margaret Lake.

David Holden was a helicopter pilot who serviced an exploration group in this area for three summers (1979-1981) from a base on this lake. R.W. Allen, BCLS, in charge, named the lake after Holden, who came from New Zealand.

KIYERA LAKE 61°47'N 138°57'W (115-G).

This is a Tuchone Indian word referring to the fish in the lake, which are a red-tailed species.

KLETSAN HILL 4,698' 61°43'N 140°58'W (115-F). An isolated hill, south of the White River and near the Yukon-Alaska boundary.

This hill takes its name from the creek on the Alaska side, a Tanana Indian name "Klet-San-Dek", meaning "Copper Creek". The name of the creek was first reported by C. Willard Hayes, USC&GS, in 1891. D.D. Cairnes, GSC, applied the name to the hill in 1913-14 when he was mapping the geology along the Yukon-Alaska boundary.

It was sometimes locally called "Klutson" or "Copper Creek" because from ancient times the Yukon Indians came here to obtain nuggets of native (pure) copper for tools, weapons and ornament.

KLINES GULCH 62°38'N 138°00'W (115-J). A tributary to Hayes Creek, which flows into the Selwyn River.

Around 1904, a prospector with this name found coarse gold, some nuggets up to two ounces, on this stream. It was said to be the only place where gold was found on the Selwyn River or its tributaries.

KLINE, later on becoming despondent, committed suicide in a most efficient manner. Using dynamite, he arranged two charges so that the first blast killed him inside his cabin while the second blast was arranged to destroy the cabin walls, allowing the three feet of soil on the roof to effectively bury him.

KLONDIKE RIVER 64°03'N 139°26'W (116-B). A large stream entering the Yukon River from the east.

The earliest reliable reports of this river were given by Frank E. Ketchum and Michael Laberge of the Western Union Telegraph Co. in 1867. This may also be the "Deer River" noted by Robert Campbell in 1851. Ketchum and Laberge were exploring a route for an overland telegraph line through B.C., the Yukon and Alaska to the Bering Sea near Nome. They reported its name as the "Deer River", from the Indian word "Chandik". In 1883 Lt. Frederick Schwatka, US Army, called it the "Reindeer River". These names were not used by the early miners from 1882 on. They were trying to twist their tongues around the Indian name "Thron-Duick" or "Tron-Deg", these words meaning, as far as can be determined, "Hammer-Water". It derived from the Indian practice of driving wooden stakes into the bed of the stream to form fish traps to catch salmon migrating upstream. The miners finally settled on the pronunciation "Clunedik", "Clundyke" or "Clondyke". Inspector Charles Constantine, NWMP, Mining Recorder at Forty Mile on the discovery of Bonanza Creek, made the spelling "Klondyke" official. Most of the miners were Americans and their usage substituted an "i" for the "y". British and some Canadian publications continued to use this spelling for some time. When the Department of the Interior issued its first report on Geographical Names in 1898, the name KLONDIKE was official.

It was one of the finest salmon streams in the Yukon and the local Indians built and maintained drying racks at its mouth. George Carmack and his party were here to catch salmon in early August 1896. It was only because of the poor run of fish that they decided to prospect up Bonanza Creek.

KLOO LAKE 60°57'N 137°52'W (115-A). Near Mile 1037 (KM1669) on the Alaska Highway.

This is a Tuchone Indian word meaning "Fish". The word "Kuua" means "Fish Trap" or "Fishing Place".

KLOO LAKE CITY 60°58'N 137°52'W (115-A). On the north side of Kloo Lake.

A small sawmill settlement was built here in 1905 to supply lumber for the Alsek diggings. It was abandoned a few years later.

KLOTASSIN RIVER 62°34'N 139°31'W (115-J). A tributary to the Donjek River.

An Indian name (not translated) first recorded by C. Willard Hayes in 1891 while travelling with the Schwatka expedition to the upper White River.

MOUNT KLOTZ 5,903' 65°24'N 140°06'W (116-F). In the Ogilvie Mountains.

This peak was named in 1945 after Dr. Otto Julius KLOTZ (1852-1923), Assistant Chief Astronomer of Canada who had carried out several geodetic surveys in western Canada. This was a sort of consolation prize as he had named a mountain in southern B.C. after himself which his superiors disallowed.

KLUANE 61°02'N 138°23'W (115-G). On the south end of Kluane Lake, near Mile 1054 (KM1707) of the Alaska Highway.

This old settlement started in 1903 with the discovery of good placer gold in the streams nearby. The first name was "Silver City" but was changed by 1904 as there was another Silver City in the White River country. This settlement was the main supply point for the area for many years but it was gradually abandoned as the Burwash Creek placer deposits assumed importance and the local creeks were worked out. The wagon road from Whitehorse was extended to the west in later years, which did away with steamboat landings here.

The first post office was opened in October 1904 with the name "Bullion Creek", and altered four months later to Kluane. It was finally closed in 1921.

Originally an Indian fishing village, the name is a Tlingit Indian name meaning "Big Fish Place" or "Whitefish Place".

The lake name was first reported by Professor Aurel Krause of the Bremen Geographical Society on his expedition in 1882. Kluane Lake is the largest in the Yukon with an area of about 154 square miles. The name KLUANE has since been given to a glacier, river, hills, ranges and a plateau.

KLUKSHU LAKE 60°19'N 137°01'W (115-A). Three miles south of Dezadeash Lake.

This name was recorded by E.J. Glave on 22 November 1890, on his first expedition into the region.

The name is a Tlingit Indian word meaning "Cohoe Salmon Lake" or "Place Where Cohoe Salmon are Caught".

KLUTLAN GLACIER 61°27'N 140°39'W (115-G). In the St. Elias Range.

This large glacier is the source of the Generc River and a major source of the White River. The native name was recorded without translation by C.Willard Hayes, USC&GS, in 1891.

KNOB CREEK 60°03'N 135°51'W (105-D). (see Morse Creek).

KNORR CREEK 65°22'N 134°39'W (105-E). A tributary to the Bonnet Plume River.

A.N. KNORR came into the Klondike in 1898. He later married a woman from Old Crow and raised sums of money in Dawson to prospect the Bonnet Plume River country. He and his wife lived here for a number of years between 1905-10 in complete isolation and seemed to have disappeared without a trace after that time. (see Margaret Lake)

KOHSE CREEK 64°33'N 133°25'W (106-C). A tributary to the Bonnet Plume River.

In the summer of 1952, E. and F. KOHSE were packers for the GSC party mapping the region, led by J.O. Wheeler. He named this creek to show his high regard for their work.

KOIDERN RIVER 62°03'N 140°27'W (115-F). Flows into the White River.

This is an old Indian word meaning "Water Lily". Miners in the area before 1915 called it "Lake Creek" from the number of ponds along its valley but the name was never adopted, This name was first noted by C. Willard Hayes, USC&GS, in 1890, on his expedition to the White and Copper Rivers.

KOOKATSOON LAKE 60°33'N 134°52'W (105-D). Two miles north of Cowley Lake.

A Tagish Indian word meaning "Ling Cod Lake".

MOUNT KOSTIUK 6,750' 61°00'N 127°58'W (95-D). West of Rock Creek.

This name was proposed in 1957 by Don Taylor, Speaker of the Yukon Legislative Assembly to honour an old and respected friend, Victor KOSTIUK.

He was born 15 April 1895 at Paltinossa, Buckovena, Austria. He came to Canada in 1904. After living in Fir Mountain, Saskatchewan he went with others to Fort St. John, B.C. in 1931. They travelled by wagon train and were three months on the way. He trapped in the southeast Yukon, worked on the Alaska Highway, the Mayo Dam and at Cassiar Asbestos. He opened and ran a gasoline station at Contact Creek Mile 590 (KM952) until his death 11 December 1965. He was a steady, hardworking man and a good neighbour.

MOUNT KULAN 62°17'N 132°28'W (105-K). East of Mount Mye.

Named after Alan KULAN. He settled here after service in the Second World War and became interested in prospecting. He was one of the discoverers of the huge Anvil silver, lead, zinc orebody near Faro, Yukon. He also found several other unique mineral deposits in the Territory, in particular, one which was later named after him called "kulanite". He was murdered in Ross River on 12 September 1977.

KUSAWA LAKE 60°21'N 136°22'W (115-A). Empties into the Takhini River.

This lake was known and described to Dr. George Davidson in 1869 by the Chilkat Chief, Koh-Klux (he led the raid on Fort Selkirk in 1852). In June 1882, the lake was visited by Dr. Arthur Krause, the first white man to see the lake. He was a geographer of the Bremen Geographical Society and brother of Aurel Krause. In 1890, it was again seen by E. Hazard Wells, Chief of the Frank Leslie Illustrated Newspaper Expedition, who renamed it Arkell Lake, after W.J. Arkell, sponsor of the expedition.

The name is a Tlingit Indian word meaning "Long, Narrow Lake". In 1898 the Board on Geographical names restored the Indian name. (see Arkell Creek)

MOUNT LABBE 64°21'N 138°16'W (116-B). Northwest of Antimony Mountain.

This was named after J. Lucien LABBE. He owned a hotel in Dawson and engaged in real estate and logging businesses in this area.

LAKE LABERGE 61°11'N 135°12'W (105-E). On the Yukon River, about fifteen miles north of Whitehorse.

In the summer of 1867, Frank E. Ketchum of St. John, New Brunswick and Michael LaBERGE of Chateaugay, Quebec, explorers for the Western Union Telegraph Company, came up the Yukon River from Fort Yukon to Fort Selkirk. They were looking for a possible route for the Collins Overland Telegraph Line being built from New York to Paris. It was never clear if LaBERGE did visit the lake but he had it described to him by the local Indians. Returning to Fort Yukon they found that the project had been terminated. William H. Dall, Director of the Scientific Corps of the Western Union Telegraph Expedition, wrote a massive report on Alaska in 1870 and gave LaBERGE's name to this lake.

In 1883, Lt. Frederick Schwatka, US Army, gave the Indian name as "Kluk-Tas-Si" with no translation. In 1882, Dr. Aurel Krause had reported the Tlingit Indian name "Tahini-Wud". A few years ago as a result of the Native Languages Project it was found that this word meant "Salmon River".

LaBICHE RIVER 60°00'N 124°06'W (95-C). In the extreme southeast corner of the Territory.

Long named after the LaBICHE family; natives whose trapping grounds have been here for many years.

LACELLE LAKE 61°23'N 137°01'W (115-H). A small lake just east of central Aishihik Lake.

In 1956, this lake was named to perpetuate the memory of Pte. Henri LACELLE, Canadian Army, who was killed in action during the Second World War.

MOUNT LADEROUTE 62°57'N 139°51'W (115-J). Northwest of Mount McClennan.

This name was proposed by James Smith, Commissioner of the Yukon Territory in 1974. He wished to commemorate Francis LADEROUTE, a pioneer farmer who homesteaded on the Yukon River in this area.

LADUE RIVER 63°10'N 140°20'W (115-N). A tributary to the White River.

This river was prospected and named by and for Joseph LADUE in the early 1880s. He had found traces of gold on it, as well as on the small creek of the same name which enters this stream just above its mouth.

LADUE, who came from New York state, was one of the first prospector entrepreneurs to come into the Yukon, crossing the Chilkoot Pass in the spring of 1882. Combining prospecting with trading and other enterprises, he was early convinced that a major goldfield would be found in the general area of the Indian and Klondike Rivers. This belief led him to encourage and grubstake prospectors to work there. He grubstaked Robert Henderson in 1894-96 and sent him up Quartz Creek to visit William Redford who was successfully mining there. He himself was one of the first to prospect the Sixtymile and Fortymile districts, although with limited success. He and Jack McQuesten prospected Bonanza Creek in early 1886 but missed the rich gold there. Loosely associated with the Alaska Commercial Company, he and Arthur Harper opened a trading post and brought in the first sawmill to the Yukon, at the mouth of the Sixty Mile River in 1894. At first, called Sixtymile Post, the name was soon changed to Ogilvie, after their friend, William Ogilvie, DLS. In early August 1896 LADUE had, by a remarkable coincidence, decided to move his sawmill from Ogilvie to the flat at the mouth of the Klondike River, where he intended to open a small trading post. He arrived there on 28 August and, realizing the potential of the new finds, staked the flat land as a townsite. He set up his sawmill and trading post, and also speculating in mining claims, quickly gained a fortune, becoming a millionaire in the next two years.

He returned to Schuyler Falls, New York in 1897 and married his childhood sweetheart. On 27 June 1901, suffering from tuberculosis, he died at his home there.

A number of other features in the Yukon were given his name, two creeks, a lake, a range of mountains and the Keno Ladue River in the Mayo district. (see Dawson City)

LAFORCE LAKE 62°41'N 132°19'W (105-K). This lake drains to the Riddell River.

In 1946, this lake received the name of a brave man, Pte. Alphonse LAFORCE, MM, of the Canadian Army. He was killed in action on 12 May 1945.

LAHCHAH MOUNTAIN 67°37'N 140°57'W (116-N). A long, low ridge twenty miles west of Old Crow.

This is an old name, a Vanta Kutchin Indian word meaning "Low Hill".

LAKE CREEK 62°26'N 140°05'W (115-J). A tributary to the White River.

Alyre Morin and Wilfred Grenier prospected this stream and in the summer of 1913 had found enough gold to warrant staking the Discovery claim. They named the stream LAKE CREEK for the number of ponds and small lakes along its course in the wide valley. On 2 March 1913 the Gold Commissioner changed the name to "Pond Creek" as the miners in the White River area were calling the Koidern River and Tchawsahmon Creek by this name. A number of years later, when names were being sorted out in this area, the name reverted to the original, LAKE CREEK.

LAKE CREEK 64°38'N 137°10'W (116-A). The west fork of Rae Creek.

This is the only "Lake" feature in the Yukon that is not a descriptive name. In 1956 this creek was named after Frederick LAKE who, with his partners Frank Rae and Afe Brown, trapped and prospected in the Hart River region during World War One and did a little mining on this creek.

MOUNT LAMBART 10,725' 61°31'N 140°58'W (115-F). In the St. Elias Range, just north of the Klutlan Glacier.

This was named after Howard Frederick John LAMBART, DLS (1880-1946), one of Canada's best mountaineers. He was born and later died in Ottawa, Ontario. He spent most of his working life with the Geodetic Survey of Canada. He was a pioneer in the development and use of aerial photography for mapping. He was the Canadian leader of the joint Canadian-American Expedition which made the first ascent of Mount Logan in 1921.

He surveyed the Yukon-Alaska boundary from 1906-1917, including the position and altitude of this mountain.

MOUNT LANDREVILLE 65°09'N 132°52'W (106-F). East of the Snake River, in the Backbone Range.

Max LANDREVILLE was a journalist who came into the Yukon in 1898. He was active politically and was chosen as one of a group to carry the miners' complaints of government inefficiency and corruption to Ottawa that same year. He was also a Yukon Councillor for the Klondike District in 1903. This hill was given his name in 1973.

MOUNT LANGHAM 62°15'N 138°03'W (115-J). South of Apex Mountain.

This peak was named in 1974 by James Smith, Commissioner of the Yukon Territory, after William LANGHAM. He was an early placer miner who took part in the first stampedes to the Beaver River and the Mount Freegold mineral finds.

LANGTON CREEK 60°00'N 136°53'W (115-A). Flows to the Tatshenshini River.

This creek was named locally after an ex-NWMP man who lived here for many years after the turn of the century.

Many years ago it was known as "Horse Canyon".

MOUNT LANSDOWNE 5,875' 60°22'N 134°31'W (105-D). Fifteen miles northeast of Carcross, on the west side of Marsh Lake.

William Ogilvie, DLS, named this feature after Henry Charles K. Petty Fitz-Maurice, Fifth Marquis of LANSDOWNE, in 1887. He was the Governor-General of Canada from 1883-1888.

LANSING 63°45'N 133°28'W (105-N). At the mouth of the Lansing River.

This was named because of its location at the confluence of the Stewart and Lansing Rivers. In 1897-98, Frank Braine, who had been a trader in northern Saskatchewan, and Percival Nash travelled through this country on their way to the Klondike from Edmonton. Disappointed in their search for gold, they returned to the vicinity of Fort Norman in the NWT to trap and trade. In 1902, they decided to return to this area to reap the fur harvest. They brought several families of MacKenzie River Indians with them, and built a trading post here. James Mervyn took over the post in 1912. The post prospered until many of the Indians died during an epidemic of influenza in the late 1920s. The post gradually lost its importance and with the coming of roads and the cessation of riverboat travel, it gradually faded into oblivion in the 1950s.

LANSING RIVER 63°45'N 133°28'W (105-N). A tributary to the Stewart River.

Samuel LANSING was one of the first prospectors in the Yukon Territory and mined the bars of the Stewart River in 1883. He prospected this stream that same year, when it received his name. He prospected widely in the Yukon and was one of the first at the Fortymile finds in 1886. He was moderately successful in the Klondike and was, for a number of years, the manager of Harper and Ladue's mining operations there. He retired in 1926 to Sumner, Washington.

LAPIE RIVER 62°02'N 132°36'W (105-K). A tributary to the Pelly River, west of Ross River.

Dr. George Mercer Dawson, G&NHSC, named this river in 1887 after one of Robert Campbell's Iroquois Indian canoemen, who had accompanied him on his exploration of the Pelly and Yukon Rivers in 1843.

LAPIERRE HOUSE 67°24'N 137°01'W (116-P). On the Bell River, near the mouth of the Rat River.

LAPIERRE HOUSE was established in 1843-44 by Chief Factor John Bell, HBC, of Fort MacPherson, as an outpost of that place, to facilitate trade with the tribes west of the Richardson Mountains.

LaPIERRE, the man who built and ran the post for the first few years, was half Iroquois and half French-Canadian. The first post was probably at the junction of what is now the Little Bell and the Bell Rivers, about thirty-five miles upstream from the present site.

After Alexander Hunter Murray built Fort Yukon in 1847, this post became a way-point between there and Fort MacPherson, used to transfer goods and furs. After the building of the second Rampart House on the Porcupine River and the supply of that place by riverboat up the Yukon River at much lower prices, LAPIERRE HOUSE fell into disuse and was abandoned by 1890.

For many years the post supplied much of the meat and fish consumed at both Fort Yukon and Fort MacPherson. Caribou were killed by the thousands and immense numbers of fish were caught and dried.

In the fall of 1847, Anne Murray, wife of Alexander Hunter Murray, gave birth to a daughter, Helen, while staying here. Anne was alone except for an Indian companion. Robert Kennicott, the brilliant young American naturalist and explorer, at that time the Director of the Scientific Corps of the Collins Overland Telegraph Co., spent about a month here in the winter of 1862, studying the natural history of the region.

Sometimes spelled "LaPierres", "Lapierres" or 'Lapiers", it was also known to HBC employees as "The Small House" and to the Indians as "Koahze" meaning "Little House".

MOUNT LAPORTE 7,050' 61°14'N 127°42'W (95-E). In the southeast corner of the Yukon Territory.

In 1972, at the request of the Commissioner of the Yukon Territory, James Smith, this mountain was named after the Hon. Pierre LAPORTE, journalist and Minister of Labour in the Quebec government. He was kidnapped and murdered by FLQ terrorists in Montreal in 1971.

LARSEN CREEK 60°10'N 125°01'W (95-C). Flows into the Beaver River.

In 1958, the long-known local name for this stream and lake was officially adopted for L. LARSEN, the first white trapper in the area, where he lived and died in his cabin at the head of the lake. (see Boucher Creek)

LASKA GULCH 63°49'N 136°19'W (115-P). A small stream off Johnson Creek.

Joe LASKA placer mined on Johnson Creek for many years in the 1930s-40s. George Ortell lived about a mile and a half away and although the two men had frequent disputes (and there were times when they hardly spoke), they were partners in a way. When one saw no smoke from the other's chimney, he investigated. Ortell said that LASKA was a great help in time of trouble. (see Ortell's Crossing)

LAST CHANCE CREEK 64°01'N 139°06'W (116-C). A tributary to Hunker Creek, two miles from its mouth.

The Discovery claim was staked on 2 October 1896 by Fred Belanger who may have named it, although a miner on this creek later wrote that a native, "Indian Sam" was the first to find gold and stake a claim.

LAST MOUNTAIN 4,407' 60°46'N 126°37'W (95-D). On the Yukon-NWT boundary.

This was named in the 1940s by G.F.G. Dalziel, big-game guide of Watson Lake and at one time owner-operator of Northern British Columbia Air Services. The hill was used by bush pilots as a landmark. (see Dalziel Creek)

LAST PEAK 6,062' 61°36'N 134°13'W (105-E). East of the Big Salmon River and south of Teraktu Creek.

In 1898, Arthur St. Cyr, DLS, surveyed the Quiet Lake-Big Salmon Lake country. He occupied ten triangulation stations on various mountain peaks within the area. This was the last one he used.

LATREILLE CREEK 60°03'N 135°02'W (105-D). Flows into the west arm of Bennett Lake.

This stream was named after Brother LATREILLE, OMI, an early day missionary in the region.

MOUNT LAURIER 5,838' 61°02'N 134°52'W (105-E). Ten miles east of the head of Lake Laberge.

Originally named "Mount Dawson" by William Ogilvie, DLS, in 1888. The name was changed in 1890 by Dawson, to honour the then Prime Minister of Canada, Sir Wilfred LAURIER.

MOUNT LEACOCK 10,200' 60°38'N 138°43'W (115-B). In the St. Elias Range, five miles east of Kaskawulsh Mountain.

This beautiful peak was named in 1970 in remembrance of Stephen LEACOCK (1876-1944), Professor of Economics at McGill University and Canada's beloved humourist and author.

LECKIE LAKE 61°33'N 129°38'W (105-H). Located between the arms of Francis Lake, at the north end.

In 1962, this lake was named to honour another of Canada's war dead. Sergeant J.C. LECKIE, Canadian Infantry Corps was killed in action during the Second World War.

LEDGE CREEK 63°40'N 134°52'W (105-M). Flows into Mayo Lake.

Gold was first discovered here and in several nearby creeks about August 1903 by a party of four Australian prospectors. They named the creeks when they were recording their claims in Dawson. The creeks were rich, for the discoverers found 175 ounces of coarse gold in a short time. (see Steep Creek and Cascade Creek)

LEGAR LAKE 62°39'N 136°33'W (115-I). About ten miles northeast of Minto.

In 1936, Dan Van Bibber reported that this name had been in local use for many years. Because of the number of pike in the lake the name may have been given by a French-Canadian prospector or trapper who fished them.

LEONARD CREEK (see California Creek).

LEOTTA CREEK 63°58'N 138°44'W (115-O). A tributary to the Klondike River.

John Scott came into the Yukon in 1897. He staked the Discovery claim on this creek and named it after his daughter in that year.

The mountain at the head of the creek was later given the same name.

MOUNT LEPAGE 62°22'N 136°24'W (115-I). Northeast of Yukon Crossing.

Aime R. "Happy" LEPAGE was a well-known woodcutter for the riverboats. He lived at Yukon Crossing for more than twenty-two years. He later prospected and mined in the Mount Freegold area. He deserved his nickname. He died on 28 November 1973, missed by all who knew him. (see Guder Creek)

LEPINE CREEK 64°05'N 139°05'W (116-B). The west fork of Rock Creek, ten miles east of Dawson.

W. LEPINE was working for the HBC when R.G. McConnell, GSC, met him on the Liard River in 1887. He had spent many years in the Yukon and NWT. Before the Klondike Rush he had gone to Forty Mile and it is believed that he prospected and lived on this stream in 1897-98.

LESAUX CREEK 63°13'N 140°46'W (115-N). A tributary to the Ladue River.

Locally named after Eugene LESAUX, a French-Canadian prospector-trapper who lived here for many years before dying in 1969.

LESLIE RIDGE 62°39'N 138°44'W (115-J). Between Dip Creek and the Klotassin River, northeast of Stevenson Ridge.

Hugh S. Bostock, GSC, gave this name in 1941 after the junior partner of a mining company on Rude Creek. They were successful miners and prospectors for many years in the district. At the start of the Second World War in 1939, LESLIE and his partner Stevenson bought an expensive radio in Dawson. They labouriously packed it and the heavy batteries it used at the time, into their camp and set up an elaborate aerial. Switching on the set, the first station they received was a German short wave propaganda program. They instantly chopped the radio to pieces and threw it outside the cabin, their patriotism totally outraged. They never bought another. (see Stevenson Ridge)

LEWES RIVER: The old name for that part of the Yukon River, above its junction with the Pelly River.

On 16 June 1843, Robert Campbell of the HBC arrived at this junction. He called the river below this point the Pelly and considered the river above it to be a tributary to the Pelly. He named it after John Lee LEWES, Chief Factor of the HBC. The local Indians told him that the headwaters of this stream formed a trade route to the coast, which undoubtedly influenced his selection of this place as the site of Fort Selkirk. By the 1880s the miners were using this name for the river as far as Lake Laberge.

In 1883, Lt. Frederick Schwatka, US Army, ignoring Campbell and the miners, named it the Yukon River. It was not until May 1945 that the Canadian government officially changed the name LEWES to the Yukon River.

In the early years the section of the Yukon from Lake Laberge to Marsh Lake was called the Thirtymile River. This was later dropped and included in the LEWES and then, the Yukon River. (see Yukon River)

LEWES (LEWIS) LAKE 60°23'N 134°50'W (105-D). On the west side of the WP&YR tracks, about fifteen miles north of Carcross.

Although still misspelled LEWES on all maps (after the old name for the Yukon River near this point), this lake received its name in the summer of 1899 from an engineering error during the construction of the railroad. A.B. LEWIS, the locating and construction engineer, while carrying out his grade survey, found that the surface of the lake was somewhat above (8 feet) the railway grade. A ditch was dug from the south end of the lake to drain away the excess water. The plug was removed in the evening and, during the night, the Force of the out-flow washed the ditch much deeper into loose gravel than had been anticipated and the lake was quickly drained by a depth of 50 or more feet. The flood washed out a considerable length of the newly constructed roadbed below the lake, holding up construction and embarrassing the engineer. The name was early mistaken for that of the Lewes River and has been so printed on maps ever since.

LEWIS LAKE 62°37'N 131°05'W (105-J). Part of the upper Ross River.

Joseph Keele, GSC, named this lake in 1907 during his explorations, after Clement S. LEWIS, son of Archbishop Lewis of Ottawa. LEWIS came into the Yukon in 1898. After various prospecting and mining ventures of limited success, he and Poole Field bought the trading post at the mouth of Ross River in 1902. Tom Smith, the owner, had built it a few years earlier. They named it "Nahanni House". Around 1906, they sold out to Taylor and Drury, Whitehorse merchants, and LEWIS managed it for them for a number of years, until about 1910. He was Justice of the Peace for the area and collected specimens for the National Museum of Canada at Ottawa.

MOUNT LEWIS 61°15'N 131°34'W (105-G). Southwest of McNeil Lake.

This name was given by Dr. George Mercer Dawson, G&NHSC, in 1887 after one of his assistants on his expedition from Dease Lake to the Yukon that year.

LIARD RIVER 60°00'N 128°35'W (105-A).

The headwaters of the mighty LIARD River are in the St. Cyr Range of mountains of the south central Yukon. The river flows southeast to cross the Yukon-B.C. boundary a few miles below Watson Lake. From there it flows east and north to join the MacKenzie River at Fort Simpson.

The early HBC traders on the MacKenzie River called this stream the "West Branch", the "Mountain River" and the "Great Current River". The MacKenzie Indians called it the "Erett-Chichi" and the "Thatradesse" and the Yukon Indians called it "Too-Ti", words all expressing its size and force.

The LIARD was first explored by John McLeod of the HBC when the company began expanding its empire westward across the Rocky Mountains. He traversed the river as far as what is now Lower Post in 1834. It was his French-Canadian voyageurs who gave it the name "Riviere aux Liards". Liard was the French name for the cottonwood (poplar) trees that still line the banks of the lower river in profusion.

The next white man on the river was Robert Campbell, also of the HBC, who from 1838-1852, opened up the route from the MacKenzie to the central Yukon. Campbell explored the Yukon Territory by way of the LIARD and its tributary, the Frances River, leading to the Pelly River and the Yukon River proper. While travelling the LIARD in 1838 Campbell did not realize that it was the same river McLeod had explored and named it the "Bell River" after Chief Trader John Bell. The name was used on some maps, but when its course was determined the old name LIARD was kept.

In 1874, a party of Cassiar miners ascended the headwaters of the river where they found and mined placer gold on a number of its tributaries. This was the first production of gold in what is now the Yukon Territory. These miners corrupted the name of the river to "Deloire" and for at least the next fifteen years they prospected its upper reaches with indifferent results.

The river is a dangerous one to travel. In 1852, the HBC abandoned the route because of the number of men lost in its rapids while trying to supply the posts at Frances Lake and Pelly Banks from Fort Simpson on the Mackenzie. Numerous prospectors were drowned in the river, especially in the Great Canyon, below Watson Lake. A number of Klondikers tried to reach the goldfields in 1897-98 by this route but few were successful, the recorded tragedies of that time only emphasizing those of earlier years.

Of scholarly interest is the number of variations of the names used for this river. Deloire, Beliore, Delyare, d'Eloir, D'Liard, Deliard, Del Liard, LIARD, Riviere des Liards, Lizzard and the Ure. Confusion in the early history also arises from the fact that the Fort Nelson River (not the Nelson River) and the Dease River, both tributaries of the LIARD, were sometimes called the Deoire River and that Delure Creek, a tributary to the Dease River, was sometimes called Deloire Creek. (see Cabin, Scurvy and Sayyea Creeks)

LIBERAL TRAIL (see Conservative Trail).

LIBERTY CREEK 62°19'N 137°06'W (115-I). A tributary to Stoddard Creek in the Mount Freegold area.

This has been a local name since 1929 when Fred Guder staked his LIBERTY claim on the creek, the first mineral find there. (see Guder Creek)

LIGHTNING CREEK 63°54'N 135°21'W (105-M). A tributary to Duncan Creek in the Mayo district.

In 1907, the discoverers of the gold on this stream gave it the name of the small riverboat "LIGHTNING", which brought miners and supplies up the Stewart River to Duncan Creek in the early 1900s.

LIL CREEK 64°31'N 138°14'W (116-B). Flows to the North Klondike River.

This creek was named after or by Harry Little, an early prospector here and in the Ogilvie Mountains.

LINDOW CREEK 63°59'N 139°13'W (115-O). A tributary to Bear Creek.

The Discovery claim was staked here on 25 August 1897. The name of the man who first staked a Discovery claim and then abandoned it is unknown.

LITHGOW CREEK 61°07'N 138°38'W (115-G). A tributary to Congdon Creek, from the south.

This creek was found to have placer gold on it when it was prospected during the rush to the Alsek country in 1903-04. The first claim was staked and the creek named in February of that year. The discoverer named it after J.T. LITHGOW who was Comptroller of the Yukon Territory from 1898-1911. He was also a Yukon Councillor from 1904-08. (see Congdon Creek)

LITTLE ATLIN LAKE 60°15'N 133°58'W (105-C). Fifteen miles north of Atlin Lake.

This lake was known to local Indians for many years as ATLIN Lake, while they called the present Atlin Lake "Taku Lake". The names were given present day usage shortly after 1900.

LITTLE BLANCHE CREEK 63°49'N 139°04'W (115-O). A tributary to Quartz Creek, from the west.

Bob Ensley staked and named this creek in October 1897. He was in love with a Dawson dance hall girl and named this stream after her. Later, in 1898, when his claim proved to be rich he induced LITTLE BLANCHE to marry him, by giving her her weight in gold dust and nuggets.

This little stream is notable as the scene of one of the tantalizing stories of gold found in the Klondike before 16 August 1896. It is claimed that in the spring of 1894 Andrew Hart and his partner Hansen prospected this creek and found payable gold. They mined it for a couple of months before running out of supplies and recovered over $2,000 in gold.

They went out to Fortymile and because no one had seen them all summer, decided to keep their find a secret. For unknown reasons they did not return and Ensley and LITTLE BLANCHE profited from the gold they left behind.

LITTLE FLETT CREEK (see Chinaidlai Creek).

LITTLE GEM GULCH 63°57'N 138°55'W (115-O). A tributary to Hunker Creek.

In October 1898, Frank Criderman was so pleased with his initial find of gold that he applied this name to the creek. The LITTLE GEM Mining Company was formed later and operated in several localities in the Yukon.

LITTLE JIMMY LAKE 60°54'N 129°43'W (105-A). About twenty miles northwest of Simpson Lake.

In 1949, LITTLE JIMMY, a local Indian, had erected a sign at his cabin here proclaiming his ownership. He had trapped from here to the East Arm of Frances Lake for many years. Named by the trader at Lower Post, Jimmy was something of a prospector. In 1937, he brought samples of high grade silver-lead ore to Anton Money at McDame Creek in the Cassiar. The samples came from the east side of Frances Lake. Money made arrangements with a Vancouver, B.C. mining firm to finance the search for the vein and others like it. The search was carried out for the next few years with some success. (see Money Creek)

LITTLE KALZAS LAKE 62°57'N 135°37'W (105-L). On Little Kalzas River, near Big Kalzas Lake.

This lake was one of the group named by Robert Campbell or one of his men in the period 1849-52. These lakes supplied many fish for Fort Selkirk. (see Big Kalzas Lake)

LITTLE RIDGE 4,482' 61°03'N 135°55'W (105-E). On the east side of Thirty-Seven Mile Creek.

Hugh S. Bostock, GSC, named this small hill after the old LITTLE River roadhouse, on the old Dawson Winter Trail, five miles to the southeast.

LITTLE SALMON RIVER 62°03'N 135°40'W (105-L). A tributary to the Yukon River, above Carmacks.

Miners in 1882 translated the Indian name for the stream and used it. In 1883, Lt. Frederick Schwatka, US Army, ignored both the Indians and the miners and renamed the river after the Hon. Charles P. Daly, President of the American Geographical Society. Dr. George Mercer Dawson, G&NHSC, disallowed the name and it was forgotten.

LITTLE VIOLET CREEK 61°25'N 134°24'W (105-E). A tributary to the South Big Salmon River.

The prospector who first found gold here was a widower who had his small daughter with him. A mining company was formed later on with this name and operated with some success.

LIVINGSTONE 61°20'N 134°20'W (105-E).

A small settlement near the mouth of Livingstone Creek came into being in the summer of 1898 to service the miners in the newly found goldfields of the area. It was connected to Lake Laberge by a 40 mile long winter trail and a little later by a 16 mile wagon road to Mason Landing on the Teslin River. The settlement flourished for many years. It contained stores, blacksmith shop, hotel, dance hall and a small red light district. It decayed with the depletion of the goldfields and improved transportation, finally ending in the late 1930s.

LIVINGSTONE CREEK 61°22'N 134°23'W (105-E). A tributary to the South Big Salmon River.

Joseph E. Peters prospected this area before the Gold Rush and, it is claimed, sank a prospect shaft on this creek in 1894. His find was not impressive as he continued prospecting in the surrounding area. There is some evidence that George Black gave him some financial assistance which led to Black's interest in the area. Peters later mined for many years on LIVINGSTONE and other nearby creeks.

In the late summer of 1899, George Black and his partner Sam H. Lough prospected the creek and found rich, coarse gold. In four weeks before freeze-up they recovered $3,600 in raw gold. He named the stream after a lawyer friend, M.D. LIVINGSTONE of Whitehorse and Dawson. A later account says that the name was that of C.J. LIVINGSTONE, Manager of the Canadian Bank of Commerce in Whitehorse. It is claimed that over a million dollars in gold was taken from this stream by 1920. Placer mining is still being carried on sporadically in the area.

MOUNT LOGAN 19,850' 60°34'N 140°24'W (115-C). In the St. Elias Range.

This is the highest mountain in Canada and the second highest in North America. It was named by professor Isaac Cook Russell, USGS, in 1890. He first saw it when he was on a National Geographical Society Expedition in southeast Alaska and the southwest Yukon, in the foothills of the St. Elias Range.

He named it in honour of Sir William E. LOGAN, founder and for many years Director of the Geological and Natural History Survey of Canada.

Sir William Edmund LOGAN, KB, LLD, FRGS, FRS, was born in Montreal, Quebec, on 20 April 1798. Taken to Scotland at 14 by his father, he attended Edinburgh High School. His work on Geology in Wales (a spare time project) was so good that it was accepted *in toto* by the Geological Survey of Great Britain. When the Canadian Government decided to set up such a department in Canada, LOGAN was so highly recommended that he was chosen over others more academically qualified. He served 27 years and, mostly by his own work in the field, laid the basis of eastern Canadian geology. He received most of the scientific honours of his day. He died in Llechryd, Wales in 1875. His monument, erected in Ottawa, reads:

The Father of Canadian Geology
Founder and First Director of the Geological
Survey of Canada. 1841-1869

His name is on several other features in Canada.

This mountain was first climbed on 23 June 1925, by a joint Canadian-American Expedition, led by H.F. Lanbart, Canadian and A.H. McCarthy, American. (see Mount Hunt)

LOGAN MOUNTAINS 61°45'N 128°38'W (95-E). East of Frances Lake.

Dr. George Mercer Dawson, G&NHSC, in 1887 gave this range of mountains the Indian name "Too-Tsho" which is their name for Frances Lake, meaning "Big Lake". This name was changed in 1929 to the present name. (see Mount Logan and Mount Hunt)

LOKKEN CREEK 61°57'N 134°38'W (105-E). Flows into Walsh Creek.

This creek was named in 1936 after H.O. LOKKEN, a long-time pioneer from the Gold Rush days. He was for many years the head linesman on the Yukon Telegraph. He was always an active prospector, especially in this area.

The mountain at the headwaters of the creek was given the name by W.H. Miller, GSC, while he was mapping the area and the creek was named later.

LOMBARD PUP 63°51'N 138°53'W (115-O). The last small stream entering the headwaters of Dominion Creek, from the north.

L.H. LOMBARD found the first gold and staked the Discovery claim on July 1897. It was never very productive.

LOMOND LAKE 64°48'N 138°11'W (116-B). Five miles east of Chapman Lake.

It is so called from the profusion of Scottish heather and sedge which abounds here. (see Ranoch and Ness Lakes)

LONELY DOME 63°35'N 134°28'W (105-M). Ten miles east of the south end of Mayo Lake.

Hugh S. Bostock, GSC, named this isolated hill while mapping the area in 1940.

LONER MOUNTAIN 63°32'N 131°58'W (105-O). Between the Rogue and Hess Rivers, in the Rogue Range.

In 1973, Dr. Aro Aho, President of Dynasty Exploration Co. was working in this region. He gave the mountain this name because it was the farthest westward of the Rogue Range.

LONG'S CREEK 61°54'N 140°13'W (115-P). Flows into the Koidern River, near Mile 1150 (KM1851).

This brook was given its name in 1953 to perpetuate the name of Pilot Officer R.W. LONG, RCAF, who was killed in action during the Second World War.

LOOKOUT MOUNTAIN (see Mount Haldane).

LOOTZ LAKE 60°11'N 126°54'W (95-D). Lootz Lake and Creek flow into the Rock River.

Clem LOOTZ, a trapper, lived on the north shore of this lake for a number of years and both the lake and the creek were officially named in 1949. His family still reside at Lower Post, B.C. They spell their name LUTZ.

LORD CREEK 67°33'N 139°09'W (116-O). A tributary to the Porcupine River, near Old Crow.

David LORD, a French-Canadian, was a grand old man in his 80s when he died in Dawson in 1954. A Klondiker, he had lived and trapped with his family in this region for many years. He had lived at New Rampart House and Old Crow since since 1900. He was respected and well liked by all who knew him. (see Annett Creek)

MOUNT LORNE 60°28'N 134°42'W (105-D). On the west side of Marsh Lake.

In 1887, William Ogilvie, DLS, named this landmark after the Right Honourable Sir John Douglas Sutherland Campbell, Marquis of LORNE, who had been Governor-General of Canada from 1878-1883.

The section stop on the WP&YR was named from its proximity to this feature in 1899.

LOST HORSES CREEK 63°56'N 137°08'W (115-P). A tributary to the Little South Klondike River.

In 1947, Hugh S. Bostock's GSC party lost half their pack horses here. The time spent searching for the animals upset their schedule.

LOUIS CREEK 65°01'N 135°22'W (105-E). A tributary to Royal Creek.

This stream was probably named by the GSC about 1950, after LOUIS Brown of Mayo. He was the first big-game outfitter and guide in this region, from 1933-1970.

LOUISE LAKE 60°32'N 137°29'W (115-A). The westernmost of the Kathleen Lakes.

In 1938, George Chambers named this beautiful lake after LOUISE Davis (Mrs. Alex Dickson) who lived alone in this area for some years. The lake tends to be calm and serene and reminded Chambers of Mrs. Davis's disposition. In 1959, she was living in Champagne and had 12 living children, 45 grandchildren and 17 great-grandchildren.

LOVETT GULCH 64°01'N 139°22'W (116-B). The first small tributary from the east on Bonanza Creek, a mile above its mouth.

B.F. LOVETT was very active in the Klondike and had many mining interests. He probably staked this gulch in late 1896. He accumulated much ground on the hill between this little valley and the Klondike River. It was known as LOVETT Hill and proved very rich, with wide stretches of the White Channel gravels. (see Mint Gulch)

LOWELL GLACIER 60°18'N 138°17'W (115-A). Just north of Mount Kennedy.

Bradford Washburn named this feature in 1908 for a former and famous President of Harvard University, Abbott Lawrence LOWELL.

MOUNT LUCANIA 17,150' 61°01'N 140°28'W (115-G). In the Icefield Ranges of the St. Elias Mountains.

On 31 July 1897, Prince Luigi Amadeo, Duke of Abruzzi saw this huge mountain and named it after the Cunard liner on which he and his party crossed the Atlantic Ocean. It was first climbed on 9 July 1937 by Bradford Washburn and Robert H. Bates. (see Mount St. Elias)

LUCKY LAKE 60°02'N 128°35'W (105-A). A small lake near Mile 526 (KM1014) of the Alaska Highway, just south of Watson Lake.

This pond was named by US Army Engineer troops in 1942 during the construction of the Alaska Highway and is still so called. At that time a young woman set up a tent business and clients there referred to transactions as "a change of luck".

The lake is shallow and warms quickly in the summer. It is one of the very few lakes in the area where swimming is possible and comfortable.

LUCKY LAKE 61°30'N 127°22'W (95-E). A narrow lake almost on the Yukon-NWT boundary, on the headwaters of the Coal River.

On 20 August 1968, Dr. E.J. Roots, GSC, was in a small airplane when the engine failed. Their glide barely reached this little lake where they made a safe landing.

LUSK LAKE 66°21'N 135°15'W (106-L). At the headwaters of the Caribou River.

Isaac LUSK was a freighter who carried the mail between Dawson and Minto Bridge for many years. He was also a Yukon Councillor for South Dawson from 1912-15. This lake was given his name in 1973.

LYNX CREEK 63°59'N 135°51'W (105-M). Flows into Haggart Creek.

Originally named "Lick Creek" after a salt lick nearby, the name was corrupted to "Link Creek" and finally to LYNX. Hugh S. Bostock, GSC, was told of this by old miners in the area.

MOUNT MACAULAY 61°13'N 140°31'W (115-G). Just south of Mount Wood, in the Icefield Ranges of the St. Elias Range.

In 1958, this mountain was named after Judge Charles Daniel MACAULAY who served for many years with distinction on the Territorial Bench.

MacAULEY CREEK 60°03'N 135°14'W (105-D). Flows into the west end of the west arm of Lake Bennett.

A good gold prospect was found here in the spring of 1900 by Dr. L.S. Sugden and "Red" Rogers. They were grubstaked by Norman MacAULEY and Thomas O'Brien. MacAULEY was the builder and owner of the Miles Canyon Tramway and proprietor of the Whitehorse Hotel, and had as well many mining interests.

The mountain at the headwaters of the creek, on the Yukon-B.C. boundary was given his name at a later date.

MOUNT MacDONALD 6,750' 63°09'N 135°50'W (105-M). In the McArthur Range.

James MacDONALD, a pioneering prospector, spent his later years (he was in his 70s and 80s) searching for a lost copper mine in this area. The mountain received his name in 1972.

MOUNT MacDONALD 64°44'N 132°47'W (106-C). On the headwaters of Corn Creek.

This peak was officially named in 1973 after a well-known prospector, Allan John "Hardrock" MacDONALD. He explored much of the northern part of the Yukon from 1920-1960.

"Hardrock John" was noted as a musher, once travelling alone in the dead of winter from Mayo to Aklavik in 17 days, a journey seldom equaled.

In 1961, while he was still alive, there were requests to have his name given to a tributary of the Boswell River, which he had prospected. The request was denied. Long after his death his name was given to this mountain. (see Wiley Creek and McDonald Creek)

MACK'S FORK 63°49'N 139°03'W (115-O). A small tributary to Quartz Creek from the east, above Little Blanche Creek.

On 20 August 1897, A. MACK staked a normal sized claim at the mouth of this stream. The stream received his name but for some reason his claim was known afterward as "MACK's Discovery". It was not, for he gave Stewart's Discovery claim above him on Quartz Creek as a reference point when recording his own claim. (see Quartz Creek)

MacKINNON CREEK 62°05'N 139°50'W (115-J). A tributary to the Donjek River, south of Wellesley Lake.

Andrew MacKINNON was a prospector who lived here while he mined and trapped in the area. The name was used locally for many years and was officially adopted in 1953.

MACINTOSH CREEK 61°57'N 137°17'W (115-H). Flows into the Nisling River.

In 1965, G.W. Rowley requested this name after George Whitfield Cameron MACKINTOSH. He joined the NWMP at Prince Edward Island in 1900 and served until 1902 when he took his discharge in Whitehorse. He lived for many years at the Bear Creek trading post and died 29 November 1939, a well respected man.

MOUNT MACLENNAN 64°18'N 138°34'W (116-B). Southeast of Yin Yang Mountain.

This name was proposed by the Yukon Territorial Government to memorialize Archie, Alex, Randolph and John MACLENNAN, brothers and cousins who were pioneers of the Dawson and Mayo districts.

MacMILLAN RIVER 62°52'N 135°54'W (105-L). A major tributary to the Pelly River.

Robert Campbell of the HBC, while on his first journey down the Pelly River in June 1843, named this river after Chief Factor James McMILLAN, who had sponsored his employment with the HBC.

Correct spelling of the name is "McMillan", sometimes spelled "Macmillan" or "M'Millan".

The pass through the Rocky Mountains at the headwaters of the river was found many years before this. It was used by goldseekers in 1897-99 in their efforts to reach Dawson from Edmonton.

MacPHERSON RIVER (see Hyland River).

MacRAE 60°38'N 135°00'W (105-D). Five miles south of Whitehorse.

This small settlement was originally a section point on the WP&YR. Named after Colin MacRAE, a supporter and backer of the WP&YR during its formation and construction. The Alaska Highway contributed to its life and it is now the center of a Whitehorse Industrial Park.

McARTHUR PEAK 14,253' 60°37'N 140°13'W (115-C). About seven miles northeast of Mount Logan.

This peak was named in 1918 after James Joseph McARTHUR, DLS (1856-1925). He was in charge of survey parties of the International Boundary Commission from 1901-1924 and in 1917 was appointed Commissioner and served until 1924.

McARTHUR was one of the surveyors sent to the Yukon by the Department of the Interior in May 1897 to survey the routes to the Klondike. He travelled the Dalton Trail from Pyramid Harbor to the Yukon River and, with a minimum of instrument work, produced a very rough map. He approved the trail as being suitable for either a wagon road or a railroad. It is probable that a railway would have been built on this easier route if the WP&YR had not begun first.

He did further work in the Yukon of a much better quality. Some years after his death a small range of mountains in the south Mayo area where he had worked was named the McARTHUR Range.

McCABE CREEK 62°32'N 139°46'W (115-I). Five miles south of Minto.

After the business establishments and other services in Fort Selkirk had closed their doors, the post office closed in December 1952. The few remaining people moved up the river to where the old Whitehorse-Dawson winter stage road leaves the river near Minto. Here, near the mouth of McCABE Creek, they settled and another post office was opened on 5 December 1953 by Mrs. Alec Coward under the name McCABE Creek. In October 1970 this too was closed as the last remaining people had left.

McCABE had been a trader here in the 1920s-30s and was noted for his highly successful potato crops.

McCANN HILL 64°55'N 141°00'W (116-C). A boundary peak, south of the Tatonduc River.

Named by D.D. Cairnes, GSC, after his assistant W.S. McCANN while they were mapping the geology of the boundary country in 1912.

MOUNT McCLEERY 60°19'N 132°02'W (105-C). At the south end of Englishman's Range.

F.S. Bailey, Forest Warden at Teslin, requested this name in 1954 after Robert McCLEERY, his late admired friend. McCLEERY came in with the Klondike Rush, was a veteran of the First World War and, in 1926, built a trading post at Teslin. He operated this post until 1951. He was also a Justice of the Peace and postmaster at the same time. A small tributary to Fat Creek, across Teslin Lake, carried his name for a few years in the 1920s but was changed to "Grouse Creek". This is a better monument to a fine man. (see Grouse Creek)

McCONNELL LAKE 60°27'N 134°55'R (105-D). Twenty-five miles north of Carcross.

This lake was named after Charles McCONNELL, a '98er who settled at Robinson Station on the WP&YR, near the lake. He was the only postmaster at Robinson from 1905-1915. He died shortly after the Second World War.

McCONNELL PEAK 6,182' 61°19'N 132°25'W (105-F). At the mouth of the McConnell River.

This mountain was named about 1945 after one of Canada's foremost geological explorers, Richard George McCONNELL (1857-1942). Born in Chatham, Quebec, he graduated from McGill University with a BA. He joined the Geological Survey of Canada in 1880. He made an exploratory circuit of the Yukon Territory in 1887-88 which, while more difficult, was overshadowed by that of Dawson at the same time. He spent ten years mapping the geology of the Yukon, especially making the first authoritative study (1901) of the Klondike goldfields and the Whitehorse copper belt. His great work was the solution of the foundation of the Rocky Mountain system. He was the author of many geological reports and maps, many still in use. In 1914, he became Deputy Minister of Mines in the federal government and filled the post with distinction throughout the war years and until 1920. He died in Ottawa on 1 April 1942.

McCONNELL RIVER 61°17'N 132°30'W (105-F). A tributary to the Nisutlin River.

This was the first feature to be named after R.G. McCONNELL, GSC, and was probably designated by Morely Ogilvie, DLS, son of William Ogilvie and at the time assistant to Arthur St. Cyr, DLS, while he was surveying the east side of Teslin Lake in 1897. (see McConnell Peak)

MOUNT McCOUBREY 10,250' 61°13'N 140°05'W (115-G). To the east of the Steele Glacier.

This was named in 1970 after Alexander Addison McCOUBREY (1885-1942), surveyor and past-president of the Alpine Club of Canada (1932-1934).

MOUNT McCULLUM 5,559' 65°28'N 137°35'W (116-H). West of the Blackstone River.

In 1973, this peak was named after the Rev. Creighton McCULLUM, Anglican Minister at Mayo and Dawson in the 1920s-30s. He served as a private soldier in the First World War and as a Chaplain in the Second World War.

MOUNT McDADE 4,918' 62°07'N 137°00'W (115-I). About twenty-three miles west of Carmacks.

This was first called McDADE Hill in 1931 when George McDADE discovered rich silver-lead ore and precipitated a staking rush which uncovered many more potential ore bodies. He and Afe Brown made the first finds on Victoria Creek. The hill was officially named in 1958.

McDONALD CREEK 61°02'N 133°47'W (105-F). A tributary to the Boswell River.

This creek has had this name locally for a number of years. It is the site of the home of Allan "Hardrock John" MacDONALD, an old-time prospector in the area who was noted for his stamina and hardihood.

In 1961, G.W. Rowley, Forest Warden at Teslin, suggested the name be made official. As "Hardrock" was still alive, the request was denied. The creek was renamed "Wiley Creek". Somehow his name was misspelled here as McDonald. (see Wiley Creek and Mount MacDonald)

McDONALD CREEK 60°07'N 134°48'W (105-D). A tributary to Lake Bennett on the eastern shore, ten miles south of Carcross.

An amateur prospector of this name, late for the Gold Rush, staked a claim here on 4 February 1899. He was overly optimistic as no gold has been found on this arm of Lake Bennett.

McDOUGALL PASS 67°43'N 136°26'W (116-P). Through the Continental Divide, between the Bell and Rat Rivers.

In May 1888, William Ogilvie, DLS, named this pass after Junior Chief Trader James McDOUGALL of the HBC. Travelling out of Fort MacPherson in 1872, McDOUGALL was the first white man to discover and map the pass when he was sent by the HBC to find a more feasible route to the Yukon River than via Fort MacPherson and Lapierre House. It is thought that his clerk Thomas Scott was the first white man to actually cross it. It was used by a number of Klondike Stampeders in 1897-98 on their way from Edmonton to Dawson.

McEVOY LAKE 61°48'N 130°14'W (105-G). Northwest of Frances Lake.

Dr. George Mercer Dawson, G&NHSC, while on his survey up the Frances River and on to the Pelly, explored this area at the head of the lake and named this lake after his assistant James McEVOY, BS, ME.

MOUNT McGUIRE 5,116' 67°56'N 137°22'W (116-P). West of the Bell River.

Mr. Justice T.H. McGUIRE, the first Judge of the Court of the Provisional District of the Yukon in 1897 and for a number of years afterward, was commemorated by this designation in 1973.

McINNES HILL 64°07'N 139°24'W (115-B). The hill between Examiner Gulch and Klondike City (South Dawson).

William Oscar Smith on 16 September 1906 found enough gold here to stake a Discovery claim. He named the hill after the then Commissioner of the Yukon Territory, William Wallace Burns McINNES who was born in Dresden, Ontario on 10 April 1871. He was the son of the Hon. T.B. McINNES, Lt. Governor of British Columbia. Graduating in law, he was appointed Commissioner of the Yukon Territory on 27 May 1905 and served until 31 December 1906. He instituted an unpopular regime of government economies, cutting down the number of both civil servants and RNWMP in the Territory. His short term was noted for controversy.

He served eight years as a County Court Judge in Vancouver, B.C. He unsuccessfully ran for political office and eventually died in obscurity.

McINTYRE CREEK 60°46'N 135°06'W (105-D). A tributary to the Yukon River, northwest of Whitehorse.

On 6 July 1898, John McINTYRE of San Bernardino, California, found the first of the high-grade copper ore bodies of the Whitehorse copper belt on this creek, which received his name at this time. His first claim was named the "Copper King". The first shipment of ore from the claim was made in 1900 and contained nine tons of bornite (copper sulphide) grading 46% copper.

In the winter of 1902-03, McINTYRE was in Atlin, B.C. and had contracted to carry the mail from there to Log Cabin on the WP&YR. He and Joseph Abbey left Atlin with the mail carried by dog sled on 25 November 1902. They never arrived at Log Cabin. A long search was made and the dogs, sled and mail were found beneath the ice at Taku Arm by George Coutts and John Fountain. Abbey's body was found in the lake on 28 April and that of McINTYRE was recovered on 14 May 1903.

MOUNT McINTYRE 5,200' 60°37'N 135°08'W (105-D). Seven miles southwest of Whitehorse.

Shortly after his death in 1902, this mountain was named by D.D. Cairnes, GSC, after John McINTYRE.

MOUNT McINTYRE 64°21'N 138°41'W (116-B). Twenty-seven miles northeast of Dawson, and south of Tombstone Mountain.

Named after Angus McINTYRE who came to the Yukon in 1898 and remained until 1942. He was "Foreman of the Ditch" during the construction of the immense, seventy mile long flume and ditch built to bring large quantities of water to the hydraulic workings in the Klondike before the First World War. He died in Kelowna, B.C. in 1950 at the age of ninety.

McKAY HILL 64°22'N 135°23'W (106-D). In the eastern Ogilvie Mountains.

This was named after Thomas McKAY who prospected in this area in the 1920s. He was a Yukon Councillor for the Mayo District around 1929-30.

McKINNON CREEK 63°44'N 139°05'W (115-O). Flows into the Indian River, from the south.

Donald and Archibald McKINNON found and mined gold here from 1898-1900.

They had prospected the rocks in the vicinity and had found gold in the conglomerates. They worked until about 1915 trying to develop what they thought were huge, low-grade gold deposits. The gold values were never good enough to make a mine.

McKINNON LAKE 60°02'N 129°18'W (105-A). On Albert Creek, twenty-five miles west of Watson Lake.

Dan McKINNON trapped and prospected for many years in a wide area around here. He died near Toobally Lakes.

McLAGAN CREEK 63°41'N 136°11'W (115-P). A tributary to Minto Lake.

Miners on this creek in 1902 named it after Jack McLAGAN, the Mining Recorder for the Mayo District.

McLEAN CREEK 64°24'N 135°19'W (106-D). A tributary to Carpenter Creek.

John McLEAN was one of a group who first prospected and found silver-lead ore on Silver Hill, part of Settlemier Ridge, in late 1923.

McLELLAN CREEK 61°55'N 140°51'W (115-G). Empties into a marsh south of the Tchawsahmon Lake.

This creek is known locally as "Coal Creek" as there are a number of seams of lignite along its upper reaches. The creek was named for an early trapper, before 1913.

McLEOD CREEK 63°55'N 135°20'W (105-M). A tributary to Lightning Creek, off Galena Hill in the Mayo district.

Around 1915, Angus McLEOD found a vein of silver-lead ore on the banks of this creek.

M'CLINTOCK LAKES 60°55'N 134°30'W (105-D). A series of small lakes or ponds on the headwaters of the M'Clintock River.

These small lakes were named in November 1897 by Arthur St. Cyr, DLS, when he was surveying a route to the Klondike from Telegraph Creek in B.C. to the south end of Teslin Lake. He had finished his survey and had decided to cross overland from Teslin to Marsh Lake and determine if a trail this way would be feasible. (see M'Clintock River)

M'CLINTOCK RIVER 60°34'N 134°29'W (105-D). This stream flows into the northeast end of Marsh Lake.

Lt. Frederick Schwatka, US Army, named this river in 1883 after the most famous of the early Arctic explorers, Admiral Sir Francis Leopold M'CLINTOCK, RN (1819-1907). It is one of Schwatka's names that Dr. George Mercer Dawson, G&NHSC, allowed to stand.

McMILLAN LAKE 60°31'N 127°55'W (95-D). A mile west of Hulse (Quartz) Lake.

This little lake was named by James Harquail, President of Fort Reliance Minerals Ltd. after a trapper named McMILLAN of Lower Post, B.C. whose cabin still stands at the west end of the lake.

MOUNT McNEIL 60°08'N 135°27'W (105-D). Two miles northeast of Mount Skookum, north of the Wheaton River.

This hill was named in 1911 after Hector McNEIL, a well-known prospector in this district for many years.

McPARLON CREEK 66°05'N 137°56'W (116-I). A tributary to the East Porcupine River.

This stream was chosen in 1973 to commemorate K-98595 Cpl. George Lynn McPARLON, MM, who was killed in action at the storming of Ortona in Italy on 23 December 1943. Lynn McPARLON was born at Waldo, B.C. on 29 June 1912. He enlisted and served with the Seaforth Highlanders of Canada at Vancouver, B.C. on 18 July 1940. Through some error his name was previously spelled as "McParland".

McPARLAND CREEK (see McParlon Creek).

McPHERSON LAKE 61°54'N 129°34'W (105-H). Twenty miles north of Frances Lake.

In August 1840, Robert Campbell of the HBC, while exploring the Frances Lake country and upper Pelly River region, named this lake after Murdoch McPHERSON, Chief Factor of the MacKenzie District at the time.

McQUESTEN 63°33'N 137°24'W (115-P). Near the McQuesten River crossing of the Klondike Highway.

Shortly after the discovery of the fine gold on the Stewart River bars in 1884 the miners chose this spot, near the mouth of the McQUESTEN River, to winter over. A small settlement sprang up. The place later became a roadhouse on the winter stage trail to Dawson from Whitehorse. It was abandoned in the 1950s, but sporadically has been the site of several highway lodges. (see McQuesten River)

McQUESTEN RIVER 63°33'N 137°27'W (115-P). A major tributary to the Stewart River.

Leroy Napoleon "Jack" McQUESTEN was born in 1836 at Litchfield, New Hampshire. As a young man attracted to life in the wilds, he entered the employ of the HBC at Fort Garry in what is now Manitoba. For about two years he worked in the area between Minnesota and Hudson's Bay. Although he was six feet tall and weighed 200 pounds he was disappointed that he could not handle the standard 200 pound packs over the portages as easily as could the much smaller French-Canadian voyageurs.

He went on to California in the early years of that Gold Rush and found prospecting for gold an attractive life. Working his way north, he was on the Fraser River in B.C. when gold was first found there in 1858. He worked at the Gamble Lumber Mill near what is now Vancouver for a short period. Always moving north, he next mined in the Cariboo Country. In 1863, he left Quesnel, B.C. for the Peace River basin and, for the next ten years prospected and traded with the Indians in northeastern B.C. and into Hay River and Lake Athabaska.

In 1871, while wintering with Alfred Mayo at the mouth of the Nelson River, he met Arthur Harper and Frederick Hart. There they learned from the Hudson's Bay men of the American purchase of Alaska and decided to go there.

The parties split up in the spring of 1873 and McQUESTEN and Mayo went down the MacKenzie River to the Peel River which they followed to its headwaters, and traversed McDougall Pass to the Rat River and down the Porcupine to Fort Yukon. They arrived there on 15 August 1873. Arthur Harper and Hart arrived shortly afterward.

After spending the winter on the lower Yukon River and at St. Michaels, they came to a loose working arrangement with the Alaska Commercial Company and purchased a trading outfit from that company. On 20 August 1874 McQUESTEN, Mayo and Frank Barnfield (Bernstein) landed at the site of Fort Reliance (eight miles downriver from Dawson) on the little steamboat Arctic. Here they built their first trading post.

McQUESTEN and Mayo spent the next eight years setting up and operating trading posts along the Yukon River for the Alaska Commercial Company but always prospecting when the opportunity arose. In the winter of 1882-83 eleven miners wintered at Fort Reliance, the first to do so in the Territory. The first miners' meeting to be held in the territory took place and McQUESTEN was elected the first Mining Recorder.

He alternated trading and prospecting and was up the Stewart River in 1885 shortly after the first rich bar gold was found. The miners there at the time gave his name to the first north branch of the river.

Although he was running his trading post at Circle City, Alaska when the Klondike goldfields were found, he grubstaked others and purchased interests in claims on Eldorado and Bonanza Creeks and so participated in the new-found wealth.

He left the Yukon in late 1898 with over $300,000 and built a large home in Berkeley, California for his wife and children. He invested widely in mining interests in California and the west without losing his fortune. When the Alaska Yukon Pacific Exposition was held in Seattle in 1909, he was appointed the official representing the Yukon. While in that city he underwent an operation for bunions, contracting blood poisoning and in a few days the "Father of the Yukon" was dead.

That title had been bestowed upon him by the miners in the Yukon while he was still alive and in business in the Territory. His name was a by-word for integrity and honesty. His trust in his fellow men was unbounded and seldom wrong. Nowhere in the literature of the Yukon is it possible to find a critical or unkind word about him. It is rare anywhere to find a man as highly regarded during his own lifetime as was Jack McQUESTEN. (see Fort Reliance)

McRAE CREEK 63°46'N 136°11'N (115-P). A small tributary to Highet Creek.

J.D. McRAE found placer gold and staked the Discovery claim on this little stream on 24 June 1903, during the rush to the Mayo and Minto finds.

McTAVISH LAKE 60°00'N 128°24'W (105-A). A small lake crossing the Yukon-B.C. boundary, seventeen miles southeast of Watson Lake.

The name of this little lake was officially confirmed as that of the trapper from Lower Post, B.C. whose base camp had been here for many years.

MAGNET HILL 63°57'N 139°21'W (115-O). The hill on the west side of Bonanza Creek, one mile below Adams Gulch.

This hill was the site of some of the earliest high level diggings in the White Channel gravels. Gold was discovered here in the White Channel gravels by J.E. McKenzie in early 1897. He named the hill because of its resemblance to a horseshoe magnet.

MAGNET City, a small community of dwellings, stores, shops and a roadhouse was in place here in early 1897. Mrs. P. Rothweiler started for the Klondike by herself in the fall of 1897 but was caught by weather and spent the winter of 1897-98 at the mouth of the Stewart River. Arriving in Dawson in the spring she bought a dug-out called "Mary's Place" near No. 17 below Discovery on Bonanza Creek, rebuilt it and called it the MAGNET Hotel. From the Daily Klondike Nugget of 22 May 1901: "At 18 below Bonanza, where there was two years ago but a little coffee house, quite a village has been established. Mrs. Rothweiler was the first to see a good business opening, and has now the largest and most complete roadhouse on Bonanza.

At present, there are at this place two big roadhouses, two barbershops, a bathhouse, a butcher shop, two confectionary stores, a blacksmith shop and a laundry. In view of the numerous business places that have lately sprung up it is proposed to call the place "Magnet City"."

MAGNET City was the largest settlement between Grand Forks and Dawson.

The gulch below the hill was discovered and staked on 10 July 1897 by Peter Erussard de Ville.

MAGUNDY RIVER 62°11'N 134°21'W (105-L). Flowing into the east end of Little Salmon Lake.

This area has been the living and trapping grounds of the MAGUNDY family for many, many years.

MAIDEN CREEK 64°23'N 140°38'W (116-C). A tributary to the Fortymile River.

Andrew Jackson MAIDEN was one of the hardy prospectors who followed the trail of gold up the west coast of North America from California to the Yukon. He crossed the Chilkoot Pass in 1884 and in 1886-87 found gold on this creek during the rush to the new, coarse gold finds on the Fortymile River.

Being middle aged in a country where young men were the rule, he was nick-named "Old MAIDEN". He carried a stack of about fifty old newspapers with him on his travels, claiming that they not only improved his mind but were useful in settling arguments. His good character and open heartedness were remarked upon by his peers in a country where these qualities were taken for granted.

George Carmack claimed that Andrew MAIDEN had prospected in the Klondike in 1889 and that he had reported this to the YOOP in Forty Mile. He had found gold but not in what was then considered paying quantities. He returned here in 1896 and, being too late to stake on Bonanza or Eldorado Creeks, found good ground elsewhere. He mined here until 1906-07 when he went to Fairbanks. He died there, a respected pioneer, in 1913, at the age of 76.

MAISY MAY CREEK 63°14'N 138°49'W (115-O). Flows into the Stewart River, from the north.

In 1897, Samuel Henry and his partner Chris Sonnickson took up a homestead at the mouth of this stream and started the Maisie Mae Ranch. They grew 26 tons of hay that year and successfully continued farming for a number of years afterward, until Sonnickson's death sometime later in Klondike City, after which Henry operated the ranch on his own. He specialized in feed for horses in Dawson and the mines. In 1906 he had over 100 acres under cultivation.

The name was first spelled Maisie Mae, then Maizy May.

MOUNT MALASPINA 60°19'N 140°34'W (115-C). Eleven miles east of Mount St. Elias.

A peak in this range was given this name in 1874 by W.H. Dall, USC&GS, after Captain Don Alessandro MALASPINA, Italian navigator and explorer who, while in the service of Spain, explored the northwest coast of North America in 1791.

Professor Israel C. Russell who led an expedition to Mount St. Elias in 1890, wrote that it was impossible to decide to which peak Dall had applied the name of the great navigator, so they gave the name to this peak.

MALCOLM RIVER 69°33'N 139°37'W (117-D). Flows into the Beaufort Sea, about five miles west of Herschel Island.

Sir John Franklin, RN, during his second exploration of the Arctic coast in 1826, named this river after Admiral Sir Pulteney MALCOLM, RN (1768-1838), on 23 July.

MOUNT MALONEY (see Porphyry Peak).

MOUNT MANITOBA 11,150' 60°58'N 140°48'W (115-C). In the Centennial Range of the St. Elias Mountains.

This is one of the 13 previously unnamed and unclimbed peaks in this locality chosen to celebrate Canada's Centennial Year in 1967. (see Centennial Range)

MARGARET LAKE 65°21'N 134°30'W (106-E). Near the junction of Knorr Creek and the Bonnet Plume River.

It is believed that the cabin here was built by A.N. Knorr and his wife Julia Bonnet Plume, an Indian woman from Fort MacPherson. (see Knorr Creek, which shows a different wife. He may have had two at different times)

MARION CREEK 63°09'N 133°26'W (105-N). A tributary to Russell Creek.

In 1902, N.A.D. Armstrong named this stream after his wife. He spelled her name Marian but this may have been misspelled by geographers. She spent 18 months here in 1905-06 with her husband and friends, George and Jessica Leith. Neither woman had ever spent any time outside England and they were completely isolated here for most of the time. (see Jessica and George Creeks and Mounts Gillis and Armstrong)

MARSH LAKE 60°27'N 134°18'W (105-D). Part of the Yukon River system, this twenty mile long lake is about twenty-five miles southeast of Whitehorse.

Originally called "Mud Lake" by the first miners, it was renamed by Lt. Frederick Schwatka, US Army, in 1883 after Professor Othniel Charles MARSH (1831-1899), paleontologist at Yale University from 1866-1899. He was a founder and first President of the National Academy of Sciences for 12 years and was Chief of Vertebrate Paleontology for the USGS from 1881-1899. A wealthy man, he served Yale with no salary and left his entire estate to the University after his death.

MARSHALL CREEK 60°48'N 137°20'W (115-A). A tributary to the Dezadeash River, from the north.

Antoine and Mae Cyr were on their way to the newly found Ruby Creek goldfield in the Shakwak valley when they stopped to examine this stream. They found enough gold to stake a Discovery claim on 6 August 1903. It is thought they named the creek after one of their party.

MOUNT MARTHA BLACK 60°40'N 137°37'W (115-A). In the Auriol Range, about seven miles south of Haines Junction.

This peak was named about 1945 by Hugh S. Bostock, GSC, for Martha Munger BLACK, wife of George BLACK, MP and one time Commissioner of the Yukon Territory. When her husband was forced by ill health to retire from politics she ran for Parliament and was elected. She was a '98er coming into the Yukon in that year and was a leading personality there for the rest of her life. (see Excelsior Creek and Mount George Black)

MOUNT MARTIN 4,460' 60°08'N 124°10'W (95-C). In the extreme southeast corner of the Yukon, just west of the LaBiche River.

In 1963, this mountain was given the name of Major Ivan Harold MARTIN, MID. He was born at Sterling, Ontario on 2 August 1912 and enlisted in the Canadian Army at Chatham, Ontario on 7 December 1939. He served in Canada, Great Britain and Northwest Europe and died of wounds sustained in action on 21 August 1944.

MARY RIVER 60°51'N 133°56'W (105-C). A tributary to the Teslin River.

This stream was probably named by Morely Ogilvie, DLS, in 1897 when he was surveying a route to the Yukon River. Likely after an Indian woman of the place.

The river formed part of the "Portage Trail", an old Indian trail from the Teslin River to Marsh Lake via the M'Clintock River.

MASCOT CREEK 62°47'N 138°25'W (115-J). A tributary to the Yukon River, six miles below the Selwyn River.

Gold was found on this creek in the late fall of 1900 by two French-Canadian prospectors, Achille Massicotte and Albert Leboeuf. When they came to Dawson on 16 February 1901 and recorded their claims it was a Monday. The news got out and the whole creek was staked from end to end by Tuesday night. Massicotte's name was shortened by the Mining Recorder.

MASON HILL 67°25'N 137°40'W (116-P). West of Lapierre House.

This was named after two trapper-prospector brothers Willoughby and Reuben MASON. (see Mason Lake and Rube Creek)

MASON LAKE 66°25'N 138°54'W (116-J). Near the junction of the Fishing and Miners Rivers.

This lake was named by Professor Otto W. Geist of the University of Alaska on 27 November 1958, after the MASON brothers, Willoughby and Reuben. The brothers trapped and prospected this area from 1900 until the 1930s.

Due to a vague location the name was given to the central of the three small lakes. The creek beside the lakes and a few hundred yards to the south is probably MASON Creek. (see Rube Creek)

MASON LANDING 61°26'N 134°39'W (105-E). On the Teslin River, about twenty miles south of Hootalinqua.

This now abandoned settlement was a steamboat landing and supply point for miners on their way to and from the Livingstone Creek goldfields, from 1901-1914. A wagon road led from here to Livingstone. (see Livingstone)

MOUNT MATHESON 60°02'N 134°43'W (105-D). One and a half miles south of Montana Mountain.

This peak is the highest point in the Conrad district. It was named by D.D. Cairnes, GSC, in 1907, after H. MATHESON, who was his assistant and topographer in the area in 1907-08.

MATSON CREEK 63°43'N 140°12'W (115-N). A tributary to the Sixty Mile River.

John MATSON, a Swedish prospector, came into the Yukon in 1898. Discovering gold on this creek in the early years, he remained to mine it until he died and was buried on the claim in 1947.

MATSON's one claim to fame was his marriage on 14 July 1933, to "Klondike Kate" Rockwell, a dance hall entertainer in Dawson in 1898-99 and self-styled "Queen of the Klondike".

The Whitehorse Star of 19 January 1912 stated "The Gold Commissioner has changed the name of the South Fork of the Sixty Mile River on which the discovery was made, to MATSON Creek, after John MATSON, who first prospected and discovered gold on it fourteen years ago".

MAUNOIR BUTTE 61°31'N 135°04'W (105-E). A prominent hill on the east bank of the Yukon River (Thirty Mile River), about ten miles below Lake Laberge.

This landmark, used by riverboat pilots, was named in 1883 by Lt. Frederick Schwatka, US Army, after M. Charles MAUNOIR, Secretary of the Geographical Society of France.

MAY CREEK 61°16'N 135°54'W (105-M). A tributary to the South Big Salmon River, in the Livingstone area.

This is a long known local name after Samuel MAY who prospected this area for many years after 1903.

MAYO 63°36'N 135°54'W (105-M).

This village at the mouth of the Mayo River was started in the winter of 1902-03 after gold was discovered on Duncan, Minto and Hyatt (Highet) Creeks. The founders were Alex Nicol, Ernest Belleveau and J.D. Bell. It contained stores, stables, hotels and a sawmill. As steamboats could navigate the Stewart River from the Yukon, this was a close supply point for the miners. It grew fast enough to have the townsite surveyed in March 1903. Raoul Rinfret laid out a 180 acre townsite. The Keno Hill silver mines increased the traffic by their large ore shipments and the town was an important center for many years. A road was opened in 1949 to connect the town with the Dawson Road. In a few years the riverboats ceased running and the population dwindled to its present small size of around 400 residents.

It was also called MAYO Landing. (see Mayo Lake and River)

MAYO LAKE 63°45'N 135°02'W (105-M). The largest lake in the Mayo district.

Alexander MacDonald of New Brunswick was the first man to explore and prospect the MAYO region. In 1886 or earlier, he named this lake after Captain Alfred S. MAYO (a corruption of Mayhew) a partner of Harper and McQuesten. Together with Frederick Hart, these men were the first to realize the prospecting potential of the upper Yukon River region. The first three utilized trading as a means of supporting themselves while prospecting and because the region was rich in fur, they prospered. They built every trading post from Rampart, Alaska to Fort Selkirk. McQuesten and Harper were the traders, Mayo captained the small steamboat "New Racket", which they had bought from Ed Scheiffelin in 1883; the second one on the Yukon River.

MAYO was born in Maine and in his younger years had been a circus acrobat. He often astounded the natives with displays of his agility. Marrying a native woman, he alone of all the partners spent the rest of his life in the country, dying at Rampart on 17 July 1924.

Alexander MacDonald, the first explorer of this country, left his name nowhere. A solitary traveller, he was the first man to ascend the Beaver River (McQuesten River) and to enter the watersheds of the Peel and Wind Rivers from the south. He was found dead of natural causes in his lone camp on the banks of the Yukon River in 1894.

MAYO RIVER 63°35'N 135°54'W (105-M). A tributary to the Stewart River.

This river was named by William Ogilvie, DLS, after talking to Alexander MacDonald in 1887. He also knew Alfred MAYO well, as he was in charge of the trading post at the mouth of the Stewart River at the time.

MANDER CREEK (see Miller Creek).

MEISTER RIVER 60°19'N 129°28'W (105-A). A tributary to the upper Liard River, from the west.

This stream was known in the 1880s and later as the "Rondeau River". After 1898 the name was forgotten. In 1947 it was given the name of Pte. L. MEISTER, MM, to perpetuate his name. He was from Nova Scotia and was killed in action during the Second World War.

MELOY CREEK 62°42'N 138°48'W (115-J). Flows into Casino Creek, in the Dawson Range.

In 1970, C.D.N."Red" Taylor, P. Eng., named this creek after Jack MELOY, a Yukon prospector for nearly 50 years and the discoverer, among other things, of the porphyry-copper deposits in the Dawson Range. He was born in the state of Washington and spent most of his life in Dawson.

MENDENHALL RIVER 60°45'N 136°02'W (115-A). A tributary to the Takhini River.

This stream was probably named by E.J. Glave, the English explorer with the Frank Leslie Illustrated Newspaper Expeditions of 1890-1891. The name is that of Professor Thomas Corwin MENDENHALL (1841-1924), Superintendent of the US&GS.

The Indian name it supplanted was "Du-chu", meaning "Driftwood Creek", from the amount of wood washed down by spring floods.

MERRICE CREEK 62°23'N 136°35'W (115-I). A tributary to the Yukon River, below Yukon Crossing.

This creek was named in 1898, after Homer MERRICE, who first discovered gold on the stream. In 1908, the name was changed by mistake to "Merrit Creek". which it remained for a number of years until later corrected by the Geographical Board.

MERRIT CREEK (see Merrice Creek).

MYERS CREEK (see Murray Creek).

MOUNT MERVYN 6,387' 64°08'N 133°50'W (106-C). In the west end of the Nadaleen Range.

James H. MERVYN came into the Yukon in 1897-98. He prospected in the Stewart River country for many years and operated the trading post at Lansing from 1912 to the 1930s when an influenza epidemic killed a great many of the Indian population. The survivors moved to Fort Norman, NWT and Lansing Post was abandoned. The MERVYNs moved to Mayo. The son, Norman MERVYN, accompanied James H. Bond, big-game hunter and naturalist to the Wind River country in the summer of 1947. (see Lansing)

MICHELLE CREEK 64°59'N 137°09'W (116-A). A tributary to the Hart River.

This was named on 29 June 1956 by Forest Warden C.J. Shattuck, after an Indian trapper and prospector on this creek around 1910. Not much is known about him.

MOUNT MICHIE 5,830' 60°30'N 134°06'W (105-D). About eight miles east of Marsh Lake.

Lt. Frederick Schwatka, US Army, named this hill in 1883 during his excursion down the Yukon River. It was named after one of his teachers, Professor MICHIE of West Point. MICHIE Creek, named many years later, flows from the mountain to the M'Clintock River.

MICKEY CREEK 64°24'N 140°37'W (116-C). Flows into the Fortymile River, just above its mouth.

This creek was named in late 1886 by or after "MICKEY" O'Brien who was said to be one of the first discoverers of gold on the upper Fortymile River that year, supposedly on Franklin Bar. He is credited by others with finding O'Brien Creek on the Alaska side of the border, the first find of coarse gold in that region.

MIDNIGHT DOME 64°04'N 139°24'W (116-B). The mountain behind Dawson.

From the earliest days this hill was called "Moosehide Hill" or "Dome" and sometimes "Mooseskin Mountain", from the peculiar shape and colour of a rock slide on the side facing the Yukon River. Around 1900, the custom began of picnicking on the summit on the evening and night of 21 June to observe the sun barely setting before it rose again. The event became a yearly tradition and people began to call the hill "The Midnight Dome".

MILES CANYON 60°40'N 135°02'W (105-D). On the Yukon River, two miles south of Whitehorse.

First called "The Grand Canyon" by the early miners, this constriction was renamed by Lt. Frederick Schwatka, US Army, after his superior officer, Brigadier General Nelson A. MILES, Commander of the Department of the Columbia (which included Alaska) of the US Army, on 1 July 1883.

Although MILES CANYON was most awesome in appearance and was approached with apprehension by miners and stampeders, it was the Whitehorse Rapids immediately below which were the more dangerous. Such records as there are show only a dozen deaths by drowning up to 1896 and about the same in the following three years. Most of these were in the rapids.

John MacKenzie, in 1883, is the first man known to have run a boat through MILES CANYON and the Whitehorse Rapids. The narrowness of the channel and the velocity of the current together with the whirlpool halfway through the canyon gave a real spice of danger which made this the highlight of the whole journey to the stampeders.

The canyon and rapids were the one major obstruction to navigation on the whole Yukon River, from the head of Lake Bennett to the Bering Sea. Without them, the largest riverboats could have run freely from Carcross to St. Michaels. The WP&YR could have ended at Carcross, making it the main freight terminal of the region and obviously, making the City of Whitehorse unnecessary.

Several small to medium riverboats ran the canyon and rapids both ways. In July 1907, Fred R. Alley took a raft 132 feet long through safely.

Since the building of the power dam below, the rapids have disappeared and MILES CANYON can be navigated in safety by the smallest craft.

MILES CREEK 61°57'N 140°33'W (115-F). A tributary to the White River.

Frank R. MILES came into the Yukon in 1898. In 1900, he found native (pure) copper on this stream and gave it his name. He died in Kalispell, Montana, in 1912. The ridge along the north side of the creek was given his name many years later.

MOUNT MILLEN 67°28'N 136°25'W (116-P). Northeast of Lapierre House.

Constable Edgar "Spike" MILLEN, RCMP, was born in Belfast, Ireland in 1901 and joined the Force in 1920, volunteering for northern service. He was stationed at Aklavik and in the MacKenzie River Valley, where he was well liked.

He was killed in a gun battle with Albert Johnson, the "Mad Trapper of Rat River" on 30 January 1932, during the greatest manhunt in the history of the northwest. This mountain was named for him in 1973.

MILLER CREEK 61°22'N 134°40'W (105-E). A tributary to the Teslin River, below Mason Landing.

Henry "Hank" Summers came from California to the Yukon country in 1885, one of the first miners here. He mined on the Stewart River, the Fortymile and Sixtymile diggings and made a fortune in the Klondike.

In 1913, he found gold on this creek and when he recorded his claim he called it "Meander Creek". The Mining Recorder, who was Assistant Gold Commissioner R.C. Miller, changed it to his own name.

Summers died in Whitehorse on 6 December that same year.

MILLER CREEK 63°57'N 135°21'W (105-M). Flows from Galena Hill to Cristal Creek.

In 1924-25, Oscar MILLER found a silver-lead ore deposit on the headwaters of this stream and staked the "Dragon" claim.

MILLER CREEK 63°59'N 140°48'W (115-N). Tributary to the Sixty Mile River.

Oliver C. "Three Finger Jack" Miller came into the Yukon in 1883 among the very first prospectors. He travelled far and wide and was the first, or among the first, in three of the most important goldfields to be found here. In late 1891 he found the first payable gold on this creek, which has together with nearby creeks, produced for many years. He was among the first to find the Birch Creek goldfields in Alaska in 1893, which established Circle City. In the Minook district another creek was given his name and he was elected the first Mining Recorder there. Like many since, he seemed more interested in searching for than in mining the gold he found. He was noted for his long and arduous journeys in the Yukon and Alaska.

MOUNT MILLER 4,047' 62°11'N 136°25'W (115-I). Ten miles above Carmacks.

This was named in 1911 for the pioneer coal miner and prospector, Captain Charles E. MILLER, who first developed and mined the coal deposits near Carmacks. MILLER, who was a coal miner from Mauchunk, Pennsylvania, came to the Klondike in 1897. Although George W. Carmack of Bonanza fame had first found coal here about 1893, MILLER was the first to locate on the seams and mine them. (Carmack with Arthur Harper as a partner, had made limited attempts to mine coal at Five Finger Rapids between 1893-95 without success).

Between 1897-1900, MILLER built and operated the riverboats "Clara", "Reindeer" and "Eldorado" as well as building and running the Yukon Sawmill at Dawson City.

He located and mined the Five Fingers Mine in 1900 and the Tantalus Mine in 1903 and in two years produced 40,000 tons of coal for the riverboats. In 1905, he located the Tantalus Butte Coal Mine and estimated 5,000,000 tons of coal reserves. Miller later sold all his interests in the coal measures to the WP&YR. This mine was worked in the more recent past for the Anvil Mining Corp. of Faro.

MILLER'S RIDGE 5,021' 62°07'N 136°32'W (115-I). About fifteen miles west of Carmacks.

In 1960, Hugh S. Bostock, GSC, and Col. Cyril H. Smith, RCE, named this ridge after the late W.H. MILLER, a former Director of the Surveys and Mapping Branch of the Department of Mines and Technical Surveys.

MILLER organized and started the topographical mapping of Canada by Canadians, a task formerly performed by the US Army Engineers. It was on this ridge that he laid out his baseline for the mapping of the Carmacks and Laberge districts.

MILLHAVEN BAY 60°06'N 134°55'W (105-D). The bay on the north shore of Lake Bennett, ten miles west of Carcross.

Here, in the winter and spring of 1897-98, Otto H. Partridge, General Manager of the Bennett Lake and Klondyke Navigation Company, erected a sawmill and shipyard on the west side of the bay. They built the riverboats "Ora", "Flora" and "Nora". These were all taken through Miles Canyon and the Whitehorse Rapids and worked the Whitehorse to Dawson run until 1903. The mill continued to turn out timbers and railroad ties for the WP&YR, as well as the lumber to build Whitehorse.

MILLS CREEK 63°26'N 138°49'W (115-O). A tributary to Blackhills Creek from the west, seven miles from its mouth.

Joseph Victor MILLS found placer gold here and staked the Discovery claim on 26 January 1907.

MOUNT MILTON 62°12'N 136°15'W (115-I). Five miles north of Tantalus Butte.

This small hill was named in 1968, probably by Hugh S. Bostock, GSC, after George H. MILTON, who organized and was General Manager of the Five Fingers Coal Co., which owned all the coal deposits known in the district.

MINERS RANGE 61°09'N 135°41'W (105-E). The range of hills ten miles west of and parallel to Lake Laberge.

Dr. George Mercer Dawson, G&NHSC, on his 1887 journey back to the coast, named these hills after the miners in the Yukon whom he admired and who aided him in his work.

MINTO 62°35'N 136°52'W (115-I). On the east bank of the Yukon River, fifteen miles southwest of Pelly Crossing.

Originally an Indian settlement called "Kitl-ah-gon" meaning "Place Between the High Hills", this village, now almost totally destroyed, was a riverboat stop and a roadhouse on the Whitehorse to Dawson stage road for many years.

Lord MINTO, when Governor General of Canada, visited the Yukon with Lady MINTO in 1900 and it was in his honour that the settlement was given his name.

MINTO CREEK 63°42'N 135°52'W (105-M). The discharge for Minto Lake into the Mayo River.

Many discoveries of gold were made in this general area after the finding of rich gold on Duncan Creek. J.G. Scrivener and P.F. Haggart were two of the most active prospectors of the time. This was one of the gold bearing streams they found, staking the Discovery claim on 19 May 1903. They named the creek after Lord MINTO, Governor General of Canada, who had visited Dawson in 1900. (see Haggart, Highet and Paradise Creeks, also Minto)

MINTON CREEK 63°46'N 136°21'W (115-P). A tributary to Johnson Creek.

This was named in 1957 by Hugh S. Bostock, GSC, after Peter MINTON, who relocated No. 9 below on 21 May 1916 and remained here working the claim for many years. The original discovery of gold had been made by Mike Sed in February 1915.

MINT PUP 63°56'N 138°53'W (115-O). A short, half-mile long brook, flowing into the south side of Hunker Creek.

Gold was discovered here, the Discovery claim staked and the pup named on 7 August 1897 by B.F. Lovett.

This gulch is remarkable because of the enormous numbers of fossil bison and mastodon bones found in the gravels of its bed. The numbers were so great as to suggest that whole herds of these animals had perished in some prehistoric disaster. (see Lovett Gulch)

MIRROR CREEK 62°28'N 140°54'W (115-J). Flows into the Snag River, near Mile 1206 (KM1941).

This creek got its name in 1898 from W.J. Peters and A.H. Brooks of the USGS because of its exceptionally clear water, which is unusual in the region.

MISCHENKO LAKES 64°03'N 138°30'W (116-B). East of the North Klondike River.

These lakes formed part of the water reservoir system of the Yukon Consolidated Gold Corporation in the 1930s. They were used to supply water for hydraulicking operations in the Klondike. They were given the name of the engineer who laid out the plan.

There are three lakes in the group: Trana, Tom O'Hara and Big Lakes. The name was made official in 1979.

MIST LAKE 63°13'N 134°21'W (105-M). Southwest of Big Kalzas Lake.

In 1939, Hugh S. Bostock, GSC, and his party were on pack horses crossing the country to this location. The topographer had missed this lake when he was mapping and the geological crew had to make a long trip around the lake in a snowstorm to get to their camp site. When they suggested the name "Missed Lake", the topographer did not appreciate the irony and compromised on the present name.

MOUNT MOFFAT 61°12'N 140°02'W (115-F). In the Icefield Ranges of the St. Elias Mountains.

This undistinguished peak was named after T.B. MOFFAT (1870-1939), past-president of the Alpine Club of Canada, (1928 -1930). Named by the club in 1970.

MONEY CREEK 61°24'N 129°36'W (105-H). Flowing into the west arm of Frances Lake.

This stream was noted by Dr. George Mercer Dawson, G&NHSC, in 1887, as "Iles Brook", meaning "Salt Lick". These names were forgotten in time and around 1930, Anton MONEY, an English prospector, found gold on the stream and worked it. The name was given by local people at the time.

One of the few men to have a feature in the Yukon bear their name while still alive, MONEY was born in Albury, Surrey, England on 16 September 1900. Educated at Cranleigh he served for two years in the British Army in the First World War. He then studied Mining Engineering. He engaged with the HBC in 1923 and was sent to their post at Telegraph Creek, B.C., on the Stikine River. He soon left their employ and started his life of successful prospecting. From 1929 to 1946 most of his work was in the Frances Lake region. He was most successful in mining placer gold in Half Moon Canyon on the Finlayson River. He went on to more successful mining in the southwestern United States. He published an interesting account of his experiences entitled "This Was The North".

MONITOR CREEK 63°18'N 138°44'W (115-O). A tributary to Black Hills Creek.

This was named in July 1898 by a group of Scandinavians from Minnesota who called themselves the MONITOR Gold Mining and Trading Company. They staked claims here and named the stream but found no payable gold. (see Blueberry Creek)

MOUNT MONOLITH 64°26'N 138°32'W (116-B). In the Tombstone Range, northeast of Dawson.

This difficult peak was first climbed, and probably named, by "Bugs" McKeith in 1975.

MOUNT MONSON 62°08'N 136°24'W (115-I). Six miles northwest of Carmacks.

This was named in April 1911 after Constable MONSON of the NWMP, a long-time Yukoner.

MONSTER RIVER 64°59'N 140°56'W (116-C). A tributary to the Tatonduc River.

Known for years as "Sheep Creek", in 1956 a local name was applied. The people in the area called it the "MONSTER River" because of a transportation accident that happened here.

A transporter called a Snowfreighter, built by the R.G. LeTourneau Corp. of Texas, carrying freight from Eagle, Alaska caught fire and broke down on this creek. It was a huge machine and together with five multi-wheeled trailers was over 300 feet in length. It carried a load of 125 tons cross-country, without a road. The machine itself was 16 feet wide, with 24 wheels.

The machine remained on the creek until 1963 when it was salvaged and taken to Fairbanks, Alaska.

It had made two previous trips across the Yukon to the Dew Line Radar site near the mouth of the MacKenzie River. It was on its third trip when it met disaster. Someone who saw it gave it the name, "The MONSTER" and it stuck.

The official name is still "Sheep Creek" on maps.

MONTANA CREEK 64°01'N 139°24'W (116-B). A tributary to the Yukon River, about six miles above Dawson.

There was a stampede to this creek in January 1897. The original stakers were working for Captain John Jerome Healy, an old Indian fighter, Montana law officer and Manager of the NAT&TC, of Fort Cudahy. Because Captain Healy and most of his men were from MONTANA, they were called the MONTANA Boys, and so the creek got its name.

MONTE CRISTO GULCH 63°59'N 139°22'W (115-O). A tributary to Bonanza Creek, one-half mile above Boulder Creek.

P.H. Hebb and Edward Monohan had worked at the small, rich MONTE CRISTO Gold Mine west of Everett, Washington, before they came to the Klondike. Too late to stake claims on the main streams they turned to this small feeder. Here they found gold showings and staked their first claims on 6 July 1897.

The hill above the gulch was much richer in gold, as the White Channel gravels lay there.

Hebb later prospected many parts of the Yukon and gained the nickname "The Diamond King". (see Dixie Creek)

MONTE CRISTO ISLAND 63°55'N 139°44'W (115-O). A small island in the Yukon River, at the mouth of Garner Creek.

This small island took its name from the riverboat landing and roadhouse at the mouth of Garner Creek which was in business in 1898.

MONTREAL CREEK 63°47'N 139°25'W (115-O). A tributary to the Indian River.

Robert Picotte (whose father staked and mined No. 17 on Eldorado Creek) found the first gold here and staked the Discovery claim on 3 July 1901. He named it after his home town in Quebec.

MONUMENT ISLAND 60°01'N 134°54'W (105-D). A small island on the east side of Bennett Lake, near the Yukon-B.C. boundary.

Inspector Constantine and Staff Sergeant Charles Brown of the NWMP, the first of the Force to enter the Yukon, are said to have built their boat here in 1894. Stories of the time claim that when the first, rough survey of the Yukon-B.C. boundary was made, a temporary boundary marker, or monument, was set on this little island.

MOONEY CREEK 60°10'N 125°04'W (95-C). A tributary to Larsen Creek

In 1963, this creek was chosen to commemorate the name of Honourary Captain Thomas Edmund MOONEY, MID. He was born on 21 January 1906 at Westport, Ontario and was appointed to the Canadian Army as a Chaplain on 10 January 1942. He served in Canada, Great Britain and northwest Europe and was killed in action on 14 September 1944.

MOOSEHORN RANGE 63°07'N 140°58'W (115-N). A fourteen mile long ridge extending across the Yukon-Alaska boundary, south of the Ladue River.

This ridge was originally named "Moosehorn Mountain" by A.H. Brooks and W.J. Peters, USGS, while they were on their expedition up the White River to the Tanana in 1898.

MORLEY RIVER 60°06'N 132°29'W (105-C). Flows into the southwest corner of Teslin Lake.

In the spring of 1897, Arthur St. Cyr, DLS, of the Department of the Interior was given the task of finding and surveying a feasible wagon road or railway route from Telegraph Creek, B.C. on the Stikine River, to the head of Teslin Lake. He was also placed in charge of other surveyors engaged in defining the boundary between the Yukon and British Columbia. His assistant on the Telegraph Creek-Teslin Lake survey was W. MORLEY Ogilvie, DLS, the son of William Ogilvie, DLS.

They quickly found and surveyed a trail to the head of Teslin Lake. St. Cyr then set out for Tagish Lake and Bennett to oversee the boundary survey. MORLEY Ogilvie was instructed to survey the east shore of Teslin Lake and continue down the Teslin River to its junction with the Yukon (Lewes) River. Ogilvie carried out this task successfully and St. Cyr afterward named this river, near his starting point, for him.

Ogilvie went on to spend some years as a government surveyor in and around Dawson. By 1908 he was associated with his father as field superintendent of the Yukon Basin Gold Dredging Co. on the Stewart River. His father was president of the Company.

The names MORLEY Bay, Lake and Mount were added in the period 1930-1955. The settlement, lodge, restaurant and gasoline station were started about 1943-44 by Clyde Wann, one of the first bush pilots in the Yukon. (see Mount Wann)

MORRIS LAKE 60°27'N 131°40'W (105-B). At the head of Morley River.

Jake MORRIS, an Indian trapper, had his cabin on this lake around 1900 and for many years after.

MORRISON CREEK 63°50'N 136°06'W (115-P). A tributary to Seattle Creek.

This stream was named in the early 1900s by Hector MORRISON. Born in Zorra, Ontario in 1856, he came to the Yukon in 1894. In 1911, he found a rich deposit of silver-lead ore in Gambler's Gulch on Keno Hill. He later sold his holdings to Keno Mines and retired to Vancouver, B.C. where he died in 1930. (see Galena Creek)

MOUNT MORRISON 64°43'N 140°54'W (116-G). Two miles north of the Yukon River, just east of the Yukon-Alaska boundary.

This was called MORISON PEAK by William Ogilvie, DLS, in 1887, after a member of his survey party, William T. MORISON of Ormiston, Quebec. He worked for Ogilvie for five or six years in the Yukon, B.C. and NWT, all on exploratory surveys. After leaving Ogilvie's employ he entered theological school and became a Presbyterian Minister, serving for many years in Montreal. He died in May 1951 at age 87. The name was misspelled by map-makers.

MORSE CREEK 60°03'N 135°51'W (105-D). A tributary to Lake Bennett, just south of Dundalk Siding on the WP&YR.

An over optimistic and over enthusiastic cheechako (greenhorn, newcomer) mistook mica for gold and precipitated a small staking stampede on this brook. Richard S. MORSE was the instigator when he staked a Discovery claim and announced his find on 24 June 1899. The claim and the name were soon forgotten. The creek was later named "Knob Creek".

MOSES HILL 67°19'N 136°48'W (116-P). South of the Rat River.

This hill was named in 1973 after John MOSES. He was the Indian Special Constable who drove dog teams for the RCMP in their hunt for Albert Johnson, "The Mad Trapper", in 1932. (see Mount Sittichinli)

MOSQUITO GULCH 63°58'N 139°21'W (115-O). Flows into Bonanza Creek, opposite Boulder Creek.

A discovery claim was staked here on 1 September 1897 by L.W. Steele. The creek had been staked and named earlier, in June, but abandoned and not recorded.

MOUNTAIN INDIAN RIVER (see Firth River).

MUNROE LAKE 60°01'N 135°00'W (105-D). South of the west arm of Lake Bennett.

Alexander MUNROE was the best axeman on Arthur St. Cyr's boundary survey crew in 1899-1900. He broke his leg near here and St. Cyr named the lake after him in 1901. He named the peak on the east side of the lake, MUNROE PEAK (6,735'), at the same time.

MURRAY CREEK 62°09'N 139°22'W (115-I). A tributary to the Yukon River, from the west.

The creek was named before the turn of the century but since there was no gold found, the man who staked and named it quickly abandoned it.

The creek has been known for years by local people as "Myers Creek". Myers was a woodcutter who provided fuel for the WP&YR riverboats for many years. His cabin is at the mouth of the stream. He came into the country from Cordova, Alaska during the Chisana rush of 1913.

MURRAY CREEK 63°45'N 133°22'W (105-N). A tributary to the Stewart River, above Lansing.

"Mike" MURRAY prospected this region and the Rogue River country for many years in the early 1900s. For a number of those years he was the only white man in the region, with the exception of Frank Braine and Percy Nash, the traders at Lansing.

MURRAY CREEK 61°36'N 139°40'W (115-G). A tributary to the Donjek River.

This stream was named about 1903-04 after T.T. MURRAY who was a long-time prospector in this area and who found gold on this creek and mined it.

MOUNT MURRAY 7,093' 60°53'N 128°49'W (105-A). Twenty miles northeast of Simpson Lake, in the Logan Mountains.

The original name of this hill was "Tent Peak", given by Dr. George Mercer Dawson, G&NHSC in 1887, because of its shape. The name was regarded as redundant by the Geographical Board in 1949. They then changed it to the name of Alexander MURRAY (1810-1884), assistant to Sir William E. Logan the first Director of the Geological and Natural History Survey of Canada.

MUSH CREEK 60°18'N 137°29'W (115-A). Flows into Mush Lake.

The discovery of coarse gold in the summer of 1902 by M.I. Christner led to a staking rush to this and other nearby streams. Christner had been prospecting this area since early 1900.

MUSSELL GLACIER 60°42'N 140°54'W (115-C). A branch of the Ogilvie Glacier, in the St. Elias Range.

This feature was named in 1966 after H.S. MUSSELL, DLS, who was in charge of the International Boundary Survey party for Canada from 1910-1912.

MOUNT MYE 6,763' 62°19'N 133°01'W (105-K). Twelve miles northeast of Faro.

J.R. Johnson, GSC, named this peak in 1935 after his fiancee Myrtle "MYE" Hay. He used her nickname as it resembled that of an old trapper-prospector who lived in the area years before.

MYERS CREEK (see Murray Creek).

NADALEEN RIVER 63°58'N 133°40'W (105-N). A major tributary to the Stewart River.

In 1885, this stream was named the "Boswell River" after the first miners to see it, Thomas Boswell and perhaps his brother George, who were from Peterborough, Ontario.

About 1905, because the original name had been forgotten, or because there was another Boswell River in the Big Salmon country, the name NADALEEN was adopted. It is supposed to be an Indian name. (see Boswell River)

NAHONI RANGE 65°40'N 139°15'W (115-G). At the headwaters of the Porcupine River.

In April 1888, William Ogilvie, DLS, named these mountains because he believed them to be the home of the NAHONI (Nahanni) Indians.

NANSEN CREEK 61°59'N 137°12'W (115-H). A tributary to the Nisling River.

Captain Henry Seymour Back and his prospecting party discovered gold on this creek in July 1899, but did not work it. He returned to the region with a larger party in 1907. Re-examining the creek they found prospects worth working and the Discovery claim was staked by his son, Frank H. Back, and Tom E. Bee on 13 June 1910.

Captain Back named the stream in honour of the famous Norwegian Arctic explorer, Fridtjof NANSEN. (see Mount Nansen)

MOUNT NANSEN 5,593' 62°06'N 137°18'W (115-I). At the headwaters of Nansen Creek.

MOUNT NANSEN overlooks a richly mineralized area which was discovered by Captain Henry Seymour Back, an outstanding pioneer. He gained his rank in the American Civil War and, moving west, became an Army scout and Indian fighter, later a trader and prospector. He came into the Klondike in 1897 where he was successful. This area came to his attention in 1899. Attracted by stories of richer finds he went on to Alaska. In 1907, he returned with a large party of seven or eight men including his son Frank. They prospected the region intensively until about 1920. He was then over 80 years old. He and his men found gold and named many of the streams in this area, including this mountain, which is named after Fridtjof NANSEN, the famed Norwegian Arctic explorer.

His son, Frank H. Back, remained in the country after his father died. He continued prospecting and, in 1917, owned and operated a black fox fur farm at Carmacks. (see Discovery, Back, Hobo and Seymour Creeks)

NARCHILLA BROOK 61°51'N 129°36'W (105-H). Flows into the foot of McPherson Lake.

Warburton Pike, the English sportsman and explorer, named this stream in 1893 after his guide and companion, a Frances Lake Indian.

NARES LAKE 60°10'N 134°40'W (105-D). A small lake joining Bennett and Tagish Lakes.

Called "Moose Lake" by the earliest miners, this lake was renamed by Lt. Frederick Schwatka, US Army, in 1883, after Vice Admiral Sir George Strong NARES, RN, a famous English Arctic explorer. The mountain immediately to the northeast of the lake was also named later for NARES.

NASH CREEK 64°36'N 134°30'W (106-D). A tributary to the Wind River.

Percival NASH, prospector and trader in this area, was a partner of Frank Braine when they operated the trading post at Lansing in the early 1900s. (see Lansing)

NASRII HILL 66°39'N 135°00'W (106-L). A mountain west of the Peel River, above its junction with the Trail River.

This is a Loucheaux Indian word meaning "Clear, Barren Hill". This hill has little vegetation and was a landmark on the old Indian trail between Fort MacPherson and the central Yukon.

NATAZHAT GLACIER 61°34'N 140°54'W (115-P). A small glacier on the northwest of the St. Elias Range.

This name was reported in 1912 by Thomas Riggs, Jr., of the US International Boundary Survey. The Indian name was reported without translation by C. Willard Hayes, USGS, in 1890.

NATION RIVER 65°31'N 141°00'W (116-F). A tributary to the Yukon River, in Alaska.

This river was first noted by Lt. Frederick Schwatka, US Army, in 1883, who called it "Tahkandik". J.E. Spurr, USGS, in 1896 reported it as "Tahkandit". At the same time F.C. Schrader, USGS, noted that the early miners had already named it the NATION River. None reported a translation of the Indian name.

The stream had some notice in 1897-98 because of a coal seam found near its mouth.

NEECHEE LUK LAKE 66°54'N 134°52'W (106-L). Near Three Cabin Creek, west of Peel River.

This name is a Loucheaux Indian word meaning "Fish Out From River Lake". This refers to the numbers of grayling gathered at the mouth of the creek entering the lake; a good supply of food. The creek has the same name as the lake.

NELSON CREEK 63°37'N 134°45'W (115-M). A tributary to Mayo Lake, at the east end.

Rich placer gold was found here in 1916 by two prospectors known only as "Big Steve" and "Little Steve". One of them was surnamed NELSON.

NELSON CREEK (see Haggart Creek).

NESHAM GLACIER 61°23'N 140°51'W (115-F). A branch of the huge Klutlan Glacier.

In 1916, this name was given after E.W. NESHAM, DLS, a British member of the International Boundary Survey party of 1915.

NESKATAHIN 60°08'N 137°03'W (115-A). Three miles north of Dalton Post.

This is the site of an ancient Indian village. Occupied long before any white men saw it. It was an important meeting place for trade between the interior and coast Indians.

The first white men known to have visited were Jack Dalton and E.J. Glave of the Frank Leslie Illustrated Newspaper Expedition in 1891. Dalton realized the potential of the place and the availability of winter feed for stock and set up Dalton Post three miles below the village.

For many years the name was given as "Neskateheen" and as "Weskatahin". The miners used the accepted name. The beautiful lake nearby was given the name of the village. No translation of the name was ever recorded.

NESS LAKE 64°49'N 138°13'W (116-B). Northwest of Lomond Lake.

Given in conjunction with Lomond Lake. (see Lomond and Ranoch Lakes)

NETRO MOUNTAIN 65°10'N 137°17'W (116-H). In the Ogilvie Mountains, west of the Hart River.

Named after Joe NETRO, a well-known and long established trader in Old Crow.

Netro is a Vanta Kutchin Indian word meaning "Wolverine".

MOUNT NEVIN 60°00'N 136°10'W (115-A). Marks the boundary between the Yukon and British Columbia.

James NEVIN Wallace, DLS (1870-1941), surveyed this mountain in 1908. It was the highest peak he had crossed in two survey seasons and he had personally made more ascents than any other boundary surveyor up to that time. He was engaged in such surveys from 1907-1914.

NEWBAUER CREEK 62°02'N 137°12'W (115-I). A small tributary to Nansen Creek.

A long known local name after the prospector who worked here and in the general area from 1910-1915. The name was officially adopted in 1968.

MOUNT NEW BRUNSWICK 11,115' 60°56'N 140°40'W (115-C). In the Centennial Range of the St. Elias Mountains.

This mountain was named to celebrate Canada's Centennial Year, 1967. (see Centennial Range)

MOUNT NEWFOUNDLAND 12,040' 60°58'N 140°33'W (115-C). In the Centennial Range of the St. Elias Mountains.

This mountain was named to celebrate Canada's Centennial Year, 1967. (see Centennial Range)

MOUNT NEWTON 13,811' 60°19'N 140°52'W (115-C). In the southwest corner of the St. Elias Range.

Professor Israel C. Russell named this mountain when he mapped it with the National Geographical Society and USGS Expedition in 1890, after Professor Henry NEWTON of the Columbia School of Mines and the USGS.

Until 1964, this was the highest unclimbed peak in North America. In that year it was climbed by the Blanchard-Eichom party.

NEW ZEALAND CREEK (see Printers Creek).

NIDDERY LAKE 63°17'N 131°20'W (105-O). A small lake south of the Hess River.

Norman NIDDERY was a trapper and prospector in this area for many years. In 1946, Bernard J. Woodruff of the Geodetic Survey of Canada proposed this name in gratitude for NIDDERY's help and information about the region. (see Fido and Senoah Creeks)

NIGGERHEAD LAKES (see Enger Lakes).

NIGGERHEAD MOUNTAIN (see Eikland Mountain).

NIGGER JIM'S GULCH 63°55'N 139°15'W (115-O). A tributary to Bonanza Creek, two miles above Grand Forks.

James "Nigger Jim" Daugherty was from Virginia and gained his nickname from his accent. He was a famous figure in the Klondike and many stories were written about him. He was especially noted as a stampeder. He discovered gold and staked this little stream on 4 December 1897.

NIHTAL GIT CREEK 65°59'N 134°35'W (106-E). A tributary to the Peel River.

Formerly called "Calamites Creek" this stream reverted to its original Indian name. The name is a Loucheaux Indian word meaning "Glacier Among the Trees or Brush".

NISUTLIN RIVER 60°14'N 132°34'W (105-C). The major tributary to Teslin Lake, from the northeast.

This name was known from the earliest times. It is a Tlingit Indian word meaning "Quiet Water". It was probably first applied to the large and beautiful NISUTLIN Bay.

NOBLE CREEK 64°10'N 139°15'W (116-B). A tributary to Lepine Creek, ten miles northeast of Dawson.

George NOBLE, an early Yukoner, staked the first claim on this creek and named it. His brother, who worked in the Gold Office in Dawson, was known as "Colonel Bill".

NOGOLD CREEK 63°26'N 139°06'W (105-M). A tributary to the Stewart River, at Horseshoe Slough.

This was named by miners in 1895 who found gold colours here, but not enough to pay.

NOISY CREEK 65°53'N 134°56'W (106-E). A tributary to the Bonnet Plume River.

This is a literal translation of the Loucheaux Indian name which more fully translates as "Waterfowl Making Noise Creek". It is evidently a large nesting area.

MOUNT NOLAN 4,566' 63°59'N 140°36'W (115-N). South of the Sixty Mile River.

This was called "Dog Tooth Mountain" by the early miners on the Sixtymile creeks in the 1890s. The name was changed by the GSC in 1920. They named it after the Manager of the NAT&TC at the time.

NORDENSKIOLD RIVER 62°06'N 136°18'W (115-H). Flows into the Yukon River, at Carmacks.

This was called "Thuch-en-Dituh" meaning "Meeting Place" by the Indians who lived here. The Chilkat Indians met the interior Indians here to trade every year. The route the Chilkats used from the coast became the Dalton Trail, later the Haines Highway. Carmacks was the northern terminus of the trail.

In 1883, Lt. Frederick Schwatka, US Army, named this river after Baron Nils Adolf Erik NORDENSKIOLD (1832-1901), the famous Swedish Arctic explorer and geologist, who made the first passage northeast of the European and Asian continents in his ship the "Vega", in 1878-79.

NORDLING CREEK 64°09'N 138°32'W (116B). Flows into the North Klondike River.

Named in 1979 to commemorate Otto NORDLING. Born in 1910 in Sweden he came to Canada as a boy. He became prominent in the community life of Dawson and the Yukon. He died in 1975 in Vancouver, B.C.

NORTH CROOKED CREEK 63°16'N 136°31'W (115-P). Flows into the Stewart River, at Stewart Crossing.

Named by the Geographical Board in 1941, the only claim to distinction held by this stream is that neither of the local names was officially adopted. "Hardrock MacDonald" and "Hotstove" Douglas lived and worked here and no one called the creek Crooked. Both of these old timers were alive when it was proposed to make the name(s) official, so they were rejected. (see Mount MacDonald)

NORTHERN LAKE 62°48'N 133°44'W (105-F). Between the Salmon and Big Salmon Rivers.

Although this appears to be a descriptive name in fact it is the name of a brave Canadian. J-14566 Flight Lt. Edward NORTHERN, DFC, was born 7 December 1917 in Sheffield, England and enlisted in the RCAF at Toronto, Ontario, on 10 September 1941. He was missing from air operations on 1 May 1944 and was presumed killed in action.

MOUNT NORTHWEST 10,550' 60°59'N 140°54'W (115-C). In the Centennial Range of the St. Elias Mountains.

This was named in 1967, after the Northwest Territories to celebrate Canada's Centennial Year. (see Centennial Range)

NOTHLA HILL 67°37'N 139°17'W (116-O). Northeast of Tack Lake.

This name was supplied by Joe Netro of Old Crow. It is a Loucheaux Indian word meaning "Little Hill".

MOUNT NOVA SCOTIA 10,800' 60°56'N 140°29'W (115-C). In the Centennial Range of the St. Elias Mountains.

This was named in Canada's Centennial Year, 1967. (see Centennial Range)

NUGGET GULCH 63°53'N 139°17'W (115-O). A tributary to Eldorado Creek, two and one-half miles above Grand Forks.

Archie Shelp found good gold and staked the No. 1 claim here on 12 July 1897.

NUKON CREEK 67°04'N 137°40'W (116-P). A tributary to the Porcupine River.

This comes from the Loucheaux Indian words "Nagwan, his Creek", after the man who lived there many years ago. The NUKON family still live in the Old Crow area and are very active in sports and politics.

NUTZOTIN MOUNTAINS 62°10'N 141°30'W (115-K). In the north Kluane district.

In 1898, A.H. Brooks and W.J. Peters of the USGS explored the upper White River country.

They wrote:

> "These snow-clad mountains, which seem to be distinct from the St. Elias Chain, we have called the NUTZOTIN Mountains. After the NUTZOTIN Indians of the region".

O'BRIEN CREEK 62°38'N 140°04'W (115-K). A tributary to the White River, four miles above Donjek City.

This creek was named when Antoine Boulay staked the Discovery claim on 1 November 1913. He worked for, or was grubstaked by, Thomas O'Brien, the old Fortymiler and Klondike millionaire. Boulay found the gold on this stream when he prospected it while on his way to the new goldfields in the Chisana district in Alaska. (see Brewery Creek)

OBSERVATION MOUNTAIN 60°50'N 138°42'W (115-B). At the junction of the Slim's River and Kaskawulsh Glacier.

In June 1952, J.O. Wheeler, GSC, mapped this area using bearings from this hill to place other features nearby. A. Cameron Ogilvy of Whitehorse, a student engineer assisting Wheeler at the time, carried the transit to the summit and suggested the name.

O'CONNOR RIVER (see Kaskawulsh River).

ODIN CREEK 63°04'N 138°20'W (115-O). A tributary to Walhalla Creek, one-half mile below Alberta Creek.

"Cap" Hansen discovered gold and staked the Discovery claim in late 1898. He named the creek after his home town, ODIN, New Brunswick.

OGILVIE 63°34'N 139°45'W (115-O).

In the summer of 1894, Arthur Harper and Joseph Ladue set up a trading post on this large island in the Yukon River, opposite the mouth of the Sixty Mile River. They were taking advantage of the increased activity in the Sixtymile goldfields.

At first it was called "Sixtymile Post" but Harper and Ladue named it after William OGILVIE, DLS, of the Department of the Interior, who had surveyed the Yukon-Alaska boundary line in the Fortymile district, settled miners disputes and was the only government official visible at the time.

Ladue built and ran the first sawmill in the Yukon at this place. The post was abandoned shortly after the discovery of gold in the Klondike. (see Ogilvie Mountains)

OGILVIE MOUNTAINS 64°35'N 138°15'W (116-B). North of Dawson and encompassing the headwaters of the Ogilvie and Porcupine Rivers.

In 1966, this range of mountains was named by the Government of Canada to honour one of Canada's most outstanding men.

William OGILVIE was born in Ottawa, Upper Canada, on 7 April 1846, the son of James OGILIVIE and Margaret Halliday. He was educated in Ottawa and in 1869 was admitted to practice as a Provincial and Dominion Land Surveyor. He later became a Dominion Topographical Surveyor, passing one of the most exacting survey examinations in the world.

Between 1875-1898, he carried out many surveys and explorations in the Canadian west, the most notable of these being the first survey of the Yukon-Alaska boundary in the Fortymile district in 1887-88 and his initial surveys in the Klondike goldfields and the Dawson townsite in 1896. At this time he was the only representative of the Canadian Government (with the exception of Inspector Constantine) in the Territory, but his reputation for honesty, integrity and impartiality was such that his unofficial decisions were accepted by all.

In September 1898, he was made Commissioner of the Yukon Territory, replacing Major James Walsh, and in April 1901 he resigned. A contemporary said of him at the time: "He brought order out of chaos".

In June 1901, while on his way home to Ottawa, he went up the Yukon River on the riverboat "Susie". Leaving Skagway, Alaska, he visited Nome and, while there, rescued a young lady, a Miss Richardson, from drowning. A short time later he married her at her home in Paris, Texas. She was his second wife.

In 1908, he returned briefly to the Yukon as President of the Yukon Basin Gold Dredging Company which held extensive leases on the Stewart River. It operated with indifferent success until 1912.

William OGILVIE died in Winnipeg, Manitoba on 13 November 1912.

OGILVIE RIVER 65°51'N 137°15'W (116-H). The north branch of the Peel River.

This river was named by the Dominion Geographer, J. Johnston, in 1888 to honour William OGILVIE's great exploratory work.

OGILVIE VALLEY 61°25'N 135°18'W (105-E). The valley extending northwest from the foot of Lake Laberge to Coghlan Lake.

In 1887, Dr. George Mercer Dawson, G&NHSC, named this feature after William OGILVIE, DLS, of the Department of the Interior who carried the first accurate survey from the Lynn Canal into the interior of the Yukon Territory and gave the GSC its accurate base for geological mapping.

O.K. CREEK 64°01'N 139°31'W (116-B). Flows into the Yukon River from the northeast, five miles above Dawson.

Joseph Pellerin found the first gold and staked a Discovery claim here on 19 January 1898. He renamed it O.K. CREEK (it had formerly been called "Six Mile Creek").

OLD CROW 67°34'N 139°51'W (116-O). On the Porcupine River.

This settlement of Loucheaux Indians has been in existence since 1911. Their forefathers had lived around old Fort Yukon, established in 1847 by Alexander Hunter Murray of the HBC, at the confluence of the Porcupine and Yukon Rivers. When the HBC was driven from American territory in Alaska in 1869 the Indians, priding themselves on being "King George men" not "Boston men", moved with the Company to Old Rampart House, further up the Porcupine River and thought to be on Canadian soil. Again the post was found to be in American territory and again it was moved. The new site was called New Rampart House. In 1911, the population was devastated by an epidemic of smallpox. The survivors burned the post and moved again, this time to the junction of the Porcupine River with the Crow River.

The new settlement took its name from a noted chief of the old days, "Te-Tshini Gevtik", meaning "Walking Crow". He died in the 1870s, leaving his people a legacy of high standards and moral principles which have persisted to modern times. The settlement is in the center of the most prolific muskrat breeding grounds in the entire northwest, if not in all of Canada. In 1955, Father J.M. Mouchet of the Oblate Fathers, introduced skiing to the native people and in 20 years, some of Canada's finest young cross-country skiers have developed here.

Edith Josie, long an OLD CROW resident, has for many years contributed one of the most colourful newspaper columns in Canada, to the Whitehorse Star, which focuses on life in and around OLD CROW, written in a style all her own.

The OLD CROW Mountains north of the town and the river, were all named after the same Chief, "Walking Crow". The word Crow here refers to the northern raven, as true crows are unknown this far north.

OLD DANGER CREEK (see Danger Creek).

OLD TRAIL CREEK 63°26'N 137°49'W (115-P). A tributary to Lake Creek.

This name was suggested by the GSC in 1949, as the old trail from Stevens Roadhouse to Stewart Crossing followed this stream.

OLD WOMAN ROCK 64°31'N 140°29'W (116-C). On the Yukon River, fifteen miles below Forty Mile.

This is an Indian name known to the early miners. OLD WOMAN ROCK is on the east side of the River and Old Man Rock on the west side. The names are from an old Indian legend.

Lt. Frederick Schwatka, US Army, on his raft voyage down the Yukon in 1883, renamed these the "Rocqette Rocks" after M. Alexander de la Rocqette of the Paris Geographical Society. The name was never accepted or used.

MOUNT OLIVER WHEELER 61°12'N 140°08'W (115-F). East of the Steele Glacier, in the St. Elias Range.

In November 1970, the Alpine Club of Canada named this mountain after Sir Edward OLIVER WHEELER, KB, MC, Leg. Hon., RE (1890-1962), engineer and surveyor. He was president of the club from 1950-1954.

O'NEIL GULCH 63°55'N 139°14'W (115-O). A small valley leading into Bonanza Creek, three miles above Grand Forks.

John King staked a Discovery claim here and recorded it on 7 July 1897. It had previously been staked by a prospector named O'Neil but he had abandoned it, leaving his name on the gulch.

MOUNT ONTARIO 12,200' 60°58'N 140°44'W (115-C). In the Centennial Range of the St. Elias Mountains.

This mountain was named in 1967, to honour the province of ONTARIO during Canada's Centennial Year. (see Centennial Range)

OPHIR CREEK 63°46'N 139°20"W (115-O). A small stream flowing into Indian River, from the north.

Alexander MacDonald, Scottish mining engineer and author, named this creek in the winter of 1897 when he found good prospects of gold on it. The name OPHIR is that of the legendary place in Africa where the Queen of Sheba got her vast riches in gold and is synonymous with the idea of untold wealth.

MacDonald (not to be confused with "Big Alex" McDonald) returned to Scotland in early 1898 and wrote some vivid and highly coloured accounts of his adventures in the Klondike, including gunfights and battles with the Indians, for various newspapers. He prospected in Africa and Australia and wrote several fictionalized accounts of his travels and adventures.

ORA GRANDE GULCH 63°53'N 139°17'W (115-O). A short stream entering Eldorado Creek from the northeast, opposite Nugget Gulch.

Ransom Noblett named this gulch in Spanish for "Big Gold" on 27 September 1897. It did not live up to its name.

ORCA COVE 69°34'N 139°15'W (117-D). A small bay on the west side of Herschel Island.

This bay was named by Lt. Commander Stockton of the "USS Thetis", when he surveyed the coast of Herschel Island in 1889. He named it after the whaler "ORCA" which was in the bay at the time.

ORCHAY RIVER 62°07'N 132°55'W (105-J). A tributary to the Pelly River.

In June 1843, this stream was named by Robert Campbell, HBC, during his major journey of exploration down the Pelly River. It was named after a river of the same name in his native Perthshire, Scotland.

ORTELL'S CROSSING 63°49'N 136°23'W (115-P). On the Stewart River at Johnson Creek.

ORTELL'S CROSSING was on the trail which ran from the Stewart River, along Johnson Creek and down Highet Creek to Minto Creek and Mayo. It was first used by miners in the early 1900s to carry supplies to the new diggings on Highet and surrounding creeks. It was so named because George L. ORTELL had lived for many years near the head of Johnson Creek, at one time the only person in the area.

He came into this part of the country shortly after 1900 and spent the rest of his life near here. Well-known and highly respected for his abilities as a bushman and trapper, he assisted Joseph Keele, GSC, with his exploration and mapping of the upper Stewart country.

He died on 3 April 1943, in St. Mary's Hospital in Dawson. The manner of his death was a display of stark courage and endurance. About the end of February 1943 he froze his hands on a trip to Highet Creek, the temperature at the time being -61°F. He stopped at the cabin of a friend, Joe Laska, who convinced him to remain there while Laska went to Mayo for help. Laska, himself in his early 70s, was persuaded when he reached Minto Bridge, to rest while the roadhouse keeper arranged for someone else to go for ORTELL. Contacting the RCMP it was found that every dog team in Mayo was out on a job for the US Army. On the third day a dog team was found and the rescue mission began.

In the meantime, ORTELL had begun to worry about Laska and his safety in the intense cold. He decided to walk to Mayo to see if Laska was alive.

Twelve miles down the trail a snowshoe strap broke. With his frozen hands he was unable to repair it so he discarded the snowshoes and struggled on through the deep snow. Fatigue and the Arctic night overtook him. He was unable to light a fire. His only hope was to remain erect and to keep moving, in the hope that someone would happen by.

Too tired to walk further, he stood beside the trail and banked snow around his legs up to his knees and steeled his mind to keep standing. He knew that if he sat or lay down he would die. All through the night and into the following afternoon he stood, slowly freezing to death, only his indomitable will keeping him erect.

Dick Kimbel and Corporal d'Easum, RCMP, were stunned when they found him. They lifted him from the snow and rushed him to the nurse at Mayo who did everything possible to relieve his suffering. An airplane took him to Dawson the next day.

Both feet had to be amputated and he appealed to the Doctor to save as much as he could: "I got to hobble around some way. Figure to get me a fine catch of beaver on the McQuesten River this spring".

When he realized that he could never return to his beloved wilderness he lost heart. He gave up, for the first and last time in his life. (see Laska Creek)

MOUNT ORTELL 6,769' 63°58'N 132°49'W (105-N). In the Tasin Range, south of the Stewart River.

Joseph Keele, GSC, named this peak in 1907 after George L. ORTELL, whose help and knowledge of the region greatly aided him in his geological mapping of the area.

MOUNT OSBORNE 65°46'N 140°50'W (116-F). South of the Kandik River.

Harriet Edna OSBORNE, OBE, wife of Franklin Osborne of Dawson, was active in the Anglican Church, IODE and St. John's Ambulance. She organized the first Girl Guides in the Yukon in 1914 at Dawson. She was made an Officer of the Order of the British Empire for public service and in 1973 this mountain was named for her.

OSCAR CREEK 60°39'N 128°49'W (105-A). Flows south to False Canyon Creek, a few miles north of Stewart Lake.

The creek and lake were named in 1943 after OSCAR Stewart, a trapper and the son of a trapper, both of whom had spent many years in this area. The name had been in local use for a long time. (see Cabin and Stewart Creeks)

MOUNT OSGOODE 63°01'N 132°28"W (105-N). North of Mount Selous.

This mountain was named in 1909 after Wilfred Hudson OSGOODE (1875-1947), a member of the US Biological Survey. OSGOODE came into the Yukon in 1899 on an expedition for the US Department of Agriculture, over the White Pass and down the Yukon River. He was with F.C. Selous, the famed African white hunter and naturalist, in 1904 when they were in this region and camped on this mountain while he studied the local flora and fauna.

OTTER FALLS 61°05'N 137°00'W (115-H). On the Aishihik River at the foot of Canyon Lake.

This beautiful falls is sometimes called "Five Dollar Falls" because its picture appeared for many years on the reverse side of five dollar Canadian banknotes.

OUTFITTER LAKE 65°53'N 138°16'W (116-B). Three miles northeast of Chapman Lake.

Big-game guide and outfitter, Douglas Low, built his base camp here in the early 1970s.

PACKARD POINT 60°58'N 133°03'W (105-C). The large point at the southeast end of Quiet Lake.

During the 1920s-30s, a wealthy American construction man by this name came yearly to hunt in this area. His companies had built many of the New York City docks as well as other large construction projects. A large, impressive and friendly man, he claimed that he could build anything. He died here and his body was sent to the northeastern United States for burial.

PACKERS MOUNTAIN 4,743' 61°50'N 135°32'W (105-E). On the east side of the Chain Lakes.

A.E. Pattison was head packer for D.D. Caimes, GSC, from 1905-1917. He was a master horseman and an exceptional bushman. Possessed of a fine singing voice, he and Cairnes often gave impromptu concerts when they came to town. In 1930, he died and W.D. Cockfield, GSC, who had also worked with him, named this mountain to commemorate him and the other packers who had served the GSC in the Yukon. (see Mount Pattison)

MOUNT PAGE 4,198' 69°20'N 140°54'W (117-C). On the headwaters of the Malcolm River, twenty-five miles south of the Arctic coast.

In June 1958, this mountain was chosen to perpetuate the name of Lt. Pierre Roger Joseph PAGE, MID. He was born on 2 February 1918 at Knowlton, Quebec. He enlisted in the Canadian Army at Sherbrooke, Quebec on 10 September 1940. After serving in Canada, Newfoundland, Great Britain and northwest Europe, he died of wounds received in action on 13 August 1944.

PALMER LAKE 66°09'N 136°24'W (116-I). Immediately south of Moose Lake.

This name was proposed in 1965 by "Pat" Callison, noted bush pilot, after his friend, Phillip E. PALMER, formerly Chief Topographical Engineer with the GSC and Chairman of the Board on Geographical Names.

PAN CREEK 62°00'N 140°55'W (115-F). (see Frying Pan Creek).

PARADISE CREEK 63°42'N 136°09'N (115-P). Flows to the southeast corner of Minto Lake.

On 19 May 1903, J.G. Scrivener staked the Discovery claim on this stream and named it for its beautiful setting.

PARENT CREEK 63°50'N 135°27'W (105-M). A tributary to Duncan Creek, from the east.

During the rush to this area Dennis PARENT and G. Beaudet prospected this stream and found placer gold. They staked the Discovery claim and named the creek on 20 June 1902.

PARKER CREEK 63°42'N 138°55'W (115-O). A tributary to the Indian River, one and a half miles above Montana Creek.

Although this creek was probably named in the 1890s, it was not until 1906 that enough gold was found to warrant claim staking.

PARIS 63°49'N 138°39'W (115-O).

This was a small mining camp and settlement at the junction of Dominion and Portland Creeks in the southeast Klondike district. It had a post office from 1904-1943 but was abandoned after that date.

PARTRIDGE CREEK 60°14'N 135°08'W (105-D). Flows into the Wheaton River.

Officially named in May 1911, but locally known for at least ten years before that, this creek bears the name of Otto H. PARTRIDGE, a prominent but lesser known figure of the Klondike Gold Rush.

In 1897, PARTRIDGE, as General Manager of the Bennett Lake and Klondyke Navigation Company, brought the boilers and fittings for three small steamboats over the White Pass, the "Ora", "Dora" and "Flora". That winter he built a sawmill and shipyard at Millhaven Bay on the west arm of Bennett Lake. Early in the spring of 1898 the three boats went downriver to Whitehorse. Although there is some argument, it is likely that one of these boats was the first to navigate through Miles Canyon and the Whitehorse Rapids.

His mill and shipyard prospered and he cut timber on this and nearby creeks. PARTRIDGE was early interested in the development of the Engineer Gold Mine (hard rock) on Windy Arm of Tagish Lake. The locale suited him and he and his wife built a home on the west side of the Arm. Their home, "Ben My Chree" (Manx for "Girl of My Heart") was a showplace for tourists on the WP&YR until the early 1930s. (see Millhaven Bay)

PAT LAKE 65°06'N 136°39'W (116-H). About fifteen miles east of the Hart River.

This lake was named by bush pilot I.A. Reid for the convenience of himself and other pilots assisting mining exploration in the area. It was probably named after E.P. "PAT" Callison, noted pioneer Yukon bush pilot who landed the first aircraft on the lake. It is the only lake within a very large area that is large enough on which to land a fixed-wing aircraft.

MOUNT PATTERSON 11,300' 61°09'N 140°07'W (115-F). On the east side of the Steele Glacier, in the St. Elias Range.

This peak was named in November 1970 after John Duncan PATTERSON (1864-1940), businessman and past-president of the Alpine Club of Canada.

MOUNT PATTERSON 6,819' 61°57'N 133°52'W (105-F). North of the North Big Salmon River, in the Pelly Mountains.

This beautiful mountain was chosen in November 1951 to honour the memory of a Canadian hero, Lt. William Clark PATTERSON, MID. He was born on 22 August 1915 in Toronto, Ontario. He enlisted in the Canadian Army on 27 May 1940, at Toronto. He served in Canada and Great Britain and was killed in action during the attack on Dieppe, France on 19 August 1942.

MOUNT PATTISON 62°28'N 138°34'W (115-J). East of the Klotassin River, in the southeast Dawson Range.

A.E. PATTISON trapped and prospected this country for many years. He worked as a packer for GSC parties from 1905-1930. An excellent horseman and packer, he was liked for his cheerful disposition and ability as a bushman.

In the summer of 1930, he was, as usual, packing for the GSC. It was a bad year for flies and PATTISON, worried about his horses, stayed up at night and kept smudge fires burning to protect them from the insects. He carried on with his normal work during the day but it was too much for his health and he suffered a stroke. He was taken to Vancouver, B.C. where he died shortly afterward at the age of 64.

D.D. Cairnes, GSC, had named the mountain for him around 1916. (see Packers Mountain)

PATTON GULCH 62°45'N 138°51'W (115-J). On the north side of Patton Hill, at the head of Canadian Creek.

This gulch and the mountain above it were named in 1911 by Jack Meloy, a well-known Yukon prospector. His old friend James "Jim" PATTON had found and worked the first placer gold in the area at a much earlier date. PATTON spent many years prospecting in the Dawson Range. The name was made official in 1970. (see Meloy Creek)

PATULLO LAKE 68°03'N 139°20'W (117-A). A small lake east of Old Crow Flats.

This name was proposed by Gordon McIntyre in June 1973 as a sheet designation for the new series of topographical maps.

Dufferin PATULLO was a lawyer prominent in Dawson and Yukon politics during the Gold Rush era. He later became Premier of British Columbia, and made an unsuccessful attempt to annex the Yukon Territory in the 1930s.

PAULINE COVE 69°34'N 138°55'W (117-D). On the east side of Herschel Island.

This bay was named by Lt. Commander Stockton of the "USS Thetis", when he surveyed the coast of Herschel Island in 1889. He used the name of a whaling ship that was in the bay at the time.

PEASOUP CREEK 64°17'N 138°29'W (116-B). Crosses the Dempster Highway and flows into the North Klondike River.

This creek was named in 1969 by highway construction crews when one of their number, a French-Canadian, fell into the stream. The blunt sense of humour of his companions supplied the name.

PEEL RIVER 67°00'N 135°00'W (106-L). A tributary to the MacKenzie River.

In 1826, Sir John Franklin, RN, on his second overland expedition to the Arctic, named this large river after Sir Robert PEEL (1788-1850), Home Secretary and later, Prime Minister of Great Britain. PEEL organized and established the first police Force of the modern type. (hence British Police were called "peelers" or "bobbies")

The PEEL River was first explored by Chief Factor John Bell of the HBC in 1839, when he ascended it as far as the Snake River. He explored the Snake River, thinking it was the PEEL. In 1840-41, it was explored further by Alexander Kennedy Isbister, also of the HBC and still further in 1893 by Count V.E. de Sainville. Charles Camsell, GSC, made the first complete survey of the river in 1905.

The river was most important for many years as the only route to the lucrative fur trade of the upper Yukon Territory and the Yukon River.

PELLY BANKS 61°46'N 131°07'W (105-G). On the north side of the Pelly River, opposite the mouth of Big Campbell Creek.

On 25 July 1840, Robert Campbell of the HBC arrived here, while establishing the true course and location of the Yukon River. That day he named the Pelly River and the high bluffs across the stream after Sir John Henry PELLY (1777-1852), Governor of the HBC. Later, when Campbell wrote his report informing PELLY of his discoveries, PELLY replied calling the river and banks, "Campbell River and Banks". Campbell declined the honour but regretted his decision in later life.

In 1846, he built a trading post here, on the east bank of Campbell Creek on the Pelly, supplied from Fort Frances. It never did well. In the early winter of 1849, while Campbell was at Fort Selkirk, the post burned down, leaving the staff destitute. Two of his men died of starvation that winter and some of the Indians resorted to cannibalism to save themselves.

The post was never re-established by the HBC. Independent traders operated here for many years after 1900.

PELLY CROSSING 62°49'N 136°34'W (115-I). About twenty-five miles east of Fort Selkirk, on the Pelly River.

Situated on the Whitehorse-Dawson Road, this small settlement had two roadhouses and a trading post run by Ira Van Bibber and his partner Woolen. In 1958, the ferry across the Pelly River was replaced by a modern bridge. The settlement remains to this day.

PELLY LAKES 62°04'N 130°17'W (105-J). Two long narrow lakes at the head of Pelly River.

These lakes were named about 1840 by Robert Campbell of the HBC, when he was exploring the country, after the Governor of the HBC, Sir John Henry PELLY (1777-1852).

PELLY MOUNTAINS 61°04'N 132°30'W (105-F). The huge range of mountains that parallel the course of the Pelly River, on the south side.

These hills were named in 1887 by Dr. George Mercer Dawson, G&NHSC, while he was mapping this country for the first time.

In 1947, his nomenclature was expanded so that the PELLY MOUNTAINS now include the Big Salmon, the St. Cyr, the Glenlyon, Campbell and Simpson Ranges. (see Pelly Banks)

PELLY POST OFFICE 62°47'N 137°23'W (115-I). At the junction of the Pelly and Yukon Rivers.

Although the settlement here was always called "Fort Selkirk", the government established a post office in September 1899 and named it "PELLY POST OFFICE". It was closed in 1939.

PELLY RIVER 62°47'N 137°20'W (115-I). The major tributary to the Yukon River.

The early Indian name for this river was "Ayan" or "Iyon", after the native tribe who lived near its mouth. The latter name was used on USC&GS maps of the late 1880s.

Robert Campbell, HBC, named the stream in 1840 after Sir John Henry PELLY, Governor of the HBC.

The PELLY was one of the first streams in the Yukon to be prospected; men panned its gravels as early as 1883.

MOUNT PERKINS 6,665 60°19'N 135°07'W (105-D). In the upper Corwin Valley.

In 1905, J. PERKINS found and staked the first gold-quartz lode claims found on the mountain.

PERTHES POINT 60°09'N 134°27'W (105-D). On the north side of Tagish Lake, at the foot of Nares Mountain.

In 1883, Lt. Frederick Schwatka, US Army, as he was passing, named this point after Justus PERTHES of Gotha, Germany, a famous geographer.

MOUNT PHELPS 65°04'N 133°57'W (106-F). South of Rapitan Creek.

This was a map designation name given in 1973 for Willard PHELPS, a long-time Whitehorse lawyer and a Yukon Councillor for the Whitehorse District for a number of years in the 1930s.

PHILLIPS BAY 69°17'N 138°30'W (117-D). At the mouth of the Babbage River, on the Arctic coast.

Sir John Franklin, RN, on his second Arctic Expedition in 1826, named this bay after Thomas PHILLIPS (1770-1845), professor of painting at the Royal Academy in London.

MOUNT PIKE 62°11'N 129°39'W (105-I). At the headwaters of the Woodside River.

Named in the 1940s after Warburton PIKE, English sportsman adventurer, who explored Frances Lake and the country north of it in 1893. He named a number of other features in the area at the time. In the late 1890s he operated a trading post at Dease Lake. A monument to him is in place at the head of Dease Lake. (see Narchilla Brook, Seagull Creek and Ptarmigan Creek)

PILLAGE POINT 68°52'N 136°44'W (117-A). The point of land immediately south of Tent Island, in Shoalwater Bay.

On 7 July 1826, Sir John Franklin, RN, and his two small boats "Lion" and "Reliance" were seized in the shallow waters off this point and forced to land. The Eskimos (Inuit) robbed the boats of stores and supplies and owing only to the coolness of Franklin and Lt. Back, there was no loss of life. The Eskimos, after listening to another chief from Hudson Bay, who was accompanying Franklin, restored the goods and thereafter traded.

PILOT MOUNTAIN 6,739' 61°02'N 135°32'W (105-E). West of Lake Laberge, in the Miners Range.

This peak was named in honour of the first riverboat pilots who ran the Lewes (Yukon) River, by Hugh S. Bostock, GSC, in 1935. The pilots used this peak as a landmark.

PINGUICULA LAKE 64°41'N 133°24'W (106-C). East of the Bonnet Plume River.

In the summer of 1940, Mr. and Mrs. George Black, accompanied by Livingstone Wernecke, flew into this lake on a camping trip to the area. The large number of butterwort plants (Pinguicula vulgaris) growing around the shores of the lake suggested the name to Mrs. Black. She was an acknowledged authority on the wildflowers of the Yukon. (see Mount Martha Black and Excelsior Creek)

PIRATE CREEK 63°26'N 137°45'W (115-P). A tributary to Lake Creek.

In 1949, Hugh S. Bostock, GSC, mapped this area. He gave this name because the stream features had altered in the area. This creek had captured the headwaters of Robbed Creek and other small streams in the vicinity.

MOUNT PITTS 5,214' 62°35'N 137°35'W (115-I). Twenty-five miles west of Minto.

In June 1899, J.J. McArthur, DLS, named this peak after Harold J. PITTS, a member of his boundary survey party that year.

Nicknamed "Buffalo" PITTS, he came in to the Yukon in 1895 over the Chilkoot Pass. Arriving at Fort Selkirk he settled in to life as a trader. He operated Arthur Harper's trading post from 1897 to at least 1899. He assisted boundary survey and GSC parties in the field. He spent almost his whole time in the Yukon around Fort Selkirk and did not visit Whitehorse until 1909. He was on the riverboat which made the first successful trip up the White and Donjek Rivers in 1909.

In a letter to E.G. DeVille, Surveyor General of Canada, dated 24 September 1909 he asked that this peak be given his name. He gave as a reason: "That he was somewhat like a mule; without pride of ancestry or hope of posterity".

PLATINUM GULCH 64°01'N 135°51'W (106-D). A small tributary to Haggart Creek.

This small stream was so called by the early miners because of the amounts of platinum found mixed with the placer gold in its gravels, when it was mined in the 1920s.

PLEASANT CREEK 65°10'N 141°00'W (116-F). A tributary to Harrington Creek, in Alaska.

This name was given in 1930 by J.B. Mertie of the Geological Survey of Alaska because of its pleasant setting.

POLICE CREEK 64°24'N 135°20'W (106-D). The north fork of the Beaver River.

This stream was probably named about 1905 or a little later. One of the trails used by the RNWMP Dawson to MacPherson patrol ran along it. The trail went via the Little Wind River.

POLLEY HILL 66°51'N 136°41'W (116-I). West of the Rock River.

D-43176 Bombardier Frank POLLEY was born on 31 July 1874 at Benson, Oxfordshire, England. He enlisted in the Royal Canadian Artillery at Valcartier, Quebec on 24 September 1914, one of the first Canadians. He served in Canada, Great Britain and France and was discharged as medically unfit, from wounds received, on 30 November 1917.

He died later from the effects of his wounds. In June 1973 this mountain was named in his memory.

POOLY CANYON 60°02'N 134°37"W (105-D). On the west side of Windy Arm, south of Montana Mountain.

The canyon below the forks of POOLY Creek was named after the existing POOLY Creek.

POOLY CREEK 60°02'N 134°37'W (105-D). Flows into Windy Arm, from the south side of Montana Mountain.

This was named in early 1905 after John M. POOLY, one of the first hardrock prospectors in the Windy Arm district. POOLY gave the creek the name "Uranus Creek", after the first claim he staked there, but the GSC soon changed it to the present one.

POPCORNFISH LAKE 65°28'N 133°48'W (106-F). North of Knorr Creek.

In 1953, a GSC survey crew caught an unusually deformed fish in this lake.

PORCUPINE RIVER 67°25'N 141°00'W (116-N). This major tributary to the Yukon River leaves Canada at this point.

The ancient Indian name for this river was the "Choodeenjik" or "Porcupine Quill River".

The stream was first explored by John Bell, Chief Trader for the HBC at Fort MacPherson, in 1842 and 1844. Bell first saw the Yukon River on his second trip. He accepted the Indian name but shortened it to simply, the PORCUPINE RIVER. Shortly afterward, in 1847, he sent Alexander Hunter Murray to establish Fort Yukon at the junction of the two streams. The PORCUPINE RIVER remained a regular trading route until the transfer of Alaska to the United States in 1867. On American insistence, Fort Yukon was abandoned. The river was in limited use after this date and was totally forsaken by the Americans after 1894 when they abandoned the Territory.

The river was first surveyed and mapped by R.G. McConnell, G&NHSC, in 1888. F.F. Sparks a member of William Ogilvie's survey party in 1888, travelling from Forty Mile to Fort MacPherson, found the source of the PORCUPINE RIVER to be a small hot-spring.

PORPHYRY PEAK 61°41'N 137°45'W (115-H). Northwest of Aishihik Lake, in the Nisling Range.

For many years, until 1974, this was known as Mount Maloney. For some reason this peak was renamed at that time. (see Mount Maloney)

MOUNT PORSILD 60°05'N 136°00'W (115-A).

Thorbjoern PORSILD was born in Denmark. He came to Canada in the 1930s and spent much time with the reindeer herd in Aklavik, NWT. When this work was finished he remained in the Yukon. He was an amateur botanist of some standing and was the brother of Erling PORSILD, the famous botanist. In 1947, he and his wife took over the US Army Engineers construction camp at Johnson's Crossing and developed it into a roadhouse and restaurant.

PORTER CREEK 60°48'N 135°08'W (105-D). A tributary to the Yukon River.

This creek was named by H.E. PORTER in July 1899 when he found a rich copper ore body on the seventh of the month, which he called the "Pueblo" claim. Porter lived and prospected in this district for many years. He died while prospecting on the headwaters of the Stewart River in early June 1907. PORTER Creek Subdivision in the City of Whitehorse takes its name from this man.

PORTER LAKE 64°00'N 130°53'W (105-O). Northwest of the Thor Hills.

This lake was named by M.O. Cecile, GSC, in 1982 when his party was supplied by a Pilatus PORTER aircraft. His crew called the lake "Porter Puddle".

The Pilatus Porter aircraft is an equivalent of the DeHaviland Beaver. The aircraft was built in Great Britain by the Porter Aircraft Co. which was later sold to the Pilatus Aircraft Co. of Sweden.

PORTLAND CREEK 63°49'N 138°40'W (115-O). A tributary to Dominion Creek, four miles above Jensen Creek.

John Salme named this stream after his hometown in Oregon when he discovered gold and staked the first claim on 27 December 1897.

POTATOE CREEK 68°09'N 140°22'W (117-B). A tributary to Surprise Creek and the Old Crow River.

This name was reported by Cpl. E.A. Kirk, RCMP, in 1949. The name "Schaefer Creek" had been mistakenly applied by the International Boundary survey crew of 1911 and was shown as such on maps until 1950.

POTTER HILLS 63°41'N 130°32'W (105-O). North of Keele Lake.

M.P. Cecile, GSC, named this feature after George POTTER, a miner and prospector in this area from 1896-1946.

POVOAS MOUNTAIN 61°22'N 135°08'W (105-E). At the northeast corner of Lake Laberge.

This was named about 1908 by D.D. Cairnes, GSC, after an early prospector and miner of this name who made his home in the area.

PREJEVALSKY POINT 60°05'N 134°53'W (105-D). The point on the south side between Lake Bennett and the West Arm.

This point was named by Lt. Frederick Schwatka, US Army, in 1883 after a well-known Russian explorer of the time.

PREVOST RIVER 62°36'N 131°10'W (105-J). A tributary to the Ross River.

A French-Canadian named PREVOST was probably the first white man to travel this river. He and a partner trapped and prospected here in 1900 and at PREVOST Canyon on the Ross River in the early 1900s.

PRIEST MOUNTAIN (see Mount Cook).

PRIMROSE LAKE 60°06'N 135°40'W (105-D). A long, narrow lake east of the Takhini River.

This was probably named by George Fraser-White, DLS, of the Department of the Interior, while setting out monuments on the Yukon-B.C. boundary in 1900. Named after Captain, later Inspector P.C.H. PRIMROSE, NWMP. He was in charge of the Tagish Post which included this district in 1899-1901. The river was named later. Rose Lake, farther up the river was derived from this name. The mountain was named last of all.

MOUNT PRINCE EDWARD ISLAND 12,260 60°57'N 140°39'W (115-C). In the Centennial Range of the St. Elias Mountains.

This peak was named in honour of the province during Canada's Centennial Year, 1967. (see Centennial Range)

PRINGLE LAKE 60°08'N 136°59'W (115-A). On the west side of the Haines Junction Road, near Dalton Post.

Sgt. J.A. PRINGLE, NWMP, served at Dalton Post in the early 1900s and after being discharged, continued to live here for many years. He was a brother of John and George PRINGLE, the famous Presbyterian Ministers of the Klondike and Atlin goldfields and the First World War.

PRINTERS CREEK 61°10'N 138°24'W (115-G). Flows into Cultus Creek, on the east side of Kluane Lake.

Named "New Zealand Creek" by the first men to find gold and stake claims during the rush to the Kluane goldfields in 1903-04. By 1914 the creek was abandoned. A new find was made and another stampede to stake claims took place. The new stakers named it PRINTERS CREEK. To many of the local people it was known as "Buck-Off Creek", after an incident concerning pack horses.

MOUNT PROFEIT 64°47'N 133°04'W (106-C). West of the Snare River.

This hill was named in 1973 by Gordon McIntyre, Territorial Land Titles Agent, for the new Topographical series of maps. It is named for Alexander PROFEIT, the first schoolteacher in the Mayo district, in 1914.

PROSPECTOR MOUNTAIN 62°27'N 137°48'W (115-I). In the Dawson Range.

This name was proposed by Hugh S. Bostock, GSC, in 1943 to commemorate the prospectors of the Yukon whom he admired and respected. His liking for the working prospectors was only equalled by their respect and liking for him.

PTARMIGAN CREEK 62°06'N 130°07'W (105-H). Flows into the east end of Pelly Lake.

In 1893, Warburton Pike, the English gentleman-explorer, travelled the Liard River, Frances River and Frances Lake and explored this area. He named this creek because of the large numbers of these birds he saw here. (see Narchilla Rook and Gull Lake)

PURE GOLD GULCH 64°00'N 139°22'W (115-O). A tributary to Bonanza Creek, from the east side.

On 30 October 1897, T.M. Rogers staked the Discovery claim on this little valley. It produced some gold.

QUARTZ CREEK 63°45'N 139°07'W (115-O). Flows from King Solomon's Dome to the Indian River, in the Klondike district.

Although the mouth of Quartz Creek was seen by prospectors working on the Indian River as early as 1887, it was probably named by William "Billy" Redford who found and mined the first gold here in 1894. The creek gained its name as about 80% of its gravels are composed of white quartz pebbles from the White Channel Gravels.

William Redford was born in Devon, England in 1861 and became a sailor. While on a whaling voyage he reached the mouth of the MacKenzie River in 1891. The following year he went to southwestern Alaska and in 1893 crossed the Chilkoot Pass and went down to Forty Mile.

In late 1893 or early 1894, he was the first to find and mine the gold of this stream, initially on the bars then in the deeper gravels. He staked a Discovery claim near the mouth of Calder Creek (unnamed at the time). This was the first payable gold recorded on the east side of the Yukon River, below the Stewart River. Previous to this it had been the consensus of opinion among the miners of the region that none would be found in this part of the territory.

Joe Ladue who had a trading post at the mouth of the Sixty Mile River (Ogilvie), used Redford's find to encourage others, including Robert Henderson, to prospect the area in following years. Thus, in the summer of 1896, about twenty men worked for Redford and others mining on the stream. A number of pre-1896 miners claimed that Henderson worked for Redford in the winter of 1895-96. The men who accompanied Henderson to Gold Bottom Creek that spring all came from Quartz Creek.

Because he obtained his supplies from Ogilvie, which was only forty five miles away, and the Mining Recorder was at Forty Mile, eighty-five miles downstream, Redford did not bother to record his claim. It was safe in those days as long as he was working it. When Bonanza and Eldorado Creeks were discovered, Quartz Creek was deserted except for Redford. The overflow of men from the Klondike in the summer of 1897 threatened his claim and he went to Dawson and recorded it in September. He was not allowed a Discovery claim as one had been filed on 11 August by D.D. Stewart, higher up the creek. Someone else had evidently tried to stake Redford's claim as the Mining Recorder would not allow his Discovery claim. After examination of the facts and testimony of those who knew Redford's history, the Recorder allowed his Discovery claim.

Redford also found, when recording his claim, that the district had been divided into two mining divisions, the Klondike comprised of all streams flowing into the Klondike River and the new Indian River division contained all those streams flowing into the Indian River. This new partition was later used effectively to ignore Redford's claims to have been the first to have mined gold in the Klondike, which enhanced Henderson's claim to that honour.

His priority was acknowledged by most of the pre-1886 miners and by R.G. McConnell, GSC, the noted explorer geologist who made the first study of the Klondike goldfields and who included the south-flowing tributaries to the Indian River as part of the Klondike District.

Redford was a shy, self-effacing man who made few public claims. He mined on his Discovery claim continuously every year from 1894-1937, never making more than good wages. He died in St. Mary's Hospital in Dawson on 18 October 1944, sadly neglected by history. A settlement grew up on his claim and lasted until the 1940s. (see Readford)

QUARTZ CREEK 60°51'N 130°35'W (105-B). A tributary to the Liard River (see Everett Creek and Wasson Lake).

QUARTZ LAKE (see Hulse Lake).

QUEBEC CREEK 64°10'N 139°33'W (116-B). A tributary to the Yukon River, about two miles below Fort Reliance.

S. Villeneuve of Quebec, named this stream when he and his partners found enough gold to stake their claims.

MOUNT QUEBEC 12,300 60°56'N 140°42'W (115-C). In the Centennial Range of the St. Elias Mountains.

This was named to honour the province of QUEBEC during Canada's Centennial Year of 1967. (see Centennial Range)

QUEEN GULCH 63°57'N 139°20'W (115-O). On the east side of Bonanza Creek, halfway between Adams and Boulder Creeks.

Gold was found here by William Gillespie who staked the Discovery claim and named the location on 10 August 1897.

QUINN GULCH 63°47'N 138°55'W (155-O). A small tributary to Sulphur Creek, a mile below the settlement of Sulphur.

Gold was found and the Discovery claim staked by William QUINN on 28 August 1897.

QUINTINO SELLA GLACIER 60°34'N 141°00'W (115-C). North of the Columbia Glacier, in the St. Elias Range.

This glacier was named by His Royal Highness, Prince Amadeo of Savoy, Duke of Abruzzi, on his expedition to Mount St. Elias in 1887, after an illustrious pioneer of Italian mountain climbing.

RAABE'S HILLS 62°10'N 136°09'W (115-I). A low range of hills, a few miles northeast of Tantalus Butte.

These hills were named in 1968 after Captain George RAABE of Portland, Oregon. He had piloted riverboats between Whitehorse and Dawson from 1900-1920. "RAABE's Slough", three miles above Tantalus Butte, although misspelled on some maps, is the backwater of the Yukon River in which he laid up his boats during the winter.

RACKLA RIVER 64°07'N 134°24'W (106-D). Tributary to the Beaver River (north branch of the McQuesten River).

From 1897, this stream was called "Hell River" by the stampeders who came this way from Edmonton. The GSC however, applied the local Indian name without translation. It is swift and shallow, making for extremely difficult boating.

RADER LAKE 62°21'N 130°45'W (105-J). Twenty miles northwest of Traffic Mountain.

Louis Thomas "Slim" RADER in his earlier years was an employee of the HBC in the NWT. It is said that he accompanied Peary's North Pole Expedition in 1909 as far as the Arctic coast. In the 1920s and 30s, he trapped on the MacKenzie and Liard Rivers and moved into this part of the Yukon. He once spent a winter in the Nahanni Valley without supplies, living by his rifle. He managed the Taylor and Drury trading post at Pelly Lakes from 1938-1950. In the early 1960s, he was caretaker of the Hudson Bay Mining and Smelting Company's Wellgreen Mine at Quill Creek, after its closure.

Retiring to Haney, B.C. he died on 31 July 1967, liked and respected.

RAE CREEK 64°53'N 137°01'W (116-A). Flows north into the Hart River.

Frank RAE was an old-time trapper and prospector in this region. He had his cabin on "RAE Lake" (now "Worm Lake"). He and his partner, Fred Hoffman, worked here in the 1930s-40s.

RAILWAY SURVEY CREEK 62°10'N 134°05'W (105-L). A small creek, flowing north into the Magundy River.

In 1942, Col. James Truitt, US Army Engineers, headed a survey group on a proposed railway location through this country, naming this creek on the way. (see Truitt Creek and Truitt Peak)

RAINBOW CREEK 60°56'N 130°41'W (105-B). A tributary to the Liard River.

This stream was named by Cassiar miners who worked on it during the Sayyea Creek excitement in the 1874-80s period. (see Sayyea, Scurvy and Cabin Creeks)

RAMPART HOUSE 67°25'N 140°59'W (116-N). Just east of the Yukon-Alaska boundary, on the Porcupine River.

When the American government forced the closure of Fort Yukon after their purchase of Alaska, the HBC moved up the Porcupine River and built a new post, calling it "Rampart House". The new location was given the name because of the steep banks of the river at the location. Turner's survey of 1889 showed that this post too was on American soil. The HBC burned this post and moved again to where they were sure they were in Canadian territory. This site they called "New Rampart House".

"New Rampart House" was operated by the HBC only until 1894 when they ceased all operations in the Yukon. The people remained here until 1911 when a smallpox epidemic carried away a large part of the population. The survivors burned the post and moved upstream to a new site they named Old Crow.

Dan Cadzow, a Scot and an early Klondiker, opened a trading post at "New Rampart House" in 1905. After its destruction due to the epidemic, he moved with the others to Old Crow, where he spent the rest of his life.

RANCHERIA RIVER 60°13'N 129°08'W (105-A). A tributary to the Liard River, west of Watson Lake.

This is an old Californian or Mexican miners' term from the Spanish meaning a native village or settlement.

When Dr. George Mercer Dawson, G&NHSC, passed this river in 1887, he found that the Cassiar miners had named the stream during the Sayyea Creek excitement in 1874-76.

RANKIN CREEK 64°01'N 134°55'W (106-D). Flows into the Keno Ladue River, in the Mayo district.

This stream was named on 21 April 1945, to honour the memory of Captain Robert Lowe James RANKIN who was born on 29 May 1910 in London, England. He enlisted in Toronto, Ontario, on 3 June 1941 and served in the Canadian Army in Canada, Great Britain and Northwest Europe. He was killed in action in France on 18 July 1944.

RANOCH LAKE 62°49'N 138°14'W (115-J). Northwest of Lomond Lake.

A Scottish name in connection with Lomond Lake. (see Lomond and Ness Lakes)

RAT LAKE 60° 26' N 134° 50' W (105-D)

Located in the Watson River valley 29 kilometers north of Carcross, this marshy lake drains underground into the Watson River. The large population of muskrats has made it a popular location for trapping muskrats (an activity known as "ratting"). The current name of the lake is derived from the local slang term for muskrats. The native Tagish people called it Dzéna Méne (muskrat lake).

RAY CREEK 60°21'N 137°11'W (115-A). A tributary to Rude Creek.

Irvine RAY was a well-known miner in the Whitehorse and Mayo districts. He and his partner, Ed Barker, mined on Shorty Creek in 1946. This lake was known locally by this name for many years. The name was made official in September 1973.

MOUNT RAYMOND 66°24'N 136°10'W (116-I). In the Richardson Mountains.

Born in Digby, Nova Scotia on 22 February 1896, George Vail RAYMOND enlisted in the Canadian Army at Dawson as a private in the Yukon Infantry Company on 2 October 1916. He was appointed a Second Lieutenant in the RAF on 20 December 1917 and was killed in action on 24 July 1918. This mountain was named in his honour in 1973.

READFORD 63°47'N 139°07'W (115-O). On Quartz Creek, at the mouth of Calder Creek.

The Canadian Post office opened an office on William Redford's Discovery claim on 19 August 1905. There was a small settlement here at the time. The authorities called this first post office "Radford". It was closed from April 1934 to September 1934. On 16 November they changed the name to "Readford" after they reopened. The office was closed permanently on 31 December 1952. Two tries in 47 years and the name was misspelled both times. (see Quartz Creek)

READY BULLION GULCH 63°54'N 139°08'W (115-O). A tributary to upper Bonanza Creek.

This short stream was named on 6 November 1897 by the first staker, Peter Farrell. He named it after the READY BULLION Mine at Juneau, Alaska, where he had been employed. This little gulch produced good gold values, almost the only place on upper Bonanza Creek to do so.

REID HOUSE 63°32'N 137°25'W (115-P). Supposedly on the south bank of the Stewart River, near the mouth of the creek emptying the Reid Lakes.

All the above is supposition. The existence and location of REID HOUSE is a genuine Yukon mystery. The first map to show any of the interior features of the Yukon Territory was John Arrowsmith's map, drawn in 1854 in London, England. Arrowsmith gained all his information about the central Yukon from Robert Campbell of the HBC, the first explorer in 1853. This place was shown on Arrowsmith's map. Campbell, when interviewed later by Dr. George Mercer Dawson, G&NHSC, stated that no such place existed, although he had had a John Reid with him at Pelly Banks and Fort Selkirk in the years 1846-51. John Reid was also questioned by Dawson and denied any knowledge of a settlement although he did state that there were a number of small lakes near this location where they obtained good numbers of fish and that a small hut or shelter had been built there while fishing.

Both REID HOUSE and Reid Lakes were shown on almost every map of the territory until 1899. Reid Lakes are still there, although sometimes spelled "Reed".

MOUNT REID 60°10'N 135°27'W (105-D). On the north side of the Wheaton River, between Skookum and Barney Creeks.

This feature was named in May 1911 after Percy REID, the Mining Recorder of the Conrad Mining Division which included this area. He was well regarded by the miners of his day.

REMINGTON PUP 63°51'N 138°51'W (115-O). A very short stream entering Dominion Creek, one-half mile below upper Discovery.

On 13 August 1897, Edward REMINGTON found gold in this little gulch and staked the first claim.

RENDELL RIDGE 64°47'N 138°16'W (116-B). Part of the Puddingstone Hills.

This was named after William J. RENDELL, who surveyed the original North Fork Ditch and was involved in Klondike mining for over forty years.

The North Fork Ditch was a large hydraulic project to bring water from the headwaters of streams flowing into the Klondike River, to the mining operations of Hunker, Bonanza and other parts of the Klondike.

REVENUE CREEK 62°21'N 137°17'W (115-I). Flows into Big Creek, three miles above Seymour Creek, from the south.

This creek was named about 1940 by Fred Guder, who had sporadically mined placer gold here. Named because he said that he could always win enough gold here to grubstake himself for further prospecting. The creek has been mined successfully for a number of years. (see Guder Creek)

REVERSE CREEK 63°33'N 136°48'W (115-P). A tributary to Moose Creek.

Because this stream turns 180 degrees to reverse its flow, Hugh S. Bostock, GSC, gave it this name while he was mapping the area in 1949.

RICE CREEK 63°15'N 140°51'W (115-N). A tributary to the Ladue River, from the north.

This stream was named in May 1920 by a GSC party after an old trapper of this name who was living here.

MOUNT RICHARDS 66°04'N 136°05'W (116-I). East of Canyon Creek.

This hill was named on 22 June 1973 to honour the name and memory of R-252612 Flight Sgt. Edward Gordon Coke RICHARDS. Born 10 October 1916 at Strathmore, Alberta, he enlisted in the RCAF on 25 March 1943. He was missing, presumed killed in action on 14 March 1945.

RICHARDSON MOUNTAINS 67°00'N 136°10'W (116-P). This range parallels the Yukon-NWT boundary.

In 1825, Sir John Franklin, RN, named these mountains after Sir John RICHARDSON (1787-1865). An Arctic explorer in his own right, RICHARDSON was the surgeon and naturalist on Franklin's land expeditions of 1819-20 and 1825-27 and later commanded a boat expedition in search of Franklin in 1848.

RICHTHOFEN ISLAND 61°06'N 135°10'W (105-E). On the west side of Lake Laberge.

In 1883, Lt. Frederick Schwatka, US Army, thought this was a peninsula and gave it the name "RICHTHOFEN ROCKS". Dr. George Mercer Dawson, G&NHSC, corrected the error in 1887 but allowed the name to stand in honour of Freiherr von RICHTHOFEN of Leipzig, Germany, a famous geographer of his time.

The stream behind this island was called the "Red River" by the early miners because of the red rocks along its banks, but the name was changed between 1930-40 to "RICHTHOFEN Creek".

MOUNT RIDDELL 6,101' 62°43'N 131°16'W (105-J). South of the MacMillan River.

In 1907, Joseph Keele, GSC, hired Robert B. RIDDELL to accompany him while he mapped the geology of the headwaters of the Pelly, Ross and Gravel Rivers. It was the first exploration of much of this area. RIDDELL had been the first white man to explore and trap in a great part of this region from about 1898 on.

Keele named this mountain in recognition of RIDDELL's character and services.

RIDDELL RIVER 62°51'N 132°25'W (105-K). A tributary to the upper MacMillan River.

In 1904, Captain Frederick C. Selous, the famed African white hunter and naturalist was assisted by Robert B. RIDDELL to obtain big-game specimens for various museums. He admired RIDDELL for his hardihood in exploring this great tract of wilderness by himself, following no other white man. He noted the name of the river, which was the site of RIDDELL's home.

RIGHT HOOK CREEK 63°41'N 137°03'W (115-P). Flows into Vancouver Creek.

The outline of this creek's course when mapped suggested this name to Hugh S. Bostock, GCS, and his men in 1949.

RIGHT ON MOUNTAIN 61°06'N 138°47'W (115-G). Near the head of Congdon Creek.

This was named in October 1973 by junior members of the Yukon Scenic and Wilderness Study Project, from a then-current slang expression, "Right On", which was intended to express approval.

RINK RAPIDS 62°19'N 136°23'W (115-I). Five miles downstream from Five Finger Rapids.

This name, after Dr. Henry RINK of Christiana, Denmark, an authority on Greenland and Director of the Royal Greenland Trade at Copenhagen, was originally applied to what is now Five Finger Rapids by Lt. Frederick Schwatka, US Army, in 1883. The name was never used by riverboatmen and was transferred to this minor obstruction by Dr. George Mercer Dawson, G&NHSC, in 1887.

In the winter of 1902-03, the most dangerous rocks were blasted from the channel by P.E. Mercier, Territorial Engineer.

ROAL CREEK 64°19'N 140°00'W (116-B). Enters the Yukon River from the west, about five miles above Cassiar Creek.

This creek was named after Louis ROAL, who prospected this area and found a vein of lead-zinc ore near here in the 1920s.

ROBBED CREEK 63°24'N 137°31'W (115-P). A tributary to Lake Creek.

Hugh S. Bostock, GSC, named this creek in 1949 while mapping the area. The headwaters of this stream had been diverted by glacial action and now flow into Pirate Creek.

ROBERT SERVICE CREEK 64°27'N 138°13'W (116-B). A tributary to the North Klondike River (see Mount Robert Service).

MOUNT ROBERT SERVICE 62°25'N 138°11'W (116-B). At the headwaters of the North Klondike River.

These names were proposed in 1968 by Dr. Dirk Tempelman-Kluit, GSC, to commemorate the Bard of the Yukon, author of "The Shooting of Dan McGrew", "The Cremation of Sam McGee", "The Spell of the Yukon" and many, many others.

Service had walked and roamed around much of this area.

ROBINSON 60°27'N 134°51'W (105-D). A way station on the WP&YR, about twenty-two miles south of Whitehorse.

In late 1899, the WP&YR built a way station here while constructing the railway. It was given the name of their Labour Foreman and construction man extraordinaire, "Stikine Bill" ROBINSON.

William C. ROBINSON was from North Anson, Maine. He had followed railroad construction across the continent. In early 1898, he was General Foreman during the short-lived MacKenzie and Mann attempt to build a railroad from Glenora, on the Stikine River, to the head of Teslin Lake. He acquired his nickname on that job.

Mike Heney (The Irish Prince), the contractor who built the WP&YR, hired him in the same capacity. In addition he was put in charge of the early freighting from the Summit to Bennett and Whitehorse, using both horse teams and boats.

From 1908-1912, he assisted Heney in building the 136 mile long Copper River and Northwestern Railway from Cordova to Chitina and on to the enormously rich Kennecott Copper Mines. He continued to engage in prospecting and mining ventures in Alaska until he died on 29 September, 1926.

W.P. Grainger and H.W. Vance, prominent miners of Whitehorse, surveyed a townsite here in 1906, when the mineral wealth of the Wheaton River area to the west appeared capable of major production. A post office was open here from 1909-1915. (see McConnell Lake)

ROCK RIVER 67°18'N 137°06'W (116-P). A tributary to the Bell River.

On 19 June 1847, Alexander Hunter Murray, HBC, found and named this stream the "Blue Fish River". The name was later changed to avoid redundancy with the "Blue Fish River" near Ramparts on the Porcupine River, in Alaska.

Blue Fish was the old name for grayling.

ROCQUETTE ROCKS (see Old Woman Rock).

RODIN CREEK 63°52'N 136°16'W (115-P). A tributary to the South McQuesten River.

A prospector named RODIN, or Roden, found and mined gold on this creek in 1907.

ROGERS CREEK 62°15'N 137°08'W (115-I). A tributary to Seymour Creek.

The creek was named by Captain H.S. Back, after one of his men in 1917.

The name was changed to "Bow Creek" in 1930. (see Bow, Seymour, Discovery and Nansen Creeks)

ROGUE RIVER 63°24'N 132°30'W (105-N). A tributary to the Hess River.

This stream was probably named about 1898 by stampeders coming from Edmonton and experiencing the difficult passages through the rapids and obstructions of this stream.

ROLAND CREEK 69°22'N 138°55'W (117-D). Flows into the Spring River, on the Arctic coast.

Anker Hoidal, who spent his lifetime trapping and prospecting in the Arctic Yukon, said that this stream had been known by this name after an Eskimo (Inuit) who lived on it for more than thirty years, beginning in the 1920s. (see Anker and Hoidal Creeks)

RONDEAU RIVER (see Meister River).

ROSE CREEK 62°25'N 133°41'W (105-K). A tributary to Anvil Creek, on the north side of Rose Mountain.

Oliver ROSE came in to the Yukon over the Edmonton Trail in 1897-98. He came up the Pelly to prospect and settled here for the remainder of his life. The RNWMP reports of the time indicate that his name was probably Oliver LaRose and that his birthplace was in Quebec. They also note that he was a solitary, hard-working and well-regarded man.

In September 1905, Charles Sheldon, noted big-game hunter and naturalist, while collecting specimens for American museums in the region, met ROSE and named this stream where he lived.

ROSE MOUNTAIN 6,513' 61°21'N 133°37"W (105-K). On the north side of the Pelly River, about twelve miles west of Faro.

Oliver ROSE had his home and a small trading post at the foot of this mountain on the Pelly River. It was known as "ROSE's Cabin". Charles Sheldon, the American naturalist, gave the mountain its name on 13 September 1905.

ROSE RIVER 61°10'N 132°59'W (105-F). A tributary to the Nisutlin River, near the foot of Quiet Lake.

In the early 1900s, Oliver ROSE prospected extensively in the area between here and the Pelly River. Lapie Creek and the ROSE River give an almost complete waterway from the Pelly to Quiet Creek.

ROSEBUD CREEK 63°17'N 138°26'W (115-O). A tributary to the Stewart River.

Alexander MacDonald (not "Big Alex"), from New Brunswick, explored and prospected the Stewart River in 1887 or even earlier. He found some gold showings on this stream and named it, probably after the Battle of the Rosebud River in the Sioux Wars in the American west during the 1870s, in which it was said he took part. It is believed that he also named Black Hills Creek in the same vicinity.

ROSS CREEK 63°54'N 136°02'W (115-P). A tributary to the South McQuesten River.

An early prospector named ROSS found placer gold here and named the creek around 1898-99. He remained in the country for many years. (see the other Ross Creek)

ROSS CREEK 64°00'N 137°34'W (115-P). A tributary to the Little South Klondike River.

ROSS came into the country during the Gold Rush. He prospected and lived in the area until the 1930s. He was the first to find gold on this stream but there was not enough to pay. (see the other Ross Creek, both named for the same man)

ROSS RIVER 61°59'N 132°25'W (105-F). A settlement at the junction of the Ross and Pelly Rivers.

This settlement was established by Tom Smith around 1903 but was soon sold to Poole Field and Clement Lewis who named it "Nahanni House", because of the number of Indians from the Nahanni country in the NWT who had followed them here to trap and trade.

The post was later taken over by the Whitehorse firm of Taylor and Drury, and later operated under various owners until 1964.

ROSS RIVER 61°59'N 132°25'W (105-F). A major tributary to the Pelly River.

In 1843, Robert Campbell of the HBC made his famous first journey down the Pelly River to its junction with the (Lewes) Yukon.. During this journey he named most of the tributaries to the Pelly. This stream was named after Chief Factor Donald ROSS of the HBC.

ROWLINSON CREEK 62°03'N 136°17'W (115-I). Flows into the Nordenskiold River, three miles south of Carmacks.

D.D. Cairnes, GSC, while mapping this part of the country in 1911, recorded this name from Seymour ROWLINSON who was living and mining on this stream. He had been the first to find gold here and had been here for a number of years.

ROY LAKE 60°32'N 127°49'W (95-D). A small lake immediately east of Hulse (Quartz) Lake.

In February 1970, this lake was named by James Harquail, President of Fort Reliance Minerals Ltd., to commemorate Andrew ROY. In the summer of 1968, ROY had been camp cook for the company's exploration crew and had lost his life in an airplane crash on Hulse Lake on 2 September 1968. John Hulse, geophysicist, was also killed in this crash. (see Hulse Lake)

ROYAL MOUNTAIN 6,567' 65°01'N 135°02'W (106-E). East of the Wind River, in the Wernecke Mountains.

In September 1897, George Mitchell of Montreal and his party were trapped here by winter. They were on their way to the Klondike via Edmonton, the MacKenzie, Peel and Wind Rivers. They established a small community near the mouth of the Wind River, called "Wind City". Mitchell named this peak that winter because it reminded him of the shape of Mount Royal in Montreal.

He later published an account of his experiences under the title, "The Golden Grindstone".

RUBE CREEK 66°36'N 138°15'W (116-J). A tributary to the Porcupine River.

This name was officially proposed on 27 November 1958, by Professor Otto William Geist of the University of Alaska, after RUBE Mason. Geist stated in his application that Ruben and his brother Bill were noted trappers and "highly esteemed individuals". This area was their trapping grounds and this stream was known locally as "Mason" and "RUBE Mason Creek". (see Mason Lake and Mason Hill)

RUBY CREEK 61°05'N 137°57'W (115-H). A small stream joining Lake Creek and flowing south into the Jarvis River.

The Discovery claim on this stream was staked and the creek named by W.H. Weisdepp on 6 July 1903 and the stampede to the Shakwak Valley goldfields was on.

The Whitehorse Star on 27 July 1903 reported: "The arrival of an Indian in the town of Whitehorse in July last, with a small quantity of gold, which he said he obtained near the surface on a creek in the Shakwak district, brought this part of the Yukon into greater prominence. The Indian who made the discovery informed several other Indians who immediately started for that part. They returned after ten days and several claims were recorded on a creek they called "RUBY". A general stampede then took place, close upon five hundred persons went out and staked, returned and recorded. (Skookum Jim Mason and "Dawson" Charlie were among the first)."

The creek was worked out within a few years. During this period a small settlement of the same name grew up at the mouth of the stream, with a post office, roadhouse and stores. It died with the decline of the stream.

RUDE CREEK 62°40'N 138°43'W (115-J). A tributary to Dip Creek, in the Dawson Range.

Jens RUDE and his partner were extremely active prospectors in this area. They found good gold on this stream and staked the Discovery claim on it on 12 March 1915. They worked the gravels here for several years. (see Dip and Jens Creeks)

RUDYARD LAKE (see Sheldon Lake).

RUNT CREEK 66°16'N 141°00'W (115-K). A tributary to the Salmon Fork, across the Yukon-Alaska boundary.

This little stream got its name from surveyors of the International Boundary Commission in 1908.

RUSSELL COL 60°19'N 140°54'W (115-C). The connecting ridge between Mount St. Elias and Mount Newton.

This feature was named to honour Professor Israel C. RUSSELL, USGS, who first mapped this area and named Mount Logan. He made three expeditions to the Yukon. On the first, in 1889, he went by boat from St. Michaels to Fort Selkirk, continued up the Yukon River with a group of miners and emerged at Dyea, after exploring in the White River area. In 1890-91 he crossed the Chilkoot Pass and again ascended the White River to the Mount St. Elias region where he continued his mapping and explorations. He added greatly to the knowledge of this part of the territory. The Col was probably named in 1891 by the USGS.

RUSSELL CREEK 63°02'N 133°24'W (105-N). A tributary to the MacMillan River, just below the forks.

Thomas Duncan Gillies (or Gillis) prospected in the Yukon from 1892. In the winter of 1896-97, he was at his home in Nova Scotia when he received news of the Klondike discovery. He returned via Edmonton and the MacKenzie River, then up the Gravel (Keele) River, across the continental divide and down the MacMillan River, mistaking it for the Hess. Prospecting along the way, he found good gold showings at the mouth of this creek, which he named "Slate Creek", from the rocks thereon. He spent several weeks prospecting the stream and was caught by winter. Having few supplies and unable to raft because of the gathering ice, he was forced to walk overland to Fort Selkirk. He suffered great hardships and privations but arrived safely.

Returning the next year with partners, he was encouraged to obtain a concession which was granted to him in 1900, when he changed the name of the stream to RUSSELL CREEK. The reason for the change is not known.

Neville A.D. Armstrong, acting for an English company, bought out the concession and worked it unprofitably for many years. (see Mount Armstrong and Mount Gillis)

MOUNT RUSSELL 67°44'N 136°29'W (116-P). On the north side of MacDougall Pass, on the Yukon-NWT boundary.

This peak was named by William Ogilvie, DLS, on his journey from Forty Mile to Fort MacPherson in May 1888. It is thought that he named it after one of his crew.

RUSSELL RANGE 63°13'N 133°10'W (105-N). North of the upper MacMillan River, near the forks.

This was named near the turn of the century, or slightly earlier, after Mark RUSSELL, a noted pioneer Yukon prospector. He ranged far and wide in Alaska and the Yukon. He accompanied Dr. C.W. Hayes, USGS, and Lt. Frederick Schwatka, US Army, in 1891 from Juneau up the Taku River to Teslin Lake and on into the White River country, probably the first to make the journey.

SABBATH CREEK 63°47'N 136°21'W (115-P). A tributary to Johnson Creek from the west.

Rudolph Rasmussen found the first gold on this stream and staked the Discovery claim on 8 August 1909.

SABINE POINT 69°04'N 137°44'W (117-D). On the Arctic coast.

Sir John Franklin, RN, named this feature in 1825 after Major General Sir Edward SABINE, RA (1788-1883), a celebrated British astronomer and physicist. He was astronomer to the first John Ross expedition of 1818 and to the Parry expedition of 1819-20. He was President of the British Association in 1853 and of the Royal Society from 1861-1871.

MOUNT ST. CYR 6,725' 61°21'N 133°09'W (105-F). Ten miles north of Quiet Lake.

This mountain was named about 1901 after Arthur St. Cyr, DLS, QLS. He was sent by the Department of the Interior of the Dominion government in May 1897 to find and survey a possible wagon or railway route from Telegraph Creek on the Stikine River to the head of Teslin Lake for the expected hordes of goldseekers. The government wished it to be an all-Canadian route. This task he accomplished that summer, exploring several alternate routes and carrying his surveys not only to Teslin Lake but also along the lake and up the Teslin River to the Lewes (Yukon) River. He continued this work through 1898.

In 1899-1901, he was engaged in surveying the Yukon-B.C. boundary.

The St. Cyr Range was named later.

MOUNT ST. ELIAS 18,008' 60°18'N 140°56'W (115-C). At the southwest corner of the Yukon Territory.

This mountain, sometimes called "the corner post of Alaska", was first seen by Vitus Bering on St. Elias Day, 16 July 1741. Bering, a Dane employed by the Russian government to explore the coast of Alaska, commanded the ship "St. Peter". This mountain was the first feature in the Yukon Territory to be named by white men.

The first attempt to climb it was made by Lt. Frederick Schwatka, US Army, in 1886. His expedition was a fiasco which barely got off the beach and turned back in a few days. The peak was first climbed by Prince Luigi Amadeo of Savoy, nephew of King Humbert of Italy, and his party in the summer of 1897.

ST. GERMAIN CREEK 61°24'N 134°24'W (105-E). A tributary to the Big Salmon River.

Joseph ST. GERMAIN of Quebec, discovered payable gold and named this stream in the fall of 1900.

SALTER HILL 66°09'N 134°50'W (106-L). West of the Peel River.

This hill was given the name of Maxwell Charles SALTER, a Yukon Councillor for South Dawson from 1917-20.

SAMBO CREEK 60°24'N 129°33'W (105-A). Flows into the upper Liard River, east of Frances Lake.

"Old SAMBO" or "Old Sam" lived and trapped on this creek and the lake of the same name at its head, for many years. Interviewed in 1942, shortly before he died, he could remember white men and former black slaves (from the underground railway between the southern United States and Canada) searching for gold along the Dease River in the 1870s.

MOUNT SAMPSON 11,000' 61°12'N 140°03'W (115-F). East of the Steele Glacier, in the St. Elias Range.

Named in 1970, by the Alpine Club of Canada after Herbert E. SAMPSON (1871-1962), a lawyer and past-president of the club (1930-1932).

SAMUELSON HILL 2,057' 66°19'N 137°11'W (116-I). East of the Canoe River.

In June 1973, this hill was named in memory of Helmer SAMUELSON. Born in Dawson, he served during the Second World War. He was owner, editor and printer of the Dawson News and later, of the Whitehorse Star.

SANPETE CREEK 62°08'N 140°29'W (115-K). Crosses the Alaska Highway near Mile 1175 (KM1903).

This stream was named about the turn of the century by a prospector from SANPETE County, Utah.

SAPPER HILL 65°22'N 138°16'W (116-G). On the east side of the Ogilvie River.

James Smith, Commissioner of the Yukon Territory, in 1971 requested this name to honour the Royal Canadian Engineers for their work. In the summer of that year they had built the George Allan Jeckell Bridge over the Ogilvie River near here.

The name "SAPPER" is a nickname given to all army engineers and dates from medieval days when they were employed mostly to dig "saps" or tunnels under enemy fortifications.

MOUNT SASKATCHEWAN 11,390' 60°57'N 140°51'W (115-C). In the Centennial Range of the St. Elias Mountains.

This peak was named for the province of SASKATCHEWAN in Canada's Centennial Year of 1967. (see Centennial Range)

SATAH RIVER 67°00'N 134°28'W (106-L). A tributary to the Peel River.

The Compte V.E. de Sainville, French sportsman and explorer, named this river in 1893. He was exploring this portion of the Northwest Territories and the Yukon when he met a band of Indians whose Chief was named SATAH.

SAVAGE GULCH 63°47'N 136°19'W (115-P). A small creek flowing into Johnson Creek from Scheelite Dome.

A prospector of this name found and worked a placer gold deposit here in the early 1900s.

SAYYEA CREEK 60°45'N 130°21'W (105-B). A tributary to the upper Liard River.

This small, little known creek is the location of the first gold mined in the Yukon Territory.

Historical writings on the Yukon usually concentrate on the miners who entered the territory by way of the Chilkoot Pass and up the Yukon River. They begin with Harper and Mayo unsuccessfully prospecting the upper reaches of the White River in the fall and winter of 1873-74 from the lower Yukon and with George Holt who was the first known white man to cross the Chilkoot Pass, finding little but prospects in the summer of 1875.

The first known payable gold mined in the watershed of the Yukon River was obtained by a miner named Cummins and his three partners from a small stream about fifteen miles above Miles Canyon, in 1880.

However, in 1874, John SAYYEA and three companions came from Dease Lake up the Liard River, discovered gold on this stream and remained to mine it during the winter of 1874-75. From 115 days work they recovered seventy-seven and three sixteenths ounces of coarse gold, including nuggets of over an ounce in weight. Their find started a rush from the Cassiar goldfields in the spring of 1875 and gold was found on several nearby creeks. After SAYYEA's first find no other payable deposits were worked, due mostly to problems of water flooding the deeper gravels. There was enough encouragement to keep prospectors active in this part of the Yukon until the time of the Klondike rush. The drawback to prospecting the Yukon Territory from this direction was the extreme difficulty of the route from either the Cassiar country or the MacKenzie Valley. Either way was much more difficult and longer than by way of the Chilkoot Pass. The upper Liard Canyon was itself a much greater hazard than Miles Canyon and the Whitehorse Rapids. In fact it was mainly the dangers of this route that had influenced the HBC to abandon its posts in the region in 1852. (see Cabin, Scurvy and Squaw Creeks and also the Finlayson and Hyland Rivers)

SCHAEFFER CREEK 66°53'N 137°41'W (116-I). A tributary to the Porcupine River.

Albert E. SCHAEFFER was a German prospector and trapper who came into the Yukon in 1898 over the Edmonton Trail. He settled in this part of the country about that time, married a woman from Old Crow and settled into a life of trapping.

He died of scurvy in Dawson in 1940. (see Schaeffer Creek below and Potato Creek)

SCHAEFFER CREEK 68°09'N 140°23'W (117-C). A tributary to the Old Crow River.

This creek was named after the same Albert E. SCHAEFFER as the one above. About 1915-20, he moved his family from their previous location to this place, where the muskrats were much more prolific. Here they remained until his death.

MOUNT SCHELLINGER 65°29'N 132°39'W (106-F). East of the Snake River.

In February 1973, this mountain was named after Arthur K. SCHELLINGER who was a mining engineer with the Yukon Consolidated Gold Company for many years and from 1920-1930 worked for Keno Hill Mines Ltd. and the Treadwell Yukon Mining Company at Mayo. He was a well-known and well-regarded man. (see Keno)

SCHNABEL CREEK 60°19'N 134°59'W (105-D). Flows into Annie Lake at the big bend of the Wheaton River.

William F. SCHNABEL came in to the Yukon in 1897. In 1898, he was the first man known to prospect Gray Ridge and that summer he found a coal seam on this creek. His wife was the first white woman in this part of the country. They lived in the district until they moved to Oregon in 1914. (see Mt. Bush)

SCHWATKA LAKE 60°41'N 135°02'W (105-D). The artificial lake above the power dam on the Yukon River at Whitehorse.

This lake was formed behind the hydro-electric power plant and dam on the Yukon River at Whitehorse. The lake covers the dreaded Whitehorse and Squaw Rapids and has eliminated the swift currents through Miles Canyon. This was accomplished and the plant was put into operation in 1959.

Lt. Frederick SCHWATKA, US Army, was born 29 September 1849 in Galena, Illinois. His family moved west and he attended Willamette University in Oregon until he was accepted at West Point Military Academy from which he was graduated in 1871. Studying while serving at various western army posts, he acquired degrees in law and medicine.

In 1879-80, he led an expedition to the Canadian Arctic in search of the lost Franklin Expedition, which established his reputation as an Arctic explorer.

In 1883, under orders from General Nelson A. Miles, Commander of the Department of the Columbia (which included Alaska) and without notice to the Canadian authorities, he crossed the Chilkoot Pass and rafted down the Yukon River. Pte. Charles A. Homan, his topographer, made a rough but fairly accurate survey of the course of the river, the first to that time. SCHWATKA ignored all previous and contemporary nomenclature of the region. He seems to have assumed that no one had given names to any feature in the country before himself, so he named most of the rivers, lakes and prominent hills along his route after his superior officers and prominent academicians of his day. He discarded Robert Campbell's Lewes River and changed it to the Yukon River and named Lake Lindeman as the source of the Yukon River without investigating the Teslin or the Pelly Rivers.

Dr. George Mercer Dawson, G&NHSC, disallowed many of SCHWATKA's names but allowed others to stand because of the international figures they honoured. Another reason was that

SCHWATKA's work was incorporated into a map issued by the USC&GS in 1885. This was the best map of the region until Dawson and Ogilvie's map was issued in 1888.

SCHWATKA led an expedition in 1886 to climb Mount St. Elias, sponsored by George Jones of the New York Times. SCHWATKA was accompanied by William Libby of the College of New Jersey and by the only member of the party with alpine experience, Heywood W. Seton-Carr, an English sportsman and naturalist. It was remarked that for Seton-Carr to try to guide the 250-pound SCHWATKA up a 19,000 foot mountain would be "a quixotic enterprise". The expedition was a fiasco, getting away from the beach for only nine or ten days. Mount St. Elias remained unclimbed.

In 1891, with C. Willard Hayes, USGS, and Mark Russell (a noted pioneer prospector, who had made the trip previously), he went from Juneau via the Taku River and Teslin Lake to Fort Selkirk and on into the basin of the White River.

SCHWATKA early realized the value of publicity and rapidly published many glowing accounts of his travels, always emphasizing the hardships and dangers encountered. He became a member of many prestigious scientific societies and died in Portland, Oregon, on 2 November 1892.

SCOTCH GULCH 63°04'N 139°19'W (115-O). The first left tributary to Thistle Creek.

This small valley was named in late 1898 by one of a party of eight Scottish miners who found and staked Thistle Creek. (see Thistle Creek)

SCOTTIE CREEK 62°38'N 141°00'W (115-J). A tributary to the Chisana River, in Alaska.

W.J. Peters and A.H. Brooks, USGS, named this stream for a member of their 1898 geological survey party. Gold was found in the gravels of the creek during the Chisana Gold Rush of 1913. It was sometimes called "Scotty" or "Big Scotty Creek".

SCOUGALE CREEK 64°12'N 134°43'W (106-D). A tributary to the Beaver River.

Named in the early 1900s by and for James A. SCOUGALE, who lived and mined here.

SCOUT LAKE 60°47'N 135°25'W (105-D). The larger of two lakes, five miles west of Haeckel Hill.

This lake was officially named in 1973. A Boy Scout summer camp had been located here for a number of years.

SCOUTCAR CREEK 64°19'N 138°27'W (116-B). Crosses the Dempster Highway, into the North Klondike River.

Probably named in 1969 when highway construction workers bogged down one of these vehicles in the stream.

SCOW LAKE 68°46'N 136°38'W (117-A). In the midst of many ponds. Connects to Shoalwater Bay by a ten mile channel.

This is a local name. Bill Strong, a local resident for many years, beached his SCOW here for many winters.

SCROGGIE CREEK 63°12'N 138°51'W (115-O). A tributary to the Stewart River.

Ernest R. SCROGGIE of Rawdon, Quebec, led a party of nine prospectors into this area in the summer of 1898. On 27 August two of the men, J.G. Stephens of Deadwood, North Dakota and H. LeDuke of Quebec, found the first gold and staked the Discovery claim. The remainder of the party staked claims and the creek was named by Wealthy T. SCROGGIE, a brother of Ernest.

The creek has produced gold sporadically up to the present time.

SCURVY CREEK 60°49'N 130°33'W (105-B). A tributary to the upper Liard River.

Gold was found here in the summer of 1874 by Cassiar miners working north from Dease Lake, B.C. The journey was arduous and some miners wintered on this and neighbouring creeks rather than face the difficult trip back to the Dease Lake country.

In the following winter at least four of these men died of scurvy and were buried near the mouth of the creek, on the banks of the Liard River. The remaining men were saved by three of their number who walked to Laketon (on Dease Lake) in March 1875, for help. The Victoria Colonist of 21 July 1875, carried a letter from McDame Creek;

"I think it my duty to notify you of the great suffering of the Deloire (Liard) pioneers from the scurvy. Four have died from the said disease and ten others had a narrow escape. The only thing that saved them was three of their number coming out on the ice and getting to Laketon on 12 March, to report the suffering that four of their number endured at the time of their leaving them, I may mention the date, 12 February. We all subscribed at Laketon, and in two days we dispatched one white man and an Indian with medicine, rum, vegetables, potatoes, lime-juice, vinegar, etc. which the sick men received in sixteen days. Those who got here on the 19th inst. state that only for what was sent from here more than half of the sick men would have perished. The four who died were ailing all winter and were too far gone by the time they received the medicines.....the unfortunate men died easy deaths. They got frozen in with their boats on 25 October 1874."

SEAFORTH CREEK 60°27'N 133°34'W (105-C). Flows north across the Alaska Highway into Squanga Lake.

This is an early name thought to have been given by a trapper who had seen service in the famous SEAFORTH Highlanders Regiment. During the construction of the highway the name was changed to "John Creek" by US Army Engineers but the name soon reverted to the original.

SEAGULL CREEK 60°00'N 131°11'W (105-B). A tributary to Swift River, near Mile 734 (KM1189) on the Alaska Highway.

This was named by US Army Engineer troops during highway construction in 1942 because of the vast numbers of these birds that visited the garbage dumps nearby.

On the mountainside east of this creek about 1960, Jack Shields discovered the only gem quality topaz ever found in the Yukon.

SECRET CREEK 63°59'N 136°00'W (115-P). A tributary to Swede Creek.

Narcisse A. Lefebvre and Isaac Mallette found gold and named this stream on 7 September 1911, giving the name because the stream enters Swede Creek in such a way as to be nearly hidden from view. They mined their claims until August 1914.

MOUNT SEDGWICK 2,956' 68°53'N 139°08'W (117-A). In the Buckland Mountains, near the Arctic coast.

Sir John Franklin, RN, on his second expedition in 1826, named this mountain after Adam SEDGWICK (1785-1873), the famous British geologist.

SEGUIN LAKES 66°43'N 134°23'W (106-L). East of the Peel River.

In April 1973, this name was given to commemorate Alavie J. SEGUIN, who was a Yukon Councillor for North Dawson from 1912-1915.

MOUNT SELOUS 7,138' 62°58'N 132 28'W (105-K). North of the South MacMillan River.

This mountain, the highest peak in the Russell Range, was named around 1907 after Frederick Courtenay SELOUS, by Joseph Keele, GSC. SELOUS had hunted here in 1904 and 1906 for specimens of big-game. He was a noted naturalist as well as a famous African white hunter. Most of his hunting was for trophy specimens which were carefully preserved for various museums. From 1870-1890 he hunted areas in Africa in which no other white man had ever set foot, finding and procuring new species of animals for museums at his own expense.

He died as a Captain in the 25th Royal Fusiliers of the British Army, decorated for bravery with the DSO, leading his troops against the German Army in East Africa. He was 65 years old when he was killed.

This peak had previously been known as "Chang Mountain", a name given it by Neville A.D. Armstrong, who mined on nearby Russell Creek for many years.

SELWYN MOUNTAINS 63°00'N 130°00'W (105-I). Paralleling the Yukon-NWT boundary.

The SELWYN MOUNTAINS comprise three ranges; the Logan, Hess and Wernecke Mountains. They were named in 1901 by Joseph Keele, GSC, after Dr. Alfred Richard Cecil SELWYN (1827-1902). Born in Somerset, England, he was one of the most distinguished geologists of his time. He was with the Geographical Survey of Great Britain from 1845-1852. From then until 1869 he was Director of the Geological Survey of Australia and from that date, until he retired in 1895, he was the Director of the Geological Survey of Canada. His contribution to the science was immense in all three countries. In Canada alone he organized, expanded and directed the Geological and Natural History Survey after Confederation.

SELWYN RIVER 62°48'N 138°17'W (115-J). A small tributary to the Yukon River.

Lt. Frederick Schwatka, US Army, named this stream in 1883 after Dr. A.R.C. SELWYN, Director of the G&NHSC. There was a small settlement at the mouth of the stream from 1900 to about 1950, as a telegraph station and a wood point for riverboats.

The river was prospected in 1885 by a man named Duval, an ex-jailer from Tacoma, Washington. He returned in August 1898 and staked a Discovery claim which he soon sold. Little gold was found on the stream and it was afterwards claimed that he had salted his claim (i.e. that he had sprinkled gold dust in the gravels to make the claim appear much richer than it actually was).

SEMINOF HILLS 61°27'N 134°35'W (105-E). The range of hills on the east side of the Yukon and Teslin Rivers.

Lt. Frederick Schwatka, US Army, gave this low range of hills the name of von SEMINOF, President of the Imperial Geographical Society of Russia, in 1883. Sometimes spelled "Semenof" or "Semenov".

SEMPLE CREEK 65°52'N 136°14'W (116-H). Flows north to Peel River.

Johnny SEMPLE was a well-known trapper in the Peel River region. Born in 1888, he died in April 1980, at the age of 92.

SENOAH CREEK 63°47'N 131°15'W (105-O). A tributary to the Rogue River.

Named for SENOAH Niddery, the Indian wife of Norman Niddery. They lived here for many years. (see Niddery Lake)

SERGERENT CREEK 61°44'N 140°11'W (115-F). A tributary to the Koidern River.

This creek was named around 1923 (officially in 1949), after a French big-game hunter of this name who hunted here in 1913 and again in 1923. He was outfitted and guided by Gene Jacquot of Burwash. Buck Dixon, a well-known guide in the area, supplied the name to the GSC.

SERPENTHEAD LAKE 61°40'N 138°45'W (115-G). At the north end of Talbot Arm of Kluane Lake.

From the hills above, the outline of the lake resembles a striking snake head. Hugh S. Bostock, GSC, thought so when he was mapping the area in 1945.

SESTAK CREEK 63°25'N 139°44'W (115-O). Flows east to the Yukon River.

Named for Joseph SESTAK who prospected and mined in the Sixty Mile River area for many years.

MOUNT SETHER 5,296' 63°20'N 136°13'W (115-P). On the south side of Ethel Lake.

Although this mountain was named in June 1967, the creek, which flows from it to Ethel Lake, was prospected many years before by Ole SETHER, who found and worked on a gold-quartz vein nearby.

SETTLEMIER CREEK 64°29'N 135°17'W (106-D). A tributary to the Beaver River, in the Wernecke Mountains.

Charles SETTLEMIER was an editor of the Dawson Daily News in the 1920s. He prospected widely in the Mayo area then and into the 1930s. This creek was named when he found silver-lead ore near it in 1923. The hill on the east side of the creek was later given the name, SETTLEMIER Ridge.

SEVENTEEN MILE 63°28'N 136°18'W (115-P). On the south bank of the Stewart River.

This was the location of an old riverboat wood camp. Louis Brown's roadhouse on the old Mayo winter trail was nearby. It has long been abandoned.

SEYMOUR CREEK 62°21'N 137°11'W (115-I). A tributary to Big Creek, in the Mount Freegold area.

In 1899, Captain Henry SEYMOUR Back prospected in this area. He returned in 1910 with a party of men to re-prospect the region. In 1916, he developed gold deposits on this creek and gave it his name. His party found gold, not only here but on many nearby streams. Back originally named the main stream after the famous British First World War Commander in Chief, Field Marshall Lord Kitchener of Sudan. The east fork he named SEYMOUR. The name Kitchener was never officially adopted. (see Back, Discovery and Nansen Creeks)

SHAHTLAH MOUNTAIN 4,166' 67°37'N 140°06'W (116-N). Eight miles northwest of Old Crow village.

Named in 1973, to confirm a long used local name, the Vanta Kutchin Indian word means "Long Hair".

SHAW CREEK 64°02'N 139°33'W (116-B). A very short creek, tributary to the Yukon River, between Bryant and Montana Creeks.

A very short creek, really a gulch about one-quarter mile long. An exciting stampede took place here in September 1903 when Fred SHAW and Fred Jorgenson found good, coarse gold here. Half the population of Dawson ran all the way here to stake claims. It was named by the Mining Recorder in Dawson.

SHEEP CREEK 60°54'N 138°34'W (115-B). A tributary to the Slim's River.

The creek was named when placer gold was discovered and staked in October 1903 by the well-known prospectors Ater, Altemose, Smith and Bones.

SHEH TSOO CREEK 66°41'N 134°43'W (106-L). Tributary to the Peel River, below Zralri Island.

This is a Loucheaux Indian word meaning "Yellow Sands Creek".

SHELDON LAKE 62°42'N 131°03'W (105-J). On the Ross River, near the South MacMillan River, east of the Canol Road.

This lake was named "Rudyard Lake" by Poole Field and Clement Lewis, early traders and sometime prospectors in the area. The name was common locally until Joseph Keele, GSC, mapped the region in 1907. He renamed it for Charles SHELDON, wealthy American sportsman and amateur naturalist who had hunted and camped in this area in 1905.

MOUNT SHELDON 6,937' 62°44'N 131°05'W (105-J). Three miles north of Sheldon Lake.

In 1900, Poole Field and Clement Lewis of the Ross River trading post, "Nahanni House", named this peak "Kipling Mountain" in conjunction with Rudyard Lake at its base. Joseph Keele, GSC, however, renamed them both after Charles SHELDON in 1907.

SHELL CREEK 64°30'N 140°25'W (116-C). Flows into the Yukon River, about five miles below Forty Mile, from the east.

William Ogilvie, DLS, named this stream in the summer of 1896 when he found fossil shells in the rocks along its banks.

SHOALWATER BAY 68°55'N 136°43'W (117-A). An arm of MacKenzie Bay on the Arctic coast.

Sir John Franklin, RN, sailed into this bay in 1826 and named it after running aground several times. (see Pillage Point)

SHOOTAMOOK CREEK 60°49'N 131°00'W (105-B). A tributary to Scurvy Creek.

Billy Smith, Chief of the Tagish Band and a trapper and prospector, found gold on this creek in 1936 and named it "Shomdenook" which means "Rising Up" and probably relates to an Indian legend of a mythical golden man.

SHORTY CREEK 60°24'N 137°10'W (115-A). Flows into Alder Creek.

The man who found gold here in May or June 1896 and named the creek was an extraordinary character. "Long SHORTY" Bigelow (sometimes known as Bowers) was a pioneer in the Haines-Kluane country before 1894. He helped drive the first herd of cattle over the Dalton Trail in 1895. In 1903, he was sentenced to fifteen years at hard labour in San Quentin Penitentiary in California by a St. Michaels judge after committing armed robbery on the lower Yukon River. In 1909, he was granted a pardon when friends brought to the attention of the government the fact that he had once, in the dead of winter, hauled a crippled woman in a hand sled from the Big Salmon River to Skagway.

Returning to the Kluane country he married an Indian woman and led a quieter life. (see Howard Lake and Dalton Trail)

SHRIMP LAKE 60°11'N 128°27'W (105-A). South of Baker Lake.

A local name from the large number of fresh water shrimp found here.

SHURSHO CREEK 60°06'N 137°21'W (115-A). Flows to Onion Creek.

A Southern Tuchone Indian word meaning "Big Bear". This creek is in an area inhabited by many grizzly bears.

SHUTDUNMUN LAKE 61°07'N 137°45'W (115-H). On upper Lake Creek.

This small lake which lies on the old Indian trail between Sekulmun Lake and the Jarvis River is called, in the local Indian dialect, "The Rest Place". The name was officially adopted in July 1962.

MOUNT SIBBALD 10,050' 61°14'N 140°01'W (115-G). On the east side of the Steele Glacier.

This was named in November 1970 after Andrew S. SIBBALD (1888-1945), lawyer and past-president of the Alpine Club of Canada (1934-1938). The name was proposed by the club.

SIDNEY CREEK 60°46'N 132°57'W (105-C). A tributary to the Nisling River, below Quiet Lake.

Gold was discovered on this stream in 1902 by Jim Thompson. News of the find started a rush to the district in June and July 1905 when he first thought that he had found payable gold. He also found the first gold prospects and named Willow and Marble Creeks in the same area.

SIFTON RANGE 60°56'N 136°10'W (115-A). A small range of hills, about fifteen miles northeast of Champagne.

These hills were named before 1898, after the Hon. Clifford SIFTON, Minister of the Interior (1896-1906), who had the unprecedented task of setting up the government apparatus of the Yukon Territory in 1897-98 under the most difficult conditions. This he did with most outstanding ability and competence.

SILVER CITY (see Kluane).

SIMPSON LAKE 60°44'N 129°15'W (105-A). On the west side of the Frances River, fifty miles north of Watson Lake.

In the summer of 1834, Chief Factor John McLeod of the HBC, ascended the Liard River from the MacKenzie to the Frances River (which he named the Liard). He travelled the Frances as far north as this lake which he named after Sir George Simpson, the Governor of the HBC. This was the first lake in the Yukon Territory to be named by a white man.

SIMPSON RANGE 60°53'N 129°55'W (105-A). The mountains on the west side of Simpson Lake.

These hills were named about 1956 when the Campbell Highway (the Cantung Road at the time) was being laid out.

SIMPSON TOWER 61°24'N 129°29'W (105-H). The lone peak sitting midway between the arms of Frances Lake.

On 19 July 1840, Robert Campbell of the HBC first saw this peak and named it after Sir George Simpson, the Governor of the Company. He named the lake the same day after Sir George's wife, Frances. (see Frances Lake)

MOUNT SITTICHINLI 67°11'N 136°15'W (116-P). South of the Rat River.

Lazarus SITTICHINLI was a Special Constable of the RCMP. He drove dog teams for the RCMP patrol in the famous search for Albert Johnson, the "Mad Trapper of Rat River", in 1932. (see Moses Hill)

SIXTY MILE RIVER 63°34'N 139°46'W (115-O). A tributary to the Yukon River, fifty miles above Dawson.

In 1876, Arthur Harper, sometime partner of McQuesten and Mayo, found good showings of gold on this river. Returning to Fort Reliance, which had just been established and was the only trading post in the territory, he gave this river its name because it was sixty miles upstream from the post. Although Harper made little from his prospects, others followed him and in 1891 rich placer gold was found on tributaries of this river. (see Ogilvie)

MOUNT SKONSENG 60°57'N 127°13'W (95-D). Between the Coal and Rock Rivers.

Thoralf "Ted" SKONSENG was born in Norway. He was a noted bushman and prospector. His long-time friend and employer, Dr. Aro Aho, of Dynasty Explorations Ltd., and another friend, Laco Hunt, proposed this name for the hill in his memory.

SKONSENG died when he fell into a tub of scalding water at the Whitehorse Hotel in 1973.

SKOOKUM GULCH 63°56'N 139°20'W (115-O). A tributary to Bonanza Creek, just below its junction with Eldorado Creek.

Joseph Goldsmith had been in the Yukon for several years and was mining on American Creek in Alaska, when he heard the news of the Klondike find. Too late to stake a claim on one of the major creeks, he prospected the feeders, and found extremely rich gold on this one. He staked the first claim and named the place on 22 March 1897. He and his partner panned $2,800 in gold in the first four days and sluiced $40,000 in four months from claims No. 1 and No. 2.

SKOOKUM is a Chinook Indian word meaning "Strong".

MOUNT SKOOKUM JIM 65°11'N 139°03'W (116-G). South of the Ogilvie River.

In September 1973, the 75th Anniversary of the Klondike Gold Rush, this mountain was chosen to commemorate one of the discoverers, SKOOKUM JIM Mason.

He and George Carmack assisted William Ogilvie over the Chilkoot Pass in 1887. In 1896, with Tagish (later "Dawson") Charlie, they discovered, not the first but the richest gold in the Klondike and on the east side of the Yukon River. Although there are many arguments as to which of the three actually panned the first gold on Bonanza Creek, Jim took little or no part in them. He worked and handled his claim wisely and remained a dedicated prospector until he died. He was instrumental in finding other placer goldfields in the Yukon, such as the Kluane fields.

He died in Carcross on 23 July 1916. He left his estate not only to his family but also to help his people. He was always generous and respected by all who knew him.

SKULL RIDGE 3,106' 68°32'N 137°26'W (117-A). Fifteen miles west of Mount Gilbert Davies.

This is a very old native name and was given because of the numerous animal bones and skulls they found there, many years ago.

MOUNT SLAGGARD 61°11'N 140°35'W (115-G). In the St. Elias Range.

In July 1958, this mountain was given the name of Joseph R. SLAGGARD, a pioneer prospector in this area of the Yukon from the early 1900s. With his partners M.C. Harris and Solomon Albert (who made the original discovery) he staked the first claims containing significant amounts of copper ore at the headwaters of the White River near here in May 1905. SLAGGARD himself found the largest slab of pure native copper ever found in the territory. This specimen now stands at the MacBride Museum in Whitehorse.

SLAGGARD RIDGE 61°45'N 140°45'W (115-F). At the headwaters of the White River.

This name was given by prospectors about 1906, after Joseph R. SLAGGARD, who was instrumental in locating copper deposits in this region. (see Mount Slaggard)

SLAVIN CREEK 64°42'N 138°24'W (116-B). A tributary to the East Blackstone River.

Frank SLAVIN was an Australian. He was a heavyweight boxing champion in that country. Making his way to America, he toured with boxing troupes. Meeting Frank Boyle, they became friends and came together to the Klondike in 1898. He became a moderately successful miner.

SLEEP CREEK 61°24'N 132°33'W (105-F). Flows into Seagull Creek and then into the McConnell River.

This was named in May 1962 to honour the memory of a gallant man, J-9483 Flight Lt. Kenneth Stephen SLEEP, MID, RCAF. Born on 19 November 1922 at Lindsay, Ontario, he enlisted at Toronto in the RCAF on 10 April 1941. He served in Canada and overseas and was killed during air operations over Europe on 1 December 1944.

SLEEPY MOUNTAIN 68°42'N 138°20'W (117-A). In the Barn Mountains.

Anker Hoidal, a long-time prospector and trapper on the North Slope, reported in 1961 that the name relates to an old Eskimo legend. Long ago a woman took refuge on this mountain from men who searched for her. She had supernatural powers and cast a spell on them, putting them to sleep so she made good her escape.

MOUNT SLIM 60°56'N 134°52'W (105-D). South of Joe Creek.

Frank SLIM, an old riverboat pilot died in 1973. This hill was named shortly after to memorialize him.

SLIM'S RIVER 61°00'N 138°32'W (115-G). Flows into the southwest end of Kluane Lake.

In the early part of 1903, during the rush to the Bullion Creek (Kluane) goldfields, SLIM was drowned while attempting to cross this river. He was a prospector's pack-horse and his owner honoured him in this way.

MOUNT SLIPPER 5,583' 65°16'N 140°55'W (116-F). On the Yukon-Alaska boundary.

On 4 July 1914, D.D. Cairnes, GSC, named this peak after his assistant, E.S. SLIPPER. He had aided Cairnes in 1912 in mapping the geology along the Yukon-Alaska boundary. This is the highest point on the boundary between the Yukon and Porcupine Rivers.

SMARCH RIVER (see Smart River).

SMART RIVER 60°00'N 131°45'W (105-B). Flows south into British Columbia, in the Cassiar Mountains.

This name has been long misspelled. The river was originally and for many years up to the present time, the homesite and trapping grounds of the Smarch family, a well-known Indian family in the southern Yukon.

SMITH RIVER 60°00'N 126°23'W (95-D). A tributary to the Liard River.

In the 1820s, this river was known to the HBC. Later on they used it to supply their needs for fish and a small post named "Fort Halkett" was intermittently maintained here for a number of years into the 1850s-60s.

In the 1920s, a trapper Tom "Liard" Smith and his daughter lived here until he was drowned in the Liard. They lived at the Hot Springs, a location which gave base to many stories at the time of a tropical valley in the far north.

SNAFU CREEK 60°08'N 133°52'W (105-C). A tributary to the Lubbock River.

In 1949-50, the Canadian Army Engineers located and built the road from Jake's Corner to Atlin, B.C., a distance of 61 miles (102 km).

The name they gave this stream (the lake at its head was named later) was a catch-word widely used in the British and Commonwealth Armed Forces during the Second World War. It originated before the war, probably in the RAF. The term means "Situation Normal All Fouled Up". Anyone who served in the Armed Forces will recognize this. (see Tarfu Creek)

SNAG 62°24'N 140°22'W (115-K). Near the mouth of the stream and the White River.

The Dominion Department of Transport established a weather station and an emergency flight strip here in 1942, in conjunction with the air-lift to Russia. The coldest temperature ever officially recorded in Canada was measured here on 3 February 1947 at -81.4 degrees Fahrenheit. The station was closed in September 1966.

SNAG CREEK 62°24'N 140°22'W (115-K). A tributary to the White River.

In 1899, A.H. Brooks and W.J. Peters, USGS, named this river because of the obstacles they met while travelling along it.

SNAKE RIVER 65°59'N 134°12'W (106-E). A tributary to the Peel River.

When John Bell, Chief Trader of the HBC at Fort MacPherson, explored the lower part of this river in 1839 he named it the "Good Hope River", after Fort Good Hope on the MacKenzie River. Charles Camsell, GSC, noted in 1905 that although the name had long been changed, some of the local people still referred to it as the "Good Hope".

The name was probably changed by A.K. Isbister of the HBC in the winter of 1840-41 when he explored farther up the river. The stream is an unending series of bends and ox-bows, which could account for the name. Oddly enough, although there are no snakes in the Yukon, the Loucheaux Indian name for the river translates as "Hairy Worm River", perhaps in memory of an infestation of some sort of caterpillars.

SOLDIER CREEK 62°51'N 138°14'W (116-G). Flows northwest into Engineer Creek.

The name proposed by James Smith, Commissioner of the Yukon Territory on 4 October 1971 for the Canadian Forces Engineers who built the George Allen Jaeckell Bridge over the Ogilvie River in the summer of 1971.

SOLDIER'S SUMMIT 61°02'N 138°31'W (115-G). On the southwest shore of Kluane Lake, at the foot of Sheep Mountain.

At this spot on 20 November 1942, the Alaska Military Highway was officially opened by E.L. Bartlett of Alaska and Ian MacKenzie of Canada, eight months after the start of construction. A monument marks the spot. (see Fisher Creek)

SOMME CREEK 62°24'N 138°41'W (115-J). Flows into the Klotassin River.

D.D. Cairnes, GSC, named this creek in 1916 after the Battle of the SOMME in France, in which he lost some of his friends.

SONORA GULCH 62°40'N 138°02'W (115-J). A tributary to Hayes Creek.

George Beal found gold and staked the Discovery claim on this creek in September 1898. He named the creek after the Mexican state of SONORA where he had previously prospected.

SOUCH CREEK 61°37'N 133°45'W (105-F). A tributary to the Big Salmon River.

On 1 November 1967, this stream was honoured by the name of a Canadian hero, J-16825 Flying Officer George Allan SOUCH, DFC. He was born in Toronto, Ontario on 13 August 1916 and enlisted in the RCAF there on 7 March 1941. While serving overseas he was killed during air operations on 29 July 1943.

SOURDOUGH GULCH 64°00'N 139°22'W (115-O). A tributary to Bonanza Creek from the west, four miles above its mouth.

Fred V. Envoldsen and his partner, John P. Hering, found the first payable gold on this stream on 5 June 1901 and renamed it. It had been staked by others in 1897 who had named it "67 Pup", from its location but were unable to find enough gold and abandoned it. (see Strathcona Creek)

SPIRIT LAKE 60° 15' N 134° 44' W (105-D)

Located in the Watson River valley, eight kilometers north of Carcross, this colourful lake drains into the Watson River. Well-known for its lake trout fishing, it was called "Mbédé Méne" (rainbow/trout lake) or "Looge Zhaazhe" (little fish) in the language of the native Tagish people. The first usage of Spirit Lake was during World War II, when the beauty of the colourful lake was said to exemplify the spirit of the north.

SPRAGUE CREEK 63°50'N 136°28'W (115-P). Flows into the North McQuesten River.

Gold was found and the creek named by a miner-prospector of this name.

SQUAN LAKE 60°23'N 133°46'W (105-C). Twenty-five miles north of Teslin.

An Indian name after the man who found plentiful pike in this lake.

SQUANGA LAKE 60°29'N 133°38'W (105-C). At Mile 850 (KM1377) on the Alaska Highway.

This small, pleasant lake received its name from the Indians long ago. The name is that of a small, rounded type of whitefish of superior flavour, which abounds in the lake.

SQUAW CREEK 60°02'N 137°10'W (115-A). Flows into the Tatshenshini River.

Named "Dollis Creek" in 1898, the name was forgotten for thirty years until, in 1927 Paddy Duncan, a native of Champagne, found enough gold here to mine. He staked a claim and worked it. It is likely that he also named it at this time. He was sentenced to life imprisonment in 1936 for murder.

SQUAW CREEK 63°47'N 137°28'W (115-P). A tributary to Clear Creek.

About 5 May 1901, this creek was staked and named by W. A. MacDonald, Dan MacDonald, Edward Carroll and George Kennedy. They were too late to stake claims in the stampede to the Clear Creek gold finds but found enough here to stake and name it.

THE SQUAW TITS 5,900' 60°29'N 136°44'W (115-A). On the northeast side of Dezadeash Lake.

These rounded, twin buttes beside the Dalton Trail were named by Dalton or his men before the Klondike Gold Rush and were used as landmarks by those travelling the trail. They were first reported and mapped by J.J. McArthur, DLS, who examined the trail for the Department of the Interior in 1897. The name has been quietly dropped from the maps in recent years.

STAN LAKE 65°10'N 140°05'W (116-F). Southwest of Mount DeVille.

This lake was named for STAN Rivers, a long-time prospector in this area. It was proposed by "Pat" Callison, well-known bush pilot.

STARR CREEK 61°48'N 131°50'W (105-G). A tributary to the Pelly River.

Gilmore and Elsie STARR came into the Yukon in May 1898. They had arrived in Skagway in 1897 but Gilmore contracted spinal meningitis while packing supplies over the White Pass. They had financed their journey to the Klondike by the sale of their North Dakota homestead after it had been laid waste by a cyclone.

Arriving in Dawson in the spring of 1898, they prospected up the Klondike River and then on Eureka Creek. Elsie owned and ran the Hillside Roadhouse on Hunker Creek in 1899. They later prospected up the Pelly River and it is believed that they lived here about 1905-1910 after finding some gold in this stream.

STEAMBOAT BAR 63°36'N 137°33'W (115-P). A large gravel island in the Stewart River, about fourteen miles below the mouth of the McQuesten River.

This was the richest bar ever found on the Stewart River. It was reported that in 1885 it yielded at the rate of eight and one-half ounces of gold per man per day. The deposits, being shallow and about two feet in thickness, were quickly exhausted.

In 1885, a group of miners hired the Alaska Commercial Company's small steamboat, the "New Racket". It had been brought up the river from St. Michaels by the Schieffelin brothers of Arizona and was the second steam vessel on the Yukon River. The boat was hauled up on the bar and her engines were detached from the paddlewheel. They were made to drive a set of pumps, manufactured on the spot, which supplied water for the set of sluice boxes. With this crude machinery, the miners cleared $1,000 each in a short time and paid an equal amount to the owners of the boat. This was the first use of powered machinery to mine in the Yukon. (see Stewart River)

STEAMBOAT MOUNTAIN 6,376' 64°15'N 135°38'W (109-D). In the Ogilvie Mountains.

This was named by Tony Hollenback, an early prospector in the region because of its appearance. The name was made official in 1955.

MOUNT STEELE 16,640' 61°06'N 140°19'W (115-F). In the Icefield Ranges of the St. Elias Mountains.

J.J. McArthur, DLS, while surveying the International Boundary in July 1909, named this majestic peak after one of the most outstanding men in the history of the Yukon.

Major General Sir Samuel Benfield STEELE, KCMG, CB, MVO, was born in Purbrook, county of Simcoe, Ontario, in Upper Canada, on 5 January 1849. His father was Captain Elmes Steele, RN, and a great-uncle, Col. Samuel Steele, had served at the capture of Quebec.

He was commissioned an ensign in the 35th Simcoe Foresters at the age of 15, after serving as a private. He took part in the repulse of the Fenian Raids in 1866. To see action he reverted to the rank of corporal in the Ontario Rifles during the Red River Rebellion of 1870.

He and his two brothers enlisted at the formation of the North West Mounted Police in August 1874, when he was immediately appointed Sergeant Major of "A" Division. He took part in the Great March of 1874 and by 1878 he had reached the rank of Inspector. During the Northwest Rebellion of 1885 he commanded the cavalry composed of the NWMP and Steele's Scouts of the Alberta Field Force.

1887 saw him in command of the NWMP expedition to the Kootenays in southeastern B.C., the establishment of Fort Steele and the settling of the Indian troubles in that country. During this time he also maintained law and order during the construction of the Canadian Pacific Railway through the Rocky Mountains.

He commanded the NWMP posts on the White and the Chilkoot Passes from February to July 1898, the height of the Klondike Gold Rush. At this time he was also Magistrate and in charge of Canada Customs for the area. In July 1898, he was promoted to Lieutenant Colonel, made a member of the Council of the Yukon Territory and Commander of all NWMP Forces in the Territory. He held all these positions with honour, distinction and efficiency until September 1899. The tradition of NWMP efficiency and incorruptibility was upheld and strongly reinforced by him and his men during this time.

Together with William Ogilvie, as Commissioner of the Yukon Territory, they presented an example of integrity in government which has seldom, if ever, been achieved anywhere in this country since that time.

He raised and commanded the Lord Strathcona's Horse and again served with more than ordinary ability and distinction in the South African War from 1899-1901, winning many honours and decorations. He commanded the Transvaal Division of the South African Constabulary from 1901-1906. He resigned from the NWMP on 1 March 1903.

In 1907, he returned to Canada and, promoted to Colonel, was placed in command of Military District No. 13 (Calgary) until 1909, and of Military District No. 10 (Winnipeg) until 1914. During this period he greatly increased and developed the Canadian Militia on the prairies.

In 1914, at the outbreak of the First World War, he was promoted to Major General and made Inspector General of Western Canada. At this time he published his autobiography, "Forty Years in Canada". He organized, commanded and trained the 2nd Canadian Division from May to August 1915 and from then to July 1918 commanded Shornecliff Military District which contained nearly all the Canadian troops in England. At the same time he was Chairman of the Canadian Militia Council in Great Britain, 1915-16, which made him nearly equivalent to Commander-In-Chief of the Canadian Forces in the United Kingdom. Again he won high honours, finally being made Knight Commander of the Order of St. Michael and St. George, one of the most distinguished honours of the British Empire.

Owing to failing health he retired in July 1918. He died on 30 January 1919 at Putney, England and was buried in Winnipeg, Manitoba.

STEEP CREEK 63°42'N 134°57'W (105-M). Flows into the south arm of Mayo Lake.

This was one of several rich, gold bearing creeks found by a party of four Australian prospectors in August 1903. They named the creeks and brought fifteen ounces of gold from this stream into Dawson where it assayed a value of $19.57 to the ounce (gold was worth $20.00 per ounce at the time), probably the purest placer gold ever found in the Yukon. (see Ledge Creek)

MOUNT STENBRATEN 6,466' 64°05'N 132°08'W (106-C). Near the headwaters of the Stewart River.

In May 1973, this mountain was named after John O. "Stampede John" STENBRATEN, a noted Yukon prospector from 1904-1960. It is said that "Stampede John" took part in nearly every mining rush in the Yukon, Alaska and even into Siberia during these years.

STERLIN CREEK 60°11'N 132°55'W (105-C). Flows to Teslin Lake.

This creek and a nearby lake were named in honour of Lt. M. STERLIN, MID, who was killed in action during the Second World War.

STEVENS CREEK 60°15'N 134°58'W (105-D). A tributary to the Wheaton River.

In 1905, George STEVENS found the first quartz-gold vein on the hill above this creek. Later, in 1908, the mountain was named for him. He lived beside this creek which already had his name.

MOUNT STEVENS 60°13'N 135°01'W (105-D) (see Stevens Creek above).

STEVENS CREEK 63°00'N 138°36'W (115-J). The right fork of Scroggie Creek.

This branch of Scroggie Creek was named by or after J.G. STEVENS of Deadwood, North Dakota in the summer of 1898. STEVENS was one of a party of prospectors who explored the creek that summer. He made the original find on Scroggie Creek. (see Scroggie Creek)

STEVENSON RIDGE 4,493' 62°34'N 138°53'W (115-J). Between Dip Creek and the Klotassin River.

Hugh S. Bostock, GSC, named this ridge in 1941 after a man named STEVENSON who was a senior partner in a placer mining company on Rude Creek for many years and an active prospector in the region at the same time. (see Leslie Ridge)

STEWART CREEK 60°41'N 128°30'W (105-A). Drains Stewart Lake (see Stewart Lake and Cabin Creek).

STEWART GULCH 64°02'N 135°49'W (105-D). A small valley on the left side of Dublin Gulch.

This was named after J.S. Stewart who found and worked on a quartz-gold vein here in 1917.

STEWART LAKE 60°38'N 128°40'W (105-A). Forty miles north of Watson Lake.

An old trapper, half Indian, half black, of this name, lived here and trapped in the general area toward the Frances River for many years. He and his family were still here in 1941 and some of them are buried here. (see Cabin Creek)

STEWART RIVER 63°19'N 139°24'W (115-O). A major tributary to the Yukon River.

In the winter of 1849, Robert Campbell of the HBC at Fort Selkirk sent his "dear and gallant friend" James G. STEWART, who was also his assistant clerk, northeast of the Fort to find some Indians believed to be hunting in that area. STEWART travelled farther than anyone from the Fort had before and crossed this stream on the ice. He reported it to Campbell on his return and Campbell named it after him. STEWART was the son of the Hon. James Stewart of Montreal.

The Indians of the district reported in 1883 to Lt. Frederick Schwatka, US Army, that the river's native name was "Na-Chon-De" which was also the name of the tribe living there. Schwatka did not change the name of this large river.

Prospecting started on the river in 1884 with a few men who found encouraging signs of good, payable, fine gold on the bars. In the spring of 1885, Frank Moffatt recovered the first of this rich, bar gold. In the late summer of the same year "Slim Jim" Wynn, (or Winn), who had first come over the Chilkoot Pass in 1875, found a rich bar 100 miles upstream. Called "Wynn's Bar" it paid at $6,000 to the man for less than 50 days work. In 1886, fully 100 men were working on the bars of the STEWART and some had prospected nearly to its headwaters.

One group of miners made a deal with Mayo and McQuesten to rent the little steamer "New Racket" and used its engines to mine the gravels of Steamboat Bar. (see Steamboat Bar)

Some of the bars worked were Wynn's (Winn's), Dutch John's, Lac De Bar, Half Moon, Chapman's, Joe Jay Bar, Low Water and Black Mike's Bar. These and other bars were worked until the Klondike Gold Rush, although they were deserted for a time after the discovery of the Fortymile goldfields in late 1886. The miners in the Yukon referred to the STEWART as the "Grubstake River", because enough gold could always be won on it to provide money for supplies for another season of prospecting.

In the summer of 1886, Frederick Harper, of Harper, McQuesten and Mayo, established a trading post at the mouth of the STEWART to serve the miners upstream. Some of the miners called the post "Fort Nelson" after Pte. Edward William Nelson of the US Army Signal Service, who was said to have been there at the time, collecting specimens of the flora and fauna of the region. (He went on to make invaluable collections of the Yukon and Alaska and later became one of America's most famous naturalists). In late 1886, coarse gold, the goal of all miners, was found on the Fortymile River and most miners abandoned the STEWART for a few years. Harper moved his trading post to Forty Mile in June 1887.

In Klondike days, the settlement of the same name was revived as a wood point for riverboats, a NWMP post and a wintering place for stampeders unable to reach Dawson before the Yukon froze over. Many of these men prospected the tributaries of the river in 1897-98 and later. In July 1897, Robert Henderson staked a 40 acre townsite on the banks of the Yukon opposite the mouth of the STEWART but it never succeeded.

William Ogilvie, who had been Commissioner of the Yukon Territory from 1898-1901, became President of the Yukon Basin Gold Dredging Company, of Missouri, which held extensive leases on the STEWART and operated with limited success, 1908-1912.

David and Mary Shand ran the "Hotel Stewart", a roadhouse here, from 1900 until it burned in 1918. They rebuilt it and operated it as "Johnson's Roadhouse" until 1930. They wrote a book about their experiences there, entitled "The Summit and Beyond". (see Sullivan Island)

STOKES LAKE 62°52'N 133°47'W (105-K). On the north side of the Earn Hills.

This lake was named in April 1951, to honour the name of Lt. E.S. STOKES, MID, Cdn. Army, who was killed in action during the Second World War.

STOKES POINT 69°20'N 138°43'W (117-D). Southeast of Herschel Island, on the Arctic coast.

On 16 July 1826, Sir John Franklin, RN, named this feature after his friend Captain John L. STOKES, RN, commander of the "Acheron".

STONY CREEK 60°47'N 135°58'W (105-D). A tributary to the Takhini River.

A notable location only because a US Army Engineers maintenance camp was established here in 1942-43 during the construction of the Alaska Highway.

STOWE CREEK 63°38'N 138°59'W (115-O). A tributary to Montana Creek, from the west.

Gold was discovered and this creek named by A.F. STOWE in May 1901. The lower part of the creek was originally called "Conglomerate Creek".

STRATHCONA CREEK 63°47'N 139°32'W (115-O). A tributary to the Indian River, from the north.

On 5 January 1902, Fred Eugene Envoldsen and C.W. Williams found gold, staked and named the stream, probably in honour of the Lord STRATHCONA Horse, a Canadian cavalry regiment raised and first commanded by Col. Sam B. Steele of the NWMP. The regiment served with great distinction in the South African War (1899-1902) and in the First and Second World Wars.

Envoldsen was one of the most active prospectors in the country for many years. He was a participant in the stampede to the Firth River placer gold finds in 1948. (see Sourdough Gulch, Bertha Creek and Firth River)

MOUNT STRICKLAND 13,818' 61°14'N 140°40'W (115-G). In the Icefield ranges of the St. Elias Mountains.

This was named about 1918, after Inspector D'Arcy A. Edward STRICKLAND of the NWMP. He enlisted in 1891 and was one of the first of the Force in the Yukon, arriving at Forty Mile in July 1895 with Inspector Charles Constantine. He was the first officer in command of the detachment on the White Pass in February 1898 and later at the important Tagish Lake Post where every goldseeker was registered and passed through Customs.

He died in the service in 1908, in the midst of a distinguished career.

STRIKER LAKE 60°01'N 134°24'W (105-D). East of Windy Arm on Tagish Lake.

This was named by A.E. Swannell, BCLS, after an old-time prospector and trapper in this area. STRIKER PASS, above the lake was named at the same time.

MOUNT STUTZER 4,165' 61°58'N 136°06'W (115-H). On the east side of the Nordenskiold River, about ten miles south of Carmacks.

D.D. Cairnes, GSC, named this peak sometime in 1908 after Dr. Otto STUTZER, Assistant Professor of Geology at the Royal School of Mines in Freiberg, Germany. STUTZER had assisted Cairnes in 1908 when he mapped the geology of this area.

SUGDEN PUP 61°01'N 138°44'W (115-G). A very short valley off Bullion Creek, to the south.

Dr. L.S. SUGDEN, an American physician, was prominent in early Dawson and Yukon politics. He was also an active prospector and mining promoter, in which he was fairly successful. He took part in the first prospecting of the Bullion Creek goldfields and was the first to find gold in this small gulch in the winter of 1907-08.

In the early years of the Klondike, he went to Lake Laberge to attend a sick man. Upon his arrival he found the man dead. He was unable to bury him owing to the depth of frost in the ground. The wreck of the riverboat "Olive May" was nearby so SUGDEN cremated the body in the boiler of the boat. This incident was the basis of Robert W. Service's famous poem, "The Cremation of Sam McGee".

SULLIVAN HILL 64°21'N 135°26'W (106-D). At the headwaters of the Beaver River.

This was named after John SULLIVAN, a prospector who was one of the first men into the area during the rush to the silver-lead finds on nearby Carpenter Creek in the early 1920s. He prospected in the Mayo district from 1920-50.

Some of the older maps show this location as "McKay Hill" but this error was corrected on later maps.

SULLIVAN ISLAND 63°12'N 139°34'W (115-O). A small island, at the mouth of the White River.

This was named after an early woodcutter who supplied the riverboats about 1897 and later. David and Mary Shand built and operated a small sawmill here in May 1898, and ran it until 1900. (see Stewart River)

SULPHUR CREEK 63°39'N 138°40'W (115-O). Flows into Dominion Creek, in the Klondike.

This creek was probably named in 1896 or early 1897 for the sulphur bearing springs found near the headwaters on King Solomon's Dome, claim No. 73 above Discovery.

There were two Discovery claims filed on this creek; the first was found by a prospector named Stafford on 22 July 1897. He was mining on nearby Quartz Creek and one night had a dream of finding gold on Sulphur Creek. He told his partner the next morning, set out for Sulphur and did find gold! For some reason this claim was not recorded. However, on 24 August 1897, W.A. Miller and his partner, W.C. "Swiftwater Bill" Gates staked another Discovery claim much lower downstream and found gold in large enough amounts to start a stampede from Dawson in which the whole creek and all its tributaries were staked. Gates claim had also been staked earlier in July, but he too did not bother to record it.

Although not nearly as rich in gold as Bonanza, Eldorado or Hunker Creeks; Sulphur Creek paid steadily and well. The pay streak for much of the creek was the widest of any in the Klondike, up to 500 feet of gold-bearing gravels. The creek is still being mined successfully and profitably. (see Mount Baird)

SULPHUR SPRINGS 63°52'N 139°58'W (115-O). At the headwaters of Sulphur Creek.

These mineral springs gave Sulphur Creek its name. In the fall of 1906, a thirty mile long railroad, the Klondike Mines Railway, was completed from Dawson to this spot. SULPHUR SPRINGS was the terminus, with waiting rooms, offices, freight sheds and other conveniences.

SUMMIT CREEK 61°23'N 134°22'W (105-E). A tributary to the Big Salmon River, near Livingstone Creek.

Gold was discovered here and the stream named by a prospector named Meany in 1901. In August 1905, a gold nugget weighing 39 ounces, the largest found in the area to that time came from this creek.

SUNAGHUN CREEK 67°31'N 141°00'W (116-O). Flows into the Porcupine River, near Rampart House.

This is a Kutcha-Kutchin Indian name reported by the International Boundary Survey party of 1914. According to Professor O.W. Geist of the University of Alaska, this word means "Old Woman". The creek was so named because, according to Orth's Dictionary of Alaska Place Names, "An old woman at Rampart House could not climb the steep river bank so she used this creek as a route to obtain her firewood. Hence, Old Woman Creek".

SUNSHINE CREEK 62°47'N 138°30'W (115-J). A tributary to Isaac Creek.

This creek was named in 1915, during the rush to the Rude Creek and Dip Creek finds in the Dawson Range.

A nearby creek was named "Moonshine Creek' but its name and location have been long forgotten.

SUPER CUB CREEK 60°02'N 137°58'W (115-A). A small tributary to the Alsek River.

In August 1963, Dr. Alex Smith, GSC, named it after a small lake just over the British Columbia boundary. The lake was named because a mining company working in the area found that a Piper Super Cub was the largest aircraft that could use the lake.

SURPRISE LAKE 60°33'N 133°20'W (105-C). A very small lake about four miles north of Johnson's Crossing.

This little lake was named by the Chief of the Teslin Indian Band in 1952 when he was guiding a party of the Canadian Army Topographical Survey.

SURVEYS RANGE 63°35'N 132°12'W (105-N). Between Fido Creek and the Rogue River.

Hugh S. Bostock, GSC, named these hills in November 1970 to honour the topographical and geodetic surveyors of Canada who had prepared the maps of the Yukon. They had been uncommemorated to this time. He had originally proposed the name "Surveyors Range".

SUTTLE GULCH 64°02'N 135°50'W (106-D). Flows to Dublin Gulch.

Hugh S. Bostock, GSC, reported this local name in 1959. John SUTTLE mined in Dublin Gulch in 1898 and continued in the area until 1915. Some old maps give this name as "Stuttle Gulch". (see Dublin Gulch)

SWANSON CREEK 61°19'N 138°18'W (115-G). A tributary to Gladstone Creek, near Kluane Lake.

Named by Axel SWANSON who, with T.T. Murray, was the first to discover gold on this stream and on Gladstone Creek in 1911.

SWEDE CREEK 60°59'N 131°18'W (105-B). A tributary to the upper Liard River.

An old prospector, known only as "The Swede", lived here between 1900 and 1930. He travelled the Liard River in a beautifully built dug-out canoe, thirty feet long, which he had constructed himself. It would travel lightly through the most dangerous waters and he propelled it with a minimum of effort, the envy of all the Indians and prospectors who saw it.

SWEDE CREEK 64°01'N 139°34'W (116-B). A long tributary to the Yukon River, five miles above Dawson.

When C.A. Olafson and his group found gold and staked their claims here on 2 February 1898, the Mining Recorder at Dawson named the creek after the nationality of the men.

A stampede from Dawson resulted in over six hundred claims being staked in the following three weeks. In spite of these efforts little gold was ever mined.

For a number of years at the time a small settlement existed at the mouth of the creek. A steamboat wood point, it was also a favourite vacation camping place for Dawson residents.

SWEDE JOHNSON CREEK 61°36'N 139°24'W (115-G). A tributary to the Kluane River, near the Alaska Highway.

In August 1942, a survey crew of the US Public Roads Administration was locating a route through here for the Alaska Military Highway. One of their crew was a local Indian named Sam Johnson. A willing, congenial worker JOHNSON earned the respect of his fellows by his ability. They nicknamed him "The Sunburned Swede". Fred Johnson, the party chief thought that the name should be memorialized.

SWIM LAKES 62°12'N 132°53'W (105-K). A group of small lakes, fifteen miles east of Faro.

These lakes were given their name in he summer of 1935 by J.R. Johnson, GSC, and his survey party. They were the only lakes found that season which were warm enough for swimming.

TABOR LAKES 66°58'N 134°46'W (106-L). East of the Peel River.

These small lakes were named after Charles William Clifton TABOR in 1973. He had been a Yukon Councillor representing North Dawson from 1912-1915 and was a pioneer lawyer in the territory. He was also the husband of "Diamond Tooth" Gertie Lovejoy. TABOR died in a fire when the Yukonia Hotel burned down on 21 February 1917.

TADRU LAKE 62°28'N 135°42'W (105-L). Ten miles southeast of Tatlmain Lake.

This lake was named in 1950 by R.B. Campbell, GSC. The word is a contraction of the names Taylor and Drury, a firm of pioneer Whitehorse merchants. They operated trading posts in many of the most isolated parts of the Yukon beginning in 1899.

Isaac Taylor was born in Thirsk, Yorkshire, England and came to the Yukon with the Klondike rush in 1898 via Australia. He met William S. Drury, from Kirme, Lincolnshire, while they were working on the Discovery claim on Pine Creek in Atlin, B.C. Here they decided to go into business supplying the needs of the miners.

They opened a tent store at Bennett on 14 August 1899. They moved their store to Whitehorse when the railroad was completed in July 1900. Their venture succeeded and they expanded by opening posts in various parts of the territory. Pelly Banks in 1905, Teslin in 1906, Mayo, Carmacks and Fort Selkirk in 1919. They built a small riverboat, the "Kluane", to service these posts. In 1912, they amalgamated with Whitney and Pedlar, Whitehorse merchants who were instrumental in developing the first copper orebodies at Whitehorse, and built a large store on the Whitehorse waterfront. They had stores in 18 locations at one time and even had company coins minted in Ottawa which were in use from 1912-1950. The business was finally sold by the family in 1974.

TAGISH 60°19'N 134°16'W (105-D). On the narrows between Tagish and Marsh Lakes.

The road from Carcross to Jake's Corner on the Alaska Highway was built in late 1942 to lay the gasoline pipeline from Skagway to Watson Lake. The present settlement of Tagish grew up around the bridge that was built then. The old location during the Gold Rush years was the TAGISH Indian village about three miles south and on the east side. The NWMP built one of their most important posts in the Yukon at this place, calling it "Fort Sifton" after the then Minister of the Interior. Every traveller passing this point was required to register his party and his boat was given a number. Customs officers, sometimes police, examined all outfits. The post brought order to the rush downriver. A post office was open from 20 August 1897 to 1 October 1901.

TAGISH LAKE 60°09'N 134°24'W (105-D). A large, many-armed lake, straddling the Yukon-B.C. boundary east of Carcross.

The name is ancient and from the Indian"Ta-Gish-Ai" which is also the name of the native people who lived there. Lt. Frederick Schwatka, US Army, ignored the Indian name and designated it "Lake Bove" after a Lt. Bove of the Italian Navy. Dr. George Mercer Dawson, G&NHSC, disallowed the name, relegating it to a small island at the entrance of Windy Arm, and retained the old Indian name for the lake.

The early miners called it "Tako" or "Tahko Lake". Part of the main route to the lower Yukon River and the goldfields, two places on the lake were approached with trepidation by the miners sailing down. The mouths of Windy Arm and Taku Arm were given to sudden and furious winds and these locations were the scenes of many wrecks and drownings.

MOUNT TAGISH CHARLIE 65°53'N 139°48'W (115-G). West of the Porcupine River.

This northern peak was named in the Klondike Jubilee Year of 1973 to commemorate TAGISH CHARLIE. He, with George Carmack and Skookum Jim Mason, found the fabulous gold of Bonanza Creek on 16 August 1896 which sparked the greatest Gold Rush in history. After that date he was known as "Dawson" Charlie.

During and prior to the Gold Rush, Indians usually took English Christian names from white associates, with the tribal or band designation added (e.g. "Tagish Charlie", "Taku Jack", "Stick Jim", etc.).

TAGISH CHARLIE was the first, perhaps the only, Indian of the Yukon Territory to be given the full rights of a Canadian citizen by an Act of Parliament. He was allowed to vote, to hold public office, sue and be sued and to buy and consume spirituous liquors.

On 26 January 1908, he fell from the railway bridge at Carcross and drowned.

TAHTE CREEK 61°59'N 137°11'W (115-H). A small tributary to the Nisling River from the south.

When J.J. McArthur, DLS, made his rough survey through this country in 1897 he thought that the Nisling River was the "Tahte" of the local Indians and so mapped it. After the error was corrected this name was given to this small stream. No translation was given.

TAKHINI 60°51'N 135°27'W (105-D).

This old settlement lay at the crossing of the Takhini River, on the old Dawson Road. It was the first stop outside Whitehorse and had a NWMP post as well as a roadhouse. The roadhouse was owned and operated by W.A. Puckett. Both it and the police post were closed in May 1907.

TAKHINI HOT SPRINGS 60°53'N 135°22'W (105-D). About five miles up the present Klondike Highway, between Whitehorse and Dawson.

These hot, mineral springs were discovered and staked by W.A. Puckett, who owned the nearby Takhini Roadhouse, and Stephen Simmons in late April 1907.

The water flow then and now is about 86 gallons per minute at a temperature of 118 degrees Fahrenheit (47°C). The water is sweet and odourless, containing no sulphur. It is said to be beneficial to sufferers of arthritis and rheumatism.

TAKHINI RIVER 60°51'N 135°11'W (105-D). A large tributary to the Yukon River, about twelve miles north of Whitehorse.

This river was first noted by Dr. Aurel Krause of the Bremen Geographical Society in 1882, the first white man to explore the southwestern part of the territory. The name, recorded by Krause, is from the Tagish Indian "Tahk-Heena". "Tahk" meaning mosquito and "Heena" meaning River.

TAKIAH CREEK 67°51'N 137°58'W (116-P). Flows into Driftwood Creek.

This is a Vanta Kutchin Indian word meaning "Little".

TALBOT ARM 61°30'N 138°37'W (115-G). The large bay at the southeast end of Kluane Lake.

This bay was named in the summer of 1945 by Hugh S. Bostock, GSC, after Albert Charles TALBOT, DLS, who made the first good map of Kluane Lake and the surrounding area in 1898 while with the Department of the Interior. He liked this calm bay. He was a member of the International Boundary Commission, 1893-95. The bay had previously been known as "Little Arm".

TALLY HO MOUNTAIN 60°13'N 135°03'W (105-D). In the big bend of the Wheaton River.

Around 1906, there was much prospecting activity and a number of promising mineral finds were made in this area. Among the more successful were a group of young English prospectors who worked energetically in this vicinity. In a gulch on the west end of this hill they found good lode (vein) showings of gold-silver-lead ore which they called the "TALLY HO" claims. They explored this ground until about 1916 and were known locally as the "TALLY HO BOYS". The mountain, which had been known as "Big Bend Mountain", was soon given the name of the group. Most of them went to England in 1915-16 to enlist in the British Forces for the First World War and it was supposed that most of them were killed in the fighting, as they did not return to the Yukon.

TANTALUS BUTTE 2,568' 62°08'N 136°16'W (115-I). Five miles north of Carmacks.

This lone hill was named in 1883 by Lt. Frederick Schwatka, US Army. Because of the convolutions of the Yukon River in this area, anyone approaching the place became confused; at one point approaching the hill and at another going away, repeatedly.

George Carmack, the discoverer of Bonanza Creek, found a seam of coal on this hill in 1893 and made sporadic attempts to develop it. He was backed by Arthur Harper who had a half interest in the venture. In 1903, Captain Charles E. Miller, who had been a coal miner in Mauchunk, Pennsylvania, developed these coal deposits further. (see Mount Miller)

TARFU CREEK 60°06'N 133°53'W (105-C). A tributary to the Lubbock River.

In 1949-50, the Canadian Army Engineers located and built the road from Jake's Corner to Atlin, B.C. While surveying the route they gave this stream a name derived from a common World War Two slang expression. The word TARFU was an extension of the word Snafu: "Situation Normal All Fouled Up". TARFU means "Things Are Really Fouled Up".

The creek was named by Staff Sergeant Perkins of the Royal Canadian Engineers, chief of the survey party.

It was too bad that there was not a third creek in the neighbourhood so as to complete the triad. "Fubar" is the third and ultimate expression of confusion; "Fouled Up Beyond All Recognition". (see Snafu Creek)

TASIN RANGE 63°55'N 132°45'W (105-N). Between the Stewart and Lansing Rivers.

This range was mapped in 1907 by Joseph Keele, GSC, who retained the local name which in the Indian language means "Black" or "Dark". Mount Ortell is the highest peak in the range.

TATAMAGOUCHE CREEK 61°22'N 139°19'W (115-G). A tributary to Burwash Creek.

Ernest (Swede) Johnson, a pioneer prospector, discovered gold here and named the creek after a small place in Nova Scotia just west of Pictou, during the rush to the Kluane goldfields. It is also spelled "Taddemagooch".

TATCHUN RIVER 62°17'N 136°20'W (115-I). A tributary to the Yukon River, at Five Finger Rapids.

Dr. George Mercer Dawson, G&NHSC, retained this Indian name on his survey in 1887 but did not give a translation.

TATLMAIN LAKE 62°37'N 135°59'W (105-L). South of the Pelly River.

In the winter of 1848-49, Robert Campbell, of the HBC, while at Fort Selkirk, obtained large quantities of fish for the Fort from this lake. The whitefish here are particularly succulent and plentiful. The name is the original Indian one at that time and no translation is known.

TATONDUK RIVER 65°00'N 141°00'W (116-C). A tributary to the Yukon River, from the Ogilvie Mountains.

It was variously called "Tatondu", "Tatonduc", "Totondu" and, by the early miners, "Sheep Creek". TATONDUK is an Indian name reported by Lt. Frederick Schwatka, US Army, in 1883 as "Tatondu" and by J.E. Spurr, USGS, in 1896 as "Tatonduc". The name means "Broken Stone River" because of the numerous rocks in the channel. William Ogilvie, DLS, was the first known white man to traverse this stream when he and his men travelled its length in the spring of 1888, on their way from Forty Mile to Fort MacPherson.

TAY RIVER 62°34'N 134°22'W (105-L). A tributary to the Pelly River, from the north.

In 1848, Robert Campbell of the HBC, while making his epic journey down the Pelly River to the Yukon River, named this stream after the "River TAY" which flows through the city of Perth in Scotland, near his ancestral home.

Tay Lake was named much later and Tay Mountain (6,991'), near the mouth of the stream, was named because of its proximity.

TAYE LAKE 60°56'N 136°21'W (115-A). The source of the Mendenhall River.

Although the source of the name is not known, E.D. Kindle, GSC, reported that numerous ancient Indian artifacts (i.e. flint arrowheads, spear points and scrapers) were found at the south end of the lake under the layer of white volcanic ash which covers most of the southern Yukon.

TAYLOR CREEK 62°44'N 138°48'W (115-J). A small tributary to Casino Creek, in the Dawson Range.

This creek was named by R.J. Cathro of Whitehorse in May 1970 after C.D.M. "Red" TAYLOR, BSc, P. Eng., a veteran mining engineer for 30 years in the Yukon. He explored this area and its copper deposits very extensively.

TAYLOR HIGHWAY and SIXTYMILE ROAD. Between Dawson and Tetlin Junction, Alaska.

Originally called the "Sixtymile Road", this road was built as a wagon road from Dawson to the Sixty Mile River diggings in the early 1900s to supply the miners there.

The road has been improved and upgraded continually since the 1950s. At present it is known as the "Top of the World Highway".

Most of the construction to connect the old Sixtymile Road with Tetlin Junction was built by Ike P. Taylor, a pioneer road builder in the Yukon and Alaska. He died in 1963. The portion of the Highway in Alaska is called the TAYLOR Highway. Constructed along the mountain ridges it affords magnificent views of the country and is one of the major scenic attractions of the area.

TELFORD CREEK 63°11'N 138°58'W (115-O). Flows into the Stewart River from the south.

It is likely that this creek was named after Captain TELFORD of the RNWMP, who was the officer in charge at Mayo around 1917.

TELLURIDE CREEK 60°51'N 138°05'W (115-B). A tributary to the Jarvis River.

Tom Laird found placer gold here and named this stream during the stampede to the newly-found Alsek goldfields.

TELLURIDES are a group of rare minerals formed from tellurium, gold, sulphur, iron and other elements. None have ever been found in this area and it is probable that Laird named this stream after the gold-mining camp of Telluride, Colorado, where he may have worked earlier.

TEMPEST MOUNTAIN 61°18'N 140°11'W (115-G). On the north side of the Steele Glacier, in the St. Elias Mountains.

This peak was officially named in November 1970 by the Alpine Club of Canada. It was first climbed on 26 August 1941 by Anderson Bakewell. The name describes the weather conditions met on the climb.

TENT ISLAND 68°55'N 136°33'W (117-A). On the Yukon-NWT boundary, near Shoalwater Bay.

On Friday 7 July 1826 Sir John Franklin, RN, with his two small boats, "Lion" and "Reliance", sailed close to this island where they discovered several hundred Eskimo camped in tents. (see Pillage Point)

TENT MOUNTAIN (see Mount Murray).

TESLIN LAKE 60°15'N 132°58'W (105-C). A large lake in the south central Yukon, straddling the Yukon-B.C. boundary.

This beautiful lake retains its Indian name although slightly changed: "Tes-Lin-Too" meaning "Long, Narrow Water". The first white men known to have seen the lake were "Ike" Powers, a noted pioneer prospector, and eight or nine companions who came from Juneau and up the Taku Inlet and River then overland to the head of the lake in either 1876 or 1877, and did a limited amount of prospecting around the lake. The next white men here were Charles Munroe and his three companions who followed Powers' route in 1880 and also prospected the lake and some of its tributaries. It was long thought that Michael Byrne of the Western Union Telegraph Company had explored north from Telegraph Creek on the Stikine River, to the head of the lake in 1869 but opinion now is that he had reached Atlin Lake.

As part of an All-Canadian Route to the Klondike, many people travelled from Glenora and Telegraph Creek, 160 miles to the head of the lake. There they built boats and sailed down to the Teslin River, on to the Lewes (Yukon) and down to Dawson. By using this route they missed the dangerous Miles Canyon and Whitehorse Rapids as well as the frightening storms of the Chilkoot Pass. The little steamer "Anglian" was built at the head of the lake and was launched on 13 June 1898.

Although there had been temporary settlements at the south end of the lake (in British Columbia) in 1897-98 and an HBC post there until 1903 or 1904, the first trading post set up on that part of the lake that was in Yukon Territory was built by Tom Smith in 1903 at the mouth of the Nisutlin River. He came from Dawson in the little steamer "Quick", piloted by Captain Henry Henderson, brother of Robert Henderson. The post was operated by Taylor and Drury for many years until about 1955 and a settlement has existed here ever since. The construction of the Alaska Highway through the village confirmed its life.

On maps of the 1880s the lake was sometimes called "Aklen", "Ahklen" and "Arklun". Dr. George Mercer Dawson, G&NHSC, officially retained the ancient Indian name in 1887.

TESLIN RIVER 61°34'N 134°54'W (105-E). A major tributary to the Yukon River.

The Indians of the very early days had several names for this stream. Michael Byrne of the Western Union Telegraph Company, although he did not see the river, was told that it was the "Hootalinkwa" or "Hootaliqua". The first miners to prospect up the river from the Yukon in 1881 called it the "Iyon" after the tribal name of the natives living at its mouth. The USC&GS map of 1884 used this name. Lt. Frederick Schwatka, US Army, while on his 1883 excursion named it the "Newberry River" after Professor Newberry of New York. This name was never accepted or used. The Tagish Indians called it "Nas-A-Thane" meaning "No Salmon", although there are many in the river and lake. Some early maps mistakenly named it the "Tahko River".

This was the first major tributary to the Yukon River to be prospected. Fine gold was found in many of the gravel bars along it, but no coarse gold was ever located.

It was one of the major routes to the Klondike goldfields in 1897-98. After Teslin Lake was reached the river was clear sailing down to Dawson and all major obstacles were bypassed.

TETLIT CREEK 66°44'N 135°23'W (106-L). A tributary to the Road River.

This was named in 1962 by B.S. Norford, GSC, after the TETLIT Band of Indians who live in the area.

THAAGA CREEK 61°22'N 137°01'W (115-H). Flows to Aishihik Lake.

This is a Tuchone Indian word meaning "Gravel". It describes the bed of the stream which is quite shallow.

THATCHELL CREEK 61°34'N 137°35'W (115-H). Flows into the northwest corner of Sekulmun Lake.

Recorded by the GSC field crew in 1956, this is an old Indian name meaning "Hide Scraper". The Indians for untold years came here to obtain a certain type of shale rock from which were fashioned good scrapers to work animal hides.

THETIS BAY 69°34'N 139°01'W (117-D). On the east side of Herschel Island.

Lt. Commander Charles Stockton, USN, in the survey ship "USS THETIS" charted much of the Arctic coast and the shores of Herschel Island in 1889. He named this bay after his ship and many of the island features after the whalers he found there. The bay is one of the very few safe anchorages to be found on the western Arctic coast and was much used by wintering whalers, from 1885-1905.

THISTLE CREEK 63°04'N 139°29'W (115-O). A tributary to the Yukon River, just above the mouth of the Stewart River.

In the summer of 1898, a party of eight Scottish prospectors examined this stream and found good payable gold. The two discoverers, Murdoch McIver and Robert Haddow each staked a Discovery claim on 28 September 1898. They named the creek after their Scots emblem, the THISTLE. Robert Henderson bought or otherwise acquired a 50% interest in McIver's Discovery claim. Their party prospected the neighbouring streams and named several of them. Thomas Barton, one of the original party, died in Dawson in 1926.

THISTLETON 63°04'N 139°30'W (115-O). On the Yukon River, at the mouth of Thistle Creek.

This village and steamboat landing was in existence by October 1898. The leading establishment was the Seattle Hotel, owned by William Kramer. A supply point for the miners on the surrounding creeks, it faded quickly as the gold gave out.

THOMAS CREEK 68°11'N 140°38'W (117-B). Flows south into the Old Crow River.

Neil MacDonald, living at Old Crow, a grandson of the first Anglican minister of Fort Yukon, Robert MacDonald, stated that a local Indian named THOMAS had erected a caribou fence on this stream. It was several miles long and was used to trap caribou to kill them. The animal was the Indians' most important source of food.

The remains of the fence can still be seen.

THOMAS GULCH 64°03'N 139°23'W (116-B). A very short stream entering the Klondike River from the south, one mile upstream from Bonanza Creek.

D.W. Thomas found enough gold here to stake the first claim on 20 November 1897 but it did not pay when it was dredged in 1912-14.

THOMAS RIVER 61°34'N 129°28'W (105-H). Joins the Anderson River.

This stream was named in July 1840 by Robert Campbell of the HBC after THOMAS Simpson, a friend of Campbell's in the Company.

THOMPSON CREEK 63°55'N 135°41'W (105-M). Flows north into the South McQuesten River.

This was likely named by or for Ogden Pickett THOMPSON, who came to the Yukon in 1898 and spent a number of years in this immediate area. He left here in 1914 and lived at Johnson Creek in the Mayo district where he made a new and profitable discovery which he mined for some further time. He was known as a good, hard-working prospector.

THOROUGHFARE CREEK 63°41'N 137°05'W (115-P). Flows into Vancouver Creek.

Hugh S. Bostock, GSC, gave this name to the creek in the summer of 1949. The old Conservative Trail to Clear Creek runs along the banks of this stream. (see Conservative Trail)

THORPE CREEK 62°02'N 125°37'W (95-C). Flows into the Crow River.

On 2 February 1966, this small stream was named after William George THORPE (1892-1955). He was, for many years, in charge of the map collection in the Department of Lands and Forests at Victoria, B.C. He was supervisor of map production for B.C. from 1951-1955.

THORSEN CREEK 63°08'N 139°33'W (115-O). Flows into the Yukon River.

Ivan Burian of Stewart River reported that an old-timer of this name lived on this creek for a long time in the early days.

THRASHER BAY 69°33'N 139°12'W (117-D). On the southwest side of Herschel Island.

This bay was named by Lt. Commander Charles Stockton, USN, of the survey ship "USS Thetis", when he surveyed the coast of Herschel Island in 1889. The name is that of a whaler which was anchored in the bay at the time.

THREE BARREL LAKE 64°57'N 136°06'W (116-A). In the Wernecke Mountains.

This small, one mile long lake was named in the early 1960s by "Pat" Callison, member of a pioneer Yukon family and a noted bush pilot. He kept a gasoline cache on the lake for his aircraft during mining exploration in the area.

THREE KINGS CREEK (see Gay Creek).

THE THREE GUARDSMEN 61°11'N 137°13'W (115-H). A group of three peaks on the south shore of Ittlemit Lake, southwest of Aishihik Lake.

These three prominent peaks were named by miners travelling the Dalton Trail in the 1830s, who used them for landmarks. Named after the Three Musketeers in Alexander Dumas famous novel of that name. They are, from east to west, Mount Athos, Mount Porthos and Mount Aramis.

THUNDER MOUNTAIN 6,193' 60°32'N 128°24'W (105-A). Ten miles southeast of Stewart Lake.

This name was proposed in August 1978 by Don Taylor who lives at Stewart Lake, near the mountain. He was, for many years, the Speaker of the Yukon Legislative Assembly.

The old trail from Lower Post to Fort Frances passed by the base of the hill. The name has been used locally for a number of years as the mountain seems to be a locus for storms.

MOUNT TIDD 5,563' 62°09'N 130°54'W (105-J). West of the Pelly Lakes.

Sergeant Claude Britoff TIDD, RCMP, came to the Yukon about 1915 and served at Ross River, Forty Mile, Old Crow, Mayo and Dawson. His entire enlistment was spent in the Yukon.

TIDIGEH LAKE 66°54'N 135°04'W (106-L). A small pond on the east side of the Peel River, below Old Robert Creek.

This is a Loucheaux Indian word meaning "Seagull" from the numbers of these birds found here.

TILLEI LAKE 61°46'N 129°29'W (105-H). About twelve miles north of the west arm of Frances Lake. Drains into the Thomas River.

Dr. George Mercer Dawson, G&NHSC, although he did not visit the lake, gave its Indian name "Til-E-I-Tsho" meaning "Walking Stick River" (he actually gave the name to the creek which drains the lake). In 1887, he traversed this country and spoke to Henry Thibert, the discoverer of the Dease Lake goldfields in the Cassiar, who had been prospecting in this area in the late 1870s and early 1880s. Thibert gave him much information on the lakes and streams in the region.

TINDIR CREEK 65°19'N 141°00'W (116-F). Flows across the Yukon-Alaska boundary, to the Nation River.

This small creek was named in 1910 by a survey team on the International Boundary. Thomas Riggs of the US was in charge. This is an Indian word meaning "Moose".

TINTINA TRENCH 63°25'N 137°00'W (115-P).

The GSC gave this name, meaning "Chief" in the native language, to the broad valley north of, and parallel to the Yukon River between Forty Mile and Dawson. The valley occupies one of the largest fault zones in the Yukon geological system. It was named by R.G. McConnell, GSC, in 1901-02. He spelled it "Tin-Tin-A".

TINY ISLAND LAKE 63°51'N 134°15'W (105-M). Fifteen miles east of Mayo Lake.

Hugh S. Bostock, GSC, named this small lake in 1940 while investigating the area for strategic minerals for the Canadian War effort.

TIZRA CREEK 67°03'N 137°30'W (116-P). Drains Whitefish Lake.

A long-known local name. TIZRA is a Vanta Kutchin Indian word which describes a certain type of whitefish.

TLOGOTSHO RANGE 60°56'N 124°40'W (95-C). At the headwaters of the LaBiche River.

This is a Kaska Indian word referring to "Larger Grassy Hills".

TOLE CREEK 60°01'N 137°12'W (115-A). A tributary to the Tatshenshini River, below Silver Creek.

After "Old TOLE" a prospector who led prospecting parties in this area for many years after 1900. (see Whitestone River)

TOM CREEK 60°11'N 129°01'W (105-A). About eight miles west of Watson Lake, flowing into the Liard River.

This is a long-used local name after "Liard TOM", an Indian trapper whose cabin is at the mouth of the stream. He appeared in an article written about the district in the National Geographic magazine of May 1942.

TOMBSTONE MOUNTAIN 8,200' 64°24'N 138°41'W (115-B). About thirty-three miles northeast of Dawson, at the head of the Tombstone River.

This peak was named "Mount Campbell" by William Ogilvie, DLS, in 1896 after the great explorer of the central Yukon.

The Klondikers who spread out through these valleys in their search for gold in 1897-98, having no maps of the area and unaware of its name, called it TOMBSTONE mountain because of its singular resemblance to a grave marker. It is a rectangular shaft of black basalt, 600 feet wide, that rises 2,000 feet above the surrounding ridge.

Since that time much argument has gone on concerning its exact location. In 1968 Dr. Dirk Tempelman-Kluit, GSC, determined that they were both the same mountain. The Geographical Board of Canada decided to retain the miner's name. However, both before and after that date, many maps, both government and others, still call this peak "Mount Campbell". (see Mount Campbell and Campbell Creek)

TOM O'HARA LAKE 64°03'N 138°31'W (116-B). Southwest of Big Lake.

One of the Mischenko Lakes. This small lake was incorporated into the water supply system needed for hydraulic mining in the Klondike. TOM O'HARA was a foreman on the project which was built in the 1930s. (see Mischenko and Trana Lakes)

TOOBALLY LAKES 60°17'N 126°17'W (95-D). Two lakes at the head of the Smith River, in the southeastern corner of the Yukon Territory.

These two lakes were known, named and fished in the 1830s to supply food for the HBC trading post at Fort Halkett which was at the junction of the Smith and Liard Rivers. (see Smith River)

TOOTSEE RIVER 60°07'N 130°18'W. A tributary to the Rancheria River, from the south.

This is a Kaska Indian word meaning "Loon".

TOO-TSHO RANGE (see Logan Mountains).

TORONTO CREEK 63°46'N 139°07'W (115-O). A tributary to Quartz Creek.

Herbert W. Savage of Toronto, Ontario, named this little stream when he found enough gold on it to stake the first claim on 3 January 1898.

TOULEARY CREEK 62°56'N 139°13'W (115-J). Flows into the Yukon River from the east, just above Kirkman Creek.

Grant and Albert Kirkman found gold here in the summer of 1898, staked the Discovery claim on 26 July and named the creek after their home town of Tulare, California. Someone spelled the name phonetically. (see Kirkman Creek)

TOWATA LAKE 62°41'N 136°21'W (115-I). On Mica Creek, nine miles north of Tatlmain Lake.

This is a Tuchone Indian word meaning "Crooked". It refers to the meanderings of Mica Creek which winds into and out of the lake.

TOWER PEAK 5,672' 61°17'N 133°13'W (105-F). On the north side of Big Salmon Lake.

Because of its distinctive appearance, Arthur St. Cyr, DLS, gave this mountain its name while surveying and mapping the Quiet Lake-Big Salmon Lake country in 1898.

TRAATSANH SPRING 66°29'N 135°04'W (106-L). Just north of Trail River.

This is a Loucheaux Indian word meaning "Stinking Water". This refers to the odour of the sulphurous waters of this mineral spring.

TRAFFIC MOUNTAIN 6,739' 62°07'N 130°25'W (105-J). The lone peak within the junction, formed by the Pelly River and Lakes.

This prominent and long-known landmark is another Yukon mystery. Although probably named by Robert Campbell of the HBC or one of his men and shown on a map in 1849 and nearly all maps since, there has been no record found yet of what or whom the name represents.

TRAIL RIVER 66°40'N 134°40'W (106-L). A tributary to Peel River.

This is an English version of the local Indian name, which was "People's Trail". It is so called because the Indians ascended this stream on foot on their way across country from the Peel to the Bonnet Plume River. The stream is wild and unnavigable so all must walk the length of the river.

TRANA LAKE 64°04'N 138°30'W (116-B). North of Big Lake.

This lake was part of a water storage system to regulate water to the "Big Ditch", the water supply to the Yukon Consolidated Gold Corp.'s power house. This lake is one of three utilized for this purpose which make up the Mischenko Lakes. This lake was named after Edward TRANA a supervisor on the project. Built in the 1930s, it was abandoned in the 1950s. (see Mischenko and Tom O'Hara Lakes)

TREADGOLD CREEK 64°45'N 138°22'W (116-B). Flows into the Blackstone River.

This creek was named after Arthur Newton Christian TREADGOLD. He was a direct descendant of Sir Isaac Newton. An Oxford University Don (Professor) he came to the Yukon in 1898, representing English interests. He formed the Granville Mining Company and accumulated large properties in the Klondike. A take-over attempt by Canadian and other interests led to his loss of control and the longest court case in Canadian history. The battle went as far as the Privy Council in London and dragged on to the 1940s, although TREADGOLD lost effective control around 1932.

He travelled widely in the Yukon and in 1899 wrote a most comprehensive report on the industry and the country.

TRESIDDER CREEK 63°29'N 136°14'W (115-P). Enters the Stewart River, about ten miles above Stewart Crossing.

In September 1941, the Geographic Board of Canada confirmed this old local name. Charles TRESIDDER was an old-timer who had trapped and lived for many years on this creek.

TRITOP PEAK 6,079' 62°13'N 137°31'W (115-I). Ten miles northwest of Mount Nansen.

Around 1910, miners in the Mount Nansen District called this hill "The Haystack". A few years later the name was changed by a GSC crew, ignorant of the local name, and the new name made official. The name comes from its appearance, the mountain has three summits.

TROMBLEY CREEK 62°40'N 138°36'W (115-J). A small tributary to Dip Creek, in the Dawson Range.

This brook was named on 16 September 1915, during the staking rush to Rude Creek. Timothy TROMBLEY (Tromblay) was from Quebec and an active prospector in many parts of the Yukon.

TROPICAL CREEK 60°05'N 126°19'W (95-D). Flows into the Smith River, south of Toobally Lakes.

This was named by the personnel of an oil exploration company in 1949. The luxuriant vegetation along the banks of the stream is caused by the waters of a hot spring there.

TRUITT CREEK 64°12'N 134°22'W (105-L). Flows into the east end of Little Salmon Lake.

This creek was named by a survey team of the US Army Engineers in the summer of 1942. Col. James J. TRUITT was in charge of location surveys for a proposed railway from Prince George, B.C. to Fairbanks, Alaska, which was intended to supplement or replace the Alaska Military Highway then being constructed.

Section "A" of the Trans Canadian, Alaska and Western Railway was between the above points. Section "B" was to be carried from Fairbanks to Nome, Alaska. On section "A" actual field surveys were carried out by 24 teams comprised of 556 men. They started early in May and completed the surveys by October 1942.

It was estimated that the railroad from Prince George to Fairbanks would be by way of Finlay Forks and Lower Post, B.C., then to Ross River, the Five Finger Rapids and west to Fairbanks. The line was to have been approximately 1417 miles in length and estimated to cost about $111,000,000 at that time.

After the defeat of the Japanese Forces in the Aleutian Islands and the successful construction of the Alaska Military Highway, the railway project was dropped in favour of improving the highway.

The present Campbell Highway (between Watson Lake and Carmacks) used these surveys as a guide to location. (see Railway Survey Creek and Truitt Peak)

TRUITT PEAK 6,799' 62°17'N 134°15'W (105-L). In the Glenlyon Range, at the headwaters of Truitt Creek.

Col. James J. TRUITT, US Army Engineers, was on an inspection flight of survey parties on the routes of the Trans Canadian, Alaska and Western Railway and the Canol Road in the early spring of 1942. He was returning to Whitehorse by aircraft when the pilot of the bomber they were flying allowed him to take over the controls. He had never flown an aircraft before and nearly crashed into this mountain. The pilot flew the rest of the way. After landing, the aircraft crew suggested they name this peak after him as a joking reminder of his only attempt at flying. The survey crews accepted the name. The name was later confirmed and made official in 1946. The survey parties later used the name for the creek below the peak.

TSIH MOUNTAIN 66°55'N 135°47'W (106-L). A long ridge on the east side of the Richardson Mountains.

A Loucheaux Indian word meaning "Nose Mountain", from the shape of the slope. It was a landmark on the Fort MacPherson-Fort Yukon trail.

TSUSHO CREEK 61°27'N 137°05'W (115-H). Flows west to Aishihik Lake.

A Tuchone Indian word meaning "Big Spruce".

TTHOH CREEK 66°38'N 135°22'W (106-L). A tributary to the Road River.

A Loucheaux Indian word meaning "Big Boulder", probably from the name of the mountain near the stream, which is called "TTHOH Mountain".

TUCHITUA RIVER 60°56'N 129°12'W (105-A). Flows into the upper canyon of the Frances River.

An Indian name, probably Kaska, reported by Dr. George Mercer Dawson, G&NHSC, in 1887 as "Too-Tshi-Too", meaning "Whitefish".

TUMMEL RIVER 62°45'N 135°04'W (105-L). A tributary to the Pelly River, from the south.

Robert Campbell of the HBC, on his exploration of the Pelly River in the summer of 1840, named this stream after a river of the same name near his home in Perthshire, Scotland.

TURNER LAKE 66°11'N 134°15'W (106-L). West of the Peel River.

This was named in 1973 after John TURNER who had been a Yukon Councillor for the Bonanza District from 1915-17.

MOUNT TURNER 65°24'N 136°15'W (116-H). East of the Hart River.

This peak was named in May 1973 to commemorate Constable F. TURNER, RNWMP. Although retired, he volunteered to be a member of the Dempster Patrol. They searched for and found the bodies of Inspector Fitzgerald and his three men who had become lost and starved to death in the Peel River country in the winter of 1911. (see Dempster Highway)

TUSTLES LAKE 61°45'N 129°I3'W (105-H). Fifteen miles northeast of the west arm of Frances Lake.

This was named by Dr. George Mercer Dawson, G&NHSC, in 1887, from the Indian name "TUSTLES-TO", for which he provided no translation.

TWELFTH OF JULY CREEK 61°10'N 138°04'W (115-G). A tributary to Fourth of July Creek.

During the start of the rush to the Kluane Lake goldfields, Charles Racine discovered gold and staked the Discovery claim on this stream, eight days after Tagish "Dawson" Charlie staked that of Fourth of July Creek.

TWO BEAVER LAKE 64°45'N 137°25'W (116-A). West of Rae Creek.

This little lake received its name in the summer of 1954 when two DeHaviland Beaver aircraft supplied mining exploration groups based here.

TWO LADDER CREEK 60°01'N 131°44'W (105-B). A tributary to the Smart River.

In the 1930s, two local Indian prospectors sank a shaft on the shore of what was then known as "Dorsey Lake". It was deep enough to need two ladders to reach the bottom.

Local people changed the name to "Two Ladder Lake". In 1963, the Geographical Board of Canada disallowed that name and restored that of "Dorsey". To compensate, they gave the name TWO LADDER to this creek, about ten miles away.

TWOPETE CREEK 62°41'N 133°52'W (105-K). A tributary to the Tay River, from the south.

J.R. Johnson, GSC, in 1935 noted this name in local use. Two Swedish prospectors and trappers lived here. Both had the given name of "Peter". The mountain was named later.

TYERS RIVER 61°14'N129°15'W (105-H). Flows into the south end of Frances Lake.

This river was named by Robert Campbell of the HBC, probably around 1840 when he was building Fort Frances. The original Indian name is not known and this is likely a Scottish name.

TYRRELL CREEK 61°55'N 138°01'W (115-G). A tributary to the Nisling River.

This stream was officially named in 1955 after Joseph Burr TYRRELL, BSc, GSC, who travelled this stream when he mapped the geology of the area, including the Nisling River, in 1898.

MOUNT TYRRELL 4,747' 63°43'N 140°04'W (115-N). Between the Sixty Mile and Yukon Rivers.

Joseph Burr TYRRELL (1858-1957) served the GSC from 1880-1898 and was a noted exploration geologist in the Northwest Territories and the Yukon. He was born in Weston, Ontario on 1 November 1858 and was educated at Upper Canada College and the University of Toronto. He won scholarships and graduated with distinction. He took an active part in the militia and served with the Queen's Own Rifles and later, in the Governor General's Foot Guards. He was a crack shot with both rifle and pistol.

After resigning from the GSC he practiced as a mining engineer in Dawson for seven years. His hobby, for which he became well-known, was researching and writing about the men of the early fur trade and their explorations in Northern Canada. He went on to successfully establish a profitable gold mine in Kirkland Lake, Ontario amid other ventures. He died at Agincourt, Ontario.

ULU MOUNTAIN 10,160' 60°14'N 138°46'W (115-B). Ten miles southeast of Mount Kennedy.

Named after the "ULU", the Eskimo (Inuit) knife which is also the symbol of the Arctic Winter Games. The peak was first climbed on 6 March 1970 by "Monty" Alford, Louis Lambert Scott Foster and Jim Boyde, to celebrate the newly established games which embrace people from the NWT, Alaska and the Yukon.

URANUS CREEK (see Pooly Creek).

VADZAIH KAN CREEK 66°42'N 137°03'W (116-I). A tributary to the Eagle River.

A Loucheaux Indian word meaning "Caribou Hill Creek".

VAN BIBBER CREEK 60°48'N 136°44'W (115-A). Flows to the Dezadeash River.

Alex VAN BIBBER was a big-game guide and outfitter in the Kluane country. H.S. Bostock and E.D. Kindle of the GSC noted him in their reports for his ability and assistance in the field during their mapping expeditions in the 1940s.

MOUNT VAN BIBBER 6,456' 63°03'N 135°37'W (105-M). In the McArthur Range, about thirty-five miles south of Mayo.

This name was requested by Mrs. D. J. Fulton of Cranbrook, B.C. in March 1967 to commemorate her father, Ira VAN BIBBER.

Ira VAN BIBBER with his two brothers, Theodore and Patrick, came from West Virginia to the Klondike in 1898. Ira loved the country and married an Indian wife. They trapped for three years in the then almost totally unknown Nahanni country. He became one of the best big-game guides in the Yukon. He made his home for most of these years at Pelly Crossing and this mountain is in the midst of the region where he hunted and trapped. After more than sixty years in the Yukon he died, leaving many descendants to carry on his name and traditions.

VAN CLEAVES HILL 63°49'N 135°32'W (105-M). Six miles west of Mayo Lake.

VAN CLEAVE, prospector and trapper, lived for years at the foot of this mountain.

MOUNT VANCOUVER 15,700' 60°20'N 139°41'W (115-B). A boundary line peak in the St. Elias Range.

In 1874, Professor W.H. Dall who was with the Western Union Telegraph Company expedition as a scientific director, named this peak. He named it in honour of Captain George Vancouver, RN (1758-1798).

Captain Vancouver, in command of the sloop "Discovery" and accompanied by Lt. W.R. Broughton in command of the tender "Chatham", made an exploring and surveying voyage from England to southeastern Alaska and around the world from 1790-1795.

Vancouver's expedition, among his other accomplishments, added a wealth of knowledge and place names to previously ill-defined coastal features of southeastern Alaska and the coast of British Columbia. He respected the names he found and the nomenclature of his charts was generally accepted.

This mountain was first climbed by N.E. Odell, A.Bruce, Bill Hainsworth, Bob McCarter and Robertson on 5 July 1949.

MOUNT VANIER 6,049' 60°37'N 136°02'W (115-A). At the northeast corner of Kusawa Lake.

Georges VANIER, DSO, MC and Bar, MID, Legion of Honour (France), Order of Merit (US), BA, LLD, was born in Montreal on 23 April 1888.

VANIER was educated in law at Laval University but found an early aptitude for military life. In 1914, he helped found the 22nd French Canadian Battalion, the famous "Van Doos". In 1920, the Battalion was made the Royal 22nd Regiment.

He served overseas in France from 1915-1918 with high distinction, winning many decorations for bravery and losing his right leg in battle in August 1918. He continued as a soldier, attending Staff College at Camberly, England in 1922. In 1925, he was promoted to Lieutenant Colonel and given command of the Royal 22nd Regiment.

His diplomatic career began about this time he was chosen as a Canadian delegate to the League of Nations in 1927 and made Minister to France in 1939, holding the post until 1942. He was a part of the highest Allied war councils and a major figure in Canadian diplomacy during the War and after.

On 3 August 1959 he was appointed Governor General of Canada.

He was the first French-Canadian to hold the post and was popular in all parts of the country, serving with distinction. He died on 5 March 1967.

VAN GORDA (see VAN GORDER).

VAN GORDER CREEK 62°13'N 133°22'W (105-K). A tributary to the Pelly River, near Ross River.

Del Charles VAN GORDER was born in Ord City, Nebraska on 4 March 1876. He came to the Yukon about the turn of the century, attracted by the stories of gold.

In the early years he gravitated to the upper Pelly River country where he prospected and trapped for many years, often with Ira Van Bibber. Around 1910, he became the manager of the Taylor and Drury trading post at Pelly Banks. Leaving there about 1944, he took over their post at Ross River until 1949. He retired to Teslin where he died, a respected pioneer, on 21 November 1953. That same year Allan Kulan found a large lead-zinc-silver ore body near this creek. In July 1971, the new school at Faro was given Van Gorder's name.

His name was often misspelled "Van Gorda" and as such will be found on many maps.

VEESHRIDLAH MOUNTAIN 67°08'N 139°21'W (116-O). On the headwaters of Lord Creek, in the Keele Range.

This is an old Vanta Kutchin Indian word meaning "Dark", which describes the appearance of this hill.

MOUNT VERMILION 61°20'N 131°30'W (105-G). East of McNeil Lake.

This was named by S. Gordey, GSC, in 1976 because of the brilliant red-orange gossan (iron rusted rock) which colours the southeast slopes of this mountain.

VERONICA CREEK 63°41'N 138°35'W (115-O). A tributary to Dominion Creek, from the south.

Gold was found here and the Discovery claim staked on 22 March 1901 by William Gerbracht and William Kandall. The creek was probably named earlier.

VICHI TIK TSIIVII CREEK 66°31'N 136°59'W (116-I). A tributary to the Eagle River.

This is a Loucheaux Indian word meaning "Spruce on Top of a Hill", describing a forested summit.

VICTOR CREEK 62°38'N 133°50'W (115-J). A tributary to Dip Creek.

Gold was found here and a Discovery claim was staked on 16 September 1915 by Timothy Trombley and Henry Detraz. They named it "Galena Creek" but the name was changed by the Mining Recorder in Dawson as there was already a "Galena Creek" in the territory. (see Trombley Creek)

VICTORIA CREEK 60°31'N 137°27'W (115-A). Flows into Louise Lake, the westernmost of the Kathleen Lakes.

Peter Ehret found the first placer gold in this creek in the summer of 1902. When he recorded the Discovery claim on 24 May, the Mining Recorder, Inspector A.E.G. MacDonnell, NWMP, named the stream in honour of the day, Queen Victoria's birthday.

MOUNT VINES 64°50'N 138°16'W (116-B). North of Rendell Ridge.

This was named for Lionel VINES, a pioneer airman in the Yukon, who was killed in a crash in the area sometime in the 1930s. The mountain was known as "Pilot Peak" by other bush pilots of the time.

VIRGIN CREEK 60°25'N 137°26'W (115-A). A tributary to Victoria Creek, ten miles west of Dezadeash Lake.

To quote the Whitehorse Star of 19 August 1905: "Thomas Laird arrived yesterday from Virgin Creek, of which he is the discoverer, in the Kluane district. He has taken out enough gold to pay good wages all summer." Laird made his find in June.

There is some evidence that an earlier prospector in the area, William Trettin, had actually named the creek in 1903 during the rush to the Kluane diggings. Perhaps a play on words.

VITRIH CREEK 66°23'N 134°19'W (106-L).

A Loucheaux Indian word meaning "Flintstone". The ancient Indians gathered this rock for tool and weapon making purposes.

VITTREKWA RIVER 67°00'N 135°36'W (106-L). Crosses the Yukon-NWT boundary, in the Richardson Mountains.

In 1900, and later, an Indian of this name lived on this river. The Dawson-MacPherson Patrol of the RNWMP camped at his cabin. They spelled his name "Vitchiquah" which, in the Loucheaux language, means "No Cry". The VITTREKWA family still trap on the upper reaches of the river.

VOLCANO MOUNTAIN 4,063' 62°55'N 137°23'W (115-I). Eleven miles north of Fort Selkirk.

Hugh S. Bostock, GSC, in 1935 reported in GSC Memoir No. 189: "This is probably the only well-preserved volcano and crater of its size in Canada."

VON WILCZEK CREEK 62°36'N 136°54'W (115-I). Enters the Yukon River, north of Rink Rapids from the east.

Lt. Frederick Schwatka, US Army, named this stream in the summer of 1883 after Graf VON WILCZEK of Vienna, Austria, but called it a "River".

The Geographical Board of Canada changed the designation to "Creek" in July 1960 and at the same time gave the same name to the small lakes on the upper reaches of the stream.

VOREEKWA LAKES 67°08'N 138°17'W (116-O). Southeast of Sharp Mountain.

These were named in 1973 as a map designation. Enquiries of the natives of Old Crow concerning the origins of the name brought the answer that it is a Vanta Kuchin Indian word meaning "No Name". Some field man had his leg pulled on this one!

MOUNT VOWLES 61°25'N 136°11'W (115-H). East of Aishihik Lake.

D.D. Cairnes, GSC, while mapping the geology of the area in 1910, named this landmark on the Dalton Trail after Stanley Tom VOWLES, RNWMP No.4206. He enlisted in the Force in 1904 and resigned in 1908. Most of his service was spent in this area, where Cairnes knew him.

VUNNUTULE LAKE 67°39'N 139°42'W (116-O). On the east side of Old Crow River, five miles north of Old Crow.

This is another Loucheaux Indian word. The translation means "A Lake with an Island Occupying Most of its Area".

VUNTA CREEK 67°55'N 136°33'W (116-P). A small tributary to Fish Creek, north of the McDougall Pass.

This was named in the summer of 1962 by B.S. Norford, GSC, after the VUNTA Band of Indians, whose trapping grounds run from here to the Porcupine River.

VYAH KIT CREEK 66°24'N 136°36'W (116-I). A tributary to the Eagle River.

A Loucheaux Indian word meaning "Caribou Snare Place Creek".

WADE LAKES 60°04'N 137°12'W (115-A). Northwest of Mount Beaton.

These were named in 1973 by the Yukon Scenic and Wilderness Study Group while using the trail along the lakeshores to Silver Creek. Flooding had raised the level of the lakes so high they had to wade through shallow flooded places.

WALHALLA CREEK 63°07'N 138°37'W (115-O). Flows into Scroggie Creek.

This was known in the earliest days as the left fork of Scroggie Creek until paying gold was found in 1912 by a prospector named LeBouef. It was believed that he had been prospecting in Australia in earlier years and named this creek after the rich goldfields of WALHALLA in the state of Victoria, Australia, which had been discovered before 1900.

MOUNT WALKER 64°17'N 138°14'W (116-B). Northwest of Antimony Mountain.

Named after Bill WALKER, finder of the antimony deposits on Antimony Mountain. He was a partner of Bob French. (see Mount French)

WALKING STICK MOUNTAIN 61°26'N 131°29'W (105-G). Northeast of McNeil Lake.

A GSC party mapping this mountain in 1976 found a WALKING STICK several hundred feet above tree line.

MOUNT WALLACE 7,726' 61°03'N 135°23'W (105-D). Southwest of Carbon Hill.

This mountain was named in 1960 to memorialize the name of Dr. Robert C. WALLACE, distinguished scholar and geologist. He was a past-president of the University of Alberta and a former Principal of Queen's University at Kingston, Ontario.

WALSH GLACIER 60°53'N 140°45'W (115-C). South of the Centennial Range, in the St. Elias Mountains.

J.J. McArthur, DLS, of the International Boundary Survey Commission named this feature after Superintendent James Morrow WALSH of the NWMP in 1900. (see Mount Walsh)

MOUNT WALSH 14,780' 61°00'N 140°01'W (115-F). A boundary marker peak in the south St. Elias Mountains.

In July 1900, J.J. McArthur, DLS, of the International Boundary Survey Commission, named this mountain after Superintendent James Morrow WALSH of the NWMP.

Born in 1841, at Prescott, Upper Canada, WALSH was one of the original Force, enlisting in 1873. After a distinguished career in the west he was called upon by the Canadian government, with almost unanimous public approval, to administer and govern the newly-formed Yukon Territory. He went to the Yukon in September 1897, armed with almost dictatorial powers. As well as being given the post of Commissioner (Governor) he was handed sole command of the NWMP in the Territory and appointed Supervisor of Customs and Mail Services.

WALSH only spent a year in the Yukon. Although there were many criticisms of his methods and ethics, there is no denying that, under almost intolerable conditions, he skillfully organized order out of chaos. He was ably assisted by some of the great names of the NWMP, such as Steele, Jarvis, Constantine, Wood, Belcher and others. He was hindered by honest but inefficient civil servants whose inability to cope with the huge number of persons flooding into the Territory led to unproven charges of government graft and corruption.

He died of a stroke on 25 July 1905 at Brockville, Ontario.

MOUNT WALTERS 3,189' 62°47'N 137°04'W (115-I). Ten miles east of Fort Selkirk.

This hill was named in 1971 to commemorate No.127 Private H. WALTERS of the Royal Regiment of Canadian Infantry, a member of the Yukon Field Force of 1898. He marched overland from Glenora on the Stikine River, to the head of Teslin Lake and came by rowboat to Fort Selkirk. He died here in service on 28 February 1899 and is buried here. (see Mounts Evans, Watson, Hansen and Corcoran)

MOUNT WANN 65°56'N 140°15'W (116-P). West of the Porcupine River.

In September 1973, this mountain was named after Clyde Gavin WANN who organized the first commercial air service in the Yukon. He carried the first air mail between Whitehorse, Mayo, Keno, Dawson, Carcross and Atlin from 1928-30. He assisted the US Army Engineers in scouting the route for the Alaska Highway and, immediately after it was opened for public travel, built some of the first tourist services on the road; at Rancheria, Morley River and Destruction Bay.

MOUNT WARD 60°07'N 135°23'W (105-D). Southwest of Carbon Hill.

Named on 2 May 1911, after Joseph WARD, a well-known prospector and miner in the south Wheaton River area.

WAREHAM LAKE 63°41'N 135°52'W (105-M). On the Mayo River, five miles above Mayo Landing.

The fore-bay or reservoir of the hydro-electric power plant here has been known locally as WAREHAM LAKE ever since it was created. After the late Rev. G.W.N. WAREHAM, who drowned in Mayo Lake some years ago. The plant was built in 1952 to provide electric power for the silver-lead mines in the region.

WASSON LAKE 60°52'N 130°27'W (105-B). On the southeast side of the Simpson Range, near the headwaters of the Liard River.

This small lake was named in February 1936 after Everett WASSON, the first bush pilot in the Yukon. He flew a Fairchild 71 for the Treadwell Yukon Mining Company from 1928-35. From 1935 until 1940 he was general manager and chief pilot of the WP&YR Aviation Division.

WASSON flew the first air search and rescue mission in Yukon history. The Burke party was lost on the upper Liard River and WASSON was called in. On 3 November 1930, he and Joe Walsh, an experienced Yukon prospector and guide, started the search. Due to a lack of knowledge of Burke's original destination, much time was lost searching in the wrong direction.

WASSON and Walsh eventually found the party on the banks of the upper Liard River on 6 December. After taking care of the survivors, Walsh had to repair the aircraft's propeller, which had been damaged on landing. The repaired propeller held and the aircraft was flown to Atlin,

B.C. Burke had died of exhaustion and exposure shortly before the party was found. The Dominion government awarded WASSON $1,500 and Walsh $500 for their hazardous efforts.

WASSON died of a heart attack in Alexander Valley, California in December 1958. (see Burke Creek and Everett Creek)

WATERS RIVER 67°24'N 137°01'W (116-P). Flows into the Bell River, at Lapierre House.

It is probable that this river was named after Corporal WATERS of the RNWMP, who assisted W.E. Cockfield, GSC, in 1917.

It was known locally as "Fool's River".

MOUNT WATES 61°14'N 140°04'W (115-F). Southeast of the Steele Glacier, in the St. Elias Mountains.

Named by the Alpine Club of Canada in 1970, after Cyril Geoffrey WATES (1884-1946), a telephone engineer and past-president of the club (1938-41).

This is the furthest south of twin peaks, the north peak being Mount Gibson.

WATSON 60°06'N 134°50'W (105-D). Opposite the West Arm of Bennett Lake.

A section point on the WP&YR. WATSON, a partner in the firm of WATSON and Church, Real Estate agents in Skagway in 1898-99. He gave much support to Heney and Hawkins of the WP&YR in their efforts to gain a right-of-way through Skagway in the early days of construction.

WATSON CREEK 63°32'N 135°09'W (105-M). A tributary to the Stewart River.

This local name has been in use since 1899, after Robert WATSON.

WATSON graduated in mathematics from the University of Toronto and came to the Yukon in 1895 or 1896. He was cheated out of a claim on Bonanza Creek in 1896 and was so soured that he formed a revulsion for all other men. He moved to this small stream, at that time almost totally isolated, and trapped for a living. While living here he made an intensive study of the works of Shakespeare as a source of modern slang. He died and was buried on the creek in 1905.

WATSON LAKE 60°04'N 128°42'W (105-A). At Mile 635 (KM1029) on the Alaska Highway, in southeast Yukon.

Frank WATSON, of Yorkshire in England, started for the Klondike in 1897 from Edmonton. Fighting his way through unmapped country he arrived on the upper Liard River in the spring of 1898. His illusions of easy gold in the Klondike were by this time completely dissipated. However, the country was appealing and he decided to stay in this part, to prospect and trap. He married an attractive Indian girl from Lower Post and from then on led an unrestricted and unhurried life. The upper Liard River and its tributaries were his trapping and prospecting grounds while his home was on the shore of WATSON LAKE. The lake had been known since the 1870s as "Fish Lake". In 1941, the area became too crowded for him when construction began on the airport and highway. He moved his family a few miles north to Windid Lake.

With the building of the Alaska Highway, most of the activity in the area moved ten miles east to what was then called "Watson Lake Wye", the site of the present town.

To quote the Alaska Highway News, Special Edition, Summer 1959: "In the spring of 1941 operations for the construction of the airport at Watson Lake were begun. First stage was the shipment of supplies by boat from Vancouver to Wrangell. It was then necessary to tranship them by riverboat and barge some 160 miles up the Stikine River to Telegraph Creek, from there by truck some 76 miles to Dease Lake but only after this section of the road had been made passable. At Dease Lake the equipment was again unloaded into barges and boats and transported down the Dease River to Lower Post on the Liard River. Here a tote road some 26 miles in length had to be built into Watson Lake to the airport site."

Two runways, approximately 5,000 feet in length, were built along with administration buildings and staff quarters for both RCAF and Department of Transport personnel. The work was completed in the autumn of 1943. The project was then handed over to the government by the contractor, General Construction Company, Ltd. A post office was opened on 1 July 1942,

Watson Lake being noted for its massive array of sign posts, it may be of interest that the first sign erected was the one put up by Carl L. Lindley of Denville, Illinois, in early 1942. He was a soldier in Company "D" of the 341st Engineers, US Army.

Frank WATSON died here but some of his family still live in the community. (see Baker Lake)

MOUNT WATSON 62°55'N 137°11'W (115-I). East of Volcano Mountain, about twelve miles northeast of Fort Selkirk.

In November 1971, this mountain was given the name of No. 125 Corporal M. WATSON of the Royal Regiment of Canada. He was a member of the Yukon Field Force of 1898. They marched overland from Glenora on the Stikine River to the head of Teslin Lake and rowed, in boats they had built, down the Teslin and Yukon Rivers to Fort Selkirk.

Known as Cpl. M. WATSON of the RRC's, it was found, after his death, that he was, in reality, the Hon. St. John Watson Beresford of Creaduff House, Athlone, Ireland. He was a nephew of Viscount Castlemain. He was 38 years of age and had been in the service for 10 or 11 years before killing himself accidentally with a service revolver in the barracks at Dawson on 28 March 1900. (see Mounts Evans, Corcoran, Hansen and Walters)

WATSON RIVER 60°11'N 134°44'W (105-D). Flows into the north end of Lake Bennett, at Carcross.

This river was named by Lt. Frederick Schwatka, US Army, in 1883 after Professor Sereno WATSON of Harvard University. As it was previously unnamed, Dr. George Mercer Dawson allowed the name to stand.

WAUGH CREEK 64°55'N 137°02'W (116-A). A tributary to the Hart River, in the Wernecke Mountains.

The Forest Warden for this area, C.J. Shattuck, stated in a letter to the CPCGN in June 1956 that: "WAUGH Creek is named after a fairly ordinary man. He was a miner and promoter who started a placer mine on this creek in 1906. About $50,000 in equipment was shipped via the MacKenzie and Peel Rivers in 1909. Some doubt exists as to whether the equipment was used or abandoned en route. At any rate, WAUGH took his own life in a hotel room in Chicago in May 1910 rather than admit his failure to his backers."

Harry F. WAUGH was born in New Brunswick and came into the Yukon in the spring of 1896 and was one of the first to stake a claim in the Klondike. He staked the first claim after Carmack and his party, locating No. 14 below Discovery, while his partner, Burpee staked No. 15 below.

WAUGH's name appears in many newspaper accounts from 1905-10 in the Yukon, all concerning his efforts to establish a viable mining operation in one of the most inaccessible and inhospitable places on the North American continent. For instance, in 1906 he and "Black" Sullivan (another Klondike original) appeared at Herschel Island with specimens of gold-bearing quartz ore and went out to Dawson on the whaler "Kar-Luk" to record their claims. He searched the country from the Ogilvie Mountains to the Arctic Slope in his quest for minerals. His partners in these ventures were almost all well-known Yukoners of wealth and experience such as "Black" Sullivan, Andrew Hunker and Thomas O'Brien, who had enough faith in his ability and integrity to back him financially for years.

WAUGH's last action in the Yukon was to assist the RNWMP in a long search for some lost men.

WAUGH may have seemed to be of "no importance", and suspect because of his willingness to gamble his own and his friend's money on such chancy adventures as looking for mines. However, his actions over the years in choosing a life of hardship in this desolate country, the regard in which he was held by his peers and his eventual suicide, all point to a man with a terrible sense of integrity and responsibility. He was certainly no "ordinary man". (see Hunker Creek)

WEBBER CREEK 62°03'N 137°13'W (115-I). A small tributary to Nansen Creek, from the east.

Charles and Jack WEBBER were coal miners at Carmacks before deciding to go prospecting. In 1912, they explored the Mount Nansen area and found gold on this stream.

WELLESLEY LAKE 62°22'N 139°50'W (115-K). This large lake is the source of the Nisling River.

Charles Willard Hayes (1859-1916), USGS geologist from 1887-1911, joined Lt. Frederick Schwatka, US Army, in his last expedition in 1891. The expedition, sponsored by a syndicate of American newspapers, was to explore the region between the Lynn Canal and the Copper River. Mark Russell, a noted prospector of his time accompanied them as their guide. Their route followed the Taku Inlet trail to Teslin Lake, along the Teslin River to the Lewes (Yukon), up the White River and over the Skolai Pass into Alaska and then down the Chitina and Copper Rivers.

Hayes made the first classification of the Alaskan physiographic provinces. For much of the area covered he gathered the first scientific information. He named this lake after WELLESLEY College in Massachusetts. The college, established in the early 1800s was named after Lord Mornington WELLESLEY, the Duke of Wellington. The "Iron Duke" was the conqueror of Napoleon's armies in the Spanish Peninsular and French Wars.

THE WEISSHORN 11,620' 60°16'N 138°54'W (115-B). In the south central St. Elias Range.

On 18 May 1976, this mountain was first climbed by a Swiss-German party consisting of Andreas Brun, Adrian Buhler, Heidi Ludi and Claus Lotscher, who named it after a Swiss Mountain.

WERNECKE 63°57'N 135°16'W (105-M). On Keno Hill.

This small mining camp was started in 1921 to serve the newly found silver-lead mines of Keno Hill. It was named for Livingstone WERNECKE, ME, Manager of the Treadwell Yukon Mining Company Ltd.

WERNECKE, an American mining engineer, was working at the Alaska Gatineau Mine at Juneau as a construction engineer in 1914. He was next employed as a geologist at the Alaska Treadwell Gold Mining Co. at the same place. He was the last man out of that huge mine when it caved in and the sea filled it forever in 1917.

His company had followed with interest the new finds of high-grade, silver-lead ore in the Keno Hill area and in 1919 sent WERNECKE there to investigate. He bought up several promising properties which were then formed into the Treadwell Yukon Mining Co.

By 1923, they were shipping high-grade ore to Kellogg, Idaho. In 1925, they had a mill in production. The concentrated ores were shipped by horse and wagon to Mayo Landing, by WP&YR riverboats to Whitehorse and by rail to Skagway. From Skagway the ore went to Seattle and then again by rail to Idaho. Clearly, this ore had to be very rich to pay for this expensive handling and still yield a profit. Although operations were suspended from 1927-32, WERNECKE, as well as managing the mines in an excellent manner, continued to explore and send out prospectors to find more mines. He had an abiding faith that large and rich mineral deposits would be found in the mountains to the east of the Mayo district and paralleling the Yukon-NWT boundary, a theory that proved to be correct.

The Treadwell Yukon Mining Co. suspended operations permanently in 1942 due to the difficulty in obtaining labour and supplies during the war years. The little settlement had been abandoned about 1933 when the ore was exhausted in the nearby mines.

Livingstone WERNECKE was killed in an airplane crash somewhere between Juneau and Ketchikan in 1941. His death may have influenced the company in its decision to suspend all operations. The Wernecke Mountains, in whose hidden riches he firmly believed, were named at a later date in memory of this exceptional man.

WESKATAHIN (see Neskatahin).

WEST LAKE 63°42'N 132°23'W (105-N). Northwest of the Rogue River.

This name proposed by James Smith, Commissioner of the Yukon Territory after Runer WEST. He was a Swedish or Finnish trapper here in the 1940s-50s. He went mad and disappeared in the wilderness.

WEST RAT RIVER (see Bell River).

MOUNT WESTMAN 5,905' 64°06'N 134°11'W (106-D). East of the junction of the Beaver and Rackla Rivers.

In November 1964, this mountain was chosen to commemorate R101306 Warrant Officer Robert Morris WESTMAN. He was born in Regina, Saskatchewan on 21 September 1915 and enlisted in the RCAF at Vancouver, B.C. on 8 May 1941. He served in Canada and overseas and was missing, presumed killed in action on 29 April 1943.

WHEATON RIVER 60°07'N 134°53'W (105-D). Flows into the north end of Lake Bennett.

This river was named by Lt. Frederick Schwatka, US Army, in 1883 after Brevet Major General Frank WHEATON, US Army.

MOUNT WHITE 60°18'N 133°57'W (105-C). Two miles south of Jake's Corner.

William Ogilvie, DLS, during his survey of the Yukon River in 1887, named this bald hill after the then Minister of the Interior, the Hon. Thomas WHITE, who had supported the exploration and survey of the Yukon. Ogilvie had already named the "White Pass" after the same man.

WHITEHORSE 60°43'N 135°03'W (105-D). The capital of the Yukon Territory.

Situated at the upper limits of feasible steamboat navigation on the Yukon River and the terminus of the WP&YR, a settlement began here in 1900. As well as controlling the shipping of the territory it became a supply point and communications center for the southern Yukon. The discovery and exploitation of the rich copper ore bodies nearby, from 1899-1920, also helped to stimulate the business and growth of the town.

Many fanciful stories have been and are being told about the origin of the name WHITEHORSE. It is probable that the first miners in 1880-81 fancied a resemblance to white horses' manes in the white waters of the rapids below Miles Canyon. The name was in common use by 1887. The foot of the rapids made a natural stopping place for those who had braved their dangers. Few people dared these hazards with loaded boats, the majority preferring to unload and carry (portage) their goods around the dangerous waters. The boats were either let down on ropes or taken through by professional pilots. In either case this location made a good place to stop and reorganize outfits before going on downriver. Most landed on the east side of the river and it was there that the first townsite of Whitehorse was surveyed in September 1899 by Paul T.C. Dumais, DLS.

The WP&YR had been granted 640 acres of land on the west side of the river for their terminus and in late 1899 laid out and surveyed a townsite which they named "Closeleigh", in honour of the Close brothers of London, England. The brothers had been instrumental in financing the construction of the railroad and the freighting operations of the company.

An outcry by the first merchants of the new town soon led to a change of heart. The WP&YR on 21 April 1900, announced that "the name of the town is to be the old, known on two continents.... WHITE HORSE".

The building of the Alaska Highway in 1942-43 assured the growth and permanence of the community. At the beginning of 1942 the population was about 500, which had increased to 8,000 by early summer when US Army Engineers and some civilian contractors arrived. This population decreased to about 3,000 by 1955 but the increasing search for oil and minerals, along with the growth of tourism and government, reversed this trend and it has grown steadily since to around 20,000.

The first post office was opened on 1 June 1900 by F.W. Cane. In March 1951, Whitehorse replaced Dawson as the capital of the Yukon Territory.

The name of the town was always spelled as two words until the Geographic Board of Canada combined them on 21 March 1957.

WHITE RANGE 60°01'N 134°31'W (105-D). On the east side of Windy Arm of Tagish Lake.

In the summer of 1899, George William Richard Montague White-Fraser, DLS, DTS, BCLS, was engaged with a crew of two men in setting boundary monuments (cairns) on the Yukon-B.C. boundary between Lake Bennett and Teslin Lake. The burst of mining activity in the region had made the immediate delineation of the boundary between the Yukon and British Columbia a necessity.

Arthur St. Cyr, DTS, in charge of the boundary survey, was following White-Fraser and cutting the actual line of the boundary, ten feet wide across country. He named this prominence after White-Fraser, but when the maps of the survey were produced in Ottawa the name Fraser had been dropped. It was never replaced. For a time between 1905-10, a period of intense mining activity, the hill was known locally as Mount Conrad (after the leading mining promoter in the district) and was even placed on a geological map of the district. This name too was eventually forgotten.

A few years ago the rest of the mountain group was included and "White-Fraser Mountain", changed to "White Mountain" then to "Mount Conrad", is now officially the WHITE RANGE.

WHITE RIVER 63°11'N 139°36'W (115-O). A major tributary to the Yukon River, from the St. Elias Mountains.

Robert Campbell of the HBC in 1850 was the first white man to see this stream and named it for the colour of its water, caused by the suspension of white, volcanic ash that it carries. The Stick Indians called the river "Yu-Kon-Hini" or "Yu-Ko-Kon-Heena" and the Chilkat Indians called it "Sand River". At the head of the stream the Tanana Indians called it the "Nasina" or "Erk-Heen" meaning "Copper River".

This was the first river to be prospected in the Yukon watershed. Arthur Harper, Frederick W. Hart, A. Gestler and George W. Fitch (or Finch) spent the winter of 1873-74 on the upper part of the river. They were searching for the source of native (pure) copper described to them by the Indians.

They did not find the deposits of copper but did find placer gold prospects which were not good enough to mine or to induce them back to the region the following summer.

This river is remarkable for the amount of sediment it carries down from its upper reaches. Some of it is silt, fed from the large glaciers of the St. Elias Mountains. Most of it comes from an extended layer of volcanic ash through which the river flows.

Great eruptions of ash from volcanoes in the St. Elias Range took place about 900-1100 A.D. covering an area about 220 by 370 miles, reaching from Alaska into the Northwest Territories. It has been estimated that about 165 cubic miles of rock in the form of ash were deposited in some places up to 100 feet in depth. It is this ash which gives the river its colour and its name.

WHITESTONE RIVER 60°01'N 137°13'W (115-A). Flows from British Columbia north into the Tatshenshini River.

This was a temporary name given to Tole Creek. It was long known locally as "Tole" or "Old Tole Creek". When it was found that he was still living, the name was changed to Whitestone. After he died, the original name was retained. (see Tole Creek)

MOUNT WHITNEY 65°38'N 139°38'W (116-G). East of the Porcupine River.

This was named after Frank A. WHITNEY, who was an early principal of the Dawson Public School in 1917-18.

WIGAN 60°40'N 135°01'W (105-D). On the WP&YR, a mile and a half north of MacRae.

An early section point and construction site of the WP&YR. It was abandoned soon after construction of the railroad was completed.

The place was named after Edward Alfred WIGAN of England. He was an early backer and shareholder of the WP&YR.

WILEY CREEK 61°02'N 133°47'W (105-F). A tributary to the Boswell River.

In May 1962, this stream was chosen to commemorate J-7234 Flight Lt. George William WILEY, MID. He was born on 24 January 1922 at London, Ontario, and enlisted in the RCAF on 4 December 1940 at Windsor, Ontario. He served in Canada and overseas and died, a prisoner of war, on 25 March 1944.

The creek had been known locally as "Hardrock MacDonald Creek" after a well-known prospector who was living there. As he was still alive, the name was disallowed. (see Mount MacDonald)

WILKINSON RANGE 62°52'N 134°10'W (105-L). A small range of hills, north of the Earn River.

These hills were named after the WILKINSON family, two generations of whom have lived and trapped in this area.

WILLIAMS CREEK 62°24'N 136°37'W (115-I). Flows into the Yukon River, five miles below Yukon Crossing.

A prospector of this name found the first gold on this stream and gave it his name in 1898. In 1907, other prospectors found quartz veins carrying good copper values on the banks of the creek, which started another staking rush to the area. A settlement called Boronite City was built at the mouth of the stream. (see Boronite City)

WILLIAMS CREEK 63°50'N 135°28'W (105-M). A tributary to Duncan Creek, in the Mayo area.

This creek was probably named by and after Frank WILLIAMS who prospected and trapped from here east to the MacKenzie Mountains. He came in 1898, one of the first men in the district and his name occurs often in the early news from the region.

WILLIAMS CREEK 64°20'N 134°50'W (106-D). A tributary to the Beaver River.

This creek was also named for Frank WILLIAMS. He assisted Charles Camsell, GSC, in his explorations of the Peel and Wind Rivers in the winter of 1904-05. Camsell held him in high regard, naming this stream for him.

MOUNT WILLIAMS 5,585' 60°46'N 135°23'W (105-D). South of the Takhini River.

J.D. WILLIAMS was a Canadian Customs Officer in Whitehorse after the First World War. He was long active as a leader in the Boy Scout movement in the Yukon. This mountain was named in his honour in November 1973.

MOUNT WILLIAMS 64°24'N 134°38'W (106-D). In the Wernecke Range, at the headwaters of Williams Creek.

W.A. Williamson was born in London, England on 9 April 1897. Coming to the Yukon he enlisted on 14 October 1916 in the Canadian Machine Gun Corps under the name WILLIAMS. He served in Canada, Great Britain and was severely wounded in France. He came back to Canada an invalid where he died of wounds on 14 August 1919. He was not the same Williams as the one for whom the creek at the foot of the mountain is named.

WILSON CREEK 60°37'N 133°30'W (105-C). Flows into the Thirtymile River.

In August 1952, this creek was officially named after George WILSON who had found gold here and mined on it for a number of years. He was a former Postmaster in Whitehorse who had turned successfully to prospecting.

WILSON LAKE 62°52'N 130°05'W (105-J). At the headwaters of the Ross River.

This was named by Joseph Keele, GSC, in 1907 when he mapped the geology of this region. Charles WILSON prospected and trapped in this area in 1904-08 and gave Keele much assistance in his work. (see Mount Wilson)

MOUNT WILSON 7,466' 62°53'N 129°42'W (105-I). At the headwaters of the Ross and Pelly Rivers, on the Yukon-NWT boundary.

Joseph Keele, GSC, named this peak, as well as the above creek, in 1907. Charles WILSON, whom most people called "Old Man WILSON", came into the Yukon with the Klondike Gold Rush. He soon gravitated to this section of the territory where he remained. Keele appreciated his wide knowledge of the country from here to the MacKenzie River Valley.

WILSON spent the rest of his life, to about 1930, searching for the Lost McHenry Gold Mine. This was a phenomenally rich deposit of placer gold supposed to be somewhere in this general area. According to Keele, McHenry was said to have been an old Dease Lake miner who penetrated this region in the late 1870s or early 1880s. After a year alone he returned to Dease Lake with forty pounds weight of coarse gold and nuggets. Various reasons were given for his failure to return to his find but he gave certain friends approximate directions to the location. Many prospectors have since searched for it without success. The area of the story overlaps the Nahanni country and may be connected with the lost gold mine stories of that area.

WIND CITY 65°43'N 135°12'W (106-E). On the west bank of the Wind River, about eight miles above the Peel River.

In the late fall of 1898, many of the gold seekers attempting to reach the Klondike from Edmonton by way of the MacKenzie, Rat, Porcupine, Peel and Wind Rivers were caught by winter and were unable to travel farther as the rivers froze. They gathered into small groups and built cabin communities to pass the winter where they were halted.

About 70 men and women were gathered at this spot. Eben McAdam, a leader, quotes in his diary: "20 September 1898. Up at seven a.m. Left for lower cache at 9:20 a.m. Back at 1:23 p.m. with last load. Have named this place WIND CITY. Expect about 10 shacks and about 40 men to put up in this place this winter". ("The Klondike Rush Through Edmonton" by J.G. McGregor)

The settlement existed from September 1898 to March 1899. To overcome the boredom of dark winter days and to avoid friction between themselves, they organized card clubs and tournaments, choirs, lectures, concerts and outdoor sports. Only two men died of scurvy despite a lack of fresh vegetables and meat. Most continued on to Dawson in the early spring although a few returned to Fort MacPherson.

WIND RIVER 65°51'N 135°18'W (106-E). A major tributary to the Peel River.

This river has had this name since ancient times. The Loucheaux Indians of the country called it this because of the furious winds which blow down its course almost constantly.

WIND RIVER TRAIL

This was a winter road built for truck haulage of oil-well drilling equipment and supplies. Beginning at a point just a few miles beyond Mayo it ran north to a point on the Bell River just a few miles short of the Arctic Coast.

Leo Proctor, of Whitehorse, was instrumental in the conception and construction of this trail and it was built by the Arctic Oilfields Transport Ltd., a subsidiary of the WP&YR. Construction was started on 12 October 1959 and was completed on 12 January 1960, for a distance of 385 miles. Over 3,000 tons of material moved over the road, the most northerly truck road in North America.

WOLF CREEK 60°37'N 134°55'W (105-D). A tributary to the Yukon River, two miles south of MacRae.

Enough gold was found here for George Stevens to stake a Discovery claim and start a staking rush in February 1914.

MOUNT WOOD 15,885' 61°14'N 140°31'W (115-F). In the St. Elias Range.

J.J. McArthur, DLS, while surveying the International Boundary in July 1900, named this peak after Inspector (later Commissioner) Zachary Taylor WOOD, NWMP.

WOOD was the grandson of the twelfth President of the United States and a graduate of the Royal Military College of Kingston, Ontario. He joined the NWMP in 1883. By 1897, he had become an outstanding officer and held the rank of Inspector. Chosen to go to the Yukon, he was for a period in charge of the Dawson detachment and earned a lasting reputation for his cool, efficient and totally successful maintenance of law and order in those turbulent times. He soon rose to command the RNWMP and died in 1915.

WOODBURN CREEK 63°08'N 136°15'W (115-P). Runs into Crooked Creek, south of Stewart Crossing.

A miner of this name was the first to find gold and to stake a claim on this stream in 1915. A sizeable rush took place with this creek and others around it being claimed.

WOODCHOPPER CREEK 64°19'N 140°00'W (116-C). Flows into the Yukon River.

Probably named after a man who lived here for many years, earning his living by cutting boiler wood for the riverboats.

WOODCUTTERS RANGE 62°21'N 136°17'W (115-I). North of Tatchun Lake.

Named by Hugh S. Bostock, GSC, after the woodcutters who supplied fuel to the steamboats on the Yukon River.

WOODSIDE RIVER 62°02'N 139°33'W (105-J). Flows into the Pelly Lakes.

This was named in 1909 after Major Henry WOODSIDE. He came into the Yukon in 1898 and took an active part in Dawson and Yukon political affairs. He was the Yukon Census Commissioner in 1901 and was editor of the Yukon Midnight Sun Newspaper in the early 1900s. He was active in promoting mining exploration in the territory and spent much time in the bush. He had an anti-American bias and strongly pushed Robert Henderson's claim to be the first man to discover the gold of the Klondike. He was instrumental in having the Canadian government recognize the claim and award Henderson a pension and other benefits.

WORKBOAT PASSAGE 69°32'N 139°12'W (117-D). A channel on the southwest shore of Herschel Island.

Named after the "CSS Richardson", the boat that was used in coastal surveys at this place by the Marine Sciences Division in 1965.

MOUNT WORTHINGTON 60°35'N 137°23'W (115-A). In the Auriol Range.

This was named in June 1968 after one of Canada's most distinguished professional soldiers, Major General Frederick Frank WORTHINGTON, CB, MC, MM, CD. He was born in Peterhead, Scotland on 17 September 1889. Enlisting in the Canadian Army at Montreal, Quebec on 17 March 1916, as a private, he won a battlefield commission in France and several decorations for bravery. He enlisted again on 1 September 1939 and was instrumental in developing armoured fighting vehicles for the Canadian and Allied Armies. He organized and commanded the 5th Canadian Armoured Division until 1943. He served until his retirement on 18 March 1943 and died on 5 December 1967.

WOUNDED MOOSE CREEK 63°37'N 138°42'W (115-O). Flows north into the Indian River, in the Klondike District.

There is some evidence that this stream was named by Robert Henderson when he prospected it in March or April 1895. No payable gold was found on it. The mountain at its headwaters was later given the same name.

WRIGHT CREEK (see Kirkland Creek).

YIDITSHUU LAKE 66°57'N 134°59'W (106-L). Four miles west of the Tabor Lakes, on the west side of Three Cabin Creek.

An uncertain translation of this Loucheaux Indian word gives a meaning of "Something Soft".

YIN YANG CREEK 64°18'N 138°28'W (116-B). A tributary to the North Klondike River.

The name was reported by Dr. Dirk Templeman-Kluit, GSC, in 1968. He said it had been named by men constucting the Dempster Highway.

YOKE MOUNTAIN 7,377' 68°07'N 138°43'W (116-B). On the north side of the Tombstone River.

Named in 1968 by Dr. Dirk Templeman-Kluit, GSC, because of its shape.

YOUTH CREEK 63°53'N 135°47'W (105-M). Flows to Haldane Creek.

This stream was named by Dr. R.W. Boyle, GSC, after the young members of his crew.

YUKON CROSSING 62°21'N 136°29'W (115-I). On the Lewes (Yukon) River, near Rink Rapids.

This little settlement was at the point where the old Whitehorse-Dawson Road crossed the Lewes (Yukon) River. During the summer months a ferry operated here. A roadhouse and telegraph station were also here. The settlement was abandoned with the end of the riverboat era and the building of the new highway to Dawson.

MOUNT YUKON 10,600' 60°59'N 140°58'W (115-C). In the Centennial Range of the St. Elias Mountains.

This peak was named in 1967 to honour the YUKON Territory during Canada's Centennial year of 1967. (see Centennial Range)

THE YUKON RIVER

The YUKON RIVER is the focal point of Yukon History. It provided the only feasible access by itself and its tributaries to almost 70% of the territory, and for many years was the main route for people and traffic. In those days, life in the territory was governed by the periods when the river was open or frozen. The summer was a time of bustling activity and the riverboats carried prospectors and freight to all parts of the Territory. In the winter men settled in to mine their summer prospects, to trap in their chosen areas and above all, to pass away the long, cold, dark winter. Limited to horse and dog teams, transportation was slow and costly in the winter. The cold brought movement to a minimum.

As well as access, the river provided food. Its magnificent runs of salmon, as well as other fish, formed the major proportion of the diet of the native peoples, most of whom lived along the waterways.

The name YUKON was given by the HBC trader, John Bell, who in 1846 descended the Porcupine River from the MacKenzie Delta to its junction with the Yukon. He called it the "Youcon", his version of the Loucheaux Indian word "Yughoo", meaning "the Greatest River" or "Big River". At this junction in 1847 Alexander Hunter Murray established the first HBC post on the river, Fort Yukon.

The estuary of the Yukon had been explored in 1835-38 by the Russian Glasunov, who named it the "Kwikhpak", the Aleut Eskimo word meaning "Great River". The Tanana Indians called it "Niga-to", with the same meaning.

Robert Campbell of the HBC, the first explorer of the south and central Yukon region, reached the headwaters of the Pelly (the main branch of the Yukon) in 1840 by way of the Liard and Frances Rivers. In 1848, he descended the Pelly to the Yukon River, the upper part of which he called the Lewes River and the lower part, below the junction, the Pelly. In the same year he began construction of Fort Selkirk and floating downstream, arrived at Fort Yukon. This journey established the course and fact of a new and great trade route through the Yukon and Alaska territories. Although he had named the river the "Pelly", he now adopted that given by John Bell and the river was known as the "Yukon" from its mouth to Fort Selkirk.

The GSC gives the length of the river from the foot of Marsh Lake to the Bering Sea as 1979 miles. Other authorities, using the Pelly or Teslin River branches, argue for total distances up to 2300 miles. It is navigable by large riverboats from its mouth to Whitehorse (before the bridge was built at Carmacks). It was the last major river to be explored in North America, the fourth longest and the fifth largest in volume of water flow.

Since the advent of cheaper and more regular transport by road and airplane the river has reverted to the wilderness and is now much the same as it was a century ago, before the coming of the white man, perhaps more so, as the native Indians who once lived along its banks have now mostly moved to the settlements. The last riverboat to carry freight and passengers ceased scheduled operations in 1956. However, as the main part of the "Trail of '98", the river acquired a glamour which it will never lose.

THE YUKON TERRITORY

In 1670, the Hudson's Bay company (The Governor and Company of Adventurers Trading Into Hudson's Bay) was given its Charter by King Charles II of England. This charter gave them, in effect, outright control of northern Quebec, Ontario and all of what is now middle, western and Arctic Canada. To quote the charter "The true and absolute Lords and Proprietors".

It was not until early in the 19th century that they began to realize just how vast an empire they had been given. They gradually relinquished parts of it to the established governments of eastern Canada as these governments developed and lands became colonized. With the Deed of Surrender in 1869 of Rupert's Land and the old Northwest Territories, the Hudson's Bay Company became a wholly commercial enterprise with no powers of government. After the passing of this Act the Yukon was made a provisional district of the NWT, to be governed from the NWT capital of Regina.

This situation lasted until the tremendous influx of people to the Yukon after the discovery of gold on the Fortymile River in late 1886. The Dominion government, in the next few years, decided to assume a more direct role in the affairs of the territory. This was started by sending in Inspector Charles Constantine and 20 men and 2 officers of the NWMP in 1894-95 as well as a Canadian Customs Agent. Constantine was appointed Dominion Agent for the Territory. The Order-in Council effecting this action also demarked the Yukon as a separate district of the NWT, encompassing 482,515 sq. km (186,300 sq. miles).

In 1897, the Dominion Government was forced into action because of the huge preponderance of American nationals in the population of the Yukon; a figure often set at 75%. They appointed Major James Morrow Walsh as the Chief Executive Officer of the Yukon Territory (which was not yet in existence). Thomas Fawcett was appointed Gold Commissioner, Dominion Agent and Mining Recorder. T.H. McGuire was made Judge of the Court of the Yukon Provisional District.

In June 1898, "An Act to Provide for the Government of the Yukon Territory" was passed, which made the Yukon, for the first time, a separate territory. It also provided a council composed of six senior officials, all taking orders from Ottawa with all ties to Regina being severed.

In 1900, two of the Council were elected from the general public. In 1902 all five were elected. In later years the total number of councillors was increased to seven and then to twelve. The Commissioner has always been appointed by Ottawa.

YUSEZYU RIVER 61°35'N 129°43'W (105-H). Two miles east of Frances Lake.

An Indian name noted by Dr. George Mercer Dawson, G&NHSC, in 1887 with no translation.

ZRALRII ISLAND 66°44'N 134°44'W (106-L). An island in the Peel River.

This is a Loucheaux Indian word meaning "Dark or Unlucky Island".